The History
of the
National Theatre

by John Elsom

Theatre Outside London
Erotic Theatre
Post-War British Theatre

The History
of the
National Theatre

JOHN ELSOM AND
NICHOLAS TOMALIN

JONATHAN CAPE
THIRTY BEDFORD SQUARE LONDON

First published 1978
© 1978 by John Elsom and Claire Tomalin

Jonathan Cape Ltd, 30 Bedford Square, London WC1

British Library Cataloguing in Publication Data

Elsom, John
The history of the National Theatre.
1. National Theatre—History
I. Title   II. Tomalin, Nicholas
792'0941   PN2595

ISBN 0-224-01340-8

Printed in Great Britain by
Ebenezer Baylis and Son Limited
The Trinity Press, Worcester, and London

Contents

v

Illustrations

ILLUSTRATIONS

Preface

NICHOLAS TOMALIN was killed on October 17th, 1973, on the Golan Heights during the Yom Kippur war. He had been with two other journalists in an armoured car, and they had stopped to survey the scene. Tomalin stayed by the car, while the others wandered a few yards away. A heat-seeking rocket blew up the car.

Among Tomalin's papers in London was a partly written book on the National Theatre's history, together with a mass of notes, press-cuttings, tapes and transcripts from interviews. He had never been professionally involved in the theatre, not even as a theatre critic; but he had a good general knowledge of the theatre scene, as of so many other matters. His particular interest, however, was in the way in which a national institution developed—the background politics, the methods of raising money and support, the rivalries and the pursuit of achievement. He had first become involved with the story as a member of the *Sunday Times* 'Insight' team; but the book was not going to be just a collection of well-researched articles. It was to be something far more substantial, for Tomalin believed that the creation of the National Theatre provided, in miniature, a portrait of our times.

I never met Nicholas Tomalin. The invitation from Tom Maschler of Jonathan Cape to continue and complete the book came as a surprise to me, more so because I seem to have been one of the few theatre critics around who did not even know that the book was there to be finished. I was very pleased to be asked, of course, but I accepted the invitation with some caution. I knew, for example, that Tomalin's literary style was different from my own—and his approach to the theatre. I was a supporter of the National Theatre movement, whereas Tomalin had maintained a greater detachment. I was also slightly sceptical about his 'portrait-of-our-times' approach, in that, while almost any social topic (whether it be housing or subsidizing the arts)

ix

can provide such a picture, I needed to be convinced that the National Theatre offered a more specific reflection.

There was also the matter of what type of book might emerge. Tomalin had written his history up to the end of the Second World War; but I did not want the book to fall into two separate Tomalin/Elsom sections. It would be necessary, therefore, to rewrite the book from beginning to end, incorporating his work into mine and undertaking a collaboration with someone whose presence would only be known to me through his words on paper, his handwriting in the notes, his voice on tapes. Claire Tomalin had generously given me a free hand to rewrite her husband's work, as I felt necessary; but being offered that freedom was not quite the same thing as feeling uninhibitedly free about accepting it.

In the event, however, only the first chapter stands more or less as Tomalin wrote it, with minor additions and editorializing from me. That does not mean, however, that his contribution ended there, or even with the paragraphs incorporated from his original completed draft; for, as it happened, Tomalin's whole approach proved illuminating to me, even when it was expressed in a jotted sentence on a random scrap of paper. I found myself agreeing with him, where I had thought to disagree; and quarrelling with him over a minor point. I developed a respect for his judgment, an appreciation for his style, and finally felt that this book had indeed been a collaborative effort, though weighted (perhaps unfortunately for the reader) in my favour.

Both of us are indebted to those connected with the National Theatre company, the various boards and the theatre profession in general who have talked so extensively about their memories, hopes and disappointments. A list of those interviewed would be long indeed and I am aware that the views expressed through this book must inevitably cause some dissension. There will be those who, despite their contributions, will probably feel that their efforts on the National Theatre's behalf have not been properly appreciated by me. Whatever their feelings about this book, however, my gratitude to them remains.

JOHN ELSOM

I

Moving Stone

LATE in July 1973, James Hotson, a stonemason, and Fred Clapp, his assistant, moved the foundation stone of the Shakespeare Memorial National Theatre from the grass mound just south of the Thames, London, where it had been standing for fifteen years. On the evening of July 24th, they prised off the two side pieces and capping slab which a foundation stone, without the comfort of other foundations around it or a theatre above it, needs as protection from rain, atmosphere and vandals. They chipped away the cement which held it to its brick base, and levered it up on to two scaffolding tubes. Next morning, Wednesday, they rolled it slowly along two wooden joists, using the scaffolding tubes as rollers, until it was in place on a lorry sent by the contractors, McAlpine. Then they took it off to the stone renovator's yard.

The foundation stone is made of Portland stone. It is four feet long, three feet high and one foot thick. A portion of it at the front has been cut away to give the impression of a scroll, curling as if with old age away from the block behind it. On this, in gold letters still in a remarkable state of preservation, is carved:

> To the Living Memory of
> WILLIAM SHAKESPEARE
> on a site provided by the
> London County Council, in
> conformity with the National
> Theatre Act MCMXLIX and in the
> year of the Festival of Britain,
> this foundation stone for
> THE NATIONAL THEATRE
> was laid on XIII July MCMLI by
> HER MAJESTY THE QUEEN

In front of the stone, as a kind of official apology, someone had

I

placed a varnished wooden board, screwed to metal supports, again covered with gold letters, which read:

> With the agreement of Her Majesty
> Queen Elizabeth the Queen Mother,
> this foundation is placed here
> temporarily, pending its transfer to
> the National Theatre now being built
> on the South Bank immediately downstream
> of Waterloo Bridge.

Fred Clapp unscrewed this board, and tucked it under his arm.

As anyone familiar with Roman numerals, or the Festival of Britain, would have immediately realized, the foundation stone was much older than the fifteen years it had lain 'temporarily' beside the Festival Hall. The L.C.C. put it there to keep it out of harm's way, but not out of sight. In its previous, dramatically exposed position high on the embankment walkway upstream, it was a temptation to vandals, and the more histrionic National Theatre campaigners, two of whom, Kenneth Tynan and Richard Findlater, had once staged a mock funeral ceremony for the National, standing in frock coats, heads bowed, with black ribbons on their top hats, with the stone as the tomb. In its temporary position, the Royal Festival Hall, a shining example of swiftly embodied municipal patronage, loomed above it, stilling awkward complaints of bumbling and delay.

The stone had been laid originally between the Festival Hall and the old Shot Tower. Then it was moved and laid again beside County Hall. Then moved again for safety's sake, and now it was off for a twenty-two year service. Each laying had brought another flourish of ceremony, a few more column inches in the press. The road to the National is paved with ceremonial. There was a Fleet Street choir singing Old English madrigals in 1938, for the Ceremony of the Twig and Sod in Brompton Road, when Bernard Shaw 'took seisin' of the wrong piece of land. The Boyd Neel Orchestra played for the 1951 laying, and Dame Sybil Thorndike recited some very ceremonial verses from the then Poet Laureate, John Masefield. Royalty, too, had been patient with that stone, all that hard pomp wasted, and to crown the indignity, at the very last foundation ceremony, the stone was not needed at all. The new building was to be in concrete; and so, on November 3rd, 1969, there was a Ceremonial Cement Pouring on a windy day on the South Bank.

On this moving occasion in July 1973, any more ceremony would have attracted sardonic comment. There were no rows of politicians, no elder statesmen of the theatre, no ambassadors to watch that peripatetic stone being rolled on to a lorry. There was only a camera team from London Weekend Television, the workers and a writer. This small group waited for about an hour, because the early morning schedule (intended to provide the correct light for the cameras) had upset McAlpine's arrangement for the lorry. Someone drove over a fork-lift truck from the theatre site, but it was waved away as too dangerous and undignified. Mr Hotson—who mentioned in passing that he never went to the theatre, didn't think much of it and had 'stopped all that kind of thing' in his wife when he married her—crouched over the stone, chipping stylishly at the remaining fragments of cement. The chipping achieved nothing useful, as all the necessary work had been done the night before, but with his round mallet and cold chisel he made a fine picture of traditional craftsmanship. London Weekend recorded him from various angles.

The television director took the gold-painted apology board from Fred Clapp (who also never went to the theatre) and symbolically dropped it on its face two or three times before the camera. It became clear that his film might turn out to have some ironic, even satirical, moments. A continuity assistant with dyed blue hair and purple trousers sat idly on the grass mound, taking notes: 'Unlaying of the foundation stone, take one. Unlaying of the foundation stone, take two,' and so on.

Some engineers from McAlpine's, innocently unaware of the less than respectful intentions behind the camera, drifted over from their work on the half-finished theatre to pose, in white protective helmets, as if they were helping to shift the stone. 'Have there been any mistakes in building the theatre?' asked one, Senior Engineer Kenneth Golinsky, rhetorically. 'By Christ, there have! A real shambles at times. But it's easy to criticize. It's the first time anyone has tried to do anything like this, I mean on this scale. Do you appreciate that we've got to install seventy-five toilet units, male and female, each comprising of several individual fitments?'

Meanwhile the theatre-going middle classes were walking past, fresh from Waterloo Station and their commuter trains from Surrey and Sussex. Two secretaries pointed at the stone and giggled: 'William Shakespeare! How lovely! Where's Laurence Olivier?' A Mr Peter Bland from Haslemere was interested in the stone. He remembered the newsreels of the Festival of Britain laying. Yes, he had frequently been to productions by the National at the Old Vic. Convenient for late trains. He did not like so much the far-out modern things they sometimes did. Shakespeare to Ibsen, yes: Brecht, no—not quite up to Brecht, perhaps. He didn't like some modern British playwrights either, but he refused to mention names, and strode on.

A middle-aged lady asked if these were the people who had attacked Sir Winston Churchill after he was dead and unable to answer back, and if they were, they were no better than traitors and did not deserve any money. A young man said that the theatre was dead, bourgeois and irrelevant to modern concerns. Others were, in general, approving.

On the grass mound, beneath a historic lime tree on the site of the old India Office, the foundation stone had suffered some damage. The softer parts had dissolved away in places from the polluting rain, although the lettering, protected by gold, was untouched. In the stonemason's yard, the surface would be reground and polished, leaving the stone fresh for its final resting place in the theatre foyer. When the stone had originally been cut, it was presumed that the entire building would be in smooth Portland stone, like the Festival Hall. Now it would stand out as the only piece of polished masonry in a foyer of rough, weatherboarded concrete.

The great feature of the new building, in fact, is its rough, structural look. Nowadays we tend to strip things down to their bare essentials, or what look like bare essentials. Sir Denys Lasdun, the fourth architect selected for the job and the only one to see tangible results, had spared no effort to achieve an honest, down-to-earth effect. The wooden boards moulding the concrete had been chosen for their scrupulously uneven thickness, as if straight from an untidy builder's yard. The workmen had been trained to select the boards randomly. The only walls in the National Theatre covered with smooth conventional plaster would be backstage, where the actors make up—an interesting inversion of illusion and reality.

But the new building was impressive even in 1973, a rough architectural beast which had slouched to the South Bank to be born. Still half-completed then, though 'topped out' and with its roof on, it seemed to grow out of the Thames embankment like several low cliffs or a pile of unexpected rocks, with useful paths and platforms leading to Waterloo Bridge. It looked more permanent than some of the buildings which had been finished and occupied long ago, such as that monument to an office age, the Shell Building, or the drab, windy square of County Hall.

'Good old stone buildings', said Fred Clapp, looking up appreciatively at the smooth, stone sides of the Festival Hall, 'need fixers. They cut the outside facing stones to conceal the messy, structural brickwork. They're expensive nowadays. You just can't get them. It's a dying skill.' Perhaps National Theatres, in stone or concrete, need fixers more than they need anything else. Ours would not be here without them. This National required one-and-a-quarter centuries' effort by high idealists and low fixers; and the most difficult stones to cut, or indeed to find, came from no pedantic quarry.

The National needed to find foundation stones of money (public and private), of goodwill (public and private), of argument (moral, aesthetic and political), of sites—London is littered with discarded National sites—of enthusiasm, and sometimes of inertia, for once a scheme has started, sheer apathy will often keep it rolling. In addition to fixers, the National has needed salesmen, foot-in-the-door specialists who will wedge their way in and make a nuisance of themselves, until it is less trouble to listen than to get rid of them. That was partly why the first site was bought—and the second—and why Peter Hall eventually decided to move the National company into the Lyttelton Theatre, before the building or even that theatre was ready. The shifting of the real foundation stone has been a minor inconvenience, when set against the main problem—which was how to find a firm place among the changing shoals and banks of British society where a National Theatre could safely be built.

'Mostly,' continued Fred Clapp, 'we do renovating work. Windsor Castle, the Guildhall, stately homes. Working with History. This is the first time I can recall renovating a new stone.'

'I've seen the Queen twice,' added James Hotson, 'while working on the vaulting in St George's Chapel. She was having a stroll around, very informal. If you want to write something important, be sure to say we are not paid enough for the work we do. Five years' apprenticeship, and only thirty-five pounds a week, with overtime.'

The lorry arrived. The stone was moved. It looked frail and uncomfortable bouncing on its trestles, WILLIAM SHAKESPEARE still gleaming in the morning sun.

'Off for refurbishment. Already. Amazing, if you think about it,' said Senior Engineer Golinsky. It must surely be the only foundation stone in history to have needed refurbishment before it had ever provided the foundation for anything.

2

The Prophets

THE first man to propose a National Theatre recognizably like the one which we now have was a London publisher, Effingham Wilson, in 1848. Wilson, a Yorkshireman by birth, was an ardent campaigner for many causes who (like George Holyoake, a generation later) outlived his younger reputation as a dangerous radical to arrive at a settled and venerable old age. Nevertheless, *The Times*, which once dismissed him as 'The Radical Bookseller of the Royal Exchange', did not grant him the courtesy of an obituary when he died in 1868, aged eighty-five — though his career certainly deserved a lengthy one.

He published, for example, the early works of Jeremy Bentham when nobody else dared to do so; and championed Tennyson and Browning when they were both young, unpublished poets. He produced John Wade's *Black Book*, a compilation of misdeeds, corruption and nepotism in high political and Church circles which is now widely credited with inspiring the agitation which led to the Reform Bill of 1867. The *Black Book* got him into trouble, which he faced with that brave confidence which characterized his life. He had once kicked a crooked Lord Mayor of London down his front staircase, and had survived an attempted horsewhipping from the Duke of York's aide-de-camp.

But he was not just a rebel. He was a dogged sergeant-major in the army (as he saw it) of enlightenment, putting heart into the forces of reform wherever they seemed to be flagging. He was a Whig, a close friend of the editor of the *Morning Chronicle*, the leading Liberal newspaper whose editorials he sometimes helped to frame. He endlessly lobbied Parliament and befriended political martyrs. His political views owe a debt to the Utilitarians, while his eighteenth-century Yorkshire background associates him with the dissenters, the Dissenting Academies, and even perhaps with Joseph Priestley, another stalwart of enlightenment, who discovered oxygen and had his house burnt down by an enraged Birmingham mob because he sympathized with the French

Revolution. Wilson, like Priestley, believed passionately in popular education. He helped to establish the Mechanics' Institutes, and frequently declared that every child in the land should 'have that given to it which nobody can take away from it'—namely, knowledge. As a practical step towards this end, he published cheap educational booklets, the Useful Handy Books; while, away from his trade, he rushed to support those industrial schemes (railways and gas-lighting among them) which seemed likely to benefit mankind.

Wilson's proposals for a National Theatre belong within this context, being anti-élitist, concerned with popularizing 'good drama' (particularly Shakespeare) and with educating the public through 'the standardization of the best'. His two pamphlets, both called *A House for Shakespeare: A Proposition for the Consideration of the Nation*, can also be seen in a wider perspective. In Europe, as in Britain, 1848 was a year if not for revolutions, at least for thinking seriously about revolutionary change. It was the year when, in Paris, the Communes were born— and died; when John Stuart Mill wrote *Principles of Political Economy*; and when the Pre-Raphaelite Movement began, breaking away from the stuffy establishment art, gloom and grime, to seek a new humanism, touching many subjects with light, colour and accurate observation— including those previously reserved for solemn piety.

Since the French Revolution, of course, sixty years before, the crowned heads of Europe had feared for their heads as well as their crowns; but 1848 was also the year when there was an attempt to organize the many revolutionary forces under one common ideological banner. Marx and Engels issued the Communist Manifesto and the trend of their thinking (as of others, including Mill and Wilson) was to relate the old rebelliousness to a new scientism, investing them both with an evangelical fervour not derived from religious superstition. Their very language was revealing. Just as, in the eighteenth century, the first steps towards a scientific approach were taken through the attempts to classify animals, plants, minerals or whatever into different categories (vertebrates, invertebrates, phylum and species), so in the nineteenth century there was also an endeavour to classify human beings. Some radicals might follow Marx into a classification system for people which rested upon their situations within the economic cycles of the production and exchange of goods (thus, the working *classes*); while others preferred systems dependent upon genetic, racial, cultural or even national characteristics.

All revolutionaries, however, face the problem of how not to throw out babies with bathwaters—and even sometimes to tell the difference

7

between them. One plausible baby was the cultural patronage previously provided by monarchies and aristocracies. It could be argued that royal patronage caused art to be produced which was anti-revolutionary in spirit. Nevertheless, a love for the old forms of art still existed while, generally speaking, nineteenth-century artists were as often on the side of revolution as against it. The easy way out of this dilemma was to invent a corporate identity, the Nation perhaps, which would take over the patronage function from the old royal families. Thus, Court theatres became State theatres, privately owned 'companies of players' became (as in Germany) municipal ones, and Napoleon himself on his long trek to Moscow redrafted the constitution of the Comédie-Française, previously written and endorsed by Louis XIV.

A similar situation existed in Britain, though without patronage in the form of grants. In London, there were two 'patent' theatres, in Drury Lane and Covent Garden, with a third during the summer at the Haymarket. Their generic name, Theatre Royal, indicates the court origins. Their Letters Patent (or Charters) had been granted by Charles II in 1662 and confirmed by the Theatres Act of 1737. Instead of direct patronage, these theatres had been given virtual monopolies over the production of straight drama, although non-patented houses could produce burlettas, ballets, variety bills and other entertainments.

During the 1830s, there was much agitation against these monopolies, led in Parliament by Sir Edward Bulwer Lytton, better known as the novelist Bulwer-Lytton, author of *The Last Days of Pompeii*. Bulwer-Lytton, who became the 1st Lord Lytton, was also a dramatist whose most successful play was *The Lady of Lyons* (1838) and he therefore had a vested interest in supporting the theatre. George Holyoake, another radical publisher, remembered him in his *Memoirs of an Agitator* with very mixed feelings. He was a Tory, which was not good, who had supported the Newspaper Stamp Bill of 1836 (which taxed the 'dissemination of knowledge'), which was bad, and by that means, according to Holyoake, had purchased his baronetcy—which should have placed him beyond the pale. But Lytton redeemed himself in Holyoake's eyes by speaking forcefully in the House of Commons debate which repealed the Newspaper Stamp Bill in 1855, a brilliant speech which drew Conservatives to the Liberal side and won the day. Lytton was then fifty-three, but he seemed a 'young man', 'fashionably dressed, slenderly built'.

In May 1832, Lytton proposed that a committee be formed to investigate the monopolies enjoyed by the patent theatres and the consequent injustices suffered by the non-patent houses. The House of Commons agreed, and consequently a Committee of Inquiry was formed, which introduced a reforming Bill in 1833. The monopoly situation, however, was not finally broken until the passing of a new Theatres Act in 1843; but a report drafted by Lytton on behalf of the Committee of Inquiry and submitted to the government, indicates that he had other ideas in mind than the mere breaking of a monopoly. The fear was that Drury Lane and Covent Garden, the theatres associated with Garrick, Sheridan, Kemble and Macready (as well as Shakespeare, for only in these places could his plays be performed in something like the original text), would face a sudden challenge from the riff-raff and *hoi polloi* of lesser theatres, suffering in revenue and standards accordingly.

Lytton therefore proposed that the patent houses should be assisted by tax concessions:

> Your Committee are therefore of the opinion that, in consideration of the current belief in the probable duration of the monopoly, and the ruinous expenses entailed by a system too long permitted, it should, from the date of the licensing of other theatres for the performance of regular drama, be respectfully recommended to H.M. Government to remit the fragment of the taxes upon these two theatres [thus providing the means whereby] it is probable that those theatres may ... retain such a pre-eminence over other competitors, that the assistance afforded them will not only be of service to individuals, but, through the drama, to the public itself [V. Lytton, *Life of Bulwer, 1st Lord Lytton*, p. 430].

He also tested the atmosphere on a much more contentious point, the question of state subsidies:

> Your Committee have the greater willingness to recommend to the Government this small pecuniary sacrifice, since it appears ... that the French Government devotes little short of £80,000 to the support of theatres in Paris [*ibid.*, p. 431].

In the event, however, the monopolies were abolished, but no assistance was forthcoming, which was where Wilson's *Proposition* came to be of importance. Wilson wanted to preserve the standards of the patent houses and improve on them. He thus sought a non-monarchical, anti-monopolistic equivalent to the patent houses, preserving Shakespeare and serious drama from the encroachments of popular theatre. His proposals were put forward at a time when state subsidies for the arts, though rare, were not totally unknown; and there were other sources of public support. In 1824, Parliament had granted £60,000 to the National Gallery (at George IV's instigation) to buy the Angerstein collection of paintings. During the 1830s, the National Gallery, previously housed in Pall Mall, moved to its premises in Trafalgar Square, built by public subscription. In 1845, the Municipal Museums Act was passed, allowing town councils to found and maintain museums from the rates, an interesting forerunner of the Local Government Act of 1948, which enabled councils to support theatres as well.

It was an appropriate moment to propose a National Theatre, but the deed which triggered Wilson's energy and enthusiasm came in 1847, when a group of public-spirited men, calling themselves the Shakespeare Committee, raised the money to buy for the nation what could have been Shakespeare's birthplace in Stratford-upon-Avon. Wilson thought that Shakespeare would be better remembered by buying a theatre so that his plays could be seen, and therefore proposed:

(1) that the Committee formed for the purpose of preserving to the nation the house in which our 'poet of all time' had birth, having satisfactorily effected that object, should now dissolve,

(2) that, it being generally acknowledged that the human mind receives most quickly and retains most durably, impressions made by dramatic representations, the importance and expediency are suggested of purchasing by national subscription, on the part of and for the people, some theatre wherein the works of Shakespeare, the 'world's greatest moral teacher', may be constantly performed,

(3) that the said theatre should be opened at such reasonable charges as shall be within the reach of all,

(4) that the most able manager and best working company should be engaged and constantly retained; and that only one five-act drama should be performed in the course of one evening,

(5) that the Government for the time being, or any other body of men agreed upon, should hold the said theatre in trust for the nation, appointing a committee for the management of the same,

(6) that the said National Theatre should be made to act as a great and true dramatic school, at which alike the poet and the performer, the creator and the embodier (in the highest walks of the dramatic and histrionic arts), should receive their diplomas, living genius and talent being so fostered and sustained.

This *Proposition*, however heavily worded, summarized neatly certain cardinal principles within which all future discussions about the National operated: egalitarianism, public support, moral high-mindedness, popular education, the training of talent and the pursuit of excellence.

Wilson sent off his pamphlets to various eminent people, asking for their comments. Charles Dickens replied pessimistically: 'That such a theatre as described would be but worthy of this nation, and would not stand low upon the list of its instructors, I have no doubt. I wish I could cherish a stronger faith than I have in the probability of its establishment within fifty years.' Charles Kemble, the actor, was equally gloomy: 'I read it with great pleasure, and, at the conclusion, heaved a sigh, that so much enthusiasm should be doomed to disappointment.'

But Wilson's words were not entirely wasted, for one of his pamphlets went to Lytton, who responded with typical enthusiasm: 'I think it would indeed be a most desirable object to obtain a theatre, strictly appropriated to Higher Drama. Your exertions cannot do but good.' Lord Lytton, who died in 1873, kept the National Theatre idea alive for the next twenty years, so much so that the *Morning Advertiser* in 1874 credited him with having invented it. He was the first noble, though not initially very rich, Victorian to have supported the cause, and to start a family tradition in the National's favour. His son Edward Robert became Viceroy of India and was created an earl, while his grandson, Victor Alexander, became the chairman of the Old Vic, at a time (1946) when the Old Vic formally linked itself to the National cause. His granddaughter Emily married Sir Edwin Lutyens, the architect who designed one National Theatre building which should have stood in Brompton Road, if it had ever been built.

Though Lytton soldiered on, an isolated campaigner, Wilson quickly gave up, deciding that 'the times were ... so thoroughly out of joint'. In retrospect, it seems strange that Wilson should have reached this conclusion, for this was an age for great public buildings reflecting new national institutions—from the Houses of Parliament (completed in 1857) to the Albert Hall (1871), as well as the National Gallery. Was Wilson mistaken in thinking that the fault lay in the stars? And why did Lytton not meet with more success?

There are simple answers to these questions, and a rather complicated one, though truer perhaps and more pervasive. The Crimean War intervened in the 1850s, driving thoughts of cultural patronage from the public mind. This was the first of three occasions when a war blew up the National plans. But even without the war, Wilson's *Proposition* would probably have fallen mainly on deaf ears, as Kemble and Dickens feared, for the reputation of the theatre was raffish. Queen Victoria herself was censured severely by *The Times* for crossing the threshold of a theatre, to see Dion Boucicault's *The Corsican Brothers* in 1852. Its notoriety was not just a myth maintained by Victorian prudery. In the lower regions of the theatrical profession, there was an association between actresses and prostitutes; while writers—many Romantic Revivalists amongst them—looked down on the theatre as a debased literary medium. Shelley, with *The Cenci*, was the only poet to attempt to revive and elevate the art of drama. Byron's dramatic poems were not written to be performed. Dickens, the most instinctively theatrical of novelists, never wrote a play, although he wrote sketches and scraps of plays, and revelled in reading extracts from his novels. The theatre was not a cause to attract solidly respectable, bourgeois support. Indeed the National Theatre found itself caught in a Catch-22 dilemma. Its purpose was partly to redeem the theatre from its debased circumstances, but until the theatre had been raised in public esteem, it was hard to find support for a National.

But the real problem lay in a spirit of the times, a cultural *Zeitgeist*, which can best be gauged perhaps by seeing pictures from the Great Exhibition of 1851 or handling objects from the period in antique shops. The Great Exhibition was an exact opposite to its successor, the Festival of Britain in 1951. One was a celebration of Britain's industrial power and strength, a May Day parade of ironwork, useful and useless statuary, of delicate-looking objects which almost needed a crane to lift them, something to urge on the armies of trade. The other was an attempt to raise spirits after another devastating war, a hopeful bit of flag-waving to prove that Britain could still lead the world in something. One was a statement of might, the other a pretence that we were not as weak as we seemed to be.

Even the visitors to the Great Exhibition now seem somewhat monumental, the men moving round sedately in their frock coats, high-necked cravats, top hats and muttonchops—the women swathed in fold after fold of heavy fabric. It was a world which stressed its reliable permanence, even to the extent of denying its humanity. Everything was made to last, even the inkwells and crockery; and in such an atmosphere, the theatre must have seemed light and ephemeral indeed, just a few hours of an evening, a way of passing the time before the serious business next morning of constructing eternity from wrought iron.

The theatre only became respectable in the later decades of the century, when Britain's industrial strength was already declining; and it did so partly by adopting some characteristics of the monumental age. The sets became mechanical miracles, the theatres (such as those designed by Frank Matcham) were wonderlands of ornament, while Henry Irving, at the Lyceum Theatre during the 1880s and 1890s, constructed his own style of monumental acting. His Mathias in Lewis's *The Bells* was not acting as we know it, or as the early Victorians had done, but rather an attempt to build from quick movement and sudden poses an unforgettable image of The Guilty Man.

While the theatre drifted towards monumentalism, society moved somewhat away from it. They started to meet on middle ground. The Victorians, or many of them, tried hard to humanize the consequences of the Industrial Revolution. This was expressed in many different ways: in the various Factory Acts, in the literary images of industrial Frankensteins (such as Dickens's Gradgrind), in the work of innumerable philanthropists (such as Samuel Morley, Lady Frederick Cavendish and Emma Cons, all connected with the early life of the Royal Victoria Hall and Coffee Tavern, which became the Old Vic), in a new atmosphere of liberalism and enlightenment which affected even such bulwarks of the establishment as the established Church and Eton. This change of tone can perhaps be regarded as one indirect consequence of the efforts of Wilson, Holyoake and the other reasonable agitators of former years. It can also be found in the slight relaxation of social codes and conventions during the Naughty Nineties.

Alfred Lyttelton observed this change at Eton, where he was at school from 1868 to 1875. He noticed how the former muscular aggressiveness of the school, with its old-style Christian fundamentalism, had moderated to a new seriousness and social concern. Beatings became very rare: games replaced gang-fights with the town as the local sport. Lyttelton himself was one of the finest cricketers of his generation, a wicket-keeper batsman who played with W. G. Grace against Australia, and gleefully against Grace in county matches. Lyttelton's national popularity, and he was very popular, came largely from the fact that he was a great sportsman, playing tennis, football (soccer and rugby) and golf, as well as cricket. He also came to be regarded as a fair-minded barrister, an eloquent Member of Parliament (who broke with his uncle, Gladstone, and a family tradition of Liberalism over Home Rule for Ireland) and an enlightened Colonial Secretary whose reputation was spoilt (if not ruined) by the Chinese Labour Ordinance of 1904, which seemed to countenance slavery.

Lyttelton started the second great family tradition of support for the National. His wife Edith was an ardent campaigner with him, continuing his work after his death in 1913, while his son Oliver became Lord Chandos, the first chairman of the National Theatre Board. Through

the Lyttelton family, the cause of the National drew closer to the heart
of government. Alfred Lyttelton's first wife, Laura, whom he married
in 1884 and who died in 1886, was one of the 'Three Graces', the
Tennant sisters of whom Margot married Herbert Asquith, Campbell-
Bannerman's successor as Prime Minister in 1908. Edith, his second
wife, was a member of the wealthy Balfour family; and despite Alfred's
break with Gladstone politically, he remained on good terms with the
Grand Old Man.

Alfred Lyttelton liked the theatre, but he was not a passionate
enthusiast. Edith, however, was. She was a minor dramatist of problem
plays, whose liberal sympathies were shown in two particular works,
Warp and Woof (1904), an attack on the conditions suffered by seam-
stresses, and *The Thumbscrew* (1912). She was also a close friend of
Bernard Shaw, persuading him to write *The Dark Lady of the Sonnets*
(1910) and providing him with the story. But Alfred's interest in the
theatre came before he met Edith, when he was still a struggling barrister. The Lyttelton family was not particularly rich, despite its air of
establishment opulence. His father, Lord Lyttelton, had eight children
and a country estate to maintain; and Alfred after university had to
battle along on £140 a year and what he could glean from the Bar. He
was able to go to Paris occasionally, however, and in 1882 he wrote back
to his friend Bernard Holland:

Yesterday we once more, in company of J. G. Butcher, saw *Ruy Blas*
at the [Comédie-] Française. Brohan most engagingly played the
part of the Queen, a part which is really written for her, and hardly
requires the wonderful powers of Sarah. Febvre's Don Salluste was
the new impression for me—he played superbly and looked like the
finest Velasquez; Coquelin was as ever—but so alas was Mounet
Sully, from whom we were distant only three or four short yards, as
the still reverberating drum of my ear painfully reminds me. It
always requires a fortnight or so of association with Frenchmen to
enable one to carry sympathy into the frantic methods they have of
expressing strong emotion: perhaps it is the prosaic recollections of
the Inner Temple which make it more than ever hard to appreciate
the intensity of grief which sounds itself on the high G, and must be
audible from the Française to Les Halles. Spencer, alas, has hanker-
ings for the opera, for low comedy, *Judic* and the like, and it is with
difficulty that I shall persuade him to go with sufficient frequency
to the home of all that is good in drama [Edith Lyttelton, *Alfred
Lyttelton*, p. 119].

14

This is a revealing passage, for it expresses precisely the tone and the attitudes of an educated English gentleman-about-Europe, for whom the Comédie-Française was a model of what a national theatre should be—despite the absence of the divine Sarah Bernhardt, despite the somewhat too extravagant displays of emotion.

Nor was he alone in this opinion—indeed he may have derived it from others—for in 1879 the Comédie-Française (with Sarah Bernhardt) had visited London for a season at the Gaiety Theatre. Matthew Arnold had seen the company—and was enraptured, using the occasion for one of his most famous and influential essays, on 'The French Play in London' for the August issue of the *Nineteenth Century*. During the 1870s, the National Theatre cause in Britain had emerged from one of its hibernations. In 1878, Henry Irving had written a paper on the subject which was read at a meeting of the Social Science Congress, held in October; and his well-publicized views (although they differed from Arnold's in some important respects) may have encouraged Arnold to link his general praise for the Comédie-Française with a more specific call for a National Theatre.

Arnold saw the Française as a perfect example of what was to be gained by organizing a theatre company, giving it financial stability (by means of state grants) and thus helping it to present a constant diet of fine, classic plays—which could act as a touchstone of excellence for the theatre in general. The Française also illustrated exactly what was wrong with the British theatre system, which totally relied upon competition and private enterprise. It was not that Britain lacked a tradition of good drama. On the contrary, it had 'a splendid national drama of the Elizabethan age and a later drama of the town'; and it had had 'great actors'. But 'we have gladly [taken] refuge in our favourite doctrines of the mischief of State interference, of the blessedness of leaving every man free to do as he likes, of the impertinence of presuming to check any man's natural taste for the bathos and pressing him to relish the sublime. We [have left] the English theatre to take its chance. Its present impotence is the result':

> The French Company shows us not only what is gained by organis-
> ing the theatre but what is meant by organising it. The organisation
> in the example before us is simple and rational. We have a society
> of good actors with a grant from the State on condition of their
> giving with frequency the famous and classic plays of their nation;
> and with a commissioner of the State attached to the Society and
> taking part in council with it. But the Society is to all intents and

purposes self-governing. And in connection with the Society is the school of dramatic elocution of the Conservatoire.

Arnold proposed the establishment of an exactly similar institution in London, supporting his argument with an infectious enthusiasm, which built up to a full fanfare of trumpets in the final phrases:

> Forget your clap-trap and believe that the State, the nation in its collective and corporate character, does well to concern itself about an influence so important to national life and manners as the theatre. Form a company out of the materials ready to hand in your many good actors and actors of promise. Give them a theatre in the West End. Let them have a grant from our Science and Art Department; let some intelligent and accomplished man like our friend, Mr. Pigott, your present Examiner of Plays, be joined to them as Commissioner from the Department, to see that the conditions of the grant are observed. Let the conditions of the grant be that a repertory is agreed upon ... and that pieces from this repertory are played a certain number of times in each session; as to new pieces, let your Company use its discretion. Let a school of dramatic elocution and declamation be instituted with your company ... When your institution in the West of London has become a success, plan a second of like kind in the East. The people *will* have a theatre; then make it a good one ... The theatre is irresistible; organise the theatre!

This essay has entered into the mythology of the theatre. It was quoted in virtually every parliamentary debate about the National, has been used to justify and rally political support for the subsidized repertory theatres in Britain and, in essence, Arnold's arguments (particularly those against the dangers of state interference) have been incorporated to different degrees into the arts policies of the modern Labour, Liberal and Conservative parties. Its influence was such that the more cautious and less eloquent remarks of Irving have tended to be overlooked.

Whereas Arnold wanted a tidy, coherent organization subject to some control from the state, Irving wanted 'a large, elastic and independent' institution subject to no state interference. Thus, they differed over state subsidies. 'The institutions of this country', stated Irving, 'are so absolutely free that it would be dangerous, if not destructive, to a certain form of liberty to meddle with them ... A time might come when an unscrupulous use might be made of the power of subsidy.' This unscrupulousness (though Irving did not describe it) might come in two forms: the state might interfere with the arts, encouraging a form of propaganda, while the artists concerned might make an unscrupulous use of public funds. Whereas Arnold envisaged the growth of a number of 'Nationals' (in the East as well as the West of London), Irving wanted only one—so as not to interfere with a predominantly private enterprise system. He considered the way in which a National should relate to its commercial rivals:

> As the National Theatre must compete with private enterprise, and be with regard to its means of achieving prosperity weighted with a scrupulosity which might not belong to its rivals, it should be so strong as to be able to merge, in its steady average gain, temporary losses, and its body should be sufficiently large to attempt and achieve success in every worthy branch of histrionic art [Austin Brereton, *Life of Henry Irving*, Vol. I, p. 258].

He envisaged a kind of independent public corporation, which could draw talent from all branches of the theatre, as and when it was needed, very unlike the more bureaucratic system of the Comédie-Française, with its *pensionnaires* and *sociétaires*. Arnold wanted a permanent company: Irving did not, except in certain respects. He wanted pensions for actors particularly associated with the company and systematic training for newcomers. 'The difficulties of systematization', he concluded, 'would be vast, but the advantages would be vast also.'

In retrospect, Irving's remarks seem to contain a good sense rather lacking in Arnold's essay. Two events indeed serve to justify them. Arnold mentions the name of Mr E. Smythe Pigott as a possible commissioner from the state. Mr Pigott was the friendly neighbourhood censor of the period, the man who once stated: 'I have studied Ibsen's plays pretty carefully and all the characters in Ibsen's plays appear to me morally degraded.' If such men were to act, however indirectly, as custodians of a publicly organized culture, were they likely to provide that protection against philistinism which was Arnold's chief justification for a National Theatre? Pigott and his successor, G. A. Redford, had cheerfully banned plays by Ibsen, Shaw, Granville Barker, Maeterlinck and Brieux. Under their influence, a pre-eminent institution, whose purpose was to spread 'sweetness and light', might, through that very pre-eminence, be an excellent means of spreading bitterness and shade.

The second event was that in 1880, just after the London visit, Sarah Bernhardt left the Comédie-Française. The institution was not 'elastic' enough for her. It restricted her social life, it prevented her from reaping the rewards of her fame and it also thwarted her artistic ambitions. She wanted to play Hamlet—and so she did, under her own management. Arnold thought her tempestuous and irresponsible; but her example in fact underlines a recurring problem with National Theatres. They exist partly to attract and provide expression for the highest theatrical talents; but, unfortunately, these talents often do not want to be tied down to a permanent company with its rules, regulations and benevolent supervision from the state. This dilemma still exists, and unless a totally state-supervised system is proposed where stars have no choice, it is hard to see how it can be overcome. This was why Irving's emphasis on 'elasticity' was so significant: he was apparently imagining a more loosely-knit system, where stars could come, play for a season and leave, without damaging the company management.

The main and underlying difference, however, between Arnold and Irving was this: that Arnold saw the theatre in general (and the National in particular) as a means of cultural evangelism, whereas Irving did not. The justification for the private enterprise system is that managers, whether they like it or not, have to stay in touch with popular opinion; and so the theatre achieves its own form of social appropriateness, following inevitably the shifts and changes of thought and fashion. This system Irving basically wanted to retain, although he recognized (from his own bitter experience as an actor-manager trying to find an audience for Shakespeare) that Higher Drama might be lost in the process. A National, therefore, existed to complement commercial theatre—by providing an area in society where High Drama could be attempted without worrying too much about the box-office. In deciding what High Drama was, Irving was somewhat evasive. The freedom to pursue an artistic vision was essential, but eccentricities had to be checked:

> Art can never suffer by the untrammelled and unshackled freedom of artists—more especially when the idiosyncrasies of individuals, with the consequent possible extravagance, are controlled by the wisdom and calmness of confluent opinion [*ibid.*, p. 259].

With this last, neatly balanced piece of diplomatic phrase-making, Irving avoided a major difficulty in organizing a National by declaring himself for freedom and against it simultaneously. But he clearly regarded the theatre as *reflecting* opinion—either on a popular level, through the commercial theatre, or on a highly educated one, through a possible National.

Arnold, however, once described art as 'a criticism of life'. That was its function. It helped to distinguish between the good and bad in life.

He wanted to civilize England, defining civilization somewhat loosely as 'the humanization of man in society'. He defined, with proper lack of tact, what it is to be provincial, out of touch with the kind of experience and intelligence that can only come from living among important people going about important business in a capital city. He even categorized three kinds of English provincialism—the Philistines, the Barbarians and the Populace. The Philistines were the bustling middle classes, who assumed that morality was nothing more than the rules laid down by the parson, police court, mess and company law. The Barbarians were arrogant, boisterous aristocrats, who valued nothing but stylish chivalry, good manners and field sports. The Populace, of course, were the workers:

> that vast portion ... which, raw and half-developed, has long lain half-hidden amidst its poverty and squalor, and is now issuing from its hiding place to assert an Englishman's heaven-born privilege of doing as it likes, and is beginning to perplex us by marching where it likes, meeting where it likes, bawling what it likes, breaking what it likes.

The alternative to these provincial specimens was to be a civilized man, seeking 'sweetness and light', a tag Arnold borrowed from Swift though he made it his own. It has become an embarrassing phrase, cheapened by sentimental abuse. Originally, however, it was a useful concept of morality which did not make the customary appeal to religious uplift. Those who seek sweetness and light aspire to wisdom without fanaticism. They never make the mistake of thinking that life is simple, or that everyone should think the same. They are serious, but have intellectual good manners. Their morality is strong but unobtrusive, and even their beliefs are aware of necessary contradictions and ironies.

How does one gain 'sweetness and light'? In part by exposure to art, which simultaneously teaches one both the style and the content of proper modes of living. To live in daily contact with true art, which thus relates both to conduct and aspirations, was to live within a 'culture', organized culture as opposed to anarchy:

> Those are the happy moments of humanity ... the flowering times ... when the whole of society is in the fullest measure permeated by thought, sensible to beauty, intelligent and alive.

Arnold distinguished between education, indoctrination and 'culture'. A culture does not necessarily seek to bring art to the masses, along the lines of an Effingham Wilson Handy Book, nor does it attempt to impose a set of beliefs, political or otherwise, on society. Its aims were different—really to supply a context within which education could fruitfully take place and where beliefs of all kinds could be rationally considered. A rich language, for example, was part of a national culture. This language could then be used for many purposes, among them education or indoctrination. Without a 'culture', however, men were exposed to all kinds of fanaticism, superstition and hypocrisies—simply because they had no context in which to consider them rationally, no language, no touchstones of sanity, no trained instincts for beauty or moral aspiration.

Culture, in short, was essential to civilization. It was the bulwark against barbarism. The popularity of Arnold was largely due to the way in which his arguments caught the tone of (and added several dimensions to) that philanthropic section of late-Victorian opinion which included the Lytteltons, the Lyttons, the Gladstonian Liberals, agitators like Holyoake (who, in his *Memoirs*, is at pains to stress that *his* arguments, unlike those of his barbaric opponents, were always expressed in a spirit of 'sweetness and light'), Samuel Morley, Emma Cons, Lady Frederick Cavendish and so many others. He shared and expressed all their fears about the harmful consequences of industrialization, he touched their nerves about the dangers of an ill-educated, barbaric populace. Above all, he was a non-religious evangelist—like Marx in that respect, although he chose art, rather than revolution, on which to pin his hopes.

His general beliefs, give or take a piety or two, provided an ideological basis for the political call which gathered strength over the next sixty years—that the provision of art should be a feature of the welfare state. He even anticipated the style of the Arts Council, by insisting that the state should not attempt to *control* art, not exactly, but provide a context in which art could exist and be freely available to those who wanted to enjoy it.

He was the founding father of a school of literary criticism which still exists and asserts that art, through its criticism of life, is moral in a specific sense. Without religion, without the external moral authority of a God, what is there (argues this school) to show us what is good? The answer is art, and especially literature. Its study will not necessarily make a man behave better; but it will make him wiser—and thus more likely to take better decisions. F. R. Leavis, the literary critic who founded the most influential critical magazine of the 1930s, *Scrutiny*, can be considered to belong within the Arnold tradition, and to have extended its implications to cover the minutiae of reviewing. Leavis, who taught at Downing College, Cambridge, after the Second World

War, influenced a generation of students, among them Peter Hall, Trevor Nunn and John Barton. Indeed, a loose alliance of Cambridge undergraduates from the early 1950s jockeyed for position in the National Theatre Stakes, competing against other informal groupings of, say, the non-university, professional actors and directors who had been trained in a different environment.

Arnold's importance, therefore, in the growth of the National Theatre is not confined to his specific support for it in 'The French Play in London'. He added an ethic to Effingham Wilson's *Proposition*, which raised the cause above that of mere popular education and provided a vision of a Good Life. Civilization itself needed a National Theatre. The alternative was to accept a cultural disorder—which might lead to the physical breakdown of our institutions.

His views, of course, can be attacked from many angles. They are essentially 'élitist', in that he did not believe that 'culture' spreads upwards from the 'people', but instead permeates downwards from the enlightened few. He disliked materialism, particularly that industrial and economic energy which provided the basis for Britain's strength in the nineteenth century. He may even have encouraged intelligent, but susceptible, young men to look down upon industry as being essentially philistine. A new kind of snobbery developed, in which ordinary pro-ductive work was considered debasing—although the professions (law, the Church, the universities, literature and the arts) were all right. Above all, he seemed to propagate the view that art was a one-way process of enlightenment. It criticized life, not vice versa; and therefore the to-ings and fro-ings of popular needs and opinions, whereby audiences influenced the theatre through the box-office and were in turn influenced by what they saw, that two-way process of which Irving was so well aware, was for Arnold a kind of corruption. It tarnished the pristine purity of art, reducing all its fine, uplifting qualities to mere fashion.

A National Theatre, in his view, should be above that sort of thing. It should affirm values which daily life neglects. That was the purpose of subsidy and organization, to raise the theatre above its normal transience. Ironically, however, the history of the National has tended to prove the opposite. Few causes have been so subject to the ebb and flow of opinion, few buildings have seemed so representative of their ages than those designed for the National, few commercial manage-ments have suffered from the financial uncertainties endured by those non-commercial ones who looked to the government or other philan-thropic bodies for help. Little stales faster than yesterday's idealism.

3

The Pioneers

THEORIES usually need practical examples to support them. Arnold found his model National in the Comédie-Française, although he recognized that French culture was more 'homogeneous' than the British (as was French society) and therefore no strict parallels could be drawn. Irving may have had his Lyceum Theatre in mind, which he ran from 1878 to 1899. His dedication to Shakespeare was unquestioned. At a time when Shakespeare's plays spelt box-office death to nearly all London managements, Irving staged them—and turned them into smash-hits. His *Hamlet* in 1874, his Shylock in *The Merchant of Venice* (1879) and his *Romeo and Juliet* (with Ellen Terry, 1882) won him a national, and indeed international, reputation; and proved that with the right actors and meticulous direction, Shakespeare's plays could be as popular with the public as your average pot-boiler, such as *The Bells*. Sarah Bernhardt indeed, and the rest of the Comédie-Française company, had visited the Lyceum when they were in London and were unstinting in their praise.

The very success of his brilliant Lyceum seasons played into the hands of those people who argued that a National Theatre was unnecessary. The Lyceum, in effect, *was* our National Theatre, a triumph of private enterprise, free from any hampering bureaucracy or intellectual attempts to define what, how and why it should be. It just was—and so why did we need to bring some official institution into being? One answer to this rhetorical question is provided by the unhappy end to Irving's career. In 1895 he was given official recognition by becoming the theatre's first knight; but by 1899 he had grown too old, tired and disillusioned to run the Lyceum. His health and his finances were ruined, and his final days were spent on arduous, perfunctory tours, patching up his income by trading on his name. The Lyceum is now a dance-hall, which is rather like seeing one of those magnificent *objets d'art* from the 1851 Exhibition being used as a doorstop in a pub.

During Irving's decline, nobody could take the Lyceum seriously as a model for a National, particularly not after Shaw's scathing comments on Irving's acting. During the 1880s, however, three other theatrical institutions were growing from very humble origins, and their work was to shape the National more drastically than even the Lyceum. In 1879, the Shakespeare Memorial Theatre opened at Stratford-upon-Avon, with the first of its summer festival seasons. In 1880, Emma Cons, social reformer and first woman member of the L.C.C., bought the freehold to an old bloodbath melodrama house, the Royal Victoria in Waterloo Road, which she changed into a temperance amusement-hall —which became the Old Vic. In 1888, a new theatre was built in Sloane Square, the Royal Court, on the site of an old Nonconformist chapel which had been roughly converted into a theatre.

These three theatres had different origins and objectives; and they came to acquire very dissimilar traditions. But each influenced the National by the fact of its existence. Individually, they served as small models, not for the whole National Theatre, but for significant parts of it. And they each played a practical part in its creation—either by providing ideas and people (as in the case of the Royal Court), or by amalgamation (as with the Old Vic), or by refusing to amalgamate (as with the theatre company at Stratford).

The Shakespeare Memorial Theatre was mainly the result of private initiative and patronage from a family of brewers, the Flowers of Stratford. In retrospect, it may seem natural that Stratford citizens should wish to commemorate their most famous member; but in fact, they were remarkably reluctant to do so—apart from the Flowers. Garrick had staged a famous Shakespeare Festival in 1769, which was thought to be a wild provincial adventure until it proved successful. The tercentenary of Shakespeare's birth had been celebrated in 1863 by another Festival, sponsored and organized by Mr E. F. Flower, whose son, Charles Edward Flower, wanted to establish a permanent Shakespeare Theatre in Stratford. He was prepared to provide the riverside site, and a little money, launching a national subscription for the rest. The response to this appeal was disappointing, and so Charles Flower himself supplied most of the £21,000 required. His intention was to establish regular summer seasons at the theatre, and in 1886 he was fortunate enough to enlist the services of Frank Benson, who was very much a theatrical pioneer.

Frank Benson (he was knighted in 1916) had acted with Irving, but he wanted to keep away from the trials and temptations of commercial theatre in London. He hated the star system (as many did who had acted with Irving), disliked long runs and lavish sets. He wanted to establish a company of 'all-round competence' which would specialize, not in trivial plays, but in 'Shakespeare and National Drama'. He followed the unusual practice, previously tried out by the Bancroft management at the old Prince of Wales in Tottenham Court Road, of scheduling productions deliberately for short runs, taking them off sometimes at the height of their popularity, to maintain their 'freshness' and make way for other works. Benson thus followed at least three of the precepts outlined in Wilson's *Proposition*—a permanent company, Shakespeare and National Drama, a single five-act play per evening performance—and added another of his own, the repertory principle.

Benson was very popular. He had an engaging personality, with more than a touch of the enthusiastic amateur about him, a tall, commanding, cheerful presence and an ability to make the best of his slender company resources. His company became almost as well known for the cricket they played on the lawns sloping down to the river as they were for their productions. Benson toured with his Stratford productions, bringing national publicity to the town; and after a few years they were welcomed back to the Festival Theatre each season by the mayor, corporation and town band, a civic reception which belied Stratford's reputation for provincial apathy.

Benson's company had many merits, not least a careful attention to Shakespeare's words and verse-speaking, which began the Stratford tradition for textual respect. This tradition was nurtured by Bridges-Adams in the 1920s and Sir Barry Jackson in the late 1940s; and positively flowered in the late 1950s and early 1960s, with Anthony Quayle, Glen Byam Shaw and Peter Hall. But even its most enthusiastic admirers could not claim that Benson's company had the richness, breadth, air of security or, indeed, the prestige which a forerunner of a National Theatre company could be reasonably expected to possess. And there were some cynics (notably from Leamington near by, Alfred Lyttelton's constituency) who regarded the Festival seasons as a civic publicity stunt.

In contrast, Emma Cons's Royal Victoria Hall and Coffee Tavern possessed high-minded social principle and few cultural pretensions at all. Its existence, however, was a perfect illustration of what spreading sweetness and light meant to many Victorians. The Royal Victoria stood among some of the worst slums in London, south of Waterloo Bridge, a priority area in London for redevelopment even after the Second World War. In 1850, Charles Kingsley described in *Alton Locke* how, at half-price time at the old Royal Victoria, 'the beggary and rascality of London were pouring into their low amusement from the neighbouring gin-palaces and thieves' cellars'.

Emma Cons took over this dump; her policy was simple: to provide a place of purified entertainment for family audiences, free from the temptations of liquor. As Lilian Baylis later pointed out, battered wives built the Old Vic: it was a place where they could expect refuge and decent manners. Cons's first manager was William Poel, who afterwards became known for his open-stage Shakespearian productions, although at this time the Royal Victoria had lost its licence to present plays. Cons offered songs instead, extracts from operas, music and recitations. She ran out of money, but not of support. Samuel Morley, a Nonconformist millionaire textile manufacturer and Liberal M.P. who supported many worthy causes, admired Cons, and her work at the Royal Victoria. He gave her £1,000. His support attracted money from other quarters, and so she was able to buy the theatre's lease for £2,000. Another active benefactor was Lady Frederick Cavendish, who was connected to some of the most powerful families in England. One uncle was Gladstone, another the Earl of Carlisle, and a third the Duke of Sutherland. Her father was Lord Lyttelton: she was Alfred Lyttelton's elder sister, her character transformed after the brutal murder of her husband in Phoenix Park, Dublin; a deeply religious woman, she devoted the rest of her life to philanthropic work.

By Matthew Arnold's standards, Morley, Lady Frederick, Emma Cons and her niece, Lilian Baylis (who came to assist her aunt in 1898 and stayed to take over the management of the Old Vic in 1912), would probably have ranked among the worthier branches of the philistines. They were more interested in providing genteel entertainment for the masses than in art. Their inspirations were religious, rather than aesthetic. Nevertheless, they were tenacious, dedicated and palpably did good — as opposed to merely talking about doing good. Baylis may have had only dubious tastes about the theatre, but she had a remarkable instinct for attracting the right people to help her. She persuaded actors, managers, directors, dancers, singers and choreographers to forgo West End salaries to take part in what was a labour of Christian love. She started the regular Shakespearian seasons in 1914, with Ben Greet as director, at a time when West End theatre had become, for understandable reasons, dominated by escapist drama. During the 1920s and 1930s, the Old Vic became a Mecca for those actors and directors who, quite simply, did not mind too much about money but wanted to test their skills with the Shakespearian classics —

25

Tyrone Guthrie, John Gielgud, Laurence Olivier, Ralph Richardson, Alec Guinness and Sybil Thorndike among them.

But the glories which would stem from the Old Vic were far from people's minds in the 1880s. It was then a symbol for social dedication, for working in a practical way under some of the worst conditions imaginable in London. A tradition began then of providing good entertainment at the lowest possible prices – to encourage everyone to come, thus fulfilling another of Effingham Wilson's criteria for a National. The Old Vic governors – and the Earl of Lytton was one – never lost this missionary sense of recognizing the needs of the poor and trying to help them. Even their reports were imbued with this one aim:

> It is difficult perhaps, for those not acquainted by direct contact and personal experience with the way in which the poor live, to realize the vast gulf in pecuniary value between a penny and tuppence [Annual Report of the Old Vic, 1911–12].

The result of this dedication was that even when the grind of Victorian poverty was to some extent lifted the Old Vic continued to attract audiences unlike those to be found in any West End theatre. It sought and found the affections of generations of theatre-lovers, the poorer ones mainly, the students, the nurses, the lower-middle-class families. This affection might be tinged with an amused tolerance, for many productions at the Old Vic were famous for their tattiness; but the Old Vic was the only theatre in London, other than some music-halls, which could truly claim to be a people's theatre – a place for everyone who was not too snobbish or discriminating about the niceties of productions.

The third theatre was blessed neither by Shakespeare nor poverty. Its association with the National can be regarded almost as accidental, the chance result from the presences of Granville Barker and George Devine, those pioneers for a National who happened to work there. But sometimes chances are not as random as they seem. The Royal Court was a comparatively small theatre outside the enchanted circle of the West End. It was not very successful in its original state, as a converted chapel, until first Marie Litton took it over, and then John Hare, who created a company 'of all-round excellence' including the Kendals, John Clayton and Henry Kembal. Litton and Hare both realized that the old Royal Court (like its replacement theatre in 1888) was not suitable for mechanical marvels nor for productions with large casts; and so they concentrated on small-cast comedies and farces. W. S. Gilbert was one of their writers, in his capacity as a straight dramatist; and later the Royal Court became the theatre associated with Arthur Wing

Pinero (*The Magistrate*, 1886; *Dandy Dick*, 1887; and *Trelawney of the 'Wells'*, 1898).

The significance of the Royal Court during this period was that it could not compete with the West End. It was too small, intimate and out of the way. Audiences had to be attracted by the excellence of the writing and the easy naturalness of the acting. The theatre provided an exact antidote to Irving's monumentalism and Beerbohm Tree's elaborate productions of Shakespeare during the 1900s. It started a tradition for intelligent non-pompous productions of new plays, thus tempting the livelier minds of the age who were afraid that their wits and opinions would be blunted by West End elaboration.

The liveliest of them all was Granville Barker, who started acting in 1891, at the age of fourteen. He became the Golden Boy of British theatre until his early (virtual) retirement in 1918, after his second marriage. He was, to begin with, a good actor, specializing in the roles of anguished, introverted heroes (Richard II, Edward II, Marshbanks in Shaw's *Candida* and Dubedat in *The Doctor's Dilemma*). He was the Ian McKellen or Nicol Williamson of his day. But he was also a leading dramatist—with at least four excellent plays to his credit, *The Marrying of Ann Leete*, *Waste*, *The Madras House* and *The Voysey Inheritance*. He was an outstanding director, renowned for his tact, sympathy and appreciation of new plays; but he also had the imaginative toughness to impose his directorial ideas over some of his wayward contemporary authors, among them Shaw. He freed Shakespeare from two opposing directorial dogmas, Beerbohm Tree's ornate naturalism and William Poel's slavish Elizabethan austerity.

Barker was one of the actor-directors of the Stage Society, formed in 1899 to produce plays of merit which might stand little chance in the West End. The Stage Society can be regarded as a natural ancestor of the English Stage Company after the Second World War, although there was no direct connection between them. For more than thirty years, the Stage Society pioneered for contemporary dramatists, from Britain and abroad, staging productions on Sunday evenings and using the device of the club status to avoid censorship. Hauptmann, Gorki, Gogol, Wedekind, Kaiser, Pirandello, Cocteau, Odets and, of course, Shaw all received British premières of their early plays through the Stage Society; and the *avant-garde* cosmopolitanism of the Stage Society started a tradition which led both to the experimental 'little theatres' of the 1930s and 1940s (and the fringe theatres of the 1960s), and also to Kenneth Tynan's 'spectrum of world drama' at the National of the 1960s.

Barker's best-known achievement, however, and one which stemmed naturally from his work with the Stage Society, was to run, with J. E. Vedrenne as his business manager, four extraordinary seasons at the Royal Court Theatre from 1904 to 1908, staging new plays and significant 'revivals' in repertory. These seasons established the name of Shaw as a dramatist (his work dominating them) but they also included Gilbert Murray's translations of classical Greek plays, contemporary European plays (by, say, Maeterlinck, Schnitzler and Hauptmann), plays by Ibsen and Strindberg—that notorious couple—as well as works from previously unperformed dramatists, such as John Galsworthy, St John Hankin and Barker himself.

These years were a great flowering of British theatre. The plays and dramatists discovered through them came to fill the programmes not only of struggling but ambitious provincial reps (such as the Birmingham Rep, established in 1913), but also of some West End theatres, and indeed of one section in the repertoire of the Royal Shakespeare Company (at the Aldwych) and the National. But there was a more direct link between Barker's work (at the Court and elsewhere) and the National, for in 1903, when he was only twenty-six, Barker collaborated with the theatre critic William Archer to write what became both the blueprint and the bible for the National Theatre movement.

Archer and Barker's *A National Theatre: Scheme and Estimates* (eventually published in 1907) transformed the vague and lofty dreams of Wilson and Arnold into an enterprise which looked eminently reasonable, well-substantiated and, above all, practical. It immediately convinced various eminent actor-managers (such as Sir Squire Bancroft, John Hare and H. B. Irving, Sir Henry's son), whose opposition was likely (for a National could have damaged their own independent interests) and could have proved formidable. It also appealed to businessmen, politicians, patriots and philanthropists. Winston Churchill, for example, then a Liberal M.P. and Secretary of State for the Colonies (succeeding Alfred Lyttelton, who had been ousted in the 1906 election, in that position), had chosen to speak sympathetically about the National Theatre scheme at a banquet in honour of Ellen Terry on June 17th, 1906:

I am one of those who hold that it is the duty of the State to be the generous but discriminating parent of the arts and the sciences; and if we can only divert national attention from the often senseless process of territorial expansion, and the ugly apparatus of war, to those more graceful and gentler flights of fancy and of ambition

28

which are associated with the theatre and the drama, we shall be more securely vindicated in our claim to be a civilized people. Let us think how much money can always be easily obtained for any purposes involving the destruction of life and property; let us think with what excitement and interest we witness the construction or launching of a Dreadnought. What a pity it is that some measure of this interest cannot be turned in the direction of the launching, say, of a National Theatre [quoted in Geoffrey Whitworth, *The Making of a National Theatre*, p. 58].

A copy of the Archer–Barker *Scheme* was promptly sent to Churchill, although there seems to be no record of his reactions to it. Nevertheless, it was a detailed, generally acceptable document which could be sent to a politician as a blueprint for action.

In their Introduction, Archer and Barker described the sort of theatre which it should be, in terms more reminiscent of Irving than Arnold. A National Theatre should be

an enterprise on a large scale, short of extravagance or ostentation [which] would have a far greater chance of succeeding and establishing itself in a permanent and honourable position than an enterprise on a small scale, however ably conducted ... Moreover, the National Theatre must be *its own advertisement*, must impose itself on public notice, not by poster and column advertisements in the newspapers, but by the very fact of its ample, dignified and liberal existence [William Archer and H. Granville Barker, *A National Theatre*, Preface, pp. xvii–xviii].

In other words, it should be 'large, elastic and independent'.

Perhaps because these two adventurous and progressive men of the theatre were trying to sell the operation to the conventional rich, perhaps because they realized that caution might prove the best way to succeed, or perhaps because they believed in a wider argument for the theatre than that expressed by their own commitments, they firmly opposed any policy which emphasized *avant-garde* drama:

There must be no possibility of mistaking [the National Theatre] for one of those pioneer theatres which have been so numerous of late years, here and elsewhere, and have in their way done valuable work. It must not even have the air of appealing to a specially literary and cultured class. It must be visibly and unmistakably a popular institution, making a large appeal to the whole community ... A struggling enterprise, with narrow resources, might provide a mere

29

stumbling block in the path of theatrical progress at large [*ibid.*, p. xviii].

These two men, therefore, who symbolized the *avant-garde* of their times and had been associated with many 'struggling enterprises' in worthy causes, came out against that type of theatre which had made their names. They realized that being over-experimental is the provincialism of the young, just as being over-conventional is the provincialism of the old.

They held an apparently neutral attitude towards the question of state subsidy:

It may be asked why ... we do not suggest going direct to the Government (which would, of course, mean to Parliament) for the money required. The reason is simply that we believe it would be a waste of time ... We must look to private liberality to present a central theatre in London, and to the Empire. That is not only the most probable, but, on the whole, the most desirable event [*ibid.*, p. xix].

Barker and Archer were thus not opposed, unlike Irving, to state subsidy in principle. Their view was that state help was not, at that stage, either practical or desirable—perhaps for the reason afterwards expressed in the first parliamentary debate about the National in 1913, that a government might well want to 'crown' a popular movement with financial support, but should not attempt to initiate the movement of its own accord.

This emphasis on *practicality* and *desirability* can be illustrated elsewhere from the Preface of the Archer–Barker volume. They did not want an all-purpose performing arts centre. They were against having a mixed opera and dramatic theatre, and argued that we should have a National Theatre before a National Opera House, for the simple reason that we already possessed a dramatic repertoire but not an operatic one. They appealed against over-optimism. 'There never was, and there never will be, an ideal theatre. The theatre is too complex and delicate a machine, depending upon the harmonious co-operation of too many talents and influences ... ' [*ibid.*, p. xxi]. They thus forestalled the criticism of those who, aspiring for the perfect theatre, would not even contemplate the merely good.

Their National would enjoy a rent-free theatre, and also escape taxes. It would have a large guarantee fund to ensure that it did not collapse after a couple of unsuccessful seasons, but, apart from that, it would have to make a profit.

If a theatre, freed from the burden of rent etc., cannot at least clear its working expenses season by season, the probable deduction is that the management must either be culpably extravagant or conducted on some mistaken principle. A theatre which appeals to no public or to a very narrow one, cannot be a National Theatre in any true sense of the word [*ibid.*, p. 2].

There was no existing theatre in London suitable for a National. Therefore a brand-new building had to be put up. Such a building would, of course, help the National to be its own advertisement, but there was a more practical reason. The National had to be a repertory theatre, putting on a variety of productions in an orderly manner. No existing London theatre had a sufficiently large backstage storage area to keep the necessary scenery.

Archer and Barker estimated that the whole project would require £330,000. That was the entire cost of getting a company of actors working in their new theatre. As the pound sterling in 1905 was worth roughly ten times what it was in 1970, that was the equivalent of £3,300,000 — or about a fifth of what the new theatre alone actually cost. They may have underestimated — but if we bear in mind that today's building is bigger and far more elaborate than the one they envisaged, and that both building and labour costs have risen out of all proportion to the general rate of inflation, their figures may not have been so wildly inaccurate. They calculated that the site would cost about £75,000, and that the building and equipment of the theatre (including £10,000 for stage devices) would cost about £150,000. The guarantee fund, which also absorbed the initial costs of setting up the company, was £150,000. The sites bought in 1913 and 1938 were in fact within their £75,000 allowance — although Barker would not have regarded them as ideal. In 1963, when the National Theatre company was established, its grants from the Arts Council were in fact £130,000 — well below the Archer–Barker figure for the guarantee fund, if we bear in mind the rate of inflation. The main difference between the Archer–Barker estimates and the final result lies in the cost, scale and elaboration of the National Theatre building: £16 million as opposed to £150,000 — more than a hundred times as much.

They suggested that the best way to get matters moving was to persuade one very rich man, donor A, to put up the money for the building, and then let a number of rather less rich men (donors B, C, D, etc.) club together to raise the money for the site and the guarantee fund. The man who put up £100,000 or more for the building would have his name put up in large letters in the foyer, and a special box for himself and his heirs in perpetuity, 'opposite or adjacent to' the royal box. 'But,' they insisted, 'once the mechanism of the theatre had been set in motion, this should be the sole personal privilege enjoyed by the donors' [*ibid.*, p. 7]. Donors have been known to want to become governors, and governors can sometimes be an interfering nuisance.

The question of interference, or (to put the matter less bluntly) the different rights and methods of controlling the enterprise, occupied the second section of the *Scheme*. In it, Archer and Barker anticipated many practical difficulties which might crop up in running that National, some of which actually did. They decided not to imitate the Comédie-Française, in having a government-appointed director. They plumped for the device of a board of trustees, who would appoint the director, and a general staff. Once the director had been appointed, the trustees were not to interfere. They would have the ultimate sanction of sacking the director, but 'no power to override his arrangements' other than that

> Trustees should receive and pass (if necessary with reservations and censures) the Director's quarterly or half-yearly report, artistic and financial. They should also serve as a sole Court of Appeal from the decision of the Director. Should the Trustees, on crucial questions, give a decision adverse to the Director, it would probably be held tantamount to asking for his resignation [*ibid.*, p. 11].

If this seems an obvious recommendation now, we must remember that more than half a century elapsed before such a division of responsibility was recommended by the Arts Council for repertory theatres—after many conflicts between governors, trustees and directors, of which one affected the National itself. Archer and Barker recommended that the trustees be appointed to represent different public interests—among them, those of the universities. There would be three university nominees, from Oxford, Cambridge and London. The Royal Academy would nominate one, the L.C.C. two, and nine more trustees (making a full board of fifteen members) would be nominated by the donors at first. When trustees died or retired, they would be replaced either by the other trustees nominating new members, or by the Prime Minister suggesting suitable names to the King. They should meet not more often than four times a year, or even only twice a year, unless there was an emergency—in which case they had the power to organize an extraordinary meeting, at the request of one-third of the trustees.

The general staff running the theatre would consist of five officials. The director would have absolute control over everything in and about the theatre, such as the engagement of actors and the casting of parts, save only in the selection of plays. In this area he would be forced to seek the advice of the literary manager (whose duties would include the prior vetting of new plays, the formation of the repertoire, the suggestion of plays for revival, of foreign plays and translations) and the reading committee man. This last official was a particularly interesting suggestion, a compromise between Arnold's view of having a state official supervising the selection of plays and Irving's, that there should be no official at all. The reading committee man was not a deputy *Dramaturg* and was not expected to give more than a portion of his time to the theatre. He was to remain outside the atmosphere of the theatre, a representative of public opinion. A two-thirds' majority could carry the reading committee, so if the reading committee man were a philistine, the director and the literary manager could out-vote him. But if the literary manager had eccentric, *avant-garde* or stuffy tastes, the reading committee man could support the director in opposing him. Archer and Barker rejected the idea that the director should be given absolute power over the choice of plays—or even that he should be given one play a year entirely of his own choosing: 'A strong director would never require to use this power, while a weak director ought not to be entrusted with it.' Completing the general staff was a business manager and a solicitor; and they were to be all reasonably well paid. Directors were to receive £2,000 a year, the literary manager £1,000— or £20,000 and £10,000 in 1970 terms. The trustees and governors, of course, would be unpaid.

In the third section, Archer and Barker described how a director might—or should—run the theatre. They did so by inventing a specimen repertoire of plays, and then working backwards, to determine the size of the necessary company and the facilities needed, in terms of workshops, stage staff, rehearsal rooms and so on. Their specimen repertoire envisaged a balance between Shakespeare, vital English classical drama, recent plays of merit, new plays, translations of representative works of foreign drama, ancient and modern. They then tried to cast these plays, and arrived at a company size of not less than 66 (44 men and 22 women).

Thirty years later, Barker revised the *Scheme* and particularly this section of it. He was particularly worried by one problem: how to make full use of this company not simply for economic reasons, but also to maintain the spirit of group endeavour. The chosen repertoire was infinitely more varied than that, say, of the Comédie-Française, but with this diversity came a situation whereby some productions required fairly small casts and others very large ones. In the Archer–Barker *Scheme*, only one theatre had been planned, with the result that, on those evenings when a small-cast play was scheduled, most of the company would be idle. Constant idleness would ruin the company spirit: but it was hard to see how a large company could be run effectively, offering each player a good choice of parts within a season, and thus avoiding idleness, if there were only one theatre. And so Barker revised the *Scheme* basically to use two theatres, one of which could be presenting a small-cast play, and the other a large-cast one, so that the company could be fully occupied the whole time. The two-theatre scheme offered other advantages. It enabled a director to schedule a 'difficult' or potentially unpopular play with a popular one, thus providing greater flexibility in the choice of plays.

Thus, Barker revised the repertoire, presenting an annual season of forty-nine plays in which each member of the company would have good opportunities. The repertoires of both *Schemes* anticipated remarkably the kind of selection later to be chosen by the Old Vic at the New Theatre in 1945, the Royal Shakespeare Company and the National Theatre. The opening productions, for example, were to be a cycle of Shakespearian History Plays (*Richard II*, *Henry IV*, *Parts 1 and 2*, and *Henry V*), thus anticipating the Royal Shakespeare Company's fondness for presenting Shakespearian plays in groups. They chose Congreve's *Love for Love* to represent eighteenth-century drama and *Money*, *Caste* and *Trelawney of the 'Wells'* for nineteenth-century drama. They even invented names to represent modern plays, naming one *The Chiltern Hundreds*—although it had nothing to do with William Douglas Home's much later play with the same title. That prophecy was the result of coincidence; but it was not chance that there should be similarities between the specimen repertoires and those later devised for the R.S.C. and the National. All planners of National repertoires in Britain have been strongly influenced by the specimens provided by Archer and Barker.

There are, however, also some telling differences. No National company in Britain, even with three theatres, has managed to tackle an output of forty-nine plays. Furthermore, Archer and Barker deliberately chose their plays to avoid the *avant-garde*. In their specimen lists there is no mention of plays by Gorki, Ibsen or Shaw. This was largely because they felt that the National should reflect popular opinion, and not try piously to make it better. The drama was not necessarily to be 'a criticism of life'. Indeed, they may have felt that such criticism was incompatible with the very duties and functions of a National, whose basic role was to provide the best in national drama—to make people aware of their cultural past, not dissatisfied with it. Other theatres, of course, ought to criticize their society: it was a legitimate function for the theatre to undertake—but not for the National. The National, inevitably in their opinion, should be an embodiment of a national heritage, in touch with society at large and at ease with it. The role of a rebel was not one which a National could, or should, play.

The size of the company chosen by Archer and Barker again anticipated the numbers actually employed by the National in the 1960s—and not only its size, but also its system of payment. They invented (or rather adapted from the Comédie-Française) a system whereby players could be kept loyal to the company and yet not pinned down by it. Each actor and actress would be given a basic salary, negotiated with the management each year, and a special performance fee in addition. Nobody in Britain had previously suggested such a scheme. It gave security to the actor, without allowing him to feel over-secure and thus to slacken his efforts. It was easy to reduce the pay of an inferior actor by giving him few performances, while perhaps gratifying his vanity by pretending to raise his salary. An actress enjoying a spell of high fashion and stardom could be paid a relatively low basic salary, but given large, guaranteed and frequent fees for performances. She would thus be given star money, which would not have to be maintained when she had grown old or out of fashion—but she still knew that she would have some security for the future.

There were other prophetic details. The theatre should seat about 1,350 people (although Archer and Barker later raised this figure to 1,550). This seating capacity was thus about 200 more than the largest auditorium in the new National, the Olivier, can hold; but they had evidently chosen in favour of a moderately sized auditorium, stressing intimacy rather than grandeur. Such a decision is the more remarkable when one remembers that late-Victorian and Edwardian theatres were often very large, sometimes seating as many as 4,000, and that to be 'large' was one of the Archer–Barker criteria for a National. Evidently, they believed that this largeness was more a matter of style than seating capacity. It was to be large-hearted, ample-bodied—no stinting on casts or expense, an imposing institution. But it was not to be so imposing as to intimidate people from coming. The ticket prices would be lower than those of the West End, between 1 shilling (50p in 1970 money) and 7/6 (£3·75). Authors' royalties would amount to 10 per cent of the box-office income during productions of their plays; but when an old play was revived, the equivalent sum in royalties should be paid into a pension fund for the staff and actors. Everyone would benefit from the pension fund, doorkeepers and directors alike.

The Archer–Barker *Scheme* is remarkable even today for its precision, foresight and practicality. It is, quite simply, the best blueprint for a National Theatre ever written. Their aims were deliberately modest — and they stressed the fact that no theatre could be *absolutely* flexible and that there was no perfect organization; but they had an image of British national life and a cultural tradition.

Perhaps the chief difference between their scheme and the one which eventually emerged was the way in which the money was to be raised, which influenced other matters, such as the scale of the theatre and the question of trusteeship. The Archer–Barker method for raising money was tried for about forty years, but it did not actually work — although perhaps it could have done. Eventually, the government and the L.C.C. stepped in where the angels of the City had feared to tread; but the relationship between government and the National caused many other problems which could not be fobbed off by large letters in foyers. These problems could not have been foreseen by Archer and Barker because they belonged to a political and social situation unknown in their day — nor were they quite of the character envisaged in nightmare dreams of state-run societies. The troubles were not caused by interference in artistic policies so much as by the bureaucratic procedures, the waiting, the disappointments, the balancing of one interest against another, the weighing of the National Theatre within a total arts policy for the country, that kind of problem.

After the publication of the Archer–Barker *Scheme*, the cause of the National changed its direction. It was no longer necessary to speculate about how a National should look, what it should do and be. Wilson's, Arnold's and Irving's views had been incorporated into a plan for action. All that was needed now was for the action to happen.

4

The Money-Raisers

THE first serious efforts to raise money for the National came about almost by accident. Richard Badger, a rich brewer living in semi-retirement in Eastbourne, felt that he owed a debt of gratitude to Shakespeare; and wanted to do something about it. On May 28th, 1903, while Archer and Barker were privately circulating their *Scheme*, Badger wrote to *The Times*:

> Of all the luminaries any country has produced, the brightest light is William Shakespeare, and to my thinking his countrymen have, as yet, failed to properly memorialize his marvellous talent as evidenced by his literary and sublime conceptions.
>
> In 1833 and 1834, I was a schoolboy at Stratford-on-Avon, 'with shining morning face', no doubt, and as a recognition of my good fortune at having been sent there, whereby I acquired a Shakes-pearian taste, which has been to me a life-long joy, and moreover has, I feel, been an important factor in the success of my career, I am pledged to place at my sole cost, if permitted, a statue to his memory at Stratford-on-Avon, a town well known as 'the birthplace, the home and the grave of the Bard'. Having had communications with the municipal authorities there, I am desirous before proceeding with my scheme to lay before the world, through the agency of *The Times*, an alternative one, which is to collect by voluntary contributions, a sufficient amount to cover the cost of erecting in London and at Stratford-on-Avon, a statue worthy of Shakespeare's fame. I have no doubt the requisite sum will be forthcoming if an influential, competent and Shakespeare-loving committee can be found for the realization of this project, and I shall gladly avail myself of the privilege of contributing £1,000 in aid of the effort suggested.

There were several 'Shakespeare-loving' committees around already, though none 'influential', and at first they were not interested in

Badger's scheme. Indeed, the Shakespeare Committee itself, which had bought Shakespeare's birthplace in 1847 and which Effingham Wilson had advised to disband, may still have been in existence. William Poel had formed the Elizabethan Stage Society in 1894, whose purpose was to promote Shakespearian productions in authentically Elizabethan settings; while in 1902, the London Shakespeare League was established, with Dr F. G. Furnivall, a renowned scholar, as its first president, and Professor Israel Gollancz on its council. The London Shakespeare League provided support and research for the Elizabethan Stage Society, but it also had, as one of its aims, 'to focus the movement for a Shakespeare Memorial in London'.

In August 1904, Badger wrote to *The Times* again. He had had some success from his first letter. The L.C.C., for example, had agreed to provide a site, probably on the South Bank, because Shakespeare had lived and worked in Southwark. But they were not prepared to help in fund-raising; and so, in his second letter, Badger offered to increase his endowment to £2,500, of which £500 was to be spent in an appeal for more funds. This time his offer was welcomed by the press in general, and by the London Shakespeare League in particular. Gollancz hurried off to meet Badger; and a document was drawn up in which it was agreed that a 'memorial' (not necessarily a statue) should be erected on a prominent site in London, given by the government or the L.C.C. To raise sufficient funds—for a monument on the scale of the Albert Memorial was possibly envisaged—a Shakespeare Memorial Committee was to be formed, consisting of eminent men and women from all parts of the Empire and the English-speaking world. A large public meeting was held for this purpose, in February 1905, at the Mansion House, under the chairmanship of the lord mayor of London. Furnivall proposed the crucial resolution—'that this meeting approves the proposal for a Shakespeare Memorial in London. It appoints a General Committee for the purpose of organizing the movement and determining the form of the memorial.' It was seconded by Beerbohm Tree.

Badger's original idea for a London statue had therefore changed. It had become a much larger project altogether, and it had also become much vaguer. Anything could have been a memorial. Perhaps behind the new wording we can detect the work of that assiduous committee man, Gollancz. Gollancz was professor of English literature at King's College in London, a philologist, an expert in Anglo-Saxon and the founder of a fairly successful attempt to duplicate the Académie-Française in London, the British Academy. He probably guessed that the age for pious statuary had passed—it had gone with the monumental 1850s—and he wanted to change the original conception without losing Badger's support. And so the nature of the memorial was left to the Shakespeare Memorial Committee to decide. Badger died, happy in the knowledge that his wishes would be fulfilled, leaving an additional £1,000 to the Shakespeare Memorial Trust.

The Mansion House resolution, however, ran into trouble with some eminent people, including Barrie, Pinero, Gilbert Murray, A. B. Walkley (the critic) and the Earl of Lytton, who declared that such a memorial was likely to prove 'a rubbish heap of trivialities'. But the Shakespeare Memorial Committee doggedly kept its options open, and considered each in turn. Six different schemes were proposed: a statue, an architectural monument, a small theatre to further dramatic art and literature, a National Theatre, a Shakespeare house and a Shakespeare fund. The more ambitious alternatives were ruled out, on the grounds that the committee had neither the authority nor the funds to implement them. One anonymous donor, for example, offered £13,000 if the committee would set about creating a proper National Theatre, but the committee decided that the task was beyond them. The municipality of Venice gave 1,000 lire to show 'its debt of gratitude to the English nation and its great poet'. In the end, the committee chose a rather conservative scheme, for an architectural monument with a statue, to be erected at the top of Portland Place, in the crescent of green framed by the Nash terrace houses, and displacing (by royal permission) a statue of the Duke of Kent.

The special committee, which examined this scheme, passed it on approvingly to the general committee, who turned it over to the executive committee, who worked out details for a world-wide competition among architects, and then reported back to the general committee—who decided that it was time for another full-scale open meeting at the Mansion House in March 1908. At this point, with the plans laid, the site chosen, some money raised and a target for funds (£200,000) decided on, with the architectural competition panting to be let off its leash, the Shakespeare Memorial Committee stepped on the head of a rake. The whole idea, it turned out, was hated by a large section of the theatrical and literary world.

John Hare, who had run the Royal Court so successfully in the 1870s and had been knighted for his services to the theatre in 1907, wrote a suave letter to *The Times*: 'Shakespeare ... requires no blocks of stone or marble to keep his memory green. But I venture to think that the opportunity has offered itself to associate the name of our national poet ... with the founding of a national theatre.' Others used rougher language: 'It is absurd ... ' (William Archer), 'rubbish ... ' (Robert Graves), 'a monstrously ridiculous superfluity ... ' (Professor Churton Collins), 'I do not approve ... ' (Rider Haggard), 'dumping down a heap of statuary in the Marylebone Road is ridiculous ... ' (A. W. Pinero), 'another public nuisance ... ' (A. B. Walkley). Bernard Shaw seized the chance to cut down philistines — 'from all the risks of jobbery, bathos and vulgarity that attend the monumental scheme, the National Theatre scheme is free'; and William Archer contributed a short poem on the subject:

> What needs my Shakespeare? Nothing. What need we?
> A Playhouse worthy his supremacy.
> Oh bathos! — to the Voice of all our race
> We raise dumb carven stones in Portland Place.

Alfred Austin, the poet laureate, wrote a longer poem, which is better forgotten.

The *Daily Chronicle*, whose assistant editor was S. R. Littlewood, a campaigner for the National and a future editor of *Stage*, published 54 letters on the subject, of which 44 deplored the Portland Place monument and 31 supported a National Theatre. The *Daily Chronicle* also printed a National Theatre edition, putting the cases for and against the theatre in clear terms, but deciding in favour of one. Their arguments had plainly been influenced by the Archer–Barker *Scheme*. *The Times* and *Daily News* also chipped in with lengthy correspondence sections. Within a fortnight of the Mansion House meeting, the supporters of the National Theatre launched their own rally — at the Lyceum Theatre on May 18th, 1908.

The Earl of Lytton presided and Alfred Lyttelton proposed the main resolution, which was a counterblast to the Shakespeare memorial: 'This demonstration is in favour of the establishment of a national theatre as a memorial to Shakespeare.' His speech was a model of that lyrical, confident, ironic style which characterized the Edwardians:

The first, and almost the last time I appeared on the stage was in a play by Racine, in which I was supposed to be 'the crowd'. I was taught to come up to the footlights and say, with great embarrassment, 'Moi, je suis l'assemblée'. Today, I am also one man, representing a crowd, and I assure you that I am not in the least ashamed of my client. The instincts of the multitude are perfectly sane and right on the question, not necessarily of an *official*, but of a national theatre. I am confirmed in my belief that there are not two sides to this question at all. If there were another, Mr. Bernard Shaw would be upon it. Now we have the happiness and strength of his support, Mr. Shaw, I suppose, is suffering the anguish of being for once in agreement with several other human beings.

This must have been one of the last occasions when the son of a lord, educated at Eton and Cambridge, could claim to represent the people and crack jokes about it. Sir John Hare seconded and, late in the evening, Shaw was asked to speak. He stood up—and sat down. 'If the subject be not exhausted,' he said, 'those who constitute this meeting are.'

It was a happy occasion. Lytton had really ensured its success by reading a surprise letter from Lord Plymouth, the chairman of the Shakespeare Memorial Committee's executive, at the beginning. Plymouth's letter was a gesture of friendship, regarded by the press as statesmanlike. The Shakespeare Memorial Committee had 'for various practical reasons' suggested an architectural monument, but 'the furtherance of serious drama [had] all along been one of [their] objects'. His executive, too, were therefore prepared to consider the establishment of a National Theatre instead; and Plymouth suggested that a meeting should be arranged between representatives of the Shakespeare Memorial Committee and the National Theatre supporters.

This about-turn startled everybody. It meant, after all, tearing up the plans for a world-wide architectural competition only a fortnight after they had been announced. Gollancz and Beerbohm Tree were thought to have been the diplomats causing the change of policy. Representatives from both sides accordingly did meet—with Gollancz, Beerbohm Tree, Lord Esher and Lord Plymouth among the nine representatives from the Shakespeare Memorial Committee. They met ten days after the Lyceum meeting at the House of Lords; while the first full meeting of the two committees took place at the Mansion House on July 23rd, with the lord mayor presiding. It was then decided that a new single general committee be formed, consisting of a balance between the two earlier committees. It would be known as the Shakespeare Memorial National Theatre Committee, and under this rather cumbersome title the first systematic efforts to raise a National Theatre began.

The first S.M.N.T. committee was an ideal blend of elder statesmen and young radicals, of the establishment and the rebels, of practical businessmen and academics. From the theatre, Sir Herbert Beerbohm

Tree, Johnston Forbes-Robertson; Sir John Hare represented the old guard of actor-managers, while Granville Barker and Shaw stood for the new. Successful playwrights were represented by Arthur Wing Pinero — and unsuccessful ones by Mrs Alfred Lyttelton and William Archer. The academics were Furnivall, Gollancz (the Honorary Secretary), Edmund Gosse, Sidney Lee, C. L. Gomme and H. W. Massingham. There was a useful M.P., S. H. Butcher, who could speak for them in the Commons; and two invaluable lords, Plymouth and Esher, who could hold the fort in the other House. There were enthusiastic dogsbodies — J. Comyns Carr, Sidney Colvin, W. L. Courtney and the secretary, Philip Carr, a young actor and director, who would organize anything, from a garden party to a lord mayor's parade.

They set to work with the enthusiasm of many newly formed committees. The first step was to organize a public meeting which would launch their campaign; but before that step could be taken, a proper handbook had to be printed, a popular version perhaps of the Archer–Barker booklet, which meant that the S.M.N.T. committee went through the *Scheme* in detail, to make it more sellable and impressive. Some indication of the committee work can be gleaned from Shaw's letters, unpublished but with the S.M.N.T. archives. On December 10th, 1908, for example, Shaw had to miss a committee meeting, but on the Great Northern Express to York (where he had a speaking engagement), he wrote ten pages of notes on the coming agenda, ranging from the spelling of Shakespeare's name to expressing doubts as to whether an *ex officio* governor should be replaced by co-option. The committee might, he feared, co-opt a Negro to replace the American Ambassador; and he suggested that *ex officios* should be enforced to appoint deputies.

These discussions were obviously useful and necessary, but with twenty-one members on the executive committee, many as determined and eloquent, if not as combative, as Shaw, compromises had to be found as well as difficult solutions to problems which did not occur; and the clear outlines of the original *Scheme* began to melt. A symptom of these confusing modifications can be found in the *Illustrated Handbook*, which is full of pious formulas. The committee, for example, noted that 'the common reverence for the great spiritual heirloom of our race [i.e. Shakespeare] is one of the deep-seated emotions which secure the unity of the English-speaking world'. Like most campaign literature, the *Illustrated Handbook* looks typical of its period, printed on fine coated art paper outside, thick matt paper inside, designed with copious laurel leaves and busts of Shakespeare. It has many illustrations of subsidized theatres in Lyons, Dresden, Prague, Vienna, to shame us into imitation.

There was a terse summary of the objects of the Shakespeare Memorial National Theatre, closely based on the Archer–Barker *Scheme*, and probably worded by them. The stated aims were: (i) to keep the plays of Shakespeare in its repertory; (ii) to revive whatever else is vital in English classical drama; (iii) to prevent recent plays of merit from falling into oblivion; (iv) to produce new plays and to further the development of modern drama; (v) to produce translations of representative works of foreign drama, ancient and modern; (vi) to stimulate the art of acting through the varied opportunities which it will offer to the members of the company. There were, however, two changes. The Archer–Barker estimates had been rounded up to the more resounding £500,000, with opportunities for various additional funds should anyone want to give more; and there was a conscious attempt to broaden the basis of the appeal through the appointment of governors and trustees. Trustees were requested from Scotland, Ireland and Wales—and from the five greatest (and, of course) richest provincial cities of England, with the two richest from Scotland and two more from Ireland. A trustee from the Workers' Educational Association was proposed, and *ex officio* trustees from Canada, Australia and any other federated colony. The American ambassador was to be a Trustee, for reasons not unconnected perhaps with the fact that Stratford-upon-Avon had received large sums from across the Atlantic. It was a time of agitation for women's rights, and so the committee guaranteed that at least one woman would be appointed a trustee. Shaw called her The Indispensable Woman.

While the men were talking and printing publicity pamphlets, one truly indispensable woman, Mrs Alfred Lyttelton, achieved the first substantial piece of fund-raising for the National. She was perhaps in the best position of all the members of the S.M.N.T. committee to do so, for in addition to being connected—by marriage and through her own family—to the leading social, political and philanthropic families in the country, she had also toured the country and the empire with her husband. She knew almost everyone of importance, many by affectionate private names; and, within the first few months, her drawing-room contacts had reaped a reward. She had a quiet word with Ardèle, the wife of Carl Meyer, who was extremely rich and connected by business both to the Rothschild merchant bank and the Bank of Egypt. Meyer donated £70,000 to the cause; and in 1910 he was awarded a baronetcy.

Carl Meyer's donation, which put him almost into the category of donor A, was announced at the first launching meeting for the appeal fund, organized by the S.M.N.T. committee at the Mansion House in March 1909. Apart from the value of the money itself, it also had the effect of proving the status of the S.M.N.T. committee. They were now a serious pressure group. They had a blueprint in the Archer–Barker *Scheme* as amended, an impressive fund-raising prospectus and sufficient money in the bank not to seem ridiculously overmatched by their task. Within a year, the cause of the National Theatre became fashionable. The S.M.N.T. executive committee had the bright idea of organizing a general committee, whose members would attend their various functions. It was simply a device for rallying as many eminent names as they could to the cause, without actually committing them to anything. This list, published in 1909, is a unique collection of familiar and strange names, highly evocative of the period. As with the executive committee, it was not confined to a narrow social world. It included the familiar names of writers—J. M. Barrie, Hilaire Belloc, Laurence Binyon, Robert Bridges, G. K. Chesterton, Marie Corelli, John Galsworthy, Thomas Hardy, Henry James, Jerome K. Jerome, John Masefield, Gilbert Murray, Bernard Shaw; of impresarios and actor-managers—Charles Hawtrey, Seymour Hicks, Miss Horniman, Nigel Playfair; of composers—Sir Edward Elgar, Edward German; a conclave of academics; a hustle of politicians; together with grand ambassadorial names, such as His Excellency Count Albert Mensdorff-Pouilly, His Excellency Li Chin-Fang; and even royalty: Her Royal Highness Princess Louise. Religious leaders were included: Dr Adler, Chief Rabbi. Humble poetesses: Alice Meynell; and, of course, the old guard, the Lytteltons, the Lyttons, Archer, Barker and all.

There was some opposition to the S.M.N.T. committee. Following the publication of the *Illustrated Handbook*, a circular was sent around, bearing the names of actor-managers such as Sir Squire Bancroft, Weedon Grossmith and the actor-impresario Sir Charles Wyndham, who saw the project as a threat to their interests, and they tried to enlist Pinero among their numbers. Pinero however stood firm, perhaps because Shaw had advised Mrs Alfred Lyttelton that he should be made a knight. He duly was, in November 1909, joining another knight-dramatist on the committee, Sir W. S. Gilbert.

The antagonism died away, however, as the S.M.N.T. appeal seemed to gain strength. The National Theatre cause took its place among the many similar good causes for which it was fashionable to hold parties, fêtes, exhibitions, banquets and even lord mayor's shows. Philip Carr, writing in 1951, recalled some of them:

There was the Shakespeare Pageant, written by Mrs. Alfred Lyttelton, always an enthusiastic supporter of the cause, and produced by me in the grounds of Knole Park in the pouring rain—for which Lady Sackville held me personally responsible. I well remember sheltering Ellen Terry with an umbrella behind a rhododendron before she divested herself of her mackintosh and galoshes to make her entrance on the squelching greensward as one of the Three Graces (Lillah McCarthy was another). There was the Lord Mayor's Show (in 1910) which I organized to introduce all the Shakespearian characters connected with London. Tom Heslewood will not forget that he rode in it as Richard III. I myself shall also not forget another historical costume designer, Herbert Norris, whom I persuaded to take part as Humphrey, Duke of Gloucester, carried wounded on a litter. On account of the litter, he wore modern trousers for the lower part of him which was covered by draperies. But he did not foresee that the bearers would be so slow that the litter was eliminated from the proceedings somewhere near the Mansion House, and he had to take a taxi home dressed in two centuries. There was the splendid Shakespeare Ball organized at the Albert Hall by the mother of Winston Churchill, and the Shakespeare Exhibition at Earl's Court, complete with the reproduction of the Globe Theatre, and the plays as Shakespeare staged them, more or less [*Manchester Guardian*, July 13th, 1951].

Clearly London had gone mad on Shakespeare. There were Shakespearian plaques, pottery, tassels, vellum scrolls as invitations, wax seals with Shakespeare's head. William Poel designed the model of the Globe Theatre for the Earl's Court exhibition, at which, with less historical accuracy, girls dressed as Nell Gwynn handed out oranges. The Shakespeare Ball at the Albert Hall had been organized by Mrs Cornwallis-West, and was under royal patronage, although the King and Queen themselves were unable to come. A commemorative volume was published for this occasion (at £5 5s. od. a copy!), which lost money, although the ball made some.

Shaw, at the request of Mrs Alfred Lyttelton, who also gave help with the story, wrote a short play, *The Dark Lady of the Sonnets*, which was first presented at the Haymarket Theatre on November 24th, 1910. Its plot concerned a tryst between Shakespeare and Mary Fitton (the Shavian Dark Lady), which is interrupted by Elizabeth herself, in disguise under a heavy cloak. Shakespeare approaches the Virgin Queen by mistake and covers his confusion with a plug for the National Theatre:

... since you are a queen and will none of me, nor of Philip of Spain, nor of any other mortal man, I must e'en contain myself as best I may, and ask you only for a boon of State.

ELIZABETH   A boon of State already! You are becoming a courtier like the rest of them. You lack advancement.

SHAKESPEARE   'Lack advancement.' By your Majesty's leave, a queenly phrase. (*He is about to write it down.*)

ELIZABETH   (*Striking the tablets from his hand.*) Your tablets are beginning to anger me, sir. I am not here to write your plays for you.

SHAKESPEARE   You are here to inspire them, madam. For this, among the rest, were you ordained. But the boon I crave is that you do endow a great playhouse, or, if I may make bold to coin a scholarly name for it, a National Theatre, for the better instruction and gracing of your subjects.

These activities may have been fun, perhaps, if only for those taking part, but they did not actually raise much money. By 1913, after four years' fund-raising, donor A had not been followed by donors B, C and D; Carl Meyer's £70,000 had crawled slowly towards £100,000, still far short of the £½ million required. By now, a curious mixture of hope and despondency, urgency and complacency was in the air. Most were convinced that the Shakespeare Memorial National Theatre would, sooner or later, be built. With those names on the general committee, with all those society events in its honour, how could the scheme fail? There was even a date chosen for the National's opening, the tercentenary of Shakespeare's death, April 23rd, 1916.

If there had been less money in the kitty (or more), the organizers might well have abandoned the scheme or gone ahead with it, confident that the money would eventually be found. As it was they were in a quandary. Some members of the S.M.N.T. organizing committee wondered whether it might not be better to start putting on plays in existing theatres, until the money could be raised to build a new one. But this course of action risked frittering away the sums already gleaned, without actually achieving the 'large, elastic and independent' institution which was the true object. Others thought that it would be better to buy the site, while there was the money for it, leaving the actual building until later. Sites wisely bought can be sold again; and it would keep the money away from those who wanted to spend it on productions.

The S.M.N.T. executive committee had appointed a site committee in 1909, which considered many possibilities. After about a year's deliberation, they decided that the most promising place for the theatre was by Trafalgar Square. The L.C.C. had just built their new County Hall on the South Bank; and their old offices, in Spring Gardens tucked behind Admiralty Arch, were going to be empty when they moved. The L.C.C. wanted the National Theatre to occupy the site; but the government, who needed the building to house their civil servants, were not so happy. Another year passed, while the government pondered the question. Then Archer had a brainwave. He decided that the 'finest site in Europe' was on the South Bank, near Waterloo Bridge, overlooking the river—within a few yards of where the National eventually came to be built. He wrote to Mrs Lyttelton about it, but faced the opposition of those people (including Shaw) who felt that the South Bank was too far from the centre of London, unfashionable and unsalubrious. Shaw wanted some undistinguished houses on the North Bank, where the old Whitehall Palace had stood in Elizabethan times, to be pulled down; and the National Theatre built there, right beside his London flat. The houses were eventually demolished, but the ugliest of government hulks now stands there, the Ministry of Defence.

In the meantime, the wolves were beginning to circle. Various actor-managers started to attack the committee, for not containing enough actors, for not handing out money and for getting nowhere. Alfred Lyttelton once told Philip Carr that 'in the course of a long and sometimes stormy political career he had never known committee meetings so violent as some of ours':

> There were the actor-managers who had fought shy of the whole thing at first, and then decided that it would be better not to be left out, and pretended then that they had been enthusiastic supporters from the beginning [*Manchester Guardian*, July 13th, 1951].

The problem with having as varied and representative a committee as the S.M.N.T. executive was that some members were not deeply committed in the first place but were going along for the ride, whereas others had their minds so completely made up that they were not going to be confused by too much listening. A core of good sense within the S.M.N.T. committee was provided by Gollancz, Mrs Lyttelton, Archer, Barker and sometimes Shaw, all dogged supporters; while a threatening revolt came from Sidney Low. Low submitted a formal memorandum in 1912 which argued that since the movement had obviously failed to raise the necessary money and enthusiasm to build the National in time for the tercentenary, it should now abandon its aims. It should simply build the Shakespeare Memorial, as originally planned, and hand the excess money to actors and impresarios.

As a last resort to raise the money quickly, in time to build the National by 1916, the S.M.N.T. committee decided to approach Parliament. It persuaded a sympathetic M.P., H. J. MacKinder, to introduce a Private Member's Bill on the subject; and the Commons debate, which took place on April 23rd, 1913 (St George's Day), was the first of several parliamentary debates about the National, arguably the best and certainly the widest-ranging debate about state patronage for the arts to have taken place in this country.

Its excellence was partly due to the fact that it was a Private Member's Bill. Unlike the debate in 1949, when money was actually approved, there was no assured government majority for the Bill and no opposition prepared on this occasion to comply. The individual speakers had to persuade their fellow M.P.s by the cogency of their arguments: they could not rely on the Whips. Nor, as in the debates which followed that in 1949, had the main questions been settled in committees beforehand. Nor indeed had the arguments in favour of state subsidies for the arts become so familiar and routine that a mere nod in the direction of Matthew Arnold was sufficient to carry the day. It also took place in an atmosphere of confidence about the future.

One crucial difference between the 1913 debate and subsequent ones lay in the question of the role of government. In 1913, the champions and the opponents of the National were agreed that Parliament should not attempt to initiate a 'popular' movement, but merely to 'crown' it. The cause had to have its roots in public demand, before the government intervened to help it along. The idea that government existed to 'change society' would have stubbed its toe on the charge of totalitarianism; and indeed the really enthusiastic supporters of the National, Shaw in particular, were often accused of a dictatorial do-gooding. It was not, therefore, a sufficiently persuasive argument for the Commons simply to state that the arts were good for people and that the government should thus provide them. MacKinder had to prove that, first, a broadly based movement for the National existed, and, second, the social need for the arts was such as to justify intervention. MacKinder could point to the activities of the S.M.N.T. committee and the fact that more than £100,000 had already been raised; but as an opponent, Ellis Griffith, immediately asked, was that a sufficient mark of public support?

ELLIS GRIFFITH. I am inclined to accept what was said by the Mover of the Motion ... that it was the duty of Government ... not to initiate but to crown a project of this kind. The honourable Member admitted that only £100,000 of the £500,000 has been subscribed voluntarily. The time for crowning has not yet arrived.

That, of course, was a matter of opinion, and other Members who were generally in agreement with the basic political philosophy supported MacKinder.

It was the second stage to MacKinder's argument, however, which was the more persuasive. He anticipated those familiar arguments of the 1950s and 1960s about the forthcoming age of leisure, the necessary by-product of industrialization. He did not therefore rely upon Arnold's arguments about culture being the bulwark against barbarism and philistinism. MacKinder believed, with William Morris, that industrialization had left behind a dereliction of boredom, a loss of interest in jobs and a decline in traditional craftsmanship:

H. J. MACKINDER. We have ... increased the leisure of vast masses of people. Moreover, you have at the present time ... an increasing monotony of employment. Machinery, mechanical operations, division of labour have brought that about. The result is that men are having less and less interest in [their] daily work.

He felt that this leisure should be turned to good use by making people more aware of the potentialities of life, and that a key element in this enlightenment was the theatre, precisely because it did not rely heavily upon reading:

H. J. MACKINDER. There is a revolt against the excessive use of books. There is a demand for a more concrete life in the teaching which we give, whether to children, adolescents, or adults. In science long ago, students turned to the laboratory, and away from the mere book. So it should be in literature. After all a composition was originally intended to be *delivered*, even poetry, certainly the drama. What we want is education through our Shakespeare ... not mere amusement. Our idea is that a theatre of this kind should be popular and educational, that you should allow schools opportunities for attending *en masse* and to form the whole audience on occasions.

MacKinder also agreed with Matthew Arnold, whom he quoted, that some kind of national institution was necessary to ensure the continuity

49

of a national culture, to protect, say, the language from the pressure of warring dialects.

The man who tabled the opposing amendment to MacKinder's Bill was someone who can perhaps be regarded as having a vested interest in maintaining dialect—or, if you like, a regional independence: someone who had suffered from the excessive centralization of British culture whose tendency was to destroy regional and indeed smaller national differences. Mr Lynch of County Clare was in the House as an Irish Nationalist Member, but he was not so obsessed with opposing all English institutions that he failed to argue the wider case—which was a protest against all attempts to institutionalize (or, in his phrase, Prussianize) culture:

> The same project has been tried out in other countries—France, Italy, Germany, Spain and elsewhere—and I believe that it is only in France that it has been an undoubted success, for many reasons which do not obtain to this country. You can hold no greater warning than the Berlin system ... The Schauspielhaus is one of the innumerable ways of glorifying that stupendous Prussian system. Who are the Berlin dramatists? Where is their great national drama? Where is their great inspiring work? Why, their best plays are all adaptations from French writers, and when they do adapt them, they invariably choose second-rate ones ... If such a national theatre had been in existence in Shakespeare's time, I doubt if he would have had a chance to be represented.

> ... I owe allegiance to something greater than Shakespeare, something more real and actual, and that is my aspiration for the free development of literature ... There is something in organisation, alien to what is the very spirit and essence of literature, and taking the example of our Universities, I would ask: can any man point out any great writer in the English language who has been a real and veritable product of our Universities?

> (*Interruptions:* Tennyson!)

> Well, yes, I have a prejudice against Tennyson perhaps on that very account, but I am quite content to give you a present of Tennyson.

The real danger, as Lynch saw it, was not that the cause of drama was too unimportant for governments to meddle with, but that it would simply become an excuse to glorify Britain and all things British—or, failing that, that it would fall into the hands of dons. The key problem was that of the trustees, who would start to dominate the director by being too careful in their control of public money:

I believe that if this National Theatre could be removed from a certain type of Trustee, it might possess many valuable points—the dry-as-dust Trustee, the Trustee educated in too much book-keeping, the Trustee attaching too much importance to the University, or the Trustee holding up Tennyson as a great National Poet. If he were a Trustee of flesh and blood, or a Trustee endowed with some of the spirit of Robert Burns ... if he were a Trustee who could look upon all our institutions with a candid eye and touch them fearlessly with a rod of light, then the National Theatre might be saved. What I fear is that this subject so pompously introduced—I mean, with such pomp and circumstance—will be somewhat too pompously managed.

Mr Lynch was thus arguing the traditional conservative case against the state meddling in art; but he did so from the angle of someone who feared, and had genuine reason to fear, the dominance of a centralized culture. And he, like MacKinder, was prepared to concede points to the other side, to recognize that the right sort of National could be an asset. Other speakers in the debate were equally direct, and sometimes prophetic, in their views. Mr Ponsonby, for example, insisted that we should have a Minister of Fine Arts, and was scathing with another Member who asked where the money was going to come from. 'It is perfectly ridiculous', Ponsonby retorted, 'to say that a country spending £195 million on various subjects cannot spare £200,000 to endow what I consider to be one of the most important branches of life, the encouragement of the arts.'

At the division, 96 M.P.s voted for Mr MacKinder's motion—that 'there shall be established a National Theatre, to be vested in Trustees and assisted by the State', and only 32 against. The House of Commons was in favour of the motion, but, as it happened, not enough in favour. The Speaker ruled that the question was not decided in the affirmative, because it was not supported by the majority prescribed in Standing Order No 27, which governed Private Members' Bills and required a more than two-thirds majority. Among those who voted for the Bill were Stanley Baldwin, J. R. Clynes, Keir Hardie, Sir Alfred Mond, Leo Amery and Wedgwood Benn. Tim Healy voted against.

Nevertheless, the S.M.N.T. committee were happy enough with the debate, though the outcome had been disappointing. They could regard it as paving the way for a more substantial assault upon Parliament, perhaps with government backing. It was an example of how things were done in Britain: a determined assault against the reactionaries might be beaten back at first, but a second assault would win the day. J. B. Priestley in his play *Eden End* (set in 1912, written in 1934 and produced by the National in 1973) recalled the mood of general optimism. Women would be emancipated: the Irish problem would be solved. Britain was evolving peacefully into a different sort of country: democratic, liberal, classless and civilized. There would never be another war: we had evolved beyond that state. The new employment exchanges would control the scourge of unemployment, as they seemed to be doing. The new industrial wealth would be spread around the populace. The National would be built. It was all a matter of time, stability and growth.

And so, in the autumn of 1913, the S.M.N.T. committee went ahead and bought their first site. It was in Bloomsbury, at the corner of Gower Street and Keppel Street, in the university area. The acre of land cost £50,000 and they hoped that this purchase would encourage donor B to appear. They even had drawings for the theatre, long, comparatively low and vaguely Tudor in appearance. The Bloomsbury site may not have been ideal: it was too far from the West End. But it was within a stone's throw of the Academy of Dramatic Art (which became the Royal Academy of Dramatic Art, by charter, in 1920), and this meant that at some point the Academy could be attached to the National as a training school. It was also a freehold property, which would make it easy to sell if a better site cropped up before the building began. And, of course, it protected the funds of the S.M.N.T. committee from those who would have used them for other purposes.

But donor B never came. Instead, war was declared and the S.M.N.T. committee was 'temporarily' dissolved. In 1914, most people thought that the war would be over by the winter, or the following spring, or summer, or the next winter, after a few hundred more lives, another thousand or so, perhaps at most a million. It was not until the tercentenary of Shakespeare's death, in 1916, that something was actually built on that empty site in Gower Street. It was a hut, put up by the Y.M.C.A., for the entertainment of wounded soldiers. It was known as the Shakespeare Hut.

The remnants of the S.M.N.T. committee gave their permission.

5

The Fragments

'HENRY BOWLBY's pupil room', wrote Oliver Lyttelton in his *Memoirs*, 'was a pupil room of all the talents ... all killed, except for Ronnie Knox, in the holocaust.'

He was recalling his days at Eton before the war; and that short sentence reveals the havoc wrought upon pre-war society by the massacres of 1914–18. The skeletal statistics—more than 1 million British dead, 1½ million French, 2 million Germans, 2–3 million Russians—do not tell the whole story. There was also the effect of this carnage upon the survivors. Oliver Lyttelton was twenty-one when the war ended. He had served in France with the Grenadier Guards, winning a D.S.O. in 1916 and rising to become a brigade major in 1918. He was awarded the Military Cross in 1918. But after the war, he looked around to find a job and saw that most of his friends and contemporaries had disappeared.

Society was gap-toothed. Once-prosperous firms were struggling along with old men and boys—and, of course, women, for the First World War proved that they were indeed indispensable. There was also a change in ethos: the pre-war optimism had been replaced by devastating emotions—the rigid determination to build a Better World, the sense of loss, the haunting friendships forged by fire, the clinging together of survivors and the nostalgia. The quiet, self-sacrificial philanthropy of many middle-class Edwardians had sought to moderate social evils, while at the same time maintaining an open society—in which government was merely a service industry. Now there was a growing resolution to change society itself, through central government action if necessary. That was what Shaw wanted, and he felt continually frustrated that the remembrance of better, pre-war days, now glamorized perhaps by those who had endured the trenches, kept intervening. Resolution (he thought) was being stifled by memories.

53

For Oliver Lyttelton, the memories were particularly painful. He had revered his father, who died just before the war when an untimely blow from a cricket ball led to an internal rupture. He wanted to live in a way that would not disgrace his parents; but the world had changed to make self-sacrifice also self-defeating. Few of his relatives were in commerce or industry, for example. Three of his uncles were in the Church, another in the army, a fifth in politics, like his lawyer father, Alfred. The professional careers of his father's family all involved a degree of public service; and a similar attraction towards self-denial characterized many middle- to upper-middle-class families before the war. Gerard Olivier, for example, Laurence Olivier's father, threw up a comfortable income as the headmaster of a private school to become a mere curate in Dorking. Even Dorking, however, was not enough of a sacrifice: Gerard Olivier left there quickly to work in the slum districts around Notting Hill Gate in London, then known as Nottingdale, thus reducing his family to a far from genteel poverty.

For Oliver Lyttelton, public service was not a practical possibility. He could not afford it. He risked lowering himself in the eyes of his family by going into the City, where he joined a banking firm, Brown Shipley & Co., for a salary of £180 a year and a bonus at Christmas. He became a specialist in foreign exchange dealings; and then joined the British Metal Corporation, rising rapidly (partly through the absence of contemporary rivals) to the post of general manager. Through his efforts, the British Empire entered the Second World War self-sufficient in non-ferrous metals, and he was thus appointed Controller of Non-Ferrous Metals in the Ministry of Supply in 1939. But he maintained, as best he could, the family links with those causes which his parents had supported, among them the National Theatre to which his mother was still attached. 'I have carried on her work for the National Theatre,' he wrote in his *Memoirs*, 'partly as an act of filial piety, and partly because my deep conviction is that a National Theatre must be one of the foundations of British Society.'

After the First World War, however, the whole social basis on which the National Theatre movement had previously rested, had disintegrated. About half the names on the impressive 1909 general committee list belonged to those who had either died, or lost their money, or their social positions; and the remaining ones were preoccupied with more important matters than the National. When, in July 1918, Sir Israel Gollancz called together the S.M.N.T. executive for the first time since August 1914, a decision was taken which at any rate implied a temporary shelving of their plans. The executive agreed to release

Effingham Wilson
Bookseller & Publisher,
Stationer, Engraver & Printer,
11, ROYAL EXCHANGE,
London

1 Trade advertisement of Effingham Wilson, bookseller and publisher.
Wilson was the first man to put forward a detailed scheme for a
National Theatre, in 1848

2 Edward George Earle Bulwer Lytton, 1803–73

3 The Hon. Alfred Lyttelton, 1857–1913

4 Matthew Arnold, 1856–1922

5 William Archer, 1856–1924

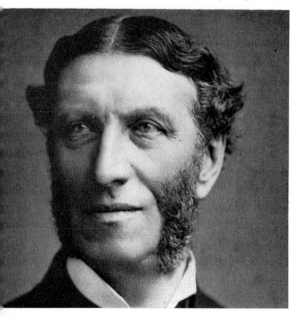

EARLY CAMPAIGNERS FOR A NATIONAL THEATRE

6 Sir Carl Meyer, 1851–1922, who donated £70,000 to the S.M.N.T. in 1909

7 Harley Granville-Barker, 1877–1946, actor, dramatist and director, co-author (with Archer) of *A National Theatre: Scheme and Estimates* (1907)

8 The Duchess of Wellington's Quadrille Party, one of the many fund-raising activities on behalf of the S.M.N.T.

9 Three posters from the 'Shakespeare's England' exhibition held at Earl's Court in 1912

10 Extract from a list of donors to the Shakespeare Memorial National Theatre Trust, March 1909

eyer, Sir Carl Bt.,	70,003.	0.	0.
~~Anonymous~~ Richard Badges	3000	c	0
orrison, Capt J. A. M..,	550.	0.	0.
Anonymous, per rs. A. Lyttelton,	500.	0.	0.
Anonymous, per rs. A. Lyttelton,	500.	0.	0.
W. Em	500	0	0
Corey, rs.	500.	0.	0.
Tennant, Sir Edward P. Bt., M.P.,	153.	0.	0.
haw, G. Bernard	108.	0.	0.
oore, Ald. A. Keatley Croydon Branch,	101.	1.	0.
orniman, E. J. M.P.,	100.	0.	0.
ea, rs. Charles Wheeley	100.	0.	0.
St. George's Society, Canada,	100.	0.	0.
J magin	100		
Nottingham Committee	81	15	6
Dodge, Miss R. H.	75.	0.	0.
Bramey Lady	75.	0.	0.
Leeds Committee,	84.	11.	0.
eyer, Col. Victor Van De	53.	0.	0.
olinsworth, C. H. A A. R.	50.	0.	0.

some money to support a company which would tour around the country, playing Shakespeare or other 'recognized classics'.

The actual company was not chosen until 1919, when W. Bridges-Adams, a young director, took over the Shakespeare Memorial Theatre at Stratford from Sir Frank Benson. The S.M.N.T. committee gave him £3,000 to form the New Shakespeare Company which would continue the summer seasons at Stratford and tour. These grants continued annually for three years; but they were not derived from the capital fund. The Y.M.C.A. was paying rent for the Bloomsbury site, £3,000, which was given directly to the company; but this decision indicated that the S.M.N.T. committee saw no immediate chance that the National Theatre would be built. It also set a risky precedent for other companies, such as the determined Old Vic, who looked enviously towards the coffers of the S.M.N.T. in their hours of need.

Fortunately, the money was still largely invested in the Bloomsbury site; but by 1922, this block of land had become a liability. The L.C.C. terminated the licence for the Y.M.C.A. huts; and so the S.M.N.T. committee thought that, with no rent coming in and no prospect for a theatre, it would be wiser to sell the site—which it did in 1922, investing the money elsewhere. As soon as the site was sold, the funds became immediately more available for needy companies; and the S.M.N.T. committee was besieged with useful suggestions as to how it could be spent.

Legalism came to its aid, prompted by Sir Israel Gollancz. A question which arose from the sale of the Bloomsbury site was whether or not the Shakespeare Memorial National Theatre was a charity—in which case its funds could only be directed towards the objects of that charity, namely the building and running of the theatre. Special approval would have been required from the Charity Commissioners to spend the money in any other way. If the Shakespeare Memorial National Theatre were not a charity, but merely an organization whose aims were 'philanthropic', then the funds could be spent in any way that the committee thought fit.

This matter was not finally decided until 1925, when two S.M.N.T. trustees, Frank C. Meyer (Carl Meyer's son) and J. Forbes-Robertson, gave an undertaking to the Treasury that the S.M.N.T. trust was indeed a charity and that its funds would be essentially used for the acquisition of a theatre. They could not finance any other company, including the New Shakespeare. There was, however, a catch. If it could be proved that the S.M.N.T. trust had failed in its aims, totally and irrevocably, then, with the approval of the Charity Commissioners,

the trust could be wound up. The money could then be diverted elsewhere. Although this meant that the S.M.N.T. funds were temporarily
kept free from marauders, this situation also tempted those who wanted
to declare the scheme a failure, so that they could lay their hands on
the money.

Those who were looking for signs of failure had no difficulty in finding
them. By 1922 there was still no donor B, and the S.M.N.T. appeals
office, opened before the war, had not reopened after it. There were no
social events, no begging letters, no ladies' committees, no debates in
the House of Commons. Gollancz was reduced to suggesting a nation-
wide collaboration with the Y.M.C.A. to produce amateur dramatics.
Nor did the committee seem responsive to suggestions. In 1923,
James K. Hackett, an American actor, through the auspices of a new
organization, the British Drama League, put forward an idea to sell
shilling shares to the public, which could then be presented to the box-
office in return for a one shilling reduction from the price of a ticket.
The S.M.N.T. considered the idea 'carefully'; and rejected it.

They also rejected an idea from William Archer, who had decided
that since the pre-war appeal had failed to raise money from the very
rich, they should now approach the second rung of the ladder. He
wanted a limited number of influential people to sign a Statement of
Principle in favour of a National Theatre, which would eventually be
backed by money. He elaborated this idea in a booklet, *The Foundation
of the National Theatre*, which was in the form of an imaginary history,
written by a historian in the impossibly distant future, 1950. He
inserted two practical suggestions into this dream—of which the first
was that an interim National Theatre company should be formed to
play in an existing theatre, which was good enough to encourage further
donations. Second, he had discovered from income tax records that
just after the First World War 7,000 people were earning more than
£10,000 a year; if one-seventh of these wealthy people could be persuaded to contribute £1,000 each to a fund, that would be £1 million;
with angelic optimism, Archer assumed that this had happened, and
also that an anonymous millionaire, a nobleman, changed heart at the
last moment. The fictional secretary of the committee arrives late for a
crucial meeting—to announce a donation of £250,000 and that the
government has offered a site by Charing Cross station. The cavalry
has arrived.

But the S.M.N.T. committee rejected both his Statement of Principle
scheme and his booklet, which was eventually published by the British
Drama League, in 1922. The truth was that the S.M.N.T. committee

was itself divided on the question of whether it should carry on. A letter from Archer (dated July 21st, 1922) to Granville-Barker reveals the dissensions:

> The Old Vickers, whom Satan fly away with, have had the unspeakable audacity to turn down my proposal at the Executive ... Really life is impossible with these people!

In fact, they had not rejected it, but the committee was so evenly divided that Archer withdrew his proposal.

The 'Old Vickers' were, of course, the members of the S.M.N.T. committee whose loyalties were being drawn away by the Old Vic; and for many years the popularity and reputation of the Old Vic was an embarrassment to the S.M.N.T. Lilian Baylis seemed to be doing on a shoestring what they had been talking about for years. Furthermore, it had acquired a heroic reputation for carrying on during the war, even during the air-raids. Miss Baylis would not accept anything less than a direct hit from a bomb as an excuse for missing a rehearsal. Sybil Thorndike was once caught in a raid as she came out of the tube at Waterloo Station. A policeman tried to stop her, but she said, 'I can't help the raid ... The curtain is up at the Old Vic, and I shan't be on for my entrance.' The policeman let her go, but the brief delay brought Miss Baylis to the pit door in a temper. 'Why on earth weren't you in before this?' Sybil Thorndike breathlessly explained. 'Raid!' snorted Miss Baylis, 'What's a raid when my curtain's up?'

The Old Vic had started its Shakespearian productions during the war, with Ben Greet as director and the Thorndikes in the company. It was the only theatre regularly to play Shakespeare during the dark days; and for many who loved the theatre, the Old Vic became a standard-bearer for civilized drama. Before the war, theatrical standards in London had been generally high, with Pinero, Maugham and Wilde among its popular dramatists, Shaw, St John Ervine, Granville Barker and Galsworthy among its more serious ones, with established actor-managers like Beerbohm Tree and Benson trying their box-offices with Shakespeare.

During the war, the theatre in London deteriorated in range and quality. This was partly due to the absence of actors on military service, but it was also because there was a theory, supported no doubt by box-office returns, that soldiers on leave with their families and girlfriends did not want to see anything as heavy as Shakespeare. They wanted light escapist musicals—like *Chu Chin Chow*, which opened in 1916 and ran for a record 2,238 performances. In 1918, a stall seat in the West

End was priceless, 'as hard to find as a box of matches'; but though the West End might be thriving, serious drama was not. In 1917, for example, there was only one Shakespeare production in the West End, H. B. Irving's *Hamlet*.

The Old Vic was thus an exceptional theatre in London, although its productions could not compare with the pre-war Shakespeares, presented by Irving or Tree. They were notoriously tatty in staging: 'not so much fustian', as Oliver Lyttelton remarked, 'as fusty'. Miss Baylis's voice could sometimes be heard from the wings, quarrelling with Ben Greet; while the smell of kippers, sausages or chops cooking in her office or in the prompt corner drifted nightly across the stage. The costumes reappeared from production to production like friendly slippers which nobody had the heart to throw away; and, during the war, some male parts had to be taken by women. One of Miss Baylis's famous prayers (for she was very religious) was 'Please God, send me some good actors—and cheap!'

But the ramshackle conditions at the Old Vic in one sense added to its attractiveness—first, because good performances often shone brighter amongst the casualness (as they do in certain fringe clubs today), and second because the Old Vic's role as a 'people's theatre' was thereby emphasized. Because the S.M.N.T. committee had become so firmly associated with pre-war society and fund-raising among the rich, it could scarcely claim to be a 'people's' movement; and because that elegant and often enlightened social veneer had been largely broken up and destroyed, the S.M.N.T. was left without a public mask.

These were the days of the 'people's' theatre, and it was not only the Old Vic which symbolized them. Many directors and actors were turning away from the West End, in order to present rudimentary productions on a shoestring to audiences of whom many had never seen a play. Lena Ashwell, for example, a famous pre-war actress and a protégée of Ellen Terry herself, formed a small company to take plays by Shakespeare, Shaw and others around the Y.M.C.A. huts and army billets in Britain and France. Basil Dean, the founder of the Liverpool Playhouse, organized entertainment parties and drama productions for the troops: his efforts during the First World War led to the establishment of ENSA during the Second. In the years before, during and after the First World War, a movement began to establish 'independent' regional reps (independent, that is, of London). Miss Horniman launched the Gaiety Theatre in Manchester in 1908, with its company of actors (including Lewis Casson and Sybil Thorndike). This produced a school of regional dramatists (among them Stanley Houghton, who wrote *Hobson's Choice*). Barry Jackson founded the Birmingham Rep from his amateur company, the Pilgrim Players, in 1913, and Basil Dean pioneered in Liverpool from 1911 onwards. If the West End seemed preoccupied with escapist musicals, the growth of the people's theatre movement and of the regional reps presented a different picture.

One young publisher, Geoffrey Whitworth, was particularly impressed by this new movement. He was a member of the firm Chatto & Windus, and in 1918 he was asked to deliver a lecture, 'A Bird's-Eye View of the History of the Stage', illustrated with lantern slides for the benefit of some munitions workers at Crayford. It was held in a Y.M.C.A. hut:

After the lecture, I was informed of a surprise item. The Crayford Reading Circle was about to perform a one-act play by Stanley Houghton. Would I not stay and hear it?

So I took my seat in the second row and waited events, expecting to be rather bored. But the first thing that happened was that the hall, which previously had been half-empty, began to fill. The billiards room was deserted. The refreshment bar soon lacked a customer. The women laid aside their knitting needles, and the men their newspapers. This was no lecture. This was real and this was earnest. This was a Play ...

Yet here were no actors in the proper sense of the word. They just sat, on a semi-circle of chairs. They were not dressed for their parts. They had not even memorised them. With books in their hands and with a minimum of action, they did not do much more than read the words of the play, pointing them with a few gestures. And yet, through the emotional sincerity of their interpretations, the characters came to life, and as I watched and listened, I felt that I was coming close to the fundamental quality of dramatic art in a way that I had never understood it before. Here was the art of the theatre reduced to the simplest terms, yet in this very reduction triumphant. Devoid of every grace and of the simplest gadgets of stage appointment, the agonists on the platform found the right echo in the hearts of their audience ...

What so distinguished the playreading at Crayford was the fact that it had been undertaken in the spirit of community enterprise. It was that which had endowed the performance with its peculiar dignity, and was it not precisely this dignity that would characterise the work of a National Theatre? In a flash I saw that a National

Theatre, for all its costly elaboration, for all its perfection of professional technique, was no more and no less than a Community Theatre writ large [Whitworth, *op. cit.*, pp. 148–9].

Inspired by this occasion, Whitworth decided to form a British Drama League, and started to sound out friends on the subject in December 1918. The first public meeting of the league was held on June 22nd, 1919, and by that time Whitworth had raised much support for it. Harley Granville-Barker had agreed to become its first chairman, with Whitworth as the honorary secretary. The clear intentions of the League were to combat the tawdry commercialism of West End theatre by encouraging signs of vitality elsewhere — by rallying the smaller amateur and professional drama groups into one co-operative organization. Whitworth hoped that 'a theatrical revival on democratic lines may be stimulated in the days to come', for 'the theatre', he added, 'was everybody's business'. Among the many aims of the British Drama League was support for a National Theatre.

The backing of the British Drama League could have been of vital importance to the S.M.N.T. committee — and to some extent it was. It provided that grass-roots support which the S.M.N.T. seemed to lack and which was so needed in its struggle with the Old Vickers, who now included the Earl of Lytton among their numbers. At successive annual conferences the British Drama League called for a National. At its first, John Martin-Harvey, an actor-manager who was judged by some to be Irving's natural successor, pointed out its social benefits in terms which seem irresistibly patriarchal:

It is the most extraordinary thing to me that no Government has ever had the vision to perceive the necessity of *beauty* in the lives of the poor. It is true that some glimmering of this need is seen in the plans of the Government in relation to better housing of the workers — plans involving the expenditure of millions. But who has the vision to see that great drama at cheap prices is the most potent instrument for the refinement of the working classes, an instrument ready to their hands at the cost of a few thousands. Let us then concentrate upon the necessity of founding a great National Theatre, build a big one in the midst of the great labouring classes, admit them to great productions of the finest work at small prices. You will have less labour unrest if you remember that man does not live by bread alone ... [*ibid.*, p. 155].

In 1922–3 the British Drama League concocted an elaborate scheme linking Hackett's shilling shares and Archer's Statement of Principle with a wider appeal to the public to be launched at the British Empire Exhibition in 1924. The S.M.N.T. committee considered and rejected it. The British Drama League launched an architectural competition for a National Theatre, in association with Hackett (who put up £250 in prize money) and the magazine, *Country Life*. The winner of this competition, W. L. Somerville of Toronto, was announced at the British Empire Exhibition; and his designs were published in *Drama*, the British Drama League's magazine, in 1924 and again in 1929, where they were subjected to a critical analysis from Granville-Barker.

These efforts were appreciated by the S.M.N.T. committee; but they did not make use of them. They could not. Their own committee was too divided; and their best supporters were drifting away to the League, Archer and Barker amongst them. By registering the S.M.N.T. trust as a charity, the committee had prevented itself from using its resources for any other purpose than the central one, and therefore it could not follow the British Drama League into all those surrounding activities which constitute a popular movement. It could, however, approach the government once more, and Parliament; and so, duly, in 1924 the S.M.N.T. committee went along to the newly elected Labour government, arguing that if the government provided a site, the S.M.N.T. had enough money to build the theatre.

Ramsay MacDonald, the new Prime Minister, made sympathetic, encouraging noises: that was his great talent as a politician. But he said that he was too busy at an Inter-Allied Conference, and could they come back later? Duly encouraged, the S.M.N.T. committee asked Shaw to become their chairman. Shaw declined regretfully and suggested Granville-Barker. Following his second marriage, however, Granville-Barker had hyphenated himself and taken to a life of literary leisure. His chairmanship of the British Drama League was a less arduous job than the S.M.N.T. committee chairmanship seemed likely to be. Barker wanted to steer clear of obvious frays.

Gollancz waited for a chance to catch Ramsay MacDonald again, but, before he could do so, the Labour government fell. The S.M.N.T. committee then tried Baldwin, the new Prime Minister, who had voted for state aid in the pre-war debate. Baldwin referred the matter, which was a specific request for a site in Whitehall Gardens, to his Commissioner of Works, Lord Peel. Peel, after two months' pondering, turned the idea down.

By now, the pre-war objections to state aid for the National Theatre had died away. Indeed, few people believed that it could be built mainly by private patronage, with a government performing the crowning ceremony. Indeed, the relationship between the theatre and successive governments had changed. Entertainments Tax had arrived. In 1916, Reginald McKenna, the Chancellor of the Exchequer, desperate to raise money for the war effort, had introduced this tax as part of the Finance (New Duties) Bill. It was intended, of course, to be a 'temporary' tax for the duration of the war, but it had a long life. It was 'adjusted' in 1917, 1918, 1919, 1921, 1922, 1923, 1924, 1931, 1935, 1940, 1942, 1943, 1946, 1947, 1948, 1949, 1950, 1952, 1953, 1954, 1955 until it was finally repealed in 1958. All these little adjustments point to the fact that Entertainments Tax had become one of those useful financial measures, like taxes on cigarettes, beer and petrol, whereby governments raise money quickly.

Successive governments came into office, promising to repeal it — but found it useful and left it alone. Ramsay MacDonald was one of the first to insist that Entertainments Tax must go. It rarely operated at less than 10 per cent of the box-office take, and sometimes rose to 20 per cent. During the First World War, theatre managers on the whole did not object to the tax. It was their contribution to the war effort. In 1916, the estimated yield from the tax was £5 million, enough to build ten National Theatres according to the Archer–Barker estimates.

This tax, however, produced some quite unforeseen changes in the structure of the theatre. It operated in a curious way. Theatre managers were asked to raise the tax themselves, by sticking a stamp on the tickets. Wealthier managements tried to absorb the cost of the tax, thus keeping ticket prices stable, whereas poorer managements were forced to pass the full cost of the tax on to their customers. This meant that the local, family-owned music halls, for example, were at a disadvantage compared to the larger chains of variety theatres; and were systematically driven out of business. Edwardian theatre was a patchwork of small managements, independent actor-managers, family theatres and medium-sized theatrical chains. By the 1920s and 1930s, this diversity was changing in favour of 'streamlining', whereby larger and larger groups of theatres were banding together, sometimes letting and subletting their buildings, marketing shows in London and sending them around on endless tours. The peak of this streamlining process came during the Second World War.

From the beginning, however, certain types of theatre claimed exemption, those presenting 'educational' drama. In 1916, David Mason, M.P., put his finger on a problem which, in different disguises, has plagued British theatre ever since. 'Where are you to draw the line', he asked in the Commons, 'between what is educational and what is amusing?' Shakespeare was, of course, educational, but what about Shaw? And can there be an educational play which is not also entertaining? Who would want to watch it, if it were dull? In place of a homogeneous theatre, in which, say, Irving could throw in a pot-boiler melodrama to finance his *Hamlet* or Tree stage *Trilby* so that he could afford *A Midsummer-Night's Dream*, the exemptions under Entertainments Tax encouraged managers to label their productions as being either 'educational' or 'popular'. A split in sensibility began then, which has continued to today, although the 'educational' tag eventually died away, to be replaced (for tax-exemption purposes) by other contrived divisions, between (during the early days of the Arts Council) the 'fine' and ordinary arts, or between the 'non-profit-distributing' and the 'commercial' companies.

Entertainments Tax also creamed off the profit from the theatre. It made the profession an even riskier undertaking. Before the First World War, for example, Sir Oswald Stoll was quite prepared to give a substantial donation, £1,500, to the S.M.N.T. committee, to benefit the profession which had served him well. After the First World War, such actor-managers were rare. It was not just a matter of poverty, but of the fact that theatres had become big business, and businesses are run by management boards with responsibilities towards shareholders.

From the narrow point of view, however, of the S.M.N.T. supporters, Entertainments Tax could have been regarded as a definite advantage. It strengthened their hands in their approaches to governments. There seemed an innate justice in the idea that governments who had benefited from taxation should give some of this money back in the form of subsidies. And by giving money to a National Theatre, a government could seem generous without actually losing much of its income. From 1916 onwards, governments inevitably were involved with the theatre as *debtors*; and even the most proudly independent actor-manager would have seemed perverse to suggest (although one or two of them still did) that in a situation where governments were taking millions of pounds annually from the theatre, some money should not be returned to the profession as grants to the National.

Despite the disappointment over the Whitehall Gardens site, the S.M.N.T. committee, usually with the support of the British Drama League, kept up its pressure on the government; and in the meantime, kept looking for sites. One turned up in St Martin's Lane, but that came to nothing. The Duke of Westminster, who had always been sympathetic to the scheme, offered them a triangular plot of grass, surrounded by roads, just north of Victoria Station. His local tenants, however, objected on the grounds that the theatre would infringe their ancient rights and lower the value of their leases. Westminster then offered an alternative site in Horseferry Road, which was much larger. The committee handled the offer with tact, helped by the fact that the duke was out of the country at the time. It was an isolated place, way outside the normal fringes of the West End, though close to Victoria Station. Shaw wrote about it to Gollancz:

> I do not like looking a gift horse in the mouth, especially when it is the only site we seem likely to get; but let us not deceive ourselves as to its eligibility. Whatever it may develop into in twenty years or so, it is at present a site on which no sane theatrical expert would dream of putting a theatre larger than the Margaret Morris theatre in Chelsea. Instead of having a crowded thoroughfare on all four sides, it stands at the crossing of two lonely roads and a condemned bridge ... In the eighteenth century it would have proved an ideal site for a gibbet. Its sole advantage from our point of view is that it is conveniently close to Mrs Lyttelton's [Whitworth, *op. cit.*, p. 136].

Shaw's enthusiasm for the project seemed to be on the wane. Before the war, he had blithely drafted a letter (never sent) to the Millionaires of England, asking them to donate £100,000 'if you can spare it'; but now he was extremely cautious about lending his name to fund-raising schemes:

> It is quite impossible for me to take part in asking people privately to give thirty thousand pounds to the S.M.N.T. They would immediately ask me why I did not give it myself. In fact Lady Meyer has already asked that. On the only occasion in my life when I asked a rich man to put money into a theatre, I offered to find half of the required sum myself, and I did so. The poor (comparatively) can make these appeals without fear of reprisals; but I, though far from being the multi-millionaire I am imagined, cannot afford to do so [*ibid.*, p. 135].

Negotiations with the Duke of Westminster petered out in 1925. In 1927, there was another proposal, this time from Lady Beecham, that the S.M.N.T. should take over the site of Dorchester House in Park Lane; but that fell apart in an atmosphere of mutual suspicion. The Foundling Hospital site in Coram's Fields was another suggestion, in 1928: also abandoned. And so it went on through much of the 1920s and 1930s; and while all these sites were being considered, the British Drama League was passing resolutions at its annual meetings deploring 'the delay in the foundation of a National Theatre' and the Old Vickers (with some help from those who wanted the money diverted elsewhere) were trying to declare the S.M.N.T. an official, total and absolute failure.

In 1928, Nigel Playfair, who had run as actor-manager some particularly successful seasons at the Lyric Theatre, Hammersmith, and was a member of the S.M.N.T. committee, put forward a formal proposal for dissolving the trust:

> I believe that, miracles apart, the trust has failed in its specific object, and that no further subscriptions of any amount worth serious consideration can now be obtained. I consider that the best policy would be to go before the [Charity] Commissioners with this frank confession, and with a strong recommendation that a new trust, if that is the correct word, should be created with the following conditions:
>
> That the Capital Sum should remain untouched until such time when it can be devoted to its original purpose, the erection of a National Theatre in London and its endowment. That, in the meantime, the Committee should be empowered to use such part of the yearly income as is not required for office expenses for the purpose of subsidising certain performances of Shakespeare's plays in London [*ibid.*, p. 141].

It sounded an eminently reasonable suggestion, a mere continuation of the policy already begun after the war with the New Shakespeare Company; but it was the thin end of the wedge. It would mean that the charitable status of the S.M.N.T. would be lost, that the funds slowly accumulating from interest would not be ploughed back into the central enterprise and that the eyes of Playfair and the Old Vickers would gleam with the hope of subsidies.

Every week, at the Old Vic, Lilian Baylis would confidently proclaim: 'All this talk about a National Theatre. We *are* a National Theatre!' Now that the war austerity had been endured, the productions at the Old Vic were improving in quality and reputation. Indeed, the Old Vic's success was such that it was expanding. 'The Old Vic', said Miss Baylis, 'is like a child almost grown up and by several sizes grown out of its clothes. The way the child has grown up has been a joy to me, and though I can only claim it as a foster-child, I may be forgiven for regarding it with motherly love' (1925). One direction in which Miss Baylis's motherly eyes were glancing for new clothes was across the river to Sadler's Wells. It was proving far too complicated to run the Old Vic as a mixed house presenting opera and Shakespeare; and Miss Baylis could not in conscience abandon either side of her activities. Someone else would have to make way.

She was supported in her aims by many who would otherwise have been sympathetic to the S.M.N.T.; and also by Reginald Rowe, an influential man, tall and commanding in appearance, an ex-rowing Blue at Oxford, whose background political activities ranged from organizing resistance to a parliamentary Bill in 1923 (which would have allowed the L.C.C. to have purchased compulsorily the Old Vic, to build two tunnel shafts for the Tube beneath it) to the 'services for housing', the eventual cause of his knighthood in 1934. Rowe was a governor of the Old Vic and, with Lilian Baylis, masterminded the Vic–Wells scheme. He was the treasurer of the Sadler's Wells Fund; and in 1928, he wrote to the S.M.N.T. proposing a wholesale 'merger' — which would have meant simply that the S.M.N.T. money would go directly into the Vic–Wells coffers:

> The Sadler's Wells scheme will undoubtedly carry out in practice essential objects of the Shakespeare Memorial Fund. Its main purpose is to provide performances of Shakespeare and of such plays, old or modern, as can be claimed to be of permanent value [*ibid.*, p. 137].

Gollancz and the S.M.N.T. committee considered his proposal seriously and appealed to the Charity Commissioners. The commissioners once again decided that buying Sadler's Wells for the Vic–Wells trust was not the same thing as building a National Theatre — and therefore not a proper use of S.M.N.T. funds.

Nor, as Mrs Lyttelton, Shaw, Archer and Oliver Lyttelton pointed out, were the causes of the Vic–Wells scheme and the National Theatre totally compatible. A 'People's Theatre' was not the same thing as a 'National Theatre'. One existed basically to educate and bring good drama to those who could not afford normally to go to the theatre. It was essentially a philanthropic enterprise, in which comparatively second-rate standards could be accepted in the pursuit of a different goal, the enlightenment of the masses. The National Theatre included this aim, certainly, but it should add another dimension. It should provide a touchstone of excellence for the theatre as a whole. It should aspire to the dramatic heights, as well as cultivate the social valleys. It needed to look outwards to other countries, other civilizations, other theatrical traditions. It had to be an external sign of British cultural prowess. An excessive do-gooding could have cut the hamstrings of ambitiousness.

And so the S.M.N.T. funds did not go to the Vic–Wells trust, which, as it happened, managed to do quite easily without them. There must have been many times when Gollancz, that dogged, persistent committee man, envied the curious way in which Baylis always seemed to get what she wanted. Whenever the Old Vic was in financial trouble, Miss Baylis would chat to God; and next morning a cheque (perhaps from the Carnegie Trust, as in 1924) would arrive on her desk. It was illogical, undemocratic and an insult to normal committee procedure; but when Miss Baylis said, quite unselfconsciously, that 'I do so believe that the moment we feel our cross, if we call on Him to help us carry it, He does indeed carry it, and we more often feel only joy: the heaviness goes', she seemed to be speaking the literal truth. One burden — that of insolvency — was lifted, continually, by various people whom one would not have suspected of being God's agents.

In contrast, the S.M.N.T. committee kept on meeting, passing resolutions and sending deputations to different government departments, without edging perceptibly nearer their goal than they had been ten years ago. And the committee were palpably waning in enthusiasm. Gollancz himself was growing old. In 1929, however, there came a glimmer of hope. Robert Young, M.P., prompted by the British Drama League, asked the Prime Minister, Ramsay MacDonald, on the rebound, in the Commons: 'Would he, in order to promote the artistic sincerity and dignity of Great Britain and to encourage the best elements in the British Theatre, consider the establishment of a national theatre on lines somewhat similar to those followed in many European countries?'

MacDonald replied that he was sympathetic to the scheme — which came as no surprise. But he added: 'There are ... serious difficulties arising partly from the number of similar schemes which are put forward. In present circumstances, therefore, I would only be holding out false hopes if I were to answer otherwise than that I regret that I cannot give a promise of Government subsidy.' James Hudson, M.P., immediately asked him: 'If those who are pressing for various schemes would come to an agreement, would the Prime Minister be prepared to reconsider the answer that he has made?' MacDonald replied: 'I think that my answer is partly an invitation for them to do so.'

The National Theatre enthusiasts, in short, should stop squabbling. Whilst the British Drama League and the S.M.N.T. committee had sometimes spoken with different voices, and grown irritable with each other, the real struggles were with the Old Vickers, and sometimes with those actor-managers who were proposing that several theatres should be linked together in one National Theatre chain. The British Drama League responded to MacDonald's call with characteristic vigour. At their 10th Annual Conference, held at Northampton in October 1929, Lord Lytton (the 2nd Earl of Lytton, and Bulwer-Lytton's grandson) called once more for the establishment of a National Repertory Theatre, while Robert Young proposed a resolution rallying all the 1,600 drama societies affiliated to the League, to 'this great object'. Whitworth read a favourable message from the Home Secretary, J. R. Clynes, and, partly to prevent the new effort from becoming bogged down in old dogmas, Young suggested that a fresh look should be taken at the scheme, redefining what was meant by a 'National'. Within a month of that conference, on November 25th, a delegation consisting of two members from the British Drama League, two from the S.M.N.T. committee and two from a parliamentary committee of sympathetic M.P.s was proposed—and duly met—with some other invited representatives: which eventually presented another report about the proposed National, not differing materially from the original Archer–Barker *Scheme* except in one respect: the committee followed Barker's latest idea, to be published in 1930 with his revised *Scheme*, that there should be two theatres within the National complex, a large and a small.

The energy for this new initiative came almost entirely from the British Drama League. In comparison, the S.M.N.T. committee presented a sadly lacklustre image. They only met twice in 1929, in spring and autumn; and for the second meeting, only three members, apart from Gollancz, bothered to turn up. Shaw himself seemed to have lost heart. During the year, he had written to Young warning him not to waste his efforts because nobody 'cared tuppence about a National Theatre'.

Shaw, under the influence of the League, recovered his enthusiasm in time for another public meeting held at Kingsway Hall on January 31st, 1930. It was held by the League as a demonstration of support for the National; and Shaw who spoke, obliquely answered the Old Vickers by saying: 'I want the State Theatre to be what St Paul's and Westminster Abbey are to religion—something to show what the thing can be at its best.' He also retorted to John Drinkwater, a member of Barry Jackson's Birmingham Rep, who had pressed hard for a national chain of regional theatres rather than one National. Shaw wanted both—a National Theatre *and* a regional chain. Perhaps because there were now firm hopes that the government would become 'involved', the plans for the National became more ambitious—two theatres not one, regional chains as well. The meeting received telegrams of support from subsidized companies abroad—from Max Reinhardt, Emile Fabre (from the Comédie-Française) and Erik Wettergreen (from the Royal Theatre, Stockholm); and was as convincing a demonstration of unity in favour of a National Theatre as any government could have wished.

Gollancz proposed the speech of thanks to the chairman, Lord Lytton, a clear sign that the S.M.N.T. committee was not in rivalry with the British Drama League. He was, according to Geoffrey Whitworth, 'at the top of his form', providing 'a ringing peroration worthy of the best days of his eloquence'. It was his last major speech, for on June 23rd, 1930, he died and the S.M.N.T. committee lost its most resilient member. Nor was the Kingsway Hall meeting successful in attracting further support from the government, for the MacDonald administration itself was overtaken by events. It was superseded by the National Government in August 1931, and then by the return of Baldwin. But the Kingsway Hall meeting served one practical purpose: it formally united the S.M.N.T. committee with the British Drama League in its pursuit of the National, and after Gollancz's death this unity was represented by the appointment of Geoffrey Whitworth, another dogged and determined committee man, to take his place.

6

The Rivals

LILIAN BAYLIS's foster-child, the Old Vic, had by now quite grown up. After six years' campaigning, it had acquired its new suit of clothes, the Sadler's Wells, which opened its doors on January 6th, 1931, under the new management, the Vic–Wells Trust. Miss Baylis became overnight the most influential theatre manager in Britain. 'This was the building', wrote Richard Findlater in his biography of Lilian Baylis, 'that was going to solve the problems of the impossibly crowded Vic; to give opera, at last, the chance to expand, and ballet the opportunity to grow; to bring sweetness and light to the working class of North London.' What was equally significant perhaps, was that the Old Vic productions were losing—indeed had lost—their air of ham and tattiness. It was now the finest classical company in London.

If the building of the Old Vic company can be attributed to the work of Ben Greet and Robert Atkins, its furnishings and decorations, in the widest sense its style, came with the arrival of Harcourt Williams in 1929. Williams got rid of the Atkins affectations ('me' for 'my'), cut down the number of productions and concentrated on improving the verse-speaking, the pace and naturalness of the company performances. He also managed to persuade Miss Baylis that low wages were not necessarily a mark of virtue. He cajoled her into paying £20 a week to a young West End actor, John Gielgud, which was then by Old Vic standards an impossibly high salary. Gielgud, who had been playing parts like Captain Allenby in *The Skull* and Nicky Lancaster (having understudied Noël Coward) in Coward's *The Vortex*, was prepared to give up his comfortable dressing rooms, 'new suits, late rising and suppers at the Savoy' in order to play in Shakespeare at the Old Vic. During his first season, 1929–30, he played Romeo, Richard II, Orlando in *As You Like It*, Hamlet and Macbeth; and by the end of it, he was starting to be regarded as the First Player of the English Stage. 'Nothing justifies a producer's methods', stated the Vic–Wells Annual

Report in 1930, 'so much as a steady increase in the size of the audience'; and box-office business was booming. *Hamlet*, for example, was being played in its entirety, always an arduous experience, but every seat was sold for it, many stood and many more were turned away.

Gielgud's success and Harcourt Williams's presence attracted other aspiring young actors to the company. Ralph Richardson joined the Old Vic in 1930, playing Hal in *Henry IV (Part 1)* and Caliban in *The Tempest* (to Gielgud's Prospero), and in the following year, Toby Belch in *Twelfth Night*, Bottom and Petruchio. Then Peggy Ashcroft joined, to play Rosalind in *As You Like It* and Juliet, with Edith Evans returning to the Old Vic to play the Nurse. Sybil Thorndike also returned, following her triumph in Shaw's *St Joan*; and by the mid-1930s, it was no longer an act of rare self-sacrifice for a popular actor to leave the comfort of the West End for the rigours of the Old Vic. Tyrone Guthrie, the most imaginative young director of the time, took over from Williams in 1933, pursuing a similar policy of trying to attract leading actors, even 'stars' like Charles Laughton; but adding a new experimentalism. It was Guthrie who invited Olivier and Michael Redgrave to join the Old Vic in 1937, and Olivier's Hamlet was based on a new psychoanalytic interpretation of the part, provided by Dr Ernest Jones in one of his essays. Hamlet, Jones's argument ran, was a classic victim of Oedipalism, loving his mother, revering an absent father and hating the present stepfather. The Old Vic could no longer be accused of sacrificing intellectualism and the arts of drama to social philanthropy. It was a daring, challenging company as well as one which offered some of the cheapest seats in town.

Olivier was three years younger than Gielgud, born on May 22nd, 1907. Unlike Gielgud, whose family connections as the great-nephew of Ellen Terry had given him an entry into the theatre and a background of some financial security, Olivier had no such advantages. Much of his childhood was spent in genuine poverty; but there had been a worse deprivation, the death of his beloved mother, Agnes, when he was only thirteen and away boarding at choir school. 'There was undoubtedly a paradise in my childhood,' Laurence Olivier has said, 'and it lasted until my mother died. This was a terrible thing. I think I've been looking for her ever since.' He had an uneasy relationship with his father at first, finding him an autocratic, forbidding man; but Sybil Thorndike, who knew the family from their days in Nottingdale, believed that Olivier derived much of his acting skill from his father, together with a rarer quality, an ability to communicate directly with ordinary people: 'To be a parson, you must have no side, no scholarly superiority. You need the common touch. Larry learnt that from his father.'

It is not merely paradoxical to add that with this common touch there was also a fierce pride, a shyness and a determination to shape his life despite circumstances—further qualities which Laurence Olivier shared with his father, Gerard. Gerard's character reminds one somewhat of Ibsen's Brand—with a similar determination, pulpit fire, zeal, coupled with an austere disdain for normal comforts which might have benefited his family. From his mother, Olivier may have inherited his continual sense of fun, the tendency to giggle on stage (half-cured by Coward in *Private Lives*), or the slightly comic touches which he introduced even into his King Lear. Olivier once chose his own epitaph: 'He's funny', which was fondly said of Archie Rice by his wife Phoebe in John Osborne's *The Entertainer*. 'Tell them that in Westminster Abbey —it's the most wonderful thing in the world to make people laugh.'

Olivier's impact upon London's theatre was less immediate than Gielgud's. In his early days he was aspiring to become a matinée idol, and sported a Ronald Colman moustache. His acting style then owed something to Gerald du Maurier, a slightly self-conscious casualness. After an apprenticeship at the Birmingham Rep in the late 1920s, he turned down the chance to play Stanhope in R. C. Sherriff's *Journey's End* in the West End, having played the part in the first two Stage Society performances at the Apollo, to take on *Beau Geste* and romantic swashbuckle in London, a production which failed disastrously. His early films in Britain and the United States during the early 1930s were also not particularly impressive, although he gained a reputation as a romantic lead. It was not until 1935 that he first made an impression as a classical actor, alternating the parts of Mercutio and Romeo with Gielgud at the New Theatre. He was Gielgud's second choice—Robert Donat had been the first.

This production of *Romeo and Juliet* presented two acting styles, side by side, in stark contrast. Gielgud was all elegance and magnificent verse-speaking: Olivier's verse-speaking was considered by many critics to be clumsy and rough—'Romeo … riding a motorbike'—but to compensate, there was a sheer imaginative virility, an animal-like quality, which caused James Agate to state that this was the most moving Romeo which he had seen. It was a production which symbolized the meeting of two theatrical traditions—the old classicism in its most highly polished form, and the new naturalistic vigour which was to supersede it. Critics were divided between those who thought

Gielgud superb and Olivier brash, and those who thought Gielgud precious and Olivier magnetically exciting. But for the general theatre-going public in the late 1930s, both actors were equally associated with the Old Vic, although by then Gielgud had become an independent actor-manager.

From the point of view of the S.M.N.T. committee, however, the success of the Old Vic came as decidedly a mixed blessing. Now that the Vic–Wells scheme had been launched, there were few direct attempts to take over their funds; but if the S.M.N.T. trust had been declared a failure, the Vic–Wells organization stood in direct line to receive the bulk of the money. It was also embarrassing to find that the leading actors of the day were more wedded to the Old Vic than to the still distant prospect of the National. In 1935, for example, Gielgud had written to the *Observer* (March 17th). He did not object, in principle, to the establishment of a national centre for dramatic art, but believed that existing buildings and institutions, if properly endowed, were good enough:

> Supposing the three institutions, Stratford, the Old Vic and Sadler's Wells were in a sense amalgamated, and endowed on a large scale as the genuine foundation of a National Theatre. In the first place, the companies would be interchangeable, and infinitely more care could be given to each production. A play could run for a month at the Old Vic, then go to Stratford, then to Sadler's Wells, and then perhaps tour for a month. Having only to produce a new play every three or four months, would give a producer much more time to put his best work into each ... To my mind, the Old Vic, subsidised and linked with Stratford-upon-Avon, has the best claims to be made the basis of a really National Theatre. If re-building there is to be—and I suppose its own building would be demolished when the great South of the River Embankment Scheme comes off—then what more suitable than that it should arise, phoenix-like, from its own ashes, on its old site, or near its own site, as the corner-stone of the scheme.

Olivier's approach, typically, was brasher, in the true Lilian Baylis tradition: 'I used to make those passionate curtain speeches [at the Old Vic] ... You know, "People talk of a National Theatre. They want to build a Great New Theatre. They have collected thousands of pounds for it. But I say, we *have* a National Theatre. And that National Theatre is *here*!" ' It was one of his *Henry V* speeches. At a Sybille Colefax party in the 1930s, Oliver Lyttelton and Lord Esher took Olivier aside. They told him that the Old Vic just was not good enough as a theatre to house a National Company. There must be something big, brand-new and impressive to show the world. It must be the best in every way — not that place in Waterloo Road, which, as Lyttelton kept stressing in that punning phrase, was not so much 'fustian as fusty'. They argued and argued with him.

For Whitworth, damaging public remarks from leading actors were, to put it mildly, very irritating:

> ... forces were at work in a section of the [S.M.N.T.] Committee which might soon succeed in a definite acceptance of the view that the Trust had failed ... I felt in my bones that on the day when the fund found itself at the mercy of applicants for help, however worthy, the National Theatre for our generation would be as good as dead, for where the corpse lies, there the ravens are gathered together [Whitworth, *op. cit.*, p. 198].

Since Gollancz's death, the S.M.N.T. committee had undergone something of a transformation. It was losing that air of social and theatrical dilettantism, and acquiring a new appearance of professional purposiveness. When the executive committee met after Gollancz's death, on November 6th, 1930, Sir Frank Meyer was in the chair, with Shaw, the mildly witty journalist Hamilton Fyfe, the energetic Labour M.P. Holford Knight, Sir Archibald Flower of the Stratford Flowers, Alfred Sutro the dramatist, Acton Bond the actor, Sir Nigel Playfair, Sir Robert Donald and Whitworth completing the committee. The Earl of Lytton, Dame Edith Lyttelton, S. R. Littlewood and Sir John Martin-Harvey were also connected with the committee, though not present on that occasion. Of these members, Meyer was primarily a financier. Due to his efforts, the S.M.N.T. funds had increased from £100,000 to £150,000 by the time of his death in 1935. Shaw was too busy to attend regularly, Playfair's loyalties were considered suspect, Fyfe provided light relief, Flower's main energies were directed towards rebuilding the Shakespeare Memorial Theatre, Stratford — which had burnt down in 1926 and opened again, totally rebuilt, in 1932 — Lytton was the chairman of the Old Vic governors which placed him in an awkward situation in the rivalry with the Vic, Bond was an actor who felt that his talents were being overlooked in the new Gielgud age, Sutro was a dramatist of the old pre-Shaw school and Holford Knight had his parliamentary duties to distract him. With the exceptions of Meyer, Dame Edith Lyttelton, Whitworth, and Shaw when he was around, the members of the S.M.N.T. committee could not claim to be wholeheartedly devoted to their task. Dame Edith, who was also an Old Vic governor, was prepared to argue the National Theatre's case even in the Old Vic committees; but she was an exception.

The first step towards changing this somewhat lacklustre committee came with Whitworth's suggestion that they should meet in the British Drama League offices at 8 Adelphi Terrace, overlooking the Thames. Proper offices themselves can change the atmosphere of an organization, and these were particularly pleasant and useful ones, close to the flats of Barrie and Shaw. Later on in the 1930s, an appeals office was established in 80 Pall Mall, a prestigious address indeed. Two younger impresarios were added to the committee: Sidney Bernstein and Sydney Carroll. Bernstein was a dynamic businessman, who had organized and built a chain of cinemas, the Granada Group, of which he was managing director. He had also built and owned the Phoenix Theatre. Carroll was better known as an incisive critic, but he had also had experience as a theatrical producer. Lewis Casson joined the committee, an ex-Old Vic man, but bringing great enthusiasm to the cause. After Frank Meyer's death, the committee acquired the services of a professional organizer and fund-raiser, Harvey Lloyd, who specialized in neat ways of raising the odd thousand here and there. Lloyd, for example, bought 700 seats overlooking the route of the Silver Jubilee procession in 1935; he sold them again for a profit of £830 to the fund. He repeated this scheme for the coronation of George VI in 1936, this time reaping £2,366. Carroll helped to organize a Shakespeare Matinée at Drury Lane, which brought in £1,800; while a Coronation Ball at the Albert Hall in May 1937 provided £4,500 to the fund.

Fund-raising therefore improved, although the money available still fell far short of the amount required. At the same time, the process of site-searching went on, but with a different emphasis. Instead of looking for sites which the government or the L.C.C. could be persuaded to contribute, the committee thought about taking over an existing theatre or hall which could be converted. Several were considered — the Junior United Services Club, the Lyceum, His Majesty's Theatre and even Drury Lane, together with places like Charing Cross Hospital, Aldridge's Repository and a site in Wilton Place. Eventually, however, these discussions homed in on the Cambridge Theatre — which could have been bought for £150,000. A deal was nearly concluded in 1934 and it was only abandoned finally in 1936.

In the background, however, a shadowy new possibility was starting to take shape. Archer had prophesied it, Barker in his revised *Scheme* had formally suggested it and Gielgud in his *Observer* letter had referred to it: the redevelopment of the South Bank. There were no formal plans at this stage, or if there were, they were locked up in the recesses of County Hall. There were merely rumours which occasionally surfaced in electioneering. Herbert Morrison was the leader of the ruling Labour group on the L.C.C. An ex-mayor of Hackney, he had a concern for London which almost amounted to a ruling passion. One of his protégés was Isaac Hayward, a quiet, determined, soft-spoken Welshman who had come to London in 1926 as a trade union official, wanting to push the Electricity Act through Parliament.

Morrison was impressed by Hayward, and wanted him on the L.C.C. 'But I don't live in London,' Hayward objected. Morrison said that did not matter. Hayward was duly offered the safe Labour seat of Rotherhithe, which became the equally safe seat of Deptford; and when Morrison rose in the ranks of the Labour Party, eventually becoming an M.P., a member of Churchill's war cabinet and Attlee's deputy leader, Hayward took over from him as leader of the Labour Party in the L.C.C. and also as leader of the L.C.C. itself. He sat on the Council for a record thirty-seven years, and was leader for seventeen of them. The South Bank scheme grew to be one of his favourite projects. He chaired the special South Bank committee meetings, and the architects' department at the L.C.C., while he was in charge, had an élite corps of planners and designers solely for the problems of the South Bank.

The South Bank certainly needed to be developed: the derelict warehouses, the rotting yards of bankrupt companies, the refuse of the industrial revolution piled up on its mud banks and the slums of Waterloo behind. But nobody knew when the development would take place or what it would entail; and most members of the S.M.N.T. shared Shaw's opinion—that a National Theatre surrounded by brothels, low-life and drunks would give quite the wrong impression to foreigners. And yet, if the National were to be given a site from the L.C.C. (which had not totally been dismissed as a possibility), there had to be some way in which the S.M.N.T. plans and those of the L.C.C. could meet on common, perhaps very common, ground.

And so the S.M.N.T. committee kept searching for sites, and early in 1937, they found one, by accident. Geoffrey Whitworth's wife heard that the French Institute was giving up a tract of land in Kensington, just at the bottom of Exhibition Road. The Royal College of Art had been offered it, but had declined; and therefore the Office of Works, who owned it, were placing it on auction. It was a strange, triangular site, only just large enough. Whitworth reported this find to the S.M.N.T. committee and they offered £50,000 for it. Another bid of

£85,000 won the auction, although the S.M.N.T. committee raised their offer to £75,000. The buyer who won the auction, however, failed to raise the deposit; and so the committee eventually bought the site for £75,000.

Many members of the S.M.N.T. committee were worried by the Kensington site. Apart from being small and triangular, it had other disadvantages. It was in an untheatrical part of town, surrounded by museums. Everyone realized that they could not fit two main theatres into this site, but Lewis Casson was convinced that they could not build even one. Shaw, however, was enthusiastic. He was convinced that the heart of London was moving steadily westwards, which would eventually have meant that Brompton Road would become the new Piccadilly. Cynics, however, were heard to point out that the Kensington site had once been a plague pit, not the best inheritance for a National.

The purchase of the site put new heart into the S.M.N.T. committee. It also kept the ravens at bay. They were left with £75,000 to build the theatre, not enough but useful as a beginning. In 1937, Lilian Baylis died and, as a gesture of friendship, the S.M.N.T. committee agreed to defer their appeal for funds, so that the Vic–Wells trust could launch its own appeal, in memory of Lilian Baylis. In the meantime, the S.M.N.T. committee searched around for an architect. They decided, after much discussion, not to hold an open competition. The difficulty here was that which later faced Lord Cottesloe and the South Bank Board in 1963. They wanted the best architect; but they also wanted the most popular one, selected in a manner least likely to attract criticism. To have appointed an architect in any way other than in open competition would have led to the charge that a closed clique was running the S.M.N.T.; but an open competition might well have deterred the most eminent architects, who would probably not enter for fear of not winning.

They solved this problem by selecting a short list of six architects, and seeing whether any of them would be interested. Sir Edwin Lutyens was an obvious choice. He was probably the most famous architect in Britain at the time, although his critics argued that his best days were past. Lutyens had designed superb country houses for rich Edwardian families, combining a William Morris delight in local stone and traditional craftsmanship with a kind of elevated Englishness —Tudor and Georgian features mingling into an imperial grandeur. From domestic architecture, he had moved easily into civic and commercial buildings, such as the headquarters of Reuters in Fleet Street and the viceroy's residence at New Delhi. He started that austere but somewhat pompous civic style which, in its lesser imitations, became known as bankers' Georgian. And, of course, Lutyens was related by marriage to the Lytton family, and so the S.M.N.T. cause was not unfamiliar to him.

But he had never before designed a theatre. Sidney Bernstein objected to his selection on that account, the only member of the S.M.N.T. committee to do so. Bernstein may also have disliked Lutyens for another reason. Bernstein was a stalwart Socialist, and the very style of Lutyens's work represented a wealthy, imperial age. In deference to Bernstein's objections, the S.M.N.T. committee decided to invite another architect to help Lutyens, with Lutyens's permission, of course. Cecil Masey, who had worked for Bernstein in building cinemas and the Phoenix Theatre, was chosen to provide the technical and stage details for Lutyens's grand scheme; and to ensure that the S.M.N.T. committee also had a voice in the proceedings. A building committee was formed, consisting of Ashley Dukes, the dramatist and theatre manager, W. Bridges-Adams from Stratford, Lewis Casson, Nicholas Hannen, Bernstein and Whitworth.

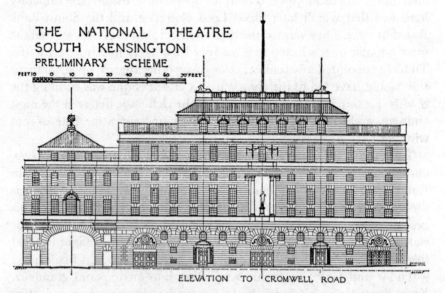

Figure 1 Lutyens's design for the National Theatre in South Kensington: Elevation to Cromwell Road

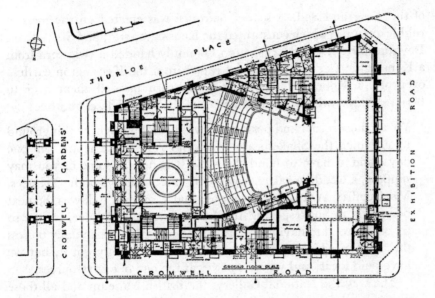

Figure 2 Ground plans of Lutyens's design for the National Theatre in South Kensington

These meetings of the building committee provided Whitworth with 'some of [his] happiest memories'. They would chat in the mornings and resort to Rosa's Edwardian Restaurant in Jermyn Street for further discussions over 'succulent beef and glasses of undiluted ale' at lunch. The result, according to Whitworth, satisfied almost everyone. Lutyens's plans, afterwards published in Volume III of *The Architecture of Sir Edwin Lutyens* (1950), looked as much like the headquarters of a large insurance company as it is decent for a theatre to be. 'The exterior', commented Whitworth, 'was in the main tradition of English architecture, yet simple and up-to-date. The interior was a marvel of concentrated amenity. Everything fitted like the mechanism of a watch.' Lutyens even found room for a small studio theatre, as well as dressing rooms and workshops.

The S.M.N.T. committee resolved that no opportunity for publicity or fund-raising should henceforward be missed. They had been too dilatory. Now was the time for a supreme effort. They decided to make a public ceremony of the legal business, the transfer of deeds for the Kensington site. They chose a symbolic day, the eve of Shakespeare's birthday, 1938; and unearthed a curious ancient ritual: the Ceremony of the Twig and Sod. A scarlet marquee was erected on the mess of rubble and mud which constituted the Kensington site; and Sir William Davison, the M.P. for Kensington, solemnly handed a twig torn from a Kensington tree lying on a sod raped from the Kensington earth — over to Sir Robert Vansittart, who in turn handed them over to Bernard Shaw, who replied on behalf of the S.M.N.T. committee:

> We are now seized and possessed lawfully and by right of this ground upon which the Shakespeare Memorial National Theatre will one day stand. I have to hand this sod — it is not, as some of you may suppose, a wedding cake — over to the representative of the Trustees, Mr. Geoffrey Whitworth. I suppose that I am here today as the next best thing to Shakespeare. At all events, as you now see, we are so far on the road to having a National Theatre that we actually possess the land on which it is to stand. We have not only got it, but we have paid for it, and we are not yet at the end of our resources.
>
> The way the National Gallery, the British Museum and all those places begin is always by a small group of people who understand the national importance, the cultural importance, of these institutions. They make a beginning, and after a time the beginning they make becomes an institution. Then the Government comes along, or rather the Government does not come along, but the created institution stands in the way of the Government, and the Government, which never wanted it, says, 'Here is something which for some reason or other, we have got to keep going.' We have got to carry this institution to the point at which the Government will be up against it.
>
> People sometimes ask me, 'Do the English people want a national theatre?' Of course they do not. They have got a British Museum, a National Gallery, a Westminster Abbey, and they never wanted any of them. But once these things stand, as mysterious phenomena that have come to them, they are quite proud of them, and feel that the place would be incomplete without them [Whitworth, *op. cit.*, p. 210].

Shaw, of course, was not to be taken seriously. He was suggesting the quite unconstitutional proposition that when persuasion and open debate in the Commons fail, moral blackmail succeeds. He was also not quite accurate historically, in that a government grant had established the National Gallery. Like many of Shaw's jokes, however, it became the received wisdom of the age, so that, by the 1950s and 1960s, it was assumed even by politicians that the best way to approach a government was to back it into a corner and then try to hit it over the head with public opinion—or a few useful editorials. Shaw's speech ended with a blatant tout for American help:

> We are gratified ... to find that the American Ambassador is present. This country owes several of its institutions to the contributions of America.

The ambassador in question was Joseph Kennedy, the father of J. F. Kennedy the future President, and it is interesting to speculate on his reactions to this tritely archaic ceremony, which was accompanied by Old English madrigals sung by the Fleet Street Choir. Kennedy's few words at the ceremony gave no encouragement to those who hoped that he might personally help—for he was rich enough to endow several National Theatres; and perhaps this spectacle may have influenced his subsequent bleak and cruel assessment of Britain's chances of survival at the onset of the Second World War.

There were of course home-orientated fund-raising schemes as well. One was launched at the Rembrandt Hotel, immediately after the ceremony. £8,000 was raised by inviting counties, boroughs, institutions and individuals to buy plaques for seats, at £100 a time. There were *thés dramatiques* at Claridge's. Once more, there was a rally, though less impressive than in 1909, of prominent names supporting the theatre. John Masefield, the poet laureate, sent a letter. Sybil Thorndike and Dame Edith Lyttelton made speeches. Everyone was relieved that the Ceremony of the Twig and Sod had not been spoilt by the expected rain. Everybody, too, was aware of darker clouds on the political horizon.

Before a brick of Lutyens's building had been laid on the Kensington site, the Second World War came; and the S.M.N.T. committee met in September 1939 to disband its staff who had become so comfortably and diligently installed at 80 Pall Mall. The Kensington site, like the one in Gower Street twenty-five years before, was added to the war effort. It was used as a triangular water tank for fire-engines.

Were they all wasted, those inter-war years? Wasn't the cause of the National Theatre back in exactly the situation of 1913, with a site (inadequate), some funds (inadequate), some support (prone to fits and starts) and with a second generation of enthusiasts getting older? What had happened, if anything? Even Whitworth the indefatigable felt defeated. The S.M.N.T. committee (though not its staff) still occasionally met, to keep the home fires burning, under the chairmanship of Dame Edith Lyttelton, for Lord Lytton was devoting his efforts to war work.

A determined optimist could have seen little gleams of hope. There were, after all, detailed architectural plans for the theatre. The basis of fund-raising and sponsorship had broadened between the wars, largely through the British Drama League's support. The principle of government aid was now being attacked less often and less stridently. These may have been minimal gains, but they could yet be significant — for future days, if and when the war was over, if and when there was something left after the London blitzes from which to reconstruct a new metropolis for the new Britain.

And yet from the dark, seminal heart of war, there sprang a curious new resolution: a determination to be done with the bickering and actually to start, at the first opportunity, with post-war reconstruction. In London, the major project to attract the utopian planners was the South Bank, which had been simmering for the past ten years. It was not simply a question of rebuilding a slummy area; it was also an attempt to use the Thames as an attractive feature of London, instead of allowing it to become a contaminated strip of watery mud. Furthermore, the south of London generally was an underprivileged area, separated by the Thames from the glittering night-life and public buildings of the north. In a sense, the first attempts to open up the South Bank came with the building of County Hall; but the new project was much more ambitious. It could almost have been regarded as London's Brasilia, a conscious attempt to alter London's pattern of social life by altering its geography.

The South Bank planners needed to construct a positive lure to tempt people away from Piccadilly and the now darkened lights of Shaftesbury Avenue; and therefore plans started to form to provide a cultural complex on the South Bank of the Thames. The first person to discuss this question with the S.M.N.T. committee was one of its trustees, J. P. Blake, who was also an alderman of the L.C.C. Blake was a quiet man, with a dry, slightly gloomy sense of humour, but someone to be trusted. He arranged a meeting at County Hall in June 1942, to discuss the possibility of building the National as part of the South Bank complex. Various members of the S.M.N.T. committee attended, as well as Lord Latham (then leader of the L.C.C.) and Bernard Shaw. Shaw provided the main opposition to the scheme, on the grounds that the South Bank was a derelict area and would remain so for the foreseeable future, quite outside the main swirl of London events. The L.C.C. were offering to swop the Kensington site (in Shaw's opinion, eminently suitable) for a larger area by the river. Sir Harold Webbe, the leader of the Conservative opposition on the L.C.C., attended the meeting; but dryly commented that he need not have done so, as the opposition could be safely left in the hands of that 'sound old Tory', Shaw.

Other members of the S.M.N.T. committee, however, did not share Shaw's opinion. They knew that the Kensington site was far from ideal, and that Archer and Barker had both suggested the South Bank. The L.C.C. asked the S.M.N.T. committee to submit plans for a theatre on the south side of Waterloo Bridge, very close to where the National now stands. Lutyens and Masey went to work again, designing a completely new theatre, incorporating two main auditoria, along the lines suggested in Barker's revised *Scheme*. These plans were eventually shown at the British Drama League's twenty-fifth anniversary exhibition at Burlington House.

But there was an obvious snag to the South Bank scheme: the Old Vic. Another major theatre by Waterloo Bridge might have drawn audiences away from the Old Vic; and in any case, the Old Vickers would not have welcomed rivals on their own territory. The former suspicion between the two had relaxed in recent years, since Lilian Baylis's death, but it had not gone completely. The S.M.N.T. committee assumed that, given half a chance, the Old Vickers would claim the S.M.N.T. money. But the Old Vic itself was in difficulties. Its theatre had been badly damaged by bombing, and the company had evacuated to Bolton and Liverpool. Guthrie was in charge and the company itself was still a strong one. But nobody knew what would happen after the war. Could the Old Vic still be patched up?

It was particularly worrying for that staunch Old Vicker Sir Reginald Rowe for, following Guthrie's regime, a new company had been formed, run by a triumvirate of Ralph Richardson, Olivier and John Burrell. Their seasons with the Old Vic company, on tour and at the New Theatre, were triumphant, including some of the most influential productions ever seen in Britain, Olivier's *Richard III* and Richardson's *Peer Gynt* among them. In 1944 and 1945, the Old Vic could claim to be the best company in the world, and it was one of those British boasts that, despite the rigours of the war, London could still provide the finest Shakespearian productions to be seen anywhere.

But where this supreme company could go after the war, when Bronson Albery asked for his theatre back, was Rowe's major worry. A few weeks before Christmas 1944, Geoffrey Whitworth received a surprise telephone-call from Rowe, inviting him to go round to Rowe's rooms in Lincoln's Inn. Whitworth accepted cautiously, fearing a repetition of the same requests for a slice of the S.M.N.T. funds.

Rowe was now an invalid. A few days after meeting Whitworth, he stumbled in the blackout, fell badly and suffered a severe shock, which caused his death. The blackout nearly prevented them from meeting at all, for Whitworth lost his way in Lincoln's Inn, groped blindly around the courtyards and little staircases, unable to read even the numbers above the doors. Eventually he found the right staircase and, at random, knocked at a door, the first one. In many epics, God or Chance has an untidy habit of interfering. The door just happened to be the right one. Rowe opened it and, surrounded by a dark and scarred London, these two now elderly men, with many years of battling for worthy causes behind them, often on opposite sides, settled down for an earnest talk in a warm room.

Rowe suggested, circuitously at first, that there should be some sort of amalgamation between the Old Vic and the plans for the National on the South Bank. Whitworth answered defensively, for he feared that Rowe simply wanted to patch up the Old Vic theatre with S.M.N.T. money. Gradually, however, they warmed to each other. Whitworth suddenly realized that Rowe wanted to throw the weight of the Old Vic esteem, public support and traditions behind the National Theatre cause, on the understanding that the existing Old Vic company would become, in some way, the nucleus of the National Theatre company. Whitworth was still cautious, in that he did not want a loose association with the Old Vic, whereby that company, among others, would sometimes use the facilities of the National. He wanted a true amalgamation, with no sniping, envy or greed. Rowe agreed, and they shook hands on it.

Their committees had, of course, to be consulted. Whitworth prepared a memorandum for the S.M.N.T. committee, which met on February 7th, 1945. After Rowe's death, the secretary of the Old Vic arranged a meeting with the S.M.N.T. committee, which led (after several other meetings) to a formal agreement, 'to effect an immediate co-operation of the two said Charities and ultimately an amalgamation to the intent that they shall then become and be administered as one body under the name of the National Theatre'. This agreement, which involved the formation of a new joint council, was formally announced after the war—at a press conference held on Monday, January 28th, 1946, at the Waldorf Hotel.

Unlike the situation at the end of the First World War, therefore, when the S.M.N.T. committee had been broken up and the plans for the National temporarily shelved, the National Theatre cause emerged from the Second World War greatly strengthened and united. In retrospect, the Waldorf Hotel press conference can perhaps be considered as the customary mixture of factual announcements (many already known) and salesmanship—but only a hardened cynic could have dismissed such announcements and such salesmen as just another pressure group. The facts in themselves were interesting enough—the patching up of an old rivalry, the swopping of the Kensington site for one on the South Bank, the adoption of Granville-Barker's scheme for two theatres in one building (the first seating 1,250 and the second 630), the twin blessings of the still embryonic Arts Council of Great Britain and the L.C.C., and the announcement of new committees.

On the platform sat Oliver Lyttelton, now M.P. for Aldershot, fresh from his triumphs as Minister of Production in Churchill's war Cabinet, who was to become the chairman of the joint council, and flanking him, on one side, sat the Earl of Lytton (for the Old Vic governors) and Viscount Esher (for the S.M.N.T. committee). Lyttelton's opening speech was jokily informal. They were putting up the banns for a marriage between the two charities, which would eventually result in a child, the new National Theatre. Esher's speech, however, was solemnly idealistic. The National Theatre would be the 'first artistic venture of our new, young, educated democracy'. In a few years' time, he forecast, the centre of London would be choked with traffic. 'How pleasant then—to enter the theatre barge, cross the cool river, dine in the theatre restaurant and afterwards attend the play.' The National Theatre would also reclaim the English language from American vulgarizations. An atmosphere of confident optimism prevailed, which had not been seen since the days before the First World War, and which was emphasized rather than diminished by the cautiously diplomatic warnings, voiced by Lyttelton and Whitworth. 'It is unlikely', Lyttelton frankly admitted, 'that the building can be completed before 1951', while Whitworth warned that the new theatre must cost at least £750,000 but more probably a full £1 million.

If we want to pinpoint a time when the National stopped being a worthy cause and became a definite project, it would be that meeting at the Waldorf Hotel. From that moment on, it would have been harder to undo the plans for the National than to carry on with them—in however desultory a fashion. This meeting demonstrated that the National now received support from all three political parties. Oliver Lyttelton, of course, represented the Tories. Lord Keynes, a Liberal, was the first chairman of the Arts Council, although it was rumoured that he would have preferred the National Theatre not to be linked with the Old Vic but with H.M. Tennent Ltd., the leading impresarios of straight plays, on whose board sat John Gielgud and H. B. Beaumont.

The support of the newly formed Labour government could be taken for granted. Attlee himself was thought to be in favour of a wholesale nationalization of the theatre system; but, in any case, the South Bank project was the particular concern of the Labour-controlled L.C.C. The first general plan for the South Bank—which included the National —had been put forward in 1943 by two L.C.C. planners, Professor Patrick Abercrombie and J. H. Forshaw. Morrison, Home Secretary in Churchill's war Cabinet, was now Leader of the House of Commons, Lord President of the Council, and very much Attlee's deputy. It was as if, quite suddenly, a large cross-section of the British political establishment had grasped the National Theatre very tightly—and would not let go. It would have taken a minor earthquake to have broken that confident, left-hand, right-hand embrace. The National was now just a matter of time.

11 Proposed buildings for a Shakespeare Memorial National Theatre in
Bloomsbury, at the corner of Gower Street and Keppel Street, *c.* 1916.
The site was bought by the S.M.N.T. committee in 1913, re-sold 1922

12 The Old Vic theatre, *c.* 1920

13 The Ceremony of the Twig and Sod. G. B. Shaw receiving the deeds of
the site of the proposed National Theatre in South Kensington, April 1938

14 G. B. Shaw and Sir E. Lutyens looking at plans for a National Theatre in Cromwell Road, South Kensington, March 24th, 1939

15 Lilian Baylis (1874–1937), who took over the management of the Old Vic in 1912

17 Edith Evans as Portia in *The Merchant of Venice*, 1925

THREE OLD VIC PRODUCTIONS:
16 John Gielgud as Richard II, 1930

18 Dame Sybil Thorndike and Laurence Olivier in *Coriolanus*, 1938

7

The Utopians

THE euphorias of victory can sometimes prove as hard to handle as the depressions of defeat. There were two famous victories in 1945: over the Axis forces and, for Socialists, the landslide electoral defeat of the Tories. At last a Labour government was in power with a sufficient majority to undertake the radical transformation of society promised in their manifestos; and when the new Parliament met, on August 1st, 1945, the assembled Labour M.P.s with their majority of 99 shocked Oliver Lyttelton as he hurried to the opposition front bench by jeering at Churchill, singing the Red Flag and chanting, 'Who are the masters now?' Lyttelton began 'to fear for [his] country'.

Around Parliament, London was devastated from bombing. The wartime austerities — rationing of clothes and food, shortages of fuel and raw materials, restrictions of all kinds — could not be lifted for many years; but there was a new optimism abroad, a determination for change, which might have depressed a staunch Tory like Lyttelton, but which intoxicated the supporters of Attlee. Those inevitable by-products of competitive capitalism — unemployment, the slump, the depressions of the 1930s — would be removed through enlightened Socialism. The commanding heights of the economy would be made answerable to Parliament and the general public through nationalization. For the first time, British society would be sensibly planned for the benefit of all. Those inhibitions about the role of government in society would be removed. The centralization of power — which during the war had led to an unprecedented control of the national income of up to 45 per cent — had won the war for the benefit of the people, and would now win the peace. The long-awaited millennium was at hand.

This excitement was widespread, operated on many levels and in curious places. At the Oxford Union, for example, in 1948, two undergraduates in their final years at university, the Hon. Anthony Wedgwood Benn and Kenneth Tynan, happily debated the proposition that 'the House would like to have it both ways', the equivalent perhaps of those student calls in the late 1960s of 'we want it [i.e. everything] now'. In the councils of the L.C.C., the South Bank plan was redrawn. The original plan, drafted in 1943, was basically an effort to tidy up the riverside. It envisaged that the National Theatre would be built roughly on the site of the present Festival Hall, that the land between County Hall and Hungerford Bridge would be primarily a leisure area, with gardens, a swimming pool, a large youth centre, and a waterfront bandstand beside Waterloo Bridge, where the National Film Theatre now stands. By March 1947 the scheme had taken on new proportions. An overall architect-planner, Dr Charles Holden, had been appointed, whose brief extended beyond that of the riverside. It now included a large development at Hammersmith, the extension of Cromwell Road to include a flyover across the Hammersmith roundabout, and a total redevelopment of the Elephant and Castle intersection. A new river wall was to be built, reclaiming a strip of land (about 100 feet wide) from the Thames mud, which would be used for walkways and gardens; while new government offices (for 10,000 people) were proposed, with concert halls, restaurants and hotels as well as the new National.

This larger project, of course, would also take much longer, particularly because all the planning procedures had to be carefully observed. The models and designs had to be on display at County Hall so that members of the public, individually or as part of various pressure groups, could inspect them and raise any objections. Nothing could be knocked down or built without at any rate the appearance of consultation; and, until the scheme as a whole had been generally approved, it was considered inadvisable to attempt any part of it, such as the National. This process could have bogged down the South Bank project indefinitely, had Herbert Morrison not been determined for quick results. Morrison was planning a great symbol for Britain's regeneration, the Festival of Britain in 1951, which would show the world that Britain, having taken it, could also make it. It would be staged on the South Bank, and as part of the festivities the first major civic building of the post-war reconstruction would be officially opened: the Royal Festival Hall.

The Festival Hall was Isaac Hayward's particular pride. He persisted in calling it that 'Music Hall', a more plebeian name, and he regarded it as 'the finest building built in Britain for the past 50 years'. It was built for £2 million, raised solely through the rates, in just over two years, a startling example of municipal efficiency. It had not been erected entirely without government help, however. Hayward had entered into a comradely pact with Morrison. Whereas Morrison was concerned to provide Britain with a symbol of its renaissance, Hayward wanted something more permanent to emerge from the Festival. He therefore offered Morrison the Festival site—and cleared the area on the rates. In return, Morrison promised Hayward that there would be no problems or red-tape with, say, the supply of building materials for the Festival Hall—which was why the building was erected in costly Portland stone and demonstrated British craftsmanship at its finest. Delays were not to be endured. The workers had to work, which was why even good Socialists showed an uncomradely impatience with troubles on the building site. There was an anecdote concerning the Minister for Works, Richard Stokes, who was once told of a shortage in shovels: 'Then the workers', he said, 'will have to lean on something else.'

Municipal patronage of the arts on this scale was itself something of a novelty. Supporting the arts through the rates was the second stage of a new approach towards the problems of public patronage. In 1942 the British Drama League had drawn up a Civic Theatre Scheme, which had suggested that, in future, local authorities and the government together should subsidize regional theatres. It was submitted to Churchill, the president of the Board of Education, and the Council for the Encouragement of Music and the Arts, CEMA, which was the forerunner of the Arts Council. It received widespread support, and in 1948 the Local Government Act allowed local authorities to raise up to (but not more than) the product of a sixpenny rate to support the arts. In theory, this could have produced about £8 million for the arts, although few councils in the age of post-war austerity chose to take advantage of this provision.

Potentially, municipal support seemed a better proposition than national patronage. The Arts Council of Great Britain had been established by Royal Charter on August 9th, 1946; but its funds for the first year amounted to only £235,000, which had to be spread among many projects throughout the country. If the National Theatre was to find the £1 million necessary, it had to look towards sources other than the Arts Council. The simplest method of raising the money remained a direct approach to the government. The launching pad for this latest and, as it proved, most successful assault on the Treasury coffers, came with a theatre conference held at Caxton Hall, Westminster, in February 1948. It was a meeting which brought together most theatre organizations which expected and wanted subsidies—such as Equity, the British

Drama League, the Conference of Repertory Theatres (CORT) and the Joint Council of the National Theatre and the Old Vic—but excluded unintentionally those which did not, such as the Society of West End Theatre Managers. On its agenda as just one of its ninety-odd resolutions, was a proposal to this effect: that the British Theatre Conference endorses the current and already well-established National Theatre Scheme. Sir Stafford Cripps, the Chancellor of the Exchequer, addressed the final session; and, to everyone's surprise, for he was renowned for his austerity measures, he indicated that the government was at last prepared to consider an increase of money to the arts in general, and was looking forward to the time when the economic situation would allow the National to be built.

Encouraged by these words, Oliver Lyttelton tabled a question in the Commons on March 23rd, inquiring whether funds would eventually be available from government sources for the National. Cripps replied with a qualified 'Yes':

> I propose to introduce legislation during the present Parliament to the effect that, if the LCC provide a suitable site for the purpose of a National Theatre, the Treasury may make a contribution not exceeding £1 million towards the cost of building the theatre.

He warned the House, however, that it would not be possible to start the building during the life of the present Parliament and that the money would necessarily be conditional in timing upon the general economic situation of the country. It would only be released subject to the approval of the Treasury.

Whitworth called 1948 'annus mirabilis'. It was the year in which the sustained campaign for the National, which had begun with the Waldorf Hotel press conference, seemed to be reaching a climax and a firm governmental decision. The propaganda in favour of the National had been ceaseless. There was now a tempting vision of a national 'art' service, along the lines of a health service. It had been bolstered by many examples, some ill-founded, from countries elsewhere in Europe, East and West. The Soviet Theatre Exhibition in 1946 stirred up a ferment of speculation about how much better things were done in Soviet Russia. J. B. Priestley had written enthusiastically that

> fine, well-equipped theatres, with repertories of first-class plays, are as common in the Soviet Union as cinemas here. And even trade unions and collective farms have their own theatres. There are playhouses everywhere, from the Arctic to the deserts of Central

Asia ... More masterpieces of world drama are shown on the Soviet stage ... than on all the stages of Britain, USA, France, Sweden, and any other country you like to mention put together [*Listener*, January 1st, 1946].

Tom Driberg, M.P., wrote excitedly in the *Municipal Journal* about a town in Czechoslovakia, Ostrava, with 30,000 inhabitants and a municipal theatre employing 500 people. It did not seem to him absurd that 1·66 per cent of the population should be actors and stage-hands, a percentage surely exceeded only by Oberammergau at passion-play time; nor that a town the size of Bratislava, another Driberg example, should subsidize its theatre by an annual grant of £215,000. A team from the joint council visited state-subsidized theatres in Stockholm and Copenhagen; and their report, though glowing, was moderate in comparison with those of other enthusiasts.

It was against this background that the National Theatre Bill was duly introduced into the House of Commons in November 1948; and passed through both Houses of Parliament without a division, by February. In comparison with the 1913 Debate, the most striking feature of the 1949 version was that there was very little discussion at all about the merits of building a National Theatre. Most M.P.s thought it an excellent idea, and those who did not were unwilling to speak. It was, of course, a Bill introduced by a government, not a private Member, and its wording was deliberately cautious. The sum, £1 million, would be given 'subject to such conditions as the Treasury may think fit'—which could mean anything and actually meant a delay of about fifteen years. The tone of the debate, however, was far less cautious. Lyttelton congratulated the government for its 'imagination and audacity' in presenting such a measure at such a time; and carried with him most of the Conservative Party. He and other speakers went through the history of the National Theatre movement, quoting Irving, Arnold and Barker where necessary. Emrys Hughes asked whether Wales and Scotland could have National Theatres too, please; and Leah Manning thought that a National would do wonders for the English language which had suffered from the American invasion. It would substitute the language of *Romeo and Juliet* for the new 'Shall us? Let's!' routine. Mr Ellis Smith of Stoke-on-Trent objected to the idea that the National should be built in London, which already had more than its fair share of good theatre. He wanted the National to be built in the north, perhaps Manchester, a view incidentally which was shared by Sidney Bernstein on the old S.M.N.T. committee. Other speakers envisaged a chain of sixpenny theatres stretching around the country; and the only serious argument against the Bill was that presented by Mr E. P. Smith of Ashford, who argued that the Chancellor was being too cautious and mean, in view of the amount which had been drawn away from the theatre by Entertainments Tax:

> ... in certain quarters there may be, and no doubt will be, some criticism of Parliament spending £1 million of the nation's money on a theatre project. I have not yet delved into the precise figures but I should not be surprised, and indeed I think it would be a conservative estimate, if the living theatre had not provided successive Chancellors of the Exchequer, during its long existence with something in the neighbourhood of £30 million of revenue ... This project will cost £1 million; and unless my arithmetic is at fault, £1 million in relation to £30 million means giving back to the theatre 3½ per cent, which is not over-generous.

In this speech alone, perhaps, can one detect the essential difference of approach traditionally associated with the Labour and Conservative Parties. The Labour Party was prepared to give grants, but rather reluctant to do away with Entertainments Tax: the Conservative Party was prepared to do away with Entertainments Tax (and eventually did so, in 1958) but more reluctant to give grants. On this occasion, however, party differences were buried. Mr Glenvil Hall, the Financial Secretary to the Treasury, who moved the Bill, stated at one point:

> This is a non-party, non-political and, I hope, non-controversial measure.

He was right. It was. Of the many speakers in favour, Benn Levy was the most eloquent.

And yet in retrospect, it seems quite extraordinary that the Bill should have been so uncontroversial. For years, the National Theatre scheme had been kicked around, subject to all kinds of delays and prevarications from the government downwards — and yet now, when there was so much post-war reconstruction to be done, when refugees from the blitz were returning to London to be put in prefabs on bomb-sites (a temporary measure which lasted for twenty-five years and more) the Bill was passed with glowing enthusiasm and no divisions. Furthermore, existing theatres in London had been damaged by the bombing. About a third had been severely damaged or destroyed, another third were suffering from dangerous-looking cracks or fallen ceilings. Basil Dean, once a sturdy supporter of the National, wanted to see these buildings repaired and preserved before the new National was started. Independent impresarios could not get hold of the money and the materials to improve their theatres. Could not the National, asked Basil Dean, make do with Drury Lane?

There were other reasonable, smaller-scale ideas. On March 27th, 1949, Mr H. B. Vincent wrote to the *Sunday Times*, pointing out that

> on the finest site in London for a National Theatre (i.e. Covent Garden), there is a fruit and vegetable market. On the finest site in London for a fruit and vegetable market (i.e. the South Bank), we therefore propose to build a National Theatre ... Before it is too late, cannot some leader of vision effect that simple exchange which will be a boon alike to the theatre-goer, the farmer and the vegetable merchant, the housewife and the citizen of London?

He was sternly rebuked by Henry Brooke, then Leader of the Conservative Party opposition in the L.C.C.:

> The County of London plan has been open to public comment for six years. Its recommendations included de-centralising Covent Garden to points right outside Inner London, and building a theatre and a concert hall on the South Bank. Nearly four years have passed since the LCC approved the plan in principle. It was agreed more than three years ago to grant a lease on the South Bank for building a National Theatre. Six months ago, it acceded to a request to proceed immediately with erecting a concert hall on a site adjoining [*Sunday Times*, April 3rd, 1949].

Mr Vincent retorted that 'not a stone has been laid'. Brooke replied sharply that 'maybe not ... but all the relevant decisions have been taken, in open session'.

Minds had been made up. They were not to be confused with new ideas. Indeed the delays surrounding the National had already been such that alternative suggestions were merely irritating. And simply to patch up London, to undertake modest unambitious schemes, was not in keeping with the spirit of the times. The Labour Party in the L.C.C. and in the Commons wanted to build a new Britain and to change London's social geography; and they were prepared to hold back minor schemes until the grand plan could be properly realized. Grand plans, unfortunately, are expensive. The Labour government became harassed by practical difficulties. Coal and steel may have been nationalized, and the National Health Service established; but the housing programme was disappointing and there was a serious balance-of-payments problem, leading to the devaluation of the pound in 1949. At the time, this was regarded as a stop-gap measure, but a pattern was established then which was doomed to recur. Ambitious government schemes had been proposed—and passed by Parliament—which proved expensive, inflexible and long-drawn-out—which in turn led to the rapid absorption of the country's resources—which had to be drawn away from the reconstruction of British industry—which in turn led to debt and borrowing from abroad.

The £1 million for the National could not be released by the Treasury, and in June 1951 there was an embargo on all buildings and the reconstruction of buildings 'used for entertainments purposes' costing more than £5,000. This meant that it became illegal to renovate existing theatres damaged by bombing. This measure did not directly affect the National Theatre, which remained government policy with bi-partisan support. The general economic condition of the country, however, did delay the theatre. It was decided that it could not be built in time for the Festival of Britain, which had been the first target date.

In the meantime, the architectural plans for the National had changed once more. Lutyens had died in 1944, and the S.M.N.T. committee had not been entirely happy with his appointed successor, Hubert Worthington, whose preliminary designs had to be drawn up in ignorance of the rest of the South Bank scheme. In 1946, a new architect was appointed by a committee which included three of the most important L.C.C. planners, Abercrombie, Forshaw and Holden. They chose an Australian architect, Brian O'Rorke, who like Lutyens had never designed a theatre before, but was best known for his interior designs for the luxury Orient liners. Cecil Masey, Lutyens's collaborator, was asked to work with him but, perhaps in disappointment at being overlooked, resigned shortly afterwards.

O'Rorke's designs suggest a building as wholly representative of 1950s civic architecture as Lutyens's would have been of the early 1930s. The National would have been a large, sleek building, with a glassed terrace overlooking the river, with two theatres inside, both proscenium arch but with different seating capacities. It would have been built in Portland stone, and it was originally intended to stand between the Festival Hall and the Shot Tower: it would have 'balanced'—or rather repeated—the impression of the Festival Hall, but with a small fly-tower instead of that curved roof which Sir Thomas Beecham compared to a 'baby's bum'.

Although the National could not be completed in time for the

Festival, it was decided that a start should be made, merely symbolic perhaps, to show the world that there was something to look forward to when the site had been cleared of marquees and temporary buildings. The ceremonial laying of the foundation stone was scheduled for Friday, July 13th, 1951. King George VI originally accepted the invitation to lay the stone, but he was trying to recover from an operation for cancer.

Queen Elizabeth took the trowel instead, and laid a trough of mortar on the stone beneath the foundation stone. Other members of the royal family, Princess Elizabeth among them, watched her, together with Prime Minister Clement Attlee, Lyttelton, Whitworth and a full parade of dignitaries. Sybil Thorndike read three verses by the poet laureate, John Masefield, which offered caution, Romantic Agony and stately rhetoric in the proportions then expected of public verse:

> Here lay we stone, that at a future time,
> May bear a House, wherein, in days to be
> Tier above tier, delighted crowds may see
> Man's passions made a plaything and sublime.
>
> Here, fellowship of lovers of the arts
> May work together, to create anew
> Worlds that a poet in his rapture knew
> Fairer than this, our hell of broken hearts.
>
> Pray therefore, brothers, as we put the stone,
> That glory from the Never-Dying Mind
> May triumph here, with vision for the blind
> Making joy daily bread and beauty known.

Queen Elizabeth's speech referred to the 'previous association' between the monarchy and Shakespeare's band of players, now to be replaced by an equally proud association between the state and the stage. The band of the Welsh Guards then played marches, which could not be broadcast with the rest of the ceremony because the Musicians' Union had blacked them. The stone was blessed and dedicated by the Archbishop of Canterbury, and nobody worried that it might be in the wrong place.

Whitworth, too, was happy. His book, *The Making of a National Theatre*, had been published in 1951, to coincide neatly with the ceremony; and when he died in September 1951, he had 'the consolation of knowing', as his obituarist Dr F. S. Boas put it, 'that he had lived to see the beginning of the end of the great project on which his heart was set'. The sun shone on the ceremonial laying, and the skies seemed to be set fair for the National, except for one small, niggling detail: British theatre in general seemed to be in a rapid decline.

Theatres were closing around the country. Managements could either not afford to renovate them or were prevented by law from doing so. There was the new threat of television. Entertainments Tax had drawn profits from the industry, which had now become increasingly centralized under one overall management, the Prince Littler Consolidated Trust, which controlled nearly half the theatres in the country. There was a dearth of new plays. The editors of the *Stage Yearbook* deplored the fact that there was no really exciting new play for Festival Year. The West End was filled with revivals of plays by dramatists whose names had been familiar before the First World War, Shaw, Maugham and Pinero among them.

This was serious enough, but what concerned the joint council directly was the state of the Old Vic. The great days of the Olivier/Richardson/Burrell regime were over, catastrophically so, for they had left behind a wake of misunderstanding, bitterness and confusion. After the triumphant seasons of 1944–5 the main Old Vic company had gone on tour, visiting the Comédie-Française in 1945, New York in 1946, and Australia and New Zealand in 1948, harvesting praise wherever they went. But when Olivier and Richardson were away, the company left holding the fort in London suffered. 1948 was a particularly bad year for the Old Vic in London. The Comédie-Française visited London for a three-week season at the Cambridge Theatre, and the critics noticed with some asperity how badly the London Old Vic compared with the French ensemble. John Burrell, in charge in London, had tried to cover up the absences of Olivier and Richardson by importing other stars, such as Sir Cedric Hardwicke, unwisely as it happened. The sole production praised by the critics was one provided by the director of the Bristol Old Vic, Hugh Hunt's *The Cherry Orchard*.

During the 1948 season, the governors of the Old Vic, among them Lord Esher who had taken over the chairmanship when the 2nd Earl of Lytton died in 1947, decided not to renew the contracts of their three artistic directors, which were due to end in June 1949. Olivier heard the news by telegram in Australia—Richardson by telegram in Hollywood. It seemed a particularly abrupt and crude form of dismissal, particularly since neither of them had undertaken tours simply for personal gain. The Old Vic had needed the money, partly to finance the new plans for the company which were the result of the intended expansion to the status of the National. Britain, too, needed the foreign exchange, and the Old Vic was the country's prize cultural export. Olivier and Richardson had for years been accepting salaries at the Old Vic far below the sums which they could have received from films. They had kept their own wages down voluntarily to £50 each a week, with small additional sums for each performance. They considered that they had built up the Old Vic to the status of an international company, sacrificing their own interests to do so.

With this treatment from the governing board, the loyalty felt by Olivier, Richardson and other members of their company to the Old Vic vanished overnight. And the general feeling of resentment spread in other directions. The Old Vic was now receiving the first few dollops of public money through the Arts Council, which was one reason why the governing board was assuming a new importance. Actors feared that with subsidies the control of the company would pass out of the hands of the 'experts' — the actors and directors — and into the clutches of benevolent, public-spirited gentlemen who knew nothing about the theatre but whose presence on bureaucratic committees attracted government support. On January 18th, 1949, Stephen Mitchell, from the Aldwych Theatre, wrote to the *Daily Telegraph*:

Sir Thomas Beecham's concern over the Arts Council's handling of the productions and affairs of Covent Garden is in fact paralleled in the theatre by the handling of the Old Vic by its Governors.

Whatever may be the qualifications of [the] Trustees [of Covent Garden], there can be little doubt that the Governors of the Old Vic, with one or two exceptions, seem even less competent to run our most important theatrical enterprise. It is disturbing that people so little qualified should be so responsible for our highest artistic endeavours and be given so much of the taxpayers' money to play around with in an industry in which they have neither trained nor laboured.

Three years ago the Old Vic had received a national position due to the work of Sir Ralph Richardson and Sir Laurence Olivier. Accordingly, one would have supposed that the ardent co-operation and continuance of these two gentlemen would have been the *sine qua non* of the Governors' policy.

It must accordingly cause surprise that, at this vital moment in the life of the Old Vic, Sir Laurence Olivier, who has just completed a great tour of Australia ... and Sir Ralph Richardson, who absented himself from the Old Vic but for one season, have been summarily dropped — politely called resigning. In their places, and presumably to make up for them, have come £30,000 of public money and the bountiful and industrious secretary of the Arts Council.

Esher's reply was published three days later. He pointed out that the 1948 Old Vic season in London had lost £26,000, a deficit which was not covered by the success of the Australian tour; and that in any case, the Old Vic organization was now much more broadly based than simply on the main company:

> This sum of £30,000, so freely thrown about, is not the correct figure of the probable application that will be made to the Arts Council for the 1949 season. But whatever the sum may ultimately be, it must be remembered that it has to cover not only the Old Vic company, but also the Young Vic company, the Old Vic Theatre School, the Bristol Old Vic Company and the Bristol Old Vic Theatre School.
>
> Mr. Mitchell's general thesis shows that he shares with Sir Thomas Beecham a lamentable ignorance of how things are run in this country. The governors of the Old Vic, like the trustees of Covent Garden, are chosen of set purpose outside the profession. Indeed, the constitution of the Old Vic forbids the appointment as governor of anyone who derives profit from the theatre.
>
> The English system of government has always been based on the principle that independent and intelligent minds, free from both profit and prejudice, should control public enterprise. But governors so appointed never should, and indeed never do, interfere with artistic direction.
>
> Since I have been a governor of the Old Vic there has never been an occasion on which the governors have interfered with experts in their own field. Our business is to appoint the artistic expert and give him a free hand ... I am convinced that if artistic experts had to appoint each other, we should fare much worse [Daily Telegraph, January 21st, 1949].

The question as to how far, if at all, the governors should 'interfere' with the artistic directorship was one which would simmer on for many years. The principle of non-interference, expressed by Esher, was generally accepted, although sometimes it was broken in practice. The non-professional status of the governors was one consequence of the Old Vic being a charity, and as grants became an increasingly important feature of theatre finance, governing boards of 'non-profit-distributing registered companies' became more influential and necessarily (to preserve the charitable status) more amateur. The board of

H. M. Tennent Ltd, a commercial company with a 'non-profit-distributing' subsidiary, Tennent Productions Ltd, had by comparison four highly professional men of the theatre: H. B. Beaumont, Sir John Gielgud, Sir Ralph Richardson and George Rylands, the Cambridge don and an expert on verse-speaking. Because the board obviously did derive income and profit from the theatre, it was regarded by the Arts Council with considerable suspicion after Lord Keynes's death. Keynes had admired the professionalism of the Tennent companies; but the new Arts Council, under its temporary chairman, Sir Ernest Pooley, was much more puritanical. They did not want to see any governing board deriving any sort of profit which might be distantly traced to public funds.

The troubles at the Old Vic were not simply to be attributed to the rows over untimely dismissals or the so-called amateurishness of the board. Under the glow of the great seasons, plans had been hatched, to which Esher referred, which had grown to quarrelsome fledglings. The governing board saw them as an attempt to establish the great, embracing organization which the National Theatre had to become. Those taking part in the schemes, however, were less concerned with the grand plan than with their practical difficulties, which were many. In 1946, three separate organizations had been started, which were nevertheless closely linked and formed a body of opinion within the Vic organization, particularly resentful of the governing board. There was an acting school, run by Glen Byam Shaw, an experimental theatre project (under Michel St Denis) and a young people's theatre (under George Devine). They had grown from an idea of St Denis, for a comprehensive Old Vic Theatre Centre, whose main purpose was to become a 'laboratory of invention'.

St Denis, a pupil of Copeau, wanted to free the theatre from the restrictions of the proscenium arch and also from those styles of cerebral, 'bourgeois' acting which seemed to him unathletic, undedicated, posing and artificial. He wanted new shapes for theatres, keeping actors and audiences 'in one room'. Devine, on an extended leave from the army, took part in the training of actors, but was also trying to organize a company to tour schools with ambitious *commedia dell'arte* productions, meeting substantial resistance from education authorities in doing so. At first, the Arts Council had encouraged these activities; and the Old Vic theatre was patched up to provide them with a cold, temporary London home, where the water dripped through the ceilings in bucketfuls. It opened as a theatre centre on Boxing Day 1946, with the Old Vic Theatre School starting at Dulwich.

99

The dedication of these three men was tireless and extraordinary. St Denis, for example, turned down an offer to become Director-General of French Radio, to stay with the centre; and Byam Shaw refused a £10,000 film offer. St Denis worked himself into his first heart attack and collapse, Devine gave up thoughts of being a full-time actor; and for a short time, the centre seemed likely to rival the Actors' Studio in New York. Few schools have provided more rigorous training for their students; and few obtained, in the long term, more spectacular results. Alan Dobie, Joan Plowright and Prunella Scales trained at the school, as did the designers Richard Negri, Voytek and Carl Toms, and the directors Frank Dunlop, Eric Thompson, Val May, Michael Cacoyannis and Peter Zadek. But the short-term results were distinctly disappointing. The Young People's Theatre had a couple of successful productions, such as *The King Stag* and *The Knight of the Burning Pestle*; but St Denis's experimental theatre programme never got off the ground, and increasingly the three pioneers realized that their aims, which involved nothing less than a transformation of the values in British theatre, were very different from the aims of the governing board – who tended to look at each venture from the angle of the National Theatre. Did they contribute to the broadly based institution, which the Old Vic/National ought to become? Were they indulging in intellectual escapades? And, above all, were they likely to lose or gain money? 'I want no meetings', said Byam Shaw, 'with hard-faced financial experts who treat one like a criminal if one is losing money, or like a genius if one is making it.' He left the dog-work on the committees to Devine, who suffered accordingly. The Old Vic governors never fully grasped what St Denis, Devine and Byam Shaw wanted or were up to. Esher could never understand St Denis's broken English, and dismissed him accordingly as a foreigner whose proper place was somewhere else.

Nor, in fairness, did the enthusiasts of the theatre centre appreciate fully the problems of the board, who wanted to maintain the London Old Vic as an outward and visible sign of the company's fitness to be regarded as an embryonic National, while furthering the regional links with the repertory companies at Bristol and Liverpool. In 1949, when the money from the Arts Council became available to the Old Vic, there was a drastic reorganization of the company. Llewellyn Rees, the drama director of the Arts Council, left his job to become the Old Vic's administrator; and Hugh Hunt was appointed artistic director. One of their first jobs was to find a permanent home for the Old Vic, for Bronson Albery could not be expected to lease them the New Theatre indefinitely; and the building on the South Bank was not expected for several years.

This meant that the Old Vic theatre had to be patched up properly and brought back into action as a public theatre, an expensive undertaking which absorbed the new funds from the Arts Council, as well as some money from the S.M.N.T. funds. The freshly decorated Old Vic opened in November 1950, looking proud and white on the outside, with a new colour scheme of grey, gold and dark red within. There was a widened proscenium arch, designed by Pierre Sonrel, and a raisable forestage. A new lighting system was installed, with the latest equipment; and the Old Vic could now be regarded as a theatre on a par with those undamaged ones in the West End.

But the renovation of the Old Vic brought the theatre centre project immediately into question. There was no room for it. Nor was there any money left over to find it new headquarters or to maintain it, even in the grotty circumstances to which it had become accustomed. Accordingly, the theatre centre had to be axed, just when its different ideas were starting to show practical results.

The founders of the centre went their different ways. St Denis became the head of the Centre Dramatique de l'Est in Strasbourg, and then was appointed artistic director of the Lincoln Center in New York, before joining the Royal Shakespeare Company as an associate director. Byam Shaw took charge of the Shakespeare Memorial Theatre in Stratford during the mid-1950s, while Devine eventually became the first artistic director of the English Stage Company at the Royal Court in 1956. The Young Vic closed in August 1951, and the Drama School in 1952.

Within three years, therefore, but stemming from decisions taken in 1948-9, the Old Vic lost its 'stars'—Olivier and Richardson—and also that creative cell, the theatre centre, which should have provided a dynamic core to the permanent company. Few companies have ever had such a team, fewer still would have treated its great talents so cavalierly and in such a philistine way. The new combination of state support and the joint council made an unhappy start.

The redecorated Old Vic opened with Hugh Hunt's *Twelfth Night*, a fair success and, for Festival year, the new administration brought back Tyrone Guthrie to direct Sir Donald Wolfit in *Tamburlaine*, an individual triumph which did not lead, as the governors had hoped, to a more permanent relationship between Wolfit, Guthrie and the company. Guthrie had the reputation of being a maverick, but the departure of Wolfit was an unexpected blow. He was perhaps the only major Shakespearian actor who could have filled the gaps left by Olivier and Richardson. The 1951 season had been designed for him—with *King Lear*, *Othello*, *The Clandestine Marriage* and *Timon of Athens* all in the programme, each demanding the heroic, boisterous playing of which Wolfit at his best was capable. But Wolfit backed out after *Tamburlaine*. He was used to running his own company and his ideas as to what a Shakespearian production should look and sound like were set fast in the grand actor-manager's mould. His place was filled by Stephen Murray (Lear), Douglas Campbell (Othello) and André Morell (Timon).

As one foundation stone for the National was being laid on the South Bank, another was therefore crumbling. The Old Vic company, the basis of the new National, was now just one of several rather second-rate and transitory teams competing for attention in an undistinguished London scene. The revival of the Old Vic's fortunes was not to come until 1953, when Michael Benthall was appointed as artistic director; and by that time, the question had ceased to be whether the Old Vic could become a proper nucleus for the new National, but whether it could survive at all.

The actors and directors who, in an ideal world, might have been expected either to stay with the Old Vic or to have been attracted to it, drifted elsewhere. The Shakespeare Memorial Theatre was one beneficiary. Sir John Gielgud went to Stratford in 1950, playing opposite Peggy Ashcroft in *Much Ado About Nothing* in a repeat of that famous Old Vic Benedick/Beatrice combination, and tackling King Lear for the first time in his career. Redgrave followed him, and Richardson, and eventually, in 1955, Laurence Olivier. The actors who had made their names with the Old Vic and had established the reputation of the Old Vic as recompense, now performed the same service for the Shakespeare Memorial Theatre. Production standards at Stratford improved, as Sir Barry Jackson (who gave Peter Brook his first Shakespearian productions) was succeeded by Anthony Quayle and Byam Shaw. While the Old Vic rambled awkwardly into the red, despite grants, Stratford thrived, building up surpluses (particularly from Gielgud's tours) which enabled it in the early 1960s to turn itself into a national company more or less on its own initiative.

The Oliviers, relieved from their ties with the Old Vic, went into business on their own account. Sir Laurence and Vivien Leigh were now the 'royalty' of British theatre, the London equivalents to the Lunts on Broadway. In 1945 they had bought a country house, Notley Abbey in Buckinghamshire, close to London, where they held house-parties at weekends, informal, jolly and distinguished, a mirror of those Edwardian house-parties which the Lytteltons had loved. Spencer Tracy, Ralph Richardson and Peter Finch were regular visitors, and Oliver Lyttelton, though not a close friend, went there on occasions. Olivier's delight on Sundays was to prune and plant trees, a substitute perhaps for those other preparations for the future which should have taken place elsewhere.

As an independent actor-manager, however, Sir Laurence Olivier was less successful. The seasons at St James's lost money, even during Festival year, when the Oliviers offered the double bill of *Antony and Cleopatra* and Shaw's *Caesar and Cleopatra*, playing in repertoire. Their losses on new plays and productions could often be offset by star appearances elsewhere, either in films or visits to Broadway. The Oliviers survived better than most the decline of British theatre during the early 1950s; but they were all too aware of the surrounding problems, and by the mid-1950s they were forced to consider selling Notley Abbey.

They had sacrificed little, however, in a material sense, by leaving the Old Vic. Indeed they had gained their independence. But they had lost perhaps that sense of social purpose and dedication which the Old Vic once provided for its supporters. Indeed this reveals the chief casualty of the Old Vic's post-war years: its damaged reputation. The Old Vic—for so long a model of what 'sweetness and light' meant in practice, a symbol of resistance during two world wars, the company which had struggled through poverty towards artistic excellence and social achievement—had now acquired a different kind of aura, of ingratitude, philistinism and bureaucratic bumbling. Even its seat prices, to the horror of Old Vic loyalists, were rising towards those of the West End.

Eventually, in the late 1950s, the disagreements were patched up. 'Can you ever forgive me?' asked Esher on one occasion, and Olivier smiled and apparently did. But the myth of the Old Vic was not so easily recaptured. What remained in Olivier's memory was not just his triumphs, but the years of struggling against the odds which were crowned, not by new opportunities, but by a snub. One anecdote serves to illustrate the change of heart. When Olivier returned to the Old Vic in 1963, now as the Director of the new National Theatre company, he looked around the auditorium and said, 'My God, how I hate this place!'

8

The Roads to Chichester

'AT LONG last,' said Lord Esher at the Times Book Club, 'after years of gestation, enough to put an elephant to shame, the National Theatre is about to be born.' He was opening an exhibition of theatre paintings, given by Somerset Maugham in 1948, which had lain around since then, with other donations to the National Theatre trust, in the vaults of County Hall. The date was March 28th, 1955; and Esher was wrong. The National Theatre was not about to be born. All that had happened was that Brian O'Rorke had nearly completed the detailed drawings for the National, which were going to be submitted to the Fine Arts Commission, for their approval. The Fine Arts Commission's seal of worthiness could then have been used to nudge the arm of government in the right direction.

Esher knew this, but he must have thought that a wildly optimistic statement at this stage might do some good, or at least no harm. If the government woke up one morning to read that the National was about to be built, they might notice that the money had not actually been released for the purpose, and phone up someone in the Treasury. It was a faint hope, but almost every other one had been tried. For ten years, from the laying of the foundation stone in 1951 to the final Treasury release of the money in 1961, there were pleas, exhortations, complaints, rallying calls and thoroughly cynical remarks from the press, every month or so, and all to no avail. Esher's remarks were among many tacks tried, no more helpful than the others.

Poking fun at the National had almost become a popular sport. Before Esher's remarks had made a small headline in *Stage*, Gerard Fay had written a sceptical piece in the *Guardian* pointing out that nothing had happened or was likely to happen. The authorities sometimes seemed to be offering copy for easy satire. There was, for example, the Saga of the Moving Foundation Stone. A few months after the ceremonial laying, the L.C.C. planners had had second thoughts. The site for the National had been chosen before the Festival Hall had been built. The Festival Hall looked much larger in life than it had done on the drawing board; and the site for the National looked cramped, sandwiched between the Hall and Waterloo Bridge. Two large buildings in Portland stone and glass would have provided a banal and very crowded riverside. Furthermore, the Ministry of Works, which had been hanging on to a site upstream of Hungerford Bridge, decided in 1952 that it was not going to be needed after all; and offered it to the L.C.C. to be included within the South Bank scheme. The L.C.C. accepted, and redrew the scheme. More space meant that the National could now be shifted across (on paper, of course) to a site nearer County Hall, while a commercial skyscraper block, the Shell Tower, could be built behind. On the old National Theatre site by Waterloo Bridge, there was now room for a conference centre.

The new South Bank scheme was shown to the press in October 1953; and just as the first scheme had left one completed section, the Festival Hall, so the second one provided other sections which barely blended with the original ideas. The Shell Building, the Art Gallery linked to the Festival Hall and the Waterloo roundabout were all ideas which came from the second scheme. Town planning on this scale takes time, and it is also subject to abrupt shifts in political thinking. A Conservative government had replaced the Labour one in the autumn of 1951; and Oliver Lyttelton was now Secretary of State for the Colonies, a post similar to the one which his father had held. The energetic utopianism of the post-war years was replaced by a different style of government altogether, one which concentrated on less radical measures, the building up of British industry among them, which accounts for the unexpected presence of the Shell block in an area previously reserved for leisure and culture. Harold Macmillan was at the Housing Department, trying to reach the target of 300,000 houses a year which Bevan had missed.

The National Theatre was still government and L.C.C. policy, which was what made the delays particularly frustrating. If there had been an attempt to shelve the National altogether, then something could have been done to change the government's mind. Campaigns could have been launched, alternatives could have been considered. As it was, however, the National simply seemed to be sliding lower and lower down the list of priorities, with art galleries and roundabouts intervening. Wolfit came out with the bright idea that 1 per cent Entertainments Tax could be devoted to the National, which would have provided plenty of money. Unfortunately for this scheme, it was now the government's intention—in time, when circumstances permitted—to abolish Entertainments Tax altogether. And so, once more, nothing could be done.

'We need a National Theatre so badly,' said Wolfit, at a meeting held by the Oxford University Dramatic Society at Worcester College in May 1956. 'There is no theatre in this country at present where young people can see a repertoire of the great classics of the language. It is only in these great plays that the great tradition of the theatre can be kept alive. I'm very worried for the younger generation. The theatre is in a very serious state of decline' [*Oxford Mail*, May 25th, 1956]. 1956 was a watershed year in post-war British theatre. Commercial television had arrived, which many feared would sound the Last Post over the body of a dying art form. The Arts Council annual report for 1956 made gloomy reading: theatres were closing around the country, the mass media and post-war austerity combined seemed to be killing them.

Wolfit was defending the actor-manager tradition in the theatre: he might have mentioned otherwise, as others sometimes did, the few signs of hope—the Shakespearian productions at Stratford perhaps, or the work of Joan Littlewood at the other Stratford (East London), on whom the mantle of Lilian Baylis (if not her religious opinions) seemed to have fallen. He also overlooked the fact that some members of the 'younger generation' felt as passionately about the National as he did. The main problem was that these 'youngsters' were at odds both with the independent actor-manager tradition which Wolfit represented, and with the West End 'establishment', as represented by the Tennent companies and the Prince Littler Consolidated Trust. They were not part of the old 'show-biz' tradition, although some wanted to be. They were university-trained young intellectuals, restlessly looking around the world of British theatre and finding it 'wanting in purpose and dignity', as Matthew Arnold had done.

One such 'youngster' was Kenneth Tynan, who joined the *Observer* in 1954 and had rapidly established the reputation of being the most brilliant critic of his generation. He had left Oxford in 1948, in a blaze of dandy glory and yellow socks, to catch the eyes of Fleet Street editors with the wit and vivid energy of his writing. He had had some practical experience in the theatre, directing a repertory season at Lichfield, and then taking over theatres just outside the West End for short seasons of, say, Victorian melodramas. He was the thinking man's anti-intellectual who, for example, loved the passion and flamboyance of 'stars' at a time when most *avant-garde* theatre-lovers were talking about permanent companies and group theatre. After the tide of 1940s utopianism had started to turn and ebb, he proclaimed himself a romantic Marxist; and later on, when Marxism itself had assumed a dour, puritanical appearance, he managed to reconcile this ardent Socialism with a flamboyant hedonism and sturdy individualism. He was the great 'imposer' of his generation, and admired 'imposing' in others. Indeed, this was a term which he borrowed from the French verb, 's'imposer', and defined it for his own purpose. It meant 'the ability not only to impose one's will upon others (although that is part of it) but to dictate the conditions—social, moral, sexual, political—within which one can operate with maximum freedom'. Much of Tynan's style of 'imposing' was directed against established bourgeois opinion, as he conceived it to be. Thus, he fought against the sexual ethics which in the 1950s thought of homosexuality as a crime and a sin: he returned to Oxford to support a friend who was enduring the ignominy of an Oscar Wilde-type trial. A bastard himself, in the literal sense of the word, he stood up for bastardy in others. In the 1960s he led the crusade against the Lord Chamberlain's Examiner of Plays, the theatre censor; and he was one of the first to take advantage of the abolition of censorship, with his production of *Oh! Calcutta!* Politically, he was prepared to defy the American establishment over Cuba, and the National Theatre Board eventually when, as the first *Dramaturg* of the National Theatre company, he chose a Hochhuth play, *Soldiers*, which accused Churchill of being an accomplice in a political assassination.

Tynan in the mid-1950s was one *enfant terrible* of British theatre. Established actors and directors (Olivier among them) feared the acid in his pen, but they read his columns. Olivier never quite forgave Tynan for a review of his *Antony and Cleopatra/Caesar and Cleopatra* season during Festival year, in which Tynan had implied that Olivier, from a mistaken chivalry, had subdued his performances to prevent overshadowing Vivien Leigh. 'A cat', he commented, 'can do more than look at a king. She can hypnotize him.'

Tynan's capacity to make enemies (selectively) was offset by the charm, warmth and liveliness of his personality. London would have been a much duller place without him. While he was making British Sunday mornings more bearable by his columns, another 'youngster' was making the theatre more literate and intelligent through his productions. Peter Hall was three years younger than Tynan, and had left Cambridge in 1953, where he too had been almost fanatically involved with university theatre. He had the opportunity to join the Tennent organization; but he chose, like Tynan, to direct in theatres outside the West End—though *less* 'outside' than Tynan: a short spell at Windsor, and a longer, much more profitable one at the Arts Theatre Club near Leicester Square. Indeed, his Arts Theatre season in 1955, which included the first British production of Beckett's *Waiting For Godot* and an outspoken play (for the period) about a homosexual relationship, *South*, can be regarded as a seminal point in 1950s theatre, almost equivalent to the arrival of the English Stage Company and *Look Back in Anger* in 1956. It was one of those hopeful signs which Wolfit chose to overlook.

Like Tynan, Hall was a supporter of state-subsidized theatre and of the National; but there the similarities start to peter away, for Hall was a born diplomat, who was only indiscreet intentionally. Hall was no dandy, no phrase-maker, no fool who would rush in where angels feared to tread. He had an intellectual's regard for literature, even poetic pieces of whimsy like John Whiting's *A Penny for a Song*, and he was steeped in the Cambridge tradition of Leavis and Rylands, social earnestness and good verse-speaking. He was not a flamboyant individualist, no hedonist, no romantic and, unlike Tynan, he had no fear of bureaucracy, except sometimes when it was in other people's hands.

Temperamentally, therefore, Hall and Tynan were like book-ends to the new generation in British theatre; but even when they seemed to be facing in opposite directions, they were both supporting a similar cause. Both had seen the Olivier–Richardson seasons at the New, the Gielgud season at the Haymarket. Both were receptive to the new ideas promulgated through the Old Vic theatre centre. Both were ambitious, and looked forward to better organization within British theatre. In calling for the National, Tynan would adapt Arnold's phrase about organizing the theatre. 'The Act', he wrote in the *Observer* on January 1st, 1956, 'is irresistible. Implement the Act': and he was referring, of course, to the National Theatre Act of 1948–9. Tynan was no bureaucrat—the reverse, a rebel—but he looked to the state for rational leadership. Hall became the most accomplished administrator in British theatre. In the army, he had lectured on management techniques to soldiers waiting to be demobbed.

Sandwiched between these two men—if that phrase does not imply an undue inferiority—were the other young individualists of British theatre: Peter Brook, whose meteoric rise as the most adventurous director of his generation began at Oxford before Tynan's time in the early 1940s; John Barton, the best Shakespearian scholar among the young directors; John Mortimer, the dramatist and barrister whose early plays were starting to be known on the B.B.C. Home Service; and Richard Findlater, the critic and theatre historian. None of them belonged exactly to the theatre establishment, although Brook after *Love's Labour's Lost* at Stratford in 1948 was in great demand as a director. They were all impatient with what they regarded as the old-boys' network in British society. None of them belonged to that group of establishment figures which constituted the S.M.N.T. committee. And indeed that committee suffered most of all from the generation gap which had so markedly emerged in the theatre. The old stalwarts had died or were growing old. Dame Edith Lyttelton died in September 1948, Shaw in 1951; and Lytton and Whitworth had gone too. Each (except Shaw) had provided family successors to carry on the cause; but their replacements on the committees were less dedicated, and perhaps more pinned down by circumstances. Oliver Lyttelton, whose support was still rock-solid, was trying to cope with a new and difficult Ministry. The 'youngsters' were not represented on the joint council, the S.M.N.T. committee or the Old Vic governors at all; and they were scathing of the inadequacies of the older generation.

Tynan and Findlater staged their ceremony of mourning for the National, standing in black frock coats with top hats and tassels, beside the foundation stone as funeral monument. In June 1956, Hall, Tynan, Flora Robson (the actress) and Benn Levy (the Labour M.P. and dramatist) totally ignored the joint council and the S.M.N.T. committee, and appealed directly to Tyrone Guthrie, asking him (in Tynan's words) to 'lead the drive into the Treasury's vaults'. Guthrie replied on the B.B.C.'s 'Brains Trust' programme and his answer was afterwards published in the theatre magazine, *Encore*:

> To avoid any coyness and nonsense, let me say that I wouldn't accept the job as director of the National Theatre. There are plenty of old duffers around who would jump at the chance. But I don't think that the National Theatre would work with an old duffer at the head of it. It needs young blood. The National Theatre may be plush, it may be a glittering institution to which the Foreign Office can take visiting diplomats. But there is no reason to believe that it will be anything more than the Old Vic could be, if the Old Vic were heavily subsidised [*Encore*, summer 1956].

The bluntness of Guthrie's reply reveals another dimension to the generation gap, a certain unwillingness on the part of the elder states-men of British theatre to lead—and thus to suffer the shafts of criticism directed against the leaders. Guthrie wanted no more battles with bureaucrats, no more sitting on dull committees, no more pleasing politicians for another round of grants. Life was too short. Nor did he want to involve himself in 'establishment' acting or productions. He thought that he knew what National theatres required: a lip-service to prevailing cultural opinion. He was through that stage, if he had ever been in it, and he had guessed pretty accurately that Britain was through it as well. The Director of the National would find himself in a 'frightful' situation. The board would expect him to be rather traditional, whereas critics like Tynan, or directors like St Denis or Devine would demand something more adventurous. There was no common ground upon which the *'avant'* and the *'derrière' gardes* could meet. Guthrie did not want to find himself in the no-man's land between two firing squads.

Furthermore, he had other plans. He had always been attracted to William Poel's ideas about staging Shakespeare's plays in Elizabethan settings. The key feature of this staging was to have the acting platform jutting out into the audience, not as a simple forestage, but so that the audience could sit around the stage, on three sides, 'embracing' the performance rather than 'confronting' it. In 1948 he seized an unlikely chance to put his theories into practice — the only previous opportunity had been a quickly improvised performance of *Hamlet* (with Olivier) in Elsinore Castle in Denmark in 1937. He had been asked to direct a forgotten classic of Scottish Renaissance theatre, Sir David Lindsay's *Ane Satyre of the Thrie Estaits* for the Edinburgh Festival; but there was no suitable theatre in Edinburgh. At one time, he wanted to find a courtyard for the purpose, but by accident he visited the Assembly Hall of the Free Church of Scotland, built like a debating hall, with a large, low platform in the centre, and rows of seating on three sides. He immediately decided that this was the place for *The Three Estates*; and the success of this production, coupled with the sheer dramatic challenge of filling a bare room with colour, light, spectacle — but without the normal conventions of a proscenium arch and ordinary scenery — fired Guthrie's imagination. Afterwards, that bubbling boiler would not subside to a more normal temperature; and so when, in the early 1950s, he was invited, again by a remote chance, to go to Canada, where a strange enthusiast, Tom Patterson, had decided off his own bat to launch a Shakespeare Festival at Stratford, Ontario, Guthrie accepted the challenge, on condition that he had some say in the Festival theatre's design. The Ontario seasons were to be staged in a large tent, with an uncompromising 'thrust' stage, Guthrie's dream made of boards and canvas.

Many critics dismissed the Ontario stage as a gimmick, but a startling and effective one. Its limitations were obvious. At any one time, a third of the audience could only see the back of the actor who was speaking; and the open stage destroyed an ordinary theatrical illusion. You could see the faces of the audience on the other side of the stage, unless you were lucky enough to be sitting directly in front. Furthermore, as Bernard Miles argued, you had to be able, if you were an actor, to 'control' the audience with your eyes. Shoulders and bottoms were not so expressive. The open stage radically changed theories about acting and stage-pictures, grouping and focal points, and, above all, audience-actor relationships—for the chief (and some would add the *only*) gain of an open stage lay in the intimate contact which developed between the public and the players. With an open stage, it was physically possible to house as many customers as was normal in a proscenium-arch theatre, but to sit them all within a close range of the main acting area. The optimum distance was considered to be within sixty-five feet. This proximity meant that a 'community' spirit could develop within the auditorium. Theatres with open stages were considered to be warm, friendly, intimate places—as opposed to the imposing, hierarchical, remote proscenium-arch theatres, with their circles rising from mere necessity and according to the ticket prices paid, tier by tier, into the dark Gods.

If there was one reason why Guthrie refused the informal offer of the National, it would probably have been that Brian O'Rorke's designs for the National contained two proscenium-arch theatres of different sizes, but not so much as a nod in the direction of the open stage. But there could have been other reasons as well. Guthrie, in some respects, was a bit of an 'old fogey': he knew that he was. He disliked, for example, the new Method school of acting—with its phony proletarianism and its *ersatz* Stanislavsky-derived 'techniques'. Unlike, say, Devine and St Denis, who would suck the yolk of Stanislavsky and throw the eggshell away, Guthrie was lofty and dismissive about what he saw as a new fad. Great plays required supreme technical prowess, voices that could run up and down the scale like yo-yos, exact understanding and precision. He believed that the Method school neglected that kind of training. He was also out of sympathy with that new rebellious school of British playwriting which was just emerging through the Royal Court theatre and whose supreme example was John Osborne's *Look Back In Anger*. If the younger generation thought that there were no causes left to fight for, Guthrie found them lacking in imagination.

The director of the National Theatre—whoever he might be, whenever he might be needed—had to be someone, in Guthrie's opinion, of an almost heroic stature: infinitely patient (to deal with committees), of an unassailable theatrical reputation (to attract the support of the political establishment) but also sufficiently flexible to absorb the ideas and styles of the new generation: a theatrical Hercules, in fact, who could carry like Atlas a world of responsibility, as well as cleaning out the Augean stables of commercialism. Perhaps the first quality demanded of your average hero is the determination to be one; and looking round the British theatrical scene, there were not many names with that talent which immediately sprang to mind.

There was, however, one such man, who was not one of Guthrie's old duffers nor a whizz-kid like Peter Brook: Sir Laurence Olivier. In the mid-1950s, Olivier's career was somewhat in the doldrums. He was much in demand, of course, as a screen actor; but his production company, having lost money during the St James's seasons, was going through a cautious spell. His 1955 performance in the title role of *Titus Andronicus* at Stratford (in Peter Brook's production) had been an outstanding triumph, in Britain and abroad; but his restless energy was looking for new worlds to conquer. Some critics felt that he was still trading on his 1940s reputation, degrading his talents by appearing in such films as *The Sleeping Prince*, opposite Marilyn Monroe; and they urged this prince of the theatre to wake up. The glamour of Notley Abbey was growing tedious and expensive to maintain. There were rumours that his marriage to Vivien Leigh was under stress, merely one more sign that his life was about to undergo another change.

The transformation, when it came, was unexpectedly sudden and complete. In 1956, Olivier had gone to the Royal Court to see *Look Back In Anger*. He hated it; but Devine tempted him back for a second visit, when Olivier recognized, perhaps through an actor's instinct, that Osborne could write vivid dialogue, was touching some social nerves and that the part of Jimmy Porter at any rate called for a star performance. He had a quiet word with Osborne, suggesting that his next script should be sent to him for consideration; and Osborne, who was writing *The Entertainer*, duly dispatched the play. Olivier immediately responded to this study of a seedy comedian in decline, the sad prop of nude revues, which was simultaneously a study of the Britain of the early 1950s, trying to creak into a post-war solvency.

Olivier's Archie Rice was a passionate, funny and supremely moving acting triumph; but it was perhaps of an even greater symbolic importance. Olivier was the first major British actor to join the new wave of

British theatre, reluctantly at first, but then with growing enthusiasm. *The Entertainer* was first staged in 1957, and then went to New York, and was made into a film.

Olivier became fascinated by the *avant-garde* of the late 1950s. He was attracted by the Absurdists, playing Berenger in Ionesco's *Rhinoceros* at the Royal Court in 1960, and Fred Midway, the greasy insurance-agent on the make in David Turner's comedy *Semi-Detached* (1962); while through his production company, he backed new plays, such as Beverley Cross's *One More River* and *Over The Bridge*, a play about union fights and religious intolerance set in Belfast. It was almost as if he were deliberately trying to shed his image as the hero-star of the Old Vic productions and as a commercial actor-manager. *Over The Bridge*, a dismal box-office failure, was the antithesis of a normal West End play.

Olivier was thus fulfilling at least one of Guthrie's criteria for a Director of the National: consciously or unconsciously. He proved that he was not an old duffer, but someone who could bridge the gap between the old and the new. And indeed, with that chameleon-like neatness which in the past had helped to change his habits and appearance according to circumstances, sporting a Colman moustache in Hollywood during the 1930s, becoming clean-shaven and square-jawed for patriotic movies during the 1940s, so now Olivier was starting to adopt the physical mannerisms and appearance of the new wave. He dressed more casually, was jocular with the Royal Court directors and entered the young set with a casual ease which cannot have been entirely instinctive. At the Royal Court, he met Joan Plowright, who was to become his third wife, following his divorce from Vivien Leigh in 1960; and he developed friendships with two young Royal Court directors, William Gaskill and John Dexter. Olivier was proving his capacity to work with the new directors, not standing too much on his dignity as a star. Brook directed him in *Titus Andronicus*, Peter Hall in *Coriolanus* at Stratford in 1959.

The change of life was thus entirely in keeping with Olivier's character: indeed, it can be regarded as a family trait, for had not Gerard Olivier shown an equal resolution to shape his life according to a sense of destiny? And behind Sir Laurence's versatility, there may have lurked an inner resolution—for Oliver Lyttelton had quietly and secretly sounded Olivier out about the possibility of becoming the National's first Director. It was during a weekend party at Notley Abbey, early in 1957, and of course the suggestion was far from official. But Olivier considered it soberly and decided that while he might not be 'the best man for the job, he was probably the only man'. In the following year, he became a trustee for the National Theatre.

His presence on the committee added muscle and resolution at a time when both were needed; for the ways of God and the government were wondrously hard to fathom. The time-scale itself seemed beyond normal human dimensions. There was for example the normal party in-fighting, a British tradition whereby parties in opposition take stances different from those adopted in government. When the Labour Party, for example, first went into opposition, its enthusiasm for the National promptly dwindled. Its Arts and Amenities Committee in 1953 (under the chairmanship of Dr Barnett Stross) decided to oppose plans for the National, on the grounds that existing theatres should be preserved instead—an argument which ran directly counter to the whole South Bank project as well as to the earlier party line on the National.

That phase died away, but gradually it was revived in a more subtle and pervasive form. By 1956, the opposition to the National was based on the law of priorities. Regional theatres were in a bad way, and they should be rescued first. Sir William Emrys Williams, the Arts Council's secretary general, took a carefully optimistic course somewhere between these points of view. He wanted regional theatres to be saved *and* the National to be built; and castigated the Conservative government for not providing enough money to do either or both. In November 1957 the British Drama League resumed its traditional call for the National (Wolfit: 'The spiritual life of the country is at stake!')—but the conference was really more worried by the closure of regional theatres. Lord Esher explained to anyone who would listen that the National Theatre committee was only waiting for the government to release the promised £1 million, and then everyone would be amazed at the remarkable speed and efficiency with which the National would be built. But since the committee had been waiting for ten years for that red-letter day, his words fell on sceptical ears.

But the Act remained on the Statute Book. Oliver Lyttelton, in the meantime, had left the Colonial Office and the House of Commons, to return to industry and take his seat in the House of Lords as Lord Chandos. He was now able to devote a little more time to the National's cause. He was growing very impatient with the delays. In 1959, weary of direct appeals to the Government, Esher and Chandos tried behind-the-scenes lobbying of M.P.s which resulted in more questions being asked in Parliament. On May 8th, 1959, a deputation from the Arts and Amenities Committees of both the Labour and Conservative

Parties had a private meeting with J. E. Simon, the Financial Secretary
to the Treasury, urging the government to implement the Act. The
theatre profession rallied in support, first through public letters to the
government via the press (signed by Olivier, Peggy Ashcroft, Edith
Evans, Lewis Casson, Sybil Thorndike, John Gielgud, Michael
Redgrave and Ralph Richardson), and then, in January 1960, through
Equity's quarterly report. Hugh Jenkins, then secretary of Equity, was
also a member of the L.C.C. which, in February 1960, sent a joint
delegation of Labour and Conservative councillors to lend their weight
to the growing clamour.

In November 1959, Sir Edward Boyle gave some government
acknowledgment of the pressure by stating in Parliament that the
Chancellor, Selwyn Lloyd, had invited the Arts Council 'to review the
priority to be given to the National Theatre within the limited total
expenditure'. The 'invitation' was one of the first jobs to drop on the
desk of Lord Cottesloe, who was appointed in 1960 to be the chairman
of the Arts Council.

Cottesloe, born in 1900, had trained as a civil engineer and served
in the army. He rowed for Cambridge during his university days in
two winning crews and was a crack shot. After the Second World War
he had become a member of the L.C.C., sitting for Hampstead, and
became involved in the post-war development of London. His particular
concern was with dockland. He was the vice-chairman of the Port of
London Authority for many years. He was also interested in the arts,
and in 1957 he became a governor of the Old Vic and Sadler's Wells
Trust, the bricks and mortar side of the organization. Cottesloe, like
Chandos, had the usefulness of someone who could walk in and out of
the corridors of power as if they belonged to him. He was also independently minded. When Sir William Emrys Williams got into trouble with
some Conservative back-benchers for handing Arts Council money
to the Royal Court and all those angry young men, it was Cottesloe,
also a Conservative, who protected Williams from their wrath.

Cottesloe was basically asked by the Treasury whether Brian
O'Rorke's theatre (or one similar) could be built on the South Bank
for £2·3 million—and whether it should be built. Cottesloe turned to
the joint council, who prepared a report—to which Cottesloe added an
enthusiastic personal recommendation. He believed that the National
should, could and must be built. The joint council report was submitted to the Chancellor in October 1960, and it envisaged the establishment of the National by 1964. The costs of the project had been
revised from the 1949 figures. While the building was estimated to

require £2,300,000 in public subsidy, its running costs were expected to need an annual grant in the region of £500,000. Among the names supporting the report were Prince Littler and Hugh Beaumont (who could be regarded as representatives of commercial theatre interests), Michael Benthall (the former artistic director of the Old Vic), Sir Fordham Flower and Peter Hall (from Stratford, where Hall had just been appointed artistic director), Sir Kenneth Clark and, inevitably, Chandos and Olivier. It represented the considered opinions of a cross-section from those who had, of recent years, doggedly supported the National cause. It filled in details left empty by previous reports, among them the intriguing possibility that the Shakespeare Memorial Theatre at Stratford might formally be linked with the National.

This idea had been floating around for some time. It had originally been suggested by Dame Edith Lyttelton in a committee meeting of the S.M.N.T. just after the war, and howled down then because the Old Vic was in such a pre-eminent position in British theatre. As the Old Vic declined and the Shakespeare Memorial Theatre gained in stature during the 1950s, the scheme had become more attractive to the joint council; and it had been unofficially discussed at Notley Abbey, with Lord Chandos, Lord Esher, Olivier, Sir Fordham Flower and Peter Hall. It was now a particularly tempting idea because the political opposition to the National had focused upon the idea that it would be better to help regional theatres first. Stratford counted as a regional theatre.

The Arts Council sent a separate report to the government, in June 1960, also supporting the National's cause but again pointing out the plight of regional theatres. No announcement, however, came from the government. One was expected on January 26th, 1961, but it never came. It was reported privately that a split had developed between those Ministers who felt that any money for the arts would be better spent in the regions and those who favoured the National. In February, the L.C.C. sent along another delegation; and then yet another party from the Labour and Conservative Arts and Amenities Committees approached the Chancellor. In March, Equity came out with a strong statement to the effect that no National Theatre company should be formed without the definite prospect of a new National Theatre building.

Finally, on Tuesday, March 21st, 1961, the government made the long-awaited announcement. It was to the effect that the money would not be released for the National, but that Arts Council funds would be increased by £450,000 to help regional theatres.

It looked as if the months of hectic lobbying (not to mention the years of desultory pleading, and the century of intermittent campaigning) had reached another dead stop; but, in fact, political matters are rarely so simple. The National Theatre had become so fully aired that it was scarcely conceivable that even the Treasury could lock it back in the cupboard. There was just too much ammunition lying around for supporters of the National to pick up and fire at their opponents. The front benches of both political parties had supported the cause from time to time; and the current refusal merely sharpened the determination of those who wanted to ensure that any politician seen eating his words would choke on them.

There was, however, one indirect change in plans, caused by the government's refusal. It stemmed, at several removes, from Guthrie's involvement with the theatre at Stratford, Ontario. A television programme about Tom Patterson's dream which became reality had been screened by the B.B.C. in Britain; and an energetic member of an amateur dramatic society in the small town of Chichester, in Sussex, Leslie Evershed-Martin, had been inspired to tackle something similar. It was a mad idea, almost as crazy as the Canadian venture; but with extraordinary persistence and a lot of luck, Evershed-Martin succeeded. He raised the money with very little help from the state, and none of the fuss which that might have entailed. The Chichester Festival Theatre was, like the Ontario model, an open-stage theatre. It was not quite the first in Britain, for discounting Poel's efforts in the 1900s and the Assembly Hall in Edinburgh, Stephen Joseph had experimented with smaller 'open-stage' theatres, before finally deciding that he preferred arena stages, with the audience sitting on four sides, instead of three.

The Chichester Festival Theatre was, however, the first large-scale, modern 'open-stage' theatre; and it opened in 1962. In the mid-1950s, anyone who suggested that the National should have an open-stage theatre instead of two proscenium-arch ones would have been dismissed as a crank—or rather as an enthusiast likely to cause unwelcome complications. But with the delays to the National, doubts were creeping in as to the wisdom, aptness and modernity of Brian O'Rorke's designs.

For a future Director of the National, the Chichester Festival Theatre offered two invaluable opportunities—first, the chance to work within an auditorium of unfamiliar shape, which might yet offer theatrical opportunities which no designer of a National ought to ignore and, second, the chance to have, as it were, a dummy run at establishing a regional company with a National repertoire. It was a place where experiments in forming a new major company could be undertaken. It was also, of course, in the 'regions', which might offset the charge that the new Director of the National Theatre simply represented metropolitan tastes and opinions.

A week before the official announcement came from the government that no money was available for the National, the Chichester Festival Theatre held its first press conference. It announced that the building was due to open in the following summer and that the first director of productions would be Sir Laurence Olivier. Olivier—who was still nothing more than a good tip for the post of the National's first Director, if and when the government decided that there should be a National—was tackling another phase in his apprenticeship for the British theatre's top job.

9

The First 'First Night'

SELWYN LLOYD, the Chancellor of the Exchequer, had made it clear in his statement to the House on March 21st, 1961, that there would be no money released for the National. Instead, more money would be given to regional theatres, to the Old Vic and to the Royal Shakespeare Theatre, Stratford-upon-Avon, which had, the day before, received its Royal Charter. It was no longer just to be known as the Shakespeare Memorial Theatre: its status had been raised by royal decree, and it could now start to regard itself as a *de facto* National Theatre, although not yet *de jure*. It was a triumph for Sir Fordham Flower, the chairman of the Stratford board, and for Peter Hall, the new artistic director. They had planned for it. In 1958, on a visit to Leningrad with the Stratford company, Flower had asked Hall whether he would consider taking over Stratford and Hall accepted, on the understanding that they should both try to transform the Shakespeare Memorial Theatre into one of the world's major permanent companies, on a size and a scale previously not seen in Britain.

'The plan', wrote Peter Brook in 1968,

> was radical and creative ... before the structure was ready [Hall] opened his grand project: suddenly, the vast company, the immense repertoire, the constant output, the excitement, the disasters, the strain all came into existence ... He was trying to create a living organism, where flexible imaginative conditions were related to flexible imaginative individuals in key positions [*Peter Hall*, by Peter Brook, R.S.C. Annual Report, 1968].

Hall intended to form an established team which would overcome the difficulties of most permanent companies by offering actors and directors flexible contracts, so that they could take on work elsewhere without losing their positions as members of the company. For those actors who feared that Stratford was a backwoods theatre, too far away from agents and television, Hall offered the tempting prospect of a London theatre (the Aldwych was eventually chosen) which would work in tandem with Stratford. The Aldwych was the Stratford company's metropolitan showcase; but it served another function. The Stratford theatre was confined, by tradition and choice, to a repertoire of Shakespeare, Elizabethan and Jacobean plays; and while such a programme was rich and exciting, it nevertheless lacked the dimension of recent and contemporary plays. This was also the time when Shakespeare was being rediscovered as 'our contemporary'; and Hall did not want his Stratford company to sink into a doublet-and-hose Bardolatry. By staging contemporary works at the Aldwych, and perhaps running experimental 'new plays' seasons at the Arts Theatre Club (his old stamping ground), Hall hoped to maintain a lively, outward-looking approach within his company, which might feed back new insights into Shakespeare's plays. Among Hall's many aims, indeed, was to bring a new brand of reasoning to Shakespeare's plays, based on detailed academic research, Cambridge-orientated, and a new, non-rhetorical verse-speaking. He chose directors who were capable of this fresh approach: John Barton, Peter Brook and that elderly, experienced innovator, Michel St Denis. The R.S.C. during the early 1960s was, as many company actors pointed out, like an extension of university life on the banks of the Avon, but without the tedious undergrad. frivolity.

This grand plan sounded — and, for a time, was — like a model for a National Theatre; but naturally it cost a lot of money. To find this money, Flower and Hall undertook their boldest gamble. They reasoned, as Shaw had done before, that once the new R.S.C. was established, governments would be forced to keep it going: they would put the R.S.C. in the way of a government's natural philistinism, so that politically it would be inconvenient to ignore the company or to be seen not to support it properly. Stratford was a comparatively wealthy company. It had more than £100,000 in the bank, the produce from foreign tours; and this money was to be used to open the Aldwych as Stratford's second theatre. Hall reasoned that while Stratford had money in the bank, no government would give it subsidies. If this money could be spent on doing something really spectacular, which no government could avoid noticing, then there was a chance of large annual grants in the future.

And so they gambled. The Aldwych under the Shakespeare Memorial Company's management opened its doors on December 15th, 1960, with *The Duchess of Malfi*, followed by *Twelfth Night* (a transfer from

Stratford) and, among other plays in an exciting first season, John Whiting's *The Devils*. Before the season was over, the risks had proved triumphantly justified. The Shakespeare Memorial Theatre had received its Royal Charter and its first government grants.

The government, therefore, as Selwyn Lloyd and Sir Edward Boyle were at pains to point out, were not just being mean and evasive when they refused funds for the National. They were proposing to spend the same amount of money, between £300,000 and £400,000, to support theatres around the regions and particularly Stratford. It was a perfectly sensible decision, and it lasted for about four months. As soon as it had been taken, there was a minor uproar. Lord Chandos immediately protested that it was an insult to the Queen Mother, who had taken all the trouble to lay the foundation stone; and Isaac Hayward (now a knight) pointed out that 'the Government is responsible to see that the site on the South Bank which the LCC has reserved for nearly 10 years is not sterilized indefinitely and lost to other cultural purposes'. Lord Cottesloe complained in the House of Lords that, without the National, the plans for the South Bank would be 'unbalanced', a typically reticent word.

Other pressures were brought to bear on the government. The joint council published the memorandum submitted to the government in October 1960. This envisaged an even grander scheme than that proposed by Hall for the Royal Shakespeare Company: a company of some 150 actors, divided into teams of which one would provide a six-month season at Stratford, a second would tour, while a third would be centred in London, playing repertory in the new National Theatre. The resources of the Old Vic and Stratford would be pooled; and the total subsidies required annually would be in the region of £230,000.

It should have been clear now, even to outside observers, that there was some division of purpose between Stratford and the joint council. The Hall–Flower scheme for Stratford had effectively forestalled the plans for the National—if the government's announcement were to be taken seriously. The government could scarcely be expected to finance the National and the R.S.C. at an unprecedentedly high level (for subsidies in Britain at that time) in the same year. Furthermore, the Stratford scheme and the joint council's memorandum were not entirely compatible. There was the knotty problem of who would control an amalgamation, should it take place.

The joint council's memorandum had partly been based upon the informal talks held at Notley Abbey on April 10th, 1959. Esher, Chandos, Fordham Flower and Hall were present, but memories of this meeting differ. Chandos was left with the firm impression that Stratford would unite with the Old Vic to become a single National company. Hall's recollections of the meeting differed from Chandos's and Olivier's: there had been no firm agreement, only speculations which committed nobody. Behind these speculations, there was a certain jockeying for position. Hall had written to Olivier, asking him to join his Stratford company, which would then become the basis for a National under Hall's directorship. Olivier and the joint council, however, had other ideas. They envisaged that the Old Vic and Stratford would be run in tandem, with Olivier probably being the man in charge and Hall and possibly George Devine as associate directors. When Olivier was at Stratford, playing Coriolanus in a Hall production in 1959, he asked Hall over lunch one day, 'I'm going to have a go at making the National ... Will you join me as Number Two?' Hall replied, 'I'm very flattered, Larry, I'd love to ... but I'm going to make my own as Number One.' It was not just a question of personal rivalry, although that was important: it was also a matter of the kind of organization which the National might become. Under Olivier, the National would have become an actors' theatre, under an actor-manager: under Hall, it could have become a director's theatre, or a scholar's, or a Cambridge impresario's. And so, when the joint council submitted its memorandum, it was, according to Hall, promising that which it could not provide—the support of Stratford; and nobody from Stratford apparently bothered to tell the government that this was a joint council error.

When the memorandum was published, it received useful support. One reason why the government refused the National may have been because London was facing local elections. If the Conservatives had come to power in the L.C.C., they might not have wished their hands to be tied by a government commitment to the immediate establishment of the National. But the Labour Party retained control of the L.C.C., and Sir Isaac Hayward went back to the task of rallying support for the South Bank scheme. Equity supported Hayward and the joint council's memorandum, so did the T.U.C., and so did the leader of the Conservative opposition on the L.C.C., Sir Percy Rugg. On June 4th, 1961, Hayward led an all-party delegation to the Commons, which added another request to the joint council's memorandum—that Sadler's Wells should be included in the overall scheme, and offered a home on the South Bank, in one of the new National's two auditoria or occupying a new custom-built opera house. A new opera house would complete the arts complex on the South Bank; and to back its demands, the L.C.C. was prepared to enter into a formal commitment that, if the £1 million were released by the Treasury, the L.C.C. would provide out of the product of a 1d. rate (spread over three or four years) the sum of £1,300,000 towards the building of the National. Some Labour supporters did not think that this commitment was sufficiently strong. Hugh Jenkins urged the L.C.C. to go ahead with the scheme without government support if necessary.

This package was tempting and politically dangerous to ignore. It seemed to streamline arts subsidies to three major existing companies, the Old Vic, Stratford and Sadler's Wells, providing them all with permanent headquarters; and would finish off the South Bank into the bargain. Faced by this determination, the government reviewed its options. On July 5th, Selwyn Lloyd indicated that he was prepared to reconsider his decisions of March 21st, and in the following week, on July 12th, 1961, he announced the government's support for the proposals submitted by the L.C.C. — with one stern proviso. The money given by the government should not exceed the original £1 million.

With Selwyn Lloyd's change of heart, there at last seemed to be political agreement all round. Ten days after the government announcement, on Friday, July 22nd, the joint council held preliminary discussions at the Grosvenor Place offices of Lord Chandos. Sir Kenneth Clark, the chairman of the joint council's executive committee, presided; and among the matters discussed was the constitution of the proposed National Theatre. The advice was sought from Arnold Goodman, later Lord Goodman, whose firm of solicitors, Goodman, Derrick & Co., was the legal firm employed by the Old Vic. Lord Chandos thought that the proposed National Theatre should be an ordinary company, limited by guarantee and (of course) non-profit-distributing. Goodman thought otherwise. He wanted the National to seek, as the Shakespeare Memorial Theatre had done, a Royal Charter; but Chandos felt that such a system might prove inflexible. Other members of the joint council supported Chandos, partly on the grounds that a Royal Charter was against the traditionally anti-monarchical line of the National Theatre movement. And so Goodman drafted a proposed constitution without such royal permission required, and sent a draft up to Stratford, where it could be discussed by Sir Fordham Flower, Peter Hall and other members of the R.S.C.'s board. In due course, Goodman followed his proposed constitution in person to Stratford, hoping to discuss the various clauses over a quiet lunch.

It was not very quiet. The Stratford board wanted to know 'rather bluntly' who was to be in charge, and would not talk about anything else. Goodman ventured the opinion that Olivier would be the National's

Director: at which point, according to Goodman, there 'seemed to be an immediate diminution of interest'. 'The atmosphere of hero-worship' at Stratford would not contemplate Peter Hall being anyone's deputy.

And so, Goodman had to turn the nose of his car back in the direction of London, bearing the sad news to the joint council that his proposed constitution would not work, had not even been discussed and that the whole package was breaking apart at the seams. Some longer-term consequences derived from this conflict. Hall, for example, became convinced that when Goodman was chairman of the Arts Council an unfairly mean attitude towards Stratford was taken, as if Goodman were determined to preserve the supremacy of the National at all costs. While welcoming the National when it was first established, Hall realized that potentially it could be a threat to other theatres, including his own. 'My biggest worry', he said, 'is that if they [i.e. the National Theatre] can afford to pay their stars £150 a week, then we may well go under. I can only manage £60 a week (for a star actor) and already the Old Vic pays £75.' Goodman did not believe that the R.S.C. was being unfairly treated; but, by the late 1960s, the disagreements between them had been resolved.

The split between Stratford and the joint council meant that the joint grant had to be divided, leaving them both underfinanced. But the immediate consequences were less serious than they might have been. Chandos was convinced that the money would not be released by the government, despite its promises, if the proposed union between the Old Vic and the R.S.C. did not take place. During the next few months rumours of disagreement spread. Equity, which had supported Sir Isaac Hayward's proposals in April, changed its mind in August, attacking the National Theatre scheme for attempting to unite the two companies. By November, the news that the R.S.C. was withdrawing from the merger had reached the press. Hayward was forced to admit that there would be further delays in building the National. By March 1962, the withdrawal of the R.S.C. had been officially confirmed. The joint council had been forced to draw up new proposals without Stratford. They had originally asked for £230,000 in grants to set up and run the joint company. Now they requested £130,000 for the National and £100,000 for the R.S.C., separate grants for separate companies, each planned to be slightly more than half the size of the joint company.

It was a compromise, and Chandos hoped that the government would accept it. The R.S.C. protested that its grant was smaller than that of the National; but Chandos pointed out that the additional

£30,000 was to set up a company, whereas the R.S.C. already had one. In fact, the National's initial subsidy was far too small.

The support for Hall at Stratford may have been one reason why the joint council's proposals for a merger had to be abandoned; but there would have been other difficulties in the way. The R.S.C.'s plans were in some respects much further advanced than those of the National. The R.S.C. had taken leases on two London theatres, the Aldwych and the Arts Theatre Club, which could not be easily broken; and its Royal Charter was not compatible with the non-royal, businessman's constitution advocated by the joint council.

Chandos need not have worried. The government did not use the R.S.C.'s withdrawal as an excuse to delay the establishment of the National. Proposals which were almost satisfactory were thrashed out between the L.C.C., the government and the joint council, and Selwyn Lloyd gave a formal 'green light' to them in July 1962. The new proposals envisaged the setting up of two Boards: the National Theatre Board (under the chairmanship of Chandos) which would supervise the National Theatre company, and the South Bank Theatre and Opera House Board, which would control the building. The idea that the National and Sadler's Wells should occupy the same building had tactfully been dropped. The plans were now that the National Theatre would occupy a 1·2 acre site by County Hall and that the Opera House would be built by Hungerford Bridge.

And so the crisis over Stratford's departure was overcome, but not without regrets. Perhaps the ideal basis for the National would have been for Olivier, Hall and Devine to work together. It was scarcely more than a dream, for Devine, like Hall, had been asked to join the National as an associate director and had refused. The very stature of Olivier, his name and reputation, provided a barrier to easy partnership. Devine and Hall may have been concerned lest their reputations should dwindle away under Olivier's shadow. But, in an ideal world, the different qualities of these three men would have provided a formidable trio. Olivier's flair would have been balanced by Hall's coolness and detachment, and both would have benefited from Devine's workmanlike approach, his lack of fuss and pomposity. Devine would have nailed their shoes to the floor, if Hall or Olivier had tried to leap over the moon.

The composition of the two boards was known by mid-July. J. B. Priestley attacked them for not containing a dramatist; but, in retrospect, and certainly in comparison with later boards, they were liberally sprinkled with people who had practical experience in the theatre and the arts. On the South Bank Theatre and Opera House Board, supposedly concerned just with bricks and mortar, sat the impresario Prince Littler, the director Norman Marshall, David McKenna and Norman Tucker (both from Sadler's Wells), while Chandos, and later Olivier, represented the National Theatre. Hayward and Rugg represented the two parties in the L.C.C. The National Theatre board contained Hugh Beaumont, Sir Kenneth Clark, Henry Moore and Derek Salberg, from the well-known Salberg family of Midland impresarios. Sir Laurence Olivier joined the boards when his appointment as the National Theatre's first Director was officially announced on August 9th, 1962 — after months of speculation in the press.

Olivier in the meantime had stayed in the background, not involving himself except when absolutely necessary with the Stratford quarrel. He was too much involved with his dummy-run at establishing the National down at Chichester. He was going through the turmoil of committees and fund-raising events, topping out ceremonies perched high on a ladder, the palaver with the press, the visits from members of the royal family interrupting rehearsals, the last-minute desperate diplomacy with the fire authorities, the luring of actors to a company which could only pay them a fraction of their commercial rates, the discipline of choking back anger when tired and nervous, the assumption of smooth diplomacy on cue when needed — and, of course, tackling his primary job, launching the first Chichester season in 1962.

He had assembled a comparatively large company of forty. He was later to be criticized at the National for not bringing more 'stars' into his team and for not holding on to the ones which he had got; but his Chichester company perhaps erred on the opposite side. It was packed with familiar names: the Cassons, Fay Compton, Michael Redgrave, Joan Greenwood, Joan Plowright, Keith Michell, John Neville, Athene Seyler, André Morell and Peter Woodthorpe. It was a tribute to Olivier's prestige and persuasiveness that they had all agreed to spend their summer at Chichester; but some critics wondered aloud during the course of the season whether some of the names were not a bit too familiar. Weren't some a bit old?

Olivier was still on trial for the National during this season. A disaster, particularly in comparison with Hall's successes at Stratford, might not have ruled him out of the running; but it would certainly have made his eventual selection more difficult. On March 12th, for example, Harold Hobson writing in the *Sunday Times* suggested seven names for the National's first Director, which included Guthrie, Hall, Brook and Gielgud, but did not mention Olivier. Olivier needed to succeed at

Chichester, and not just as an actor-director, but as a kind of leader. He was drawn a little reluctantly into making leader-like statements:

> I am not one for making pronouncements or expounding theories. I do not like talking about what I am trying to do ...

But he broke this rule to 'appraise the importance of the actor as a member of human society':

> His office — or his art — lends him as occasion provides, the importance of the philosopher, the psychiatrist or even the preacher. More simply, he must be a great understander. He must, in fact, love the person he is portraying, no matter how unsympathetic; nothing must stall or dismay his clinical appreciation of the character, no matter how antipathetic or revolting; he must make the subject real and understandable to his audience, not by any means playing *for* sympathy, but *with* sympathy, or at least, with empathy [*Sunday Times*, February 25th, 1962].

Characteristically, Olivier moved away immediately in this article from the generalized statement to his particular, technical problem — the open stage at Chichester. He was never happy with his slightly self-conscious profundities. At a visit to the Berliner Ensemble's theatre in East Berlin, he was asked to say a few words. Anyone else would have leant back on diplomatic niceties and a few jokes. Olivier started out like that, but switched to asking about their revolving stage. Why did it make so little noise? Revolves in Britain always seemed to rattle and shake. And what spirit gum did they use for beards? These workmanlike questions endeared him to the company's hearts.

And so, on this occasion, Olivier switched to the stage — 'My plan is to demonstrate the versatility of the stage through a range of styles, conventions and periods.' It was assumed that a hexagonal-shaped stage, with the audience on three sides, would be particularly suitable for Elizabethan and Jacobean drama, or indeed for all plays written before the introduction of the proscenium arch towards the end of the eighteenth century. The problems were likely to come with nineteenth-century drama, particularly naturalistic plays. Olivier's programme at Chichester included one such 'difficult' play, Chekhov's *Uncle Vanya*; but for the first two productions, he went back to the Jacobeans.

If the open stage was his main technical problem, the choice of plays was Olivier's Achilles' heel, which he was anxious to hide. Olivier was very conscious of the fact that he had not had a university education. He was worried that he might be let down by his unsystematic knowledge of literature. He therefore did some homework. He wanted to find some obscure, but stageable, Jacobean plays; and dug around the British Museum to look for them. He unearthed a (fairly) bawdy comedy by John Fletcher, *The Chances*, once enjoyed by Pepys, which had not been seen in Britain since a Drury Lane revival in 1808 and, for the second play, he chose John Ford's *The Broken Heart*, whose last British production was in 1904.

Rehearsals began in April for the July opening. Because the theatre was not yet finished, preliminary work was tackled at a church hall in Chelsea: the read-throughs, the blockings, the early book-bound rehearsals. At weekends, Olivier took the company to Chichester to work on the open stage, sorting out the practical difficulties one by one. In *Uncle Vanya*, for example, Olivier found that the open stage required about '20 per cent more movement' than a proscenium production would have done. Six weeks before the opening, the company moved down to Chichester, where they worked in the inevitable last-minute noises of banging, clattering and sawing. Everyone, it seemed, wanted Chichester to succeed—even the press. The press had been invited down to the still unfinished theatre in the last week of April; and had written enthusiastically about the beautiful parkland setting, the cobweb dome of the interior, the carefully calculated balance between space and intimacy, and the enthusiastic dedication of the Chichester supporters, who, with no state aid, had raked together the mere £170,000 to build the theatre—little more than the 1903 Barker estimates for a National.

The test of all this hopefulness, however, would come with the productions—on whether the audiences would leave the theatre as cheerfully as they had entered it. *The Chances* opened on July 3rd—and the press notices had that tone of cautious moderation which usually indicates a minor disaster. The play was considered slight, flippant, dull: but the production was carefully welcomed. The real enthusiasm was reserved for the theatre itself. For *The Broken Heart*, however, there were no punches pulled. The play was damned, and so was the production, even Olivier's performance as Bassanes. The only play left to redeem the season was the one which was supposed not to work in the theatre, *Uncle Vanya*.

It was a gloomy weekend at Chichester, after the opening of *The Broken Heart*. Joan Plowright glanced at the reviews, noticed the tone of them and did not want to read them carefully: nor did Olivier. They knew that the production had been a failure, and that concentration and determination had to be preserved for *Uncle Vanya*. Kenneth Tynan's review in the *Observer* remained virtually unread; until a

couple of days later, when Olivier received a letter from Tynan, whom
he had met on several occasions. Tynan was inquiring whether Olivier
might need a literary manager at the National, and whether he could
be considered for the post; and he mentioned his review of *The Broken
Heart*, not apologetically, but fully aware that the piece could have
seemed unfriendly. Olivier took a look at his comments.

Tynan argued that Olivier had mishandled and misunderstood the
play. Ford had composed 'a series of agonized tableaux', rather than
'a continuously developing action'; and Olivier had also failed to
appreciate 'the essential comedy' which gave tone and texture to the
tragedy. For Olivier, who had so often been accused of making tragic
characters too comic, this must have seemed a particularly unkind cut.
But the brunt of Tynan's remarks was directed against the Chichester
stage, theatre and Sir Laurence's management of it:

> Chichester is a product of our gullibility: instead of letting the whole
> audience see the actors' faces (however distantly), we now prefer to
> bring them closer to the actors' backs. The Chichester stage is so
> vast that even the proximity argument falls down: an actor on the
> opposite side of the apron is farther from one's front row seat than
> he would be from the twelfth row of a proscenium arch theatre—
> where in any case he would not deliver a crucial speech with his rear
> turned towards one's face. The more-or-less straight-edged stage ...
> remains the most cunning and intimate method yet devised for
> transmitting plays to playgoers; and it was on stages like this that
> you spent a quarter of a century polishing your technique. Alas, at
> Chichester, your silky throwaway lines ... are literally thrown away:
> they go for nothing and they die unheard. Tomorrow *Uncle Vanya*
> opens. Within a fortnight, you will have directed three plays and
> appeared in two leading parts. It is too much. Do you recall the
> triumvirate, made up of John Burrell, Ralph Richardson and your-
> self, that ruled the Old Vic in those miraculous seasons between 1944
> and 1946? Why not recruit a similar team to run the National
> Theatre—a joint directorship consisting of yourself, Peter Brook and
> Anthony Quayle? I don't wish to be dogmatic; I am merely drop-
> ping names, and hints [*Observer*, July 15th, 1962].

Olivier was not, of course, pleased with this review; but he was prepared to recognize the scholarship and intelligence of the man who had
written it. The episode illustrates two facets of their characters—that
Tynan, wanting a job at the National, was nevertheless prepared to
write a wounding review of the man who might be employing him;

and that Olivier, at a low period in his professional life, could receive such an attack and nevertheless act generously. Tynan eventually joined the National as literary manager, and he was in the habit of commenting flippantly on his selection: 'They would probably rather have me on the inside pissing out, than on the outside pissing in.' The relationship between them, as they worked together at the National, was to be close—but never sycophantic or flattering. Tynan might 'woo' Olivier to play a particular part (such as Othello), but he was also prepared sometimes to row with him.

Olivier's production of *Uncle Vanya* surprised everybody. It was the play which Olivier knew best, and, despite the nature of the stage, his understanding of it permeated the production. It was therefore the undeniable success which Chichester (and Olivier) needed. The reviews the following morning were, almost without exception, ecstatic, praising the balance between Olivier and Redgrave (Astrov and Vanya) in the main parts, the lyricism and teamwork of the company, the richness of the individual performance, the delicacy and timing of the interplay. It was also the kind of settled, established, solid-looking production which could be brought back—both into Chichester's second season and as part of the National's first repertory. Audiences would come, critics would rave and the National would have at least one feather in its cap, around which to arrange the rest of the head-dress. A good play on any type of stage is more likely to succeed than a second-rate one on an appropriate stage.

Enthusiasm was now essential. With the first Chichester season over and Olivier's appointment confirmed at the beginning of August, all efforts had to be directed towards the establishment of the National Theatre company. The opening productions at the Old Vic were now a matter of months away, and Olivier was determined that there should be no further delays.

Following Selwyn Lloyd's statement in July that money would be released for the National, the National Theatre board had reached an agreement with the governors of the Old Vic whereby the National Theatre would occupy the Old Vic theatre until its own building was ready. The initial lease was for five years, which could be renewed or ended as necessary. The existing Old Vic company would be wound up; and the last Old Vic season, the forty-ninth since Lilian Baylis had taken charge, was scheduled to end with a Jubilee production in June 1963. The National would take over from August 5th, 1963. Devine begged Olivier to consider a postponement: after 115 years, it seemed absurd to risk a false start by rushing. But Olivier wanted to snatch the tide.

But there was still so much to be done. The National Theatre had not even yet been registered as a company. It was formally incorporated under the Companies Act on February 8th, 1963. The company had no offices. It had to take up temporary offices in some huts provided at 22 Duchy Street, S.E.1, by a firm of building contractors, Sir Robert McAlpine & Sons Ltd, who were eventually chosen to build the National. There was no formal administration. In December 1962 Stephen Arlen, the Sadler's Wells administrator, was borrowed from that company to become the administrative director for the National.

The Old Vic itself had to be altered and decorated. The ten-year-old renovations were not considered sufficiently splendid for the new demands of the National; and the stage had to be altered. There were only ten weeks between the last Old Vic performance and the first of the new National. A new, large revolving stage had to be installed, designed by Sean Kenny (who had provided the Chichester set for *Uncle Vanya*); and a new forestage was built to jut out in front of the proscenium arch, replacing the front two rows of the stalls. A new sound system was provided; and the whole building had to be repainted, re-upholstered and generally turned into a fit home for the National.

It was all a frantic rush and a mess. Max Adrian, who joined the Chichester company for its second season and afterwards went to the National, called it 'sheer hell':

> I remember when we got on to the stage at the Old Vic to rehearse the *Hamlet*, the whole place was still littered with rubble and mortar, and there was a bloody enormous hole in one wall which allowed the wind to blow straight in from Waterloo Road. It was frightfully uncomfortable and chaotic. Then to add to the problems we had a very complicated, overpowering set by Sean Kenny ... a delightful and talented Irishman, but I think he went too far on that occasion. I said to him after falling over bits of the set for the hundredth time: 'I suppose this is your revenge on the English.' There were moments during rehearsals for that very first National production when I thought we'd never open [Logan Gourlay (ed.), *Olivier*, p. 37].

Sean Kenny's revolving stage, in fact, worked so arbitrarily that it was nicknamed the Revolt.

There was also the major task of building up the management team, the acting company and ensuring that there was a bank of acceptable productions upon which the National could draw to prevent a disaster in its first season. The second season at Chichester was more evenly successful than the first, with Joan Plowright playing Joan in Shaw's

St Joan (Max Adrian was the Inquisitor) and the première of a new British play, John Arden's *The Workhouse Donkey*.

Individual productions, however, were less important than the formation of the company. In Chichester's first season, Olivier had relied upon 'stars', his personal friends and largely representative of the theatre's old guard. This policy had been criticized, and in any case, Olivier now wanted to build up a permanent team—which 'stars' might be unwilling to join. He also needed others who could share his burden of running the company. On February 14th, 1963, Tynan's appointment as literary manager was discussed at the National Theatre board's meeting, and he was offered a formal contract the following week—for one year, at £46 a week, plus expenses.

Heading the management with Olivier and Tynan were two young directors from the Royal Court, John Dexter and William Gaskill, trained substitutes for the man whom Olivier really wanted, George Devine. Olivier was, in fact, seeking the support of the one company around (apart from the Royal Shakespeare Company) which represented new growth in British theatre—the English Stage Company at the Royal Court. In March 1963, a more formal liaison between the two companies had been outlined—although it never took place. The nature of this abortive 'special relationship' was described in a press statement on August 6th:

> Lord Chandos, Chairman of the National Theatre Board, and Mr. Neville Blond, Chairman of the English Stage Company at the Royal Court Theatre, announce that these two bodies have decided to co-operate in certain activities. These would include the use of a studio for the training of young actors, directors and designers, and the commissioning of new plays.

In fact, the relationship was mainly one-way, in the National's direction. Apart from borrowing Dexter and Gaskill from the Royal Court, Olivier also snaffled away some actors, Robert Stephens, Frank Finlay and Robert Lang among them. The usefulness of the Royal Court was not, however, just to be measured in terms of personalities. The actors and directors who knew each other well provided the nucleus of a settled team. The influence of Devine's new plays policy, reflected in this team, acted like spurs and reins upon Olivier. It encouraged him to take a positive approach towards new drama and, for example, Brechtian approaches to the problems of production: Olivier was not an admirer of Brecht. And it also deterred him from taking wild gambles in order to seem experimental.

'We aim', stated Olivier at his first major National Theatre press conference on August 6th, 1963, 'to give a spectrum of world drama and to develop in time a company which will be the finest in the world.' This 'spectrum' was reflected in the plays chosen for the first season, also announced on August 6th. Two productions from Chichester, *Uncle Vanya* and *St Joan*, provided the ballast of established successes. In addition, there were to be two staple classics, *The Master Builder* and *Othello*, with Redgrave as Solness and Olivier as Othello. Gaskill would direct Farquhar's *The Recruiting Officer*, and Dexter *Hobson's Choice*, a forgotten classic of its kind, whose selection indicated a refusal to be solemn and over-intellectual. Max Frisch's *Andorra* represented modern European allegorical drama, Beckett's *Play*, the absurdist *avant-garde*, and Sophocles' *Philoctetes*, Greek drama. Ancient and modern plays, British and European, adventurous and conservative, each 'good of its kind'—a spectrum of world drama indeed.

For the opening production, there seemed to be only one obvious choice—*Hamlet* with a star. Peter O'Toole was chosen, on release from heavy film commitments: the right age, the right appearance, the right fame—and perhaps a little too obvious. Olivier directed, his own commitments now limited to acting in *Uncle Vanya*, but with the cloud of *Othello* looming on the horizon, and the burden of the organization resting on his shoulders. The months of August, September and October passed in a blur of activity. Mailing lists were sent out to the members of the Vic–Wells Society, some of whom were not too pleased that the Old Vic had been snatched from them.

Bookings for the opening night flowed in. It was not going to be an over-formal event: the Chancellor, Selwyn Lloyd, would be there, but not royalty. There would not be semi-compulsory evening dress: the true festivities would be saved for the new building. But it was still going to be a great evening for British theatre, a milestone, and the seriousness of the occasion was stressed by the fact that this was not going to be a half-starved *Hamlet*, drastically cut to fit the normal limits of theatre-going endurance. It was to last for four and a half hours, beginning at 6.30 and ending at 11.00. It was still daylight as the audience drifted into the foyers and bars, now looking 'staggeringly contemporary' and far too hedonistic for Emma Cons's temperance music-hall. Where the public could not see them, painters were adding the final dabs to the decorations.

During rehearsals, O'Toole had been the only member of the company not weighed down by the general air of feverish responsibility. 'He's high-spirited,' commented Max Adrian, tactfully, what they used to call a hell-raiser. But thank God, there was someone around like him to raise our spirits and break the tensions, even if he indulged in a few schoolboys' practical jokes, like putting ice in the shower in the star dressing room, which Larry lent to him. Peter got it into his head that I couldn't get through a performance without a bottle of what he called 'green whiskey'—Irish whiskey. The truth is I loathe and detest the stuff, but he would try to pour it down my throat. The star dressing room became a sort of oasis of relaxation while he was there ... [Gourlay, *op. cit.*, p. 37].

On opening night, however, O'Toole, his hair dyed an angelic blond, restlessly wandered around in a red dressing-gown before the curtain went up, practising fencing against the shadows, muttering his lines, Sean Kenny's set, a monolithic Elsinore perched on his revolve, loomed on the still dark stage like shadowy cliffs. The cast sat around on it like seagulls. At the last minute, the trap-door grave decided to stick: teams of stage-hands rushed on to free it with oil-cans and brute force.

Olivier, who had been up half the night rehearsing, carefully put on the relaxed air of a successful actor-manager, skilfully portraying a confidence which he did not feel. He dreaded the reviews the following morning. He felt sure that a production conceived in such chaos was bound to be a disaster. In fact, he was pleasantly surprised. The production ran smoothly and even the revolve did not stick. The press were not ecstatic about the production, but they welcomed the arrival of the National Theatre company wholeheartedly. *The Times* review was a little lofty: the production contained 'good things', but 'it bears the stamp of having been put on as a means of exhibiting a number of big names in the most famous and popular work in the classical repertory. And even with the cuts restored, the result is a tired and routine performance'. O'Toole was considered a conventional Hamlet, 'his features twisted ... into an introspective melancholy'. Rosemary Harris's Ophelia was more highly praised, 'a figure of frustrated sweetness [who] ... becomes in madness a creature of sexual vindictiveness', together with Redgrave's Claudius, 'an over-friendly charmer' and Finlay's 'brilliantly inventive' First Grave-digger.

That was one of the less kind reviews. Olivier later confessed himself satisfied that there were not more of them. He thought that the critics, on this occasion, were generous. At any rate, it was a competent production: nothing had gone too badly wrong. At the end of the evening, Olivier heaved an enormous, jaw-breaking yawn of relief. A start had been made. The career of the National had begun.

IO

Interlude

MANY READERS may have suspected by now that the word 'national' in the phrase 'The National Theatre' is little more than jingoism. Its original meaning may have been vague enough, but in the intervening century between the original idea and its first realization in the early 1960s, it had been pressed into service in so many different political and theatrical causes that it had become little more than a trumpet call rallying the weary veterans and the raw recruits.

If we say that English is the 'national' language of the people who live in England, we are using the word in an observably precise sense. It is the common tongue. Can we say, however, that English is the national language of those who were born and bred in Ireland, or Wales, or the United States? Again, it is the common tongue, more freely understood and spoken than Gaelic, or Welsh, or any immigrant language in the United States; but we would only use the phrase 'national language' in this context with strict reservations. English is 'their' language through adoption, convenience, chance or perhaps conquest. It is not theirs, as it were, by 'blood', tradition and heritage.

We have therefore qualified the word 'national'. It no longer just means 'in common use', but indigenous as well, something which grew up with the country. But a national theatre is neither indigenous nor in common use. It is rather (or so the theory might run) something which a government on behalf of the nation supplies for the benefit of the people at large. In this context, we would be tempted to use the word national as we have come to employ it in such phrases as National Insurance or the National Health Service.

Here again, however, doubts and reservations intervene, for while the health service, insurance and education are at any rate intended to be used by most people in the country, the same cannot be said of a national theatre. It is obviously physically impossible. You can talk perhaps of a national theatre system, expressing the pious hope that at some time in the future nobody in Britain will live further than thirty miles from a state-subsidized theatre, whose seat prices will be kept within the means of all. You can even talk about English theatre in general, as opposed to Dutch or French theatre. But the fact cannot be ducked that when Olivier played Othello when the National company took over the Old Vic, only a very small proportion of the national population was able to see him—and that this proportion would not have been significantly greater if the seats had been given away free or if the National had gone on endless tours.

A national theatre, therefore, is not and cannot be a nation-wide institution like a health service. It cannot be freely available to all who need or would like its services. It cannot be 'national' in that sense. The question of 'values' intervenes. Audiences for Olivier's *Othello* were limited by the fact that auditoria for drama purposes cannot be massive stadiums, and because Olivier's stamina was limited, and because it was desirable to present other productions at the National as well. From the beginning, the National Theatre was expected to provide the 'best' in British theatre; and the best, unfortunately, is in short supply. Even though campaigners for the National, from Effingham Wilson onwards, would talk about the 'best' drama being accessible to everybody who wanted to see it, a moment's thought would have convinced them, if they had been willing to be convinced, that this could never be so. Drama is not that kind of mass-produced activity; and certainly not drama of the highest quality.

Should therefore this awkward term, the National Theatre, only be used for genuinely popular theatrical forms, such as the music-halls of the 1900s? Perhaps so—but unfortunately it has never been used in this context. Indeed, the supporters of the National were usually those who were directly opposed to 'popular' theatre. It was precisely because Matthew Arnold thought that popular tastes were not enlightened enough to support the best theatre that he called for a National.

But if 'national' does not mean 'popular' or 'of the people', what does it mean? Can we logically argue that there is a nation (and therefore a National) which exists apart from and superior to those people who constitute the nation? Obviously not—but we maintain this illogical pretence because it is convenient for us to do so. Because we fear that popular tastes are not enlightened enough to provide us with a theatrical institution appropriate to our image as a theatre-loving nation, we are prepared to let governments and other philanthropists do so on our behalf.

From this angle, we could suggest that the 'nationalism' of the

National Theatre consisted simply of the fact that successive generations of Labour, Conservative, Liberal and floating voters had been gradually convinced that an enlightened institution, such as the National was presumed to become, would be a credit to the country. Not to have one would be a source of shame and dishonour, lowering Britain in the eyes of countries which possessed them already. The National Theatre thus could be held to derive its honourable title by public consent, expressed democratically through the ballot box.

This argument too would be rubbish, for no constitutional means exist to test public opinion on such a specific issue. The most that can be said is that the cause was carried politically by default. No body of opinion outside Parliament had risen which could claim to represent public opinion and was powerful enough to sway M.P.s one way or the other for political reasons alone. No M.P. won or lost his seat because of his support for the National. The virtually unanimous support which the National Theatre Act received in both Houses of Parliament may or may not have reflected opinion in the country. There was just no way of knowing; and Shaw may well have been right when he insisted that 'of course' the English people did not want a national theatre, but that they would get used to one in time, and feel proud of it.

The National Theatre is thus an institution established by the few in the name of the many. To justify its title and status, however, certain criteria come into play which do not exist either in commercial theatre or among civic reps. A commercial impresario either puts on plays which he likes in the hope that the public will like them too, or he puts aside his personal preferences, relying on his marketing instincts to tell him which plays will be successful. The manager of a civic rep works to a comparatively limited public, whose tastes he must gauge if he is to be good at his job.

But 'popularity' is not good enough for the Director of a National, who also has to judge the mood of a public far larger and more nebulous than that to be found in a town or city. He has to find an image for his theatre which is socially appropriate to its status as a National. As we have seen, what is considered appropriate fluctuates sharply from time to time. For Effingham Wilson, this problem scarcely existed. His National Theatre would simply have taken over and developed the sort of 'serious' drama previously associated with the patented houses. The word 'national' for him meant the opposite to 'royal' or 'aristocratic': good art made democratic and cheaper. For much of the nineteenth century this basic outlook prevailed. The National Theatre should be established to preserve for the nation a heritage of theatre which might otherwise have been threatened by populism and commercial interests.

By the turn of the century, however, this view was being challenged. A theatre which merely preserved a national heritage would be nothing more than a museum. Barker wanted 'new plays', though not of an *avant-garde* nature, and Shaw thought that nobody would visit a theatre which simply put on old plays. But what sort of new plays? Second-rate ones which complacently assumed that society was all right as it was? Or first-rate ones, which might well upset some dearly held national fancies? Nobody wanted the dramatic equivalent to Masefield's public verse—but was it appropriate that a National Theatre should seem to be attacking the nation, or actually do so? Could liberalism, tolerance and the political sources of finance survive such an onslaught?

Can a National, in short, justify its very tenuous claims to its title when it seems un-British? Can 'appropriateness' extend that far? The content of the plays, however, is only one sort of appropriateness. It could be argued that the National exists simply to bring together the best actors, writers and directors in the country, whatever their opinions might be. The National Theatre would therefore become something like a national football team. It might not always win matches, but it represents the best that the country can do at the time.

This parallel, too, runs into difficulties, partly because in the theatre 'content' and 'skill' are often closely linked—the 'best' director is usually someone who has a clear idea as to what his production should do or say—and partly because it is not possible simplistically to decide which people in the theatre are the 'best'. The problem faced by football managers becomes much more complicated when applied to the theatre—should they have a team of 'stars' or of less individually talented players who might cohere better into a team? The National Theatre, too, had a struggle to decide whether it should have a permanent company or a permanent 'nucleus' with guest stars. Here again the question of appropriateness cut across ordinary dramatic considerations. Some felt that it was more appropriate for the National to act as a shop-window for British talent, and others—that the company itself should be a model of democracy, with full voting rights extended to all permanent company members. How matters were arranged at the National was—or became—as important as what things were being done.

The crucial test of appropriateness, however, consisted in the way the National related to its surrounding society—both to the little world of the theatre system and to the wider world of the country. Long before the National company came into existence, there had been earnest discussions as to whether another London theatre could represent the country as a whole. Early in 1961, as we have seen, the cabinet decided that regional theatres deserved preference over a metropolitan one. On a regional tour, the National company visited Cardiff, and found that their posters had been scrawled over with the telling message, '*Their* National—or ours?'

It was possible to take the sting away from such criticisms—without answering them completely—by various physical means, such as establishing close links with regional theatres and undertaking regional tours; but it was not so easy to avoid another charge, that of social élitism. Critics of the National—from both Left and Right—could fairly argue that, because the National had no basis in a popular will, it was an institution which reflected the standards and opinions of an educated, Southern, metropolitan few who were using public money to impose their views on the rest of society. They might be doing so from the best possible motives, they might not be 'imposing' in an ordinary sense but simply providing a standard against which other views could be judged. They could be as liberal, catholic and tolerant in their tastes as any well-brought-up Englishman is entitled to be; but nevertheless the fact remained—that *their* views were not shared by everyone, or even perhaps by a majority of the population, and they had claimed the right to institutionalize them under the title of a National Theatre.

How supporters of the National Theatre faced the charge of élitism depended much upon their political outlooks. To Lord Chandos, the National would become a bulwark of British society, and he could have argued that by providing a national institution to which all could aspire, the government was offering the country a symbol of its national coherence. If you have a lot of smaller theatres competing with one another, society is likely to disintegrate into mere petulance. Providing this open, competitive theatrical society with a focal point in the National was one way of reminding people that, beneath all their differences, they still belonged to One Nation, Disraeli's famous watchword for the Conservative Party.

Socialists tended to define the role of the National differently. It was there partly to redress the class bias within the existing theatrical system. The West End catered for the wealthy middle classes: it did not want to be bothered with the problems and needs of working-class men and women. To have a theatre which properly represented a cross-section of views within society, it was necessary to free the theatre from its dependence on wealth and the capitalist system. The state had to step in to fulfil this function. If there had to be a class bias within the National—and the left-wing, of course, would have said that such a bias was unavoidable—it should be towards the working-class movement. Some left-wingers might have pointed to the Lilian Baylis tradition at the Old Vic as an example of how the embryonic National catered deliberately for the needs of the poor; but others would have protested that Baylis herself was just a nineteenth-century do-gooder. The National, if it were to fulfil its social function, had to embark upon a more radical course—nothing less than the transformation of British society.

Liberals again would have reasoned differently. The purpose of the National—and indeed of the whole subsidized system—was not to transform society, which would have been a pretentious and potentially totalitarian aim, nor to provide a spurious national identity if none already existed. Its purpose was to provide a calmer area in the turbulent seas of the market economy, a harbour where theatrical artists could examine their crafts, improve them and build something better for the future in an atmosphere free from commercial harassment.

All these three views were reflected from time to time, in different degrees, in the discussion about the role of the National. But it could be argued that there were historical forces at work which were of greater importance than any single political ideology. We could, I suppose, describe these 'forces' in world terms, relating them to Britain's changing status as a commercial, military and colonial power; but if we narrow the perspective a little, and concentrate simply upon the government's control over the country's money, we can see that the ideologies had constantly to be modified according to the prevailing facts.

In the 1900s, for example, the government controlled less than 10 per cent of the national income. This meant that the government's power to influence the financial basis of society was comparatively slight. Any attempts by a government to control more than this share would have met with widespread resistance. Money was generally regarded as the language of transactions. It was the way in which one person swopped the goods and services which he could provide for those offered by someone else. Money provided the very texture of society, the common culture, so that people who did not know each other very well—and therefore could not be assumed to trust each other—nevertheless trusted sterling. They related their jobs together through this commonly accepted symbolic language, money.

To control a larger proportion of the country's money, therefore, would have left a government open to the charge of totalitarianism. It was the dangerous first step, for by trying to control money the government would also be deciding who should do business with whom, how and under what circumstances, and to what ends. You were taking away from the people the right to decide how the produce of their labour should be used; and for that reason, even worthy causes, such as the establishment of labour exchanges or the founding of a National, were opposed on the grounds that they represented a new centralization of power.

This was why the outlook of progressive (but not extreme) politicians before the First World War tended to differ from that of the generations to come. The job of government was not to take over the money economy but, first, to prevent anyone else from doing so and second, to clear up the wastes, inefficiencies and social evils left in the wake of competitive capitalism. Government was a service industry; and the achievements of the Liberal governments before the First World War have to be seen in that light. They wanted to control the power of entrenched interests within British society (such as those represented by the House of Lords) and to moderate blatant social evils by providing useful services, such as labour exchanges.

The establishment of a National Theatre occupied a shadowy area within their political ideology. To force one upon an unwilling public would have been regarded as an abuse of government power; but to respond to public initiatives was quite acceptable, and even desirable. But however the National was established, whoever established it, it would still take its place within a predominantly booming, commercial system. The entire network of small chains of theatres, independent actor-managerial enterprises and family-run music-halls was independent of government involvement; and all that even ardent supporters of the National were requesting was that one small section of this system should be set aside to preserve a national heritage of good drama.

But facts upset the plans. The arrival of the First World War, the losses among families and businesses after it, the slump, the rise of the Labour Party and the trade union movement, the assaults on sterling, and the Second World War, meant that successive British governments felt themselves forced to centralize power in a manner which would have been unthinkable in the 1900s. They were often reluctant to do so. The growth of government power often came as the result of stop-gap measures: nobody in 1916 expected Entertainments Tax to last for over forty years. By the Second World War, the government was controlling over 40 per cent of the national income, a proportion which could have declined when the war effort was over, but in fact increased. Many of the old fears about too much government control had dwindled away, or were thought exaggerated. Now it could be claimed (mainly of course, by the Labour Party) that the government could administer national resources more fairly in the interests of all; and so we find the growth of nationalization, utopianism and such projects as the South Bank.

By the 1970s, the government was effectively controlling between 58 per cent and 60 per cent of the national income; and within this situation, subsidies had ceased to be just a way of protecting a certain section of the theatre from box-office instabilities. They had become, for large sections of the theatre, a condition of survival. There was simply not the money left in private hands to support the theatrical economy in any other way. The West End itself, the last bulwark of commercialism, was largely dependent upon tourists for its survival.

In this new world, the National could not be regarded as a quiet harbour, away from the turmoils of commercialism. On the contrary, it was to be the apex of the state-supported system, the crowning glory, the top of the heap. That was its new function. The patented houses had gained their position of privilege simply by a royal decree banning all other theatres showing straight drama. The National gained its status through a subsidy system whose effects were inevitably (though unintentionally perhaps) hierarchical. Once the building of the new National had begun, once the whole scale of the enterprise had been unfolded before a waiting world, there was very little chance of another theatre rising to challenge its supremacy. The resources of the National were much superior to those allotted elsewhere, in terms of finance, building, company size and, apparently, political support.

Within twenty years, from 1956 to 1976, the commonly expressed attitudes within the theatrical profession to the new National under-went an abrupt change. In 1956, the National was an honourable cause, not lost but infinitely delayed. By 1976, it had become an object of much jealousy, a threat to lesser theatres, a symbol of privilege. Many of the policies which the National was to adopt have to be seen within this context. They were attempts to forestall criticism, to ward off resentment; and underlying all these tactical manoeuvres was the attempt to find an appropriate image for the National.

Unlike the Comédie-Française during the nineteenth century, the new National had no settled repertoire of classical plays on which it could necessarily concentrate. Our culture, as Matthew Arnold indicated, is not homogeneous enough for that. There was thus no point of departure for its work, no settled boundaries within which it could play. This freedom brought advantages and disadvantages. Many theatres, as Michael Kustow, associate director of the National, pointed out to me, 'have been hung on their manifestos'. Olivier was given the opportunity to present 'a spectrum of world drama', inviting guest directors from countries other than Britain to stage works at the Old Vic. Excellence could be pursued, regardless of parochially national considerations.

The loosely defined role of the National, however, also brought many problems, some superficial, others deep-set. There was, to begin with, no settled justification for its existence other than the excellence of its standards. It was not providing a *kind* of theatre, unlike any other to be found in this country. And so when its standards dropped, in its weaker or perhaps just more controversial seasons, the whole institution came under attack. What was it there for, if not to provide the 'best'? Furthermore, the National was always likely to be caught up in problems of national prestige. The pursuit of prestige has sometimes been regarded as the chief folly of post-imperial Britain. Was it really necessary for British theatre to build that enormous block on the South Bank, which costs so much to heat, light and man, year in, year out, expenses which have to be covered before any production can be staged in any one of its theatres? The security guards alone require a subsidy of more than £100,000, which in the early 1970s was equivalent to the entire grants given to some very productive civic reps.

Lastly, there was the awkward fact that the National, because it had no settled role, would snap up talent, initiative and sometimes sheer manpower from lesser theatres. All profitable roads, even from fringe theatres, at times seemed to lead inexorably to that Rome on the South Bank. Peter Hall would sometimes argue that the National was the heart of the theatre system, drawing in talent from the regions and elsewhere, and pumping it out again in a purified form around the circuits. From the point of view, however, of some other theatre managers in a less fortunate situation, the National could seem less like a heart than a leech, drawing off the blood of enterprise which they needed to stay alive.

We are therefore faced by several curious paradoxes. From 1848 to 1961, the period covered by the first half of this book, the National did not exist, but support for the National grew—in fits and starts, but nevertheless gradually increased. From 1961 to 1976, as the National company came into being and started to occupy its building on the South Bank, support for it started to waver, particularly within the theatrical profession, and (where it did not actually decline) became more unreliable. The atmosphere surrounding the National became altogether more cantankerous.

Nor is this phenomenon solely to be confined to the National Theatre, for it could be argued that the pursuit of national prestige ventures took place against a background of growing national uncertainty. This did not derive solely from the slump in Britain's status in the eyes of the world, but from a growing sense of internal doubt. There may also have been a scepticism about nationalism itself. Nationalism was very much a nineteenth-century reaction which had acquired an unsavoury appearance in some twentieth-century eyes.

To illustrate these dubious implications, we can take perhaps a clipping from *The Times*, dated April 23rd, 1922, the anniversary of Shakespeare's birthday. It had been cut out and stored among the S.M.N.T. committee's papers in the British Theatre Centre. It was evidently considered worth quoting in speeches:

GERMAN CLAIM TO SHAKESPEARE
A Lost English Possession
Leipzig Professor's Rhapsody

We have received a copy, in German, of the speech to be delivered today by Professor Max Förster, professor of the English language and literature, at the annual meeting of the German Shakespeare Society at Weimar.

The speaker says that over 500 special works have already been published on the subject of Shakespeare and Germany. The clearest and quickest way, he says, to show how Germany has appropriated Shakespeare's works is to look at the part played by Shakespeare in German theatrical enterprise. In 1870, there was an average of 438 German theatrical Shakespeare performances. The number slowly increased up to the first decade of this century. It then increased by sudden jumps, reaching 1,653 performances in 1906. This meant that about five Shakespeare plays were being performed every evening in Germany. Even during the war Shakespeare was much played, the number of performances in 1916 being 1,179. In the first year of peace, the number again rapidly rose to 1,349, and last year the gigantic number of 1,622 performances was attained. The significance of these figures, says Professor Förster, will only become clear to us if we turn our eyes to England and other countries. In England, where exact statistics of performances are not available, Shakespeare is scarcely played a few hundred times a year. It is still worse in other countries, such as France, Russia, and Italy, where Shakespeare only appears quite occasionally on the stage.

Professor Förster goes on to ask: How is this remarkable fact that Shakespeare is a more living factor of *Kultur* amongst us than in his own fatherland to be explained? His explanation is, first, that Germany with its high level of education, which, moreover, is of a specially literary aesthetic character, affords better soil for all theatrical culture, than a country in which the encouragement of a matter-of-fact business sense is the chief end of all education. For this reason it could only happen in England that the scion of one of the finest aristocratic families, Randolph Churchill, having been called away from a performance of *Hamlet*, should ask the actor, whom he met the following day, how the piece really ended.[*] So little did he know of the most famous piece of the most famous English poet! It was, therefore, bitter earnest mockery on the part of Bernard Shaw when in 1916 he advised his fellow-countrymen preferably to leave the 300th celebration of Shakespeare to Berlin ...

With the external causes are associated also grave inward causes, all of which are to be summed up by saying that Shakespeare in thought and sensibility stands nearer to the present-day German than to his present-day fellow countryman. How is that at all possible? Only through the whole character of the English people having entirely changed since Shakespeare's time. The political, and religious, troubles of the 17th century have changed the Englishman from the cheerful, merry, frankly epicurean man of the Renaissance time to the serious, reserved Puritan of the present, intent on business alone, while we have preserved to ourselves to a greater extent the freshness and accessibility of the Renaissance. This can be supported by many details.

Shakespeare, like the modern German, has a more thoughtful tendency than the modern Englishman with his business mind. We are accustomed to hear difficult trains of thought from the stage, as Shakespeare expects his hearers to do, while the present-day English-man expects only amusement from the theatre. Shakespearian free-dom and independence of thought appeals to us more strongly than to the Englishman, who, moreover, in his own thought moves entirely along the paths of tradition and conventions. We rejoice that

* Yes, well, we all know what an old tease Randolph was!

Shakespeare has an accessible eye for foreign nations, that he has nothing of the stupid presumption so characteristic of the modern Englishman. Shakespeare's patriotism too, glowing as it shows itself on every occasion, has nothing of the aggressive, wounding form of that of the present-day Englishman. It is more a home feeling (*Heimatsgefühl*), just as in the case of the German. There is no trace to be found in Shakespeare of that religious narrowness and hypocrisy which has made religion to the present-day Englishman a social matter and one of external form, but such beautiful toleration that even today one is in doubt as to his belief and rightly attributes to him religious indifferentism.

Shakespeare's politics also sorts better with the modern German than with English political thought. The fact that Shakespeare shows himself in his drama but slightly interested politically, and that he never deduces the developments from political grounds but only from purely human antagonisms, corresponds rather to the German than to the English conception, in which politics occupies the centre of the whole of life. Further, Shakespeare's view of the State makes an entirely strange impression on the present-day Englishman; that constitutional absolutism to which Shakespeare pays homage is farther removed from the modern English parliamentarianism with its mock-monarchy than our German form of government, both our former constitutional monarchy and our present republican pseudo-Parliamentarianism with its despotism of the party functionaries.

Finally, Shakespeare stands nearer to us also in the domain of feeling than to the coldhearted, reserved modern Englishman, whose main task in education is to suppress every exhibition of temperament, even if only in expression. Shakespeare let a man give full course to his feelings and affections. He could still laugh and weep, rejoice noisily, complain passionately, tear his hair and throw himself on the ground from pain. In ethics, again, Shakespeare shows nothing of that inflexible narrow-mindedness which presses like an incubus upon present-day England. Here too, Shakespeare is like the German idealist and individualist. A true Renaissance man, he does not base all morality on an intellectual consideration of the ethical means and ends which plays so great a part in modern English moralists, but on affection and the will springing from it. There is naturally nothing whatever in Shakespeare of the militarism and egoism of the English ethics of today. On all these grounds, Shakespeare has grown so dear to our hearts that the speaker could dare in the midst of the world war to lecture upon Shakespeare to our brave soldiers yonder in the field, in far half-Asiatic Charkoff and Kiev, as well as in the middle of the North Sea on our ironclads and by the Belgian waterside, even under the thunder of English guns. May this capacity for honouring a great man, which the German has so finely proved in the case of Shakespeare, remain to our German people.

It will then be able to attain what it now needs above all else – the closing up of its ranks as one people with a single national will. Only when that is attained will the German Phoenix rise again from the ashes [Copyright *The Times*, London].

Hmm. One begins to understand what Mr Lynch might have meant during the 1913 parliamentary debate when he talked about this 'attempt to Prussianize our literature' – although he probably did not. At all events, Professor Max Förster made it quite clear how even Shakespeare, a foreign author to him, could be twisted to the service of a national unity. And even Peter Hall, though by no means a fascist, was prone to use similar arguments when answering attacks against the National Theatre. 'We need', he wrote in 1974, 'a national reviving symbol', at a time when Britain was 'enduring a national nervous breakdown'. After the Second World War, with Weimar and its consequences in mind, such sentiments were not received with the enthusiasm which might have been expected.

II

The Best of Everything

KENNETH TYNAN, as spokesman, summarized the policy for the National. It was very simple in outline and very difficult to achieve. 'Our aim', he said at the end of the National's first season, ' ... is the best of everything.' Olivier's remarks at the August press conference in 1963 had been similar. The National would provide 'a spectrum of world drama' (a phrase but not an outlook which he had borrowed from Tynan) and build up a company which, it was hoped, would become 'the best in the world'.

These intentions sounded so vague and ambitious that they almost amounted to no policy at all. Indeed, the greatest tribute which can be paid to the first four excellent years of the National's life is that few people felt them to be excessive or ridiculous. The company might not yet be 'the best in the world', but it was on its way to being so. Its repertoire might not yet reflect the intended 'spectrum'—but the basis was there, on which time and the better opportunities of the promised new theatre could build.

The real interest of such statements, however, was that they showed what the National was not going to be. It was not, for example, going to concentrate on 'Shakespeare and National Drama'. That role in British theatre was increasingly being taken by the Royal Shakespeare Company at Stratford and the Aldwych. 1963 was a great year for the R.S.C. It was the season in which Hall staged *The Wars of the Roses* (assisted by John Barton and Frank Evans), a collation of the *Henry VI* plays and *Richard III*, which more perhaps than any other event established the R.S.C. style. Brook's production of *King Lear* was at the Aldwych, with Hall's *A Midsummer-Night's Dream* and Clifford Williams's *The Comedy of Errors*. The National was not going to invade that firmly annexed territory.

Nor was the National to become the art theatre of an intellectual élite—nor the product of one man's inspiration. It was to be large, liberal, outward-looking and catholic in its tastes. Again, Tynan described the options clearly:

> Good repertory theatres fall into two main categories. One is the kind that is founded by a great director or playwright with a novel, and often revolutionary, approach to dramatic art. He creates a style for his own special purpose. Examples of this process would include Stanislavsky's Moscow Art Theatre, Bertolt Brecht's Berliner Ensemble and Joan Littlewood's Theatre Workshop. The other category consists of theatres with a broader, less personal *raison d'être*: whose function — more basic though not more valuable — is simply to present to the public the widest possible selection of good plays from all periods and places. In this group, you can place the Schiller Theatre in West Berlin; the Royal Dramatic Theatre in Stockholm; and the National Theatre in Waterloo Road. Their aim is to present each play in the style appropriate to it ... [speech to Royal Society of Arts, March 18th, 1964].

The policy of the National — leaving aside its aspirations to excellence, which nearly all serious companies share — was thus to resist specialization, in whatever form that concentration might take, political, aesthetic or indeed company structure. No restrictions — just 'the best of everything'.

The company was thus formed to represent different views, in the hope perhaps that these would settle down into a creative harmony not devoid of dissonance or tension. The consensus principle really extended from the National Theatre Board (under its 'buccaneering High Tory' chairman, Lord Chandos) downwards to its acting team; but it was particularly noticeable in that inner core of management represented by Olivier, Tynan, Dexter and Gaskill. Each had sharply defined views, prejudices perhaps, each was capable of defending them vigorously and each had an edge of uncertainty which compelled him to listen to the others and sometimes to over-react sharply. There was within this core a certain drift to the left politically, but this would be expressed in very different ways.

Olivier, for example, was thought by the others to be a Tory in disguise. He was very much the captain of the ship, knew himself to be so and acted accordingly. He was the oldest of the four by some twenty years, representative of another generation and of the now despised actor-managers. His eagerness to cross this generation gap was obvious. His political opinions were veering towards Socialism, partly under the influence of the others and also because Joan Plowright, on whose common sense and integrity he came to rely, was then a Labour supporter. But he retained a gruff determination to lead and a stolid patriotism, which the others sometimes resented. A half-jocular, half-cynical relationship developed between Olivier and his younger assistant directors, Gaskill and Dexter, in which he would call them his 'boys' and they would retort with 'Dad'. And indeed there grew between the three of them (or four, with Joan Plowright) something very similar to a family relationship — close, often tender and protective, and sometimes bitter and quarrelsome. They were professionals of two generations, and the younger ones sometimes resented the intrusion of 'outsiders'. Tynan, being a critic and not a practising director, was sometimes regarded as an intruder; and Olivier as 'father' wanted to protect him, to make sure that he had fair treatment.

But Olivier too felt vulnerable, a character trait which he had always possessed, but which his new status exaggerated. When he was appointed to the National, he talked about the need to put on 'a heavy suit of armour', confiding to Max Adrian that he was about to become 'the most hated man in England'. He felt the strain of being the National's star actor, as well as its chief administrator, and he knew that audiences would not judge him by ordinary standards. He was commonly regarded as the best actor in the world, and every time he went on stage that reputation was at stake. This meant that sometimes he encouraged, even invited, a certain protectiveness in others, which was freely given — and sometimes abused, for once on the stage, Olivier brooked no opposition. It was not that he could not work supremely well with other actors, it was rather that they had either to be very strong to match him or that otherwise his unselfishness, pulling himself back not to distort the production, would have its own form of eye-catching reticence.

The fear was that Olivier might use the National, as Wolfit had done with his touring companies, to enhance his own reputation at the expense of others. It was an understandable fear, expressed by observers and sometimes other actors: but it was not really proved by events. Olivier did not take many major roles during his stay at the National; although the memories of the parts that he did play are so vivid that they can swamp the recollections of other productions. It is sometimes asserted that he did not wish to appear with actors of a comparable stature. *Othello* is cited as an example. The obvious casting would have included Redgrave as Iago (instead of the little-known actor then, Frank Finlay) and Rosemary Harris as Desdemona (instead of Maggie Smith). These were in fact the original intentions, but Rosemary Harris

19 The South Bank by Waterloo Bridge before the Second World War

20 Model for South Bank redevelopment, 1957. Arrow indicates National
Theatre as designed by Brian O'Rorke

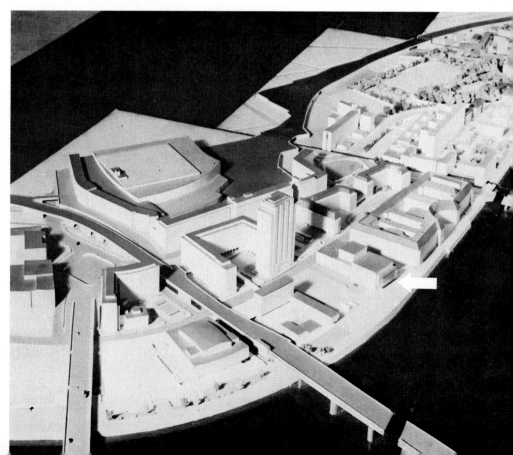

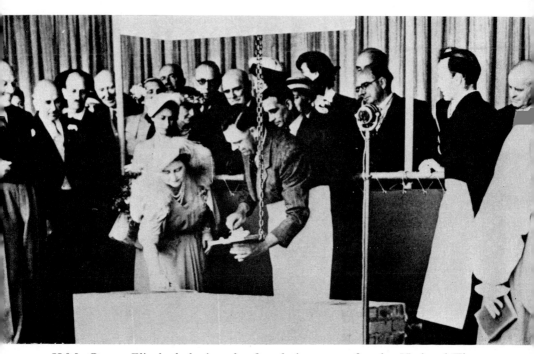

21 H.M. Queen Elizabeth laying the foundation stone for the National Theatre, 1951

22 The foundation stone on its temporary site

TO THE LIVING MEMORY OF
WILLIAM SHAKESPEARE
ON A SITE PROVIDED BY THE
LONDON COUNTY COUNCIL IN
CONFORMITY WITH THE NATIONAL
THEATRE ACT MCMXLIX AND IN THE
YEAR OF THE FESTIVAL OF BRITAIN
THIS FOUNDATION STONE FOR
THE NATIONAL THEATRE
WAS LAID ON MDCCLXX MCMLI BY
HER MAJESTY THE QUEEN

With the agreement of Her Majesty
Queen Elizabeth the Queen Mother
this foundation stone is placed here
temporarily while reconstruction
works are taking place on the
South Bank and pending a final
decision on the situation of the
National Theatre

left to join her husband's company in the United States, while Redgrave seemed to strike one of those awkward phases in an actor's career where parts become hard to memorize and the sheer energy required to play major roles night after night was lacking. Olivier's supposed 'selfishness' cannot be blamed for the fact that he took over from Redgrave in *The Master Builder*: it was a matter of necessity. Nevertheless, some leading actors were reluctant to work with Olivier; and indeed the policy of the National during its early days was to create a company not dependent on known stars who might be tempted away by better offers. The policy was to create the leading actors from within the company: Finlay was one example (First Grave-digger in *Hamlet*), Colin Blakely another (Fortinbras's Sergeant), and many more could be cited.

Within the management, Olivier certainly found opposition and was prepared to accept, and dole out, criticism. Tynan, who admired his acting extravagantly, was also prepared to be tough with him. Olivier, who respected Tynan's flair, incisiveness and sometimes sheer knowledge (for he seemed to have been everywhere and seen everything), relied upon him to be more than a literary manager — rather an early-warning system, a promoter of bright ideas, and a spokesman. Tynan sometimes thought of himself as an *éminence grise*. Chandos, who never liked Tynan particularly and became very scathing about him, defended his original selection on the grounds that he would become the 'A.F.D. — the Anti-Fuddy-Duddy' of the National's management. He would be the sceptical maverick. Tynan indeed gave that impression to the outside world. He was the one who, in 1965, shocked the B.B.C. and several Members of Parliament by first using the word 'fuck' on television. Within the company, however, he was a stalwart, whose behaviour might seem unconventional, even outrageous, but whose loyalty to Olivier was unquestioned and who was capable of dogged hard work. He might conceal his capacity for controlled intuition and careful research beneath a flamboyant façade — of, say, the romantic Marxist (whose love of individualism matched his concern for economic good order), or of the 'international hedonist', or of the dandy wit. But Tynan was the one who, having coined the phrase 'spectrum of world drama', had the tenacity to compile a reference book of the world's greatest plays, 400 of them, so that future repertoires could be planned systematically.

He realized, as other *Dramaturgs* have done, that planning programmes for the National was also a matter of finding the right 'package' — the crucial directors, actors, translators and designers. He was a potential showman, the C. B. Cochran of serious theatre; and he loved that image. The National, he would sometimes say, was about 'show-business' whereas the R.S.C. under Hall was about 'art'. That sort of inversion, defying the literary establishment (as he saw it), was typical of his style. He was not particularly perceptive in selecting new scripts or encouraging young writers. But it was largely at his instigation that, say, John Mortimer, perhaps the most skilful British writer of middle-class comedies, was invited to translate Feydeau's *La Puce à l'Oreille* (*A Flea In Her Ear*) and that Jacques Charon from the Comédie-Française was asked to direct it. At a time when Noël Coward was particularly out of fashion, Tynan put forward the idea that he should be invited to direct his *Hay Fever*, which he accepted with delight and some surprise, a success which led to other Coward revivals (in London and elsewhere). These two examples should scotch the idea that Tynan was always trying to pull the National towards a kind of revolutionary fervour, which sometimes seemed to be Chandos's impression. There was that side to him, which surfaced perhaps in the controversy over Hochhuth's *Soldiers* (would Tynan have regarded it as such a good play, if it had not seemed to attack Churchill and an establishment myth?) and more obviously in Adrian Mitchell's *Tyger*, a musical about Blake and one of Tynan's packages which went wrong. But Tynan's gift to the National lay in the variety of his enthusiasms. He was always feeling passionate about someone or something, demanding Zeffirelli to direct *Much Ado About Nothing* or Ingmar Bergman for *Hedda Gabler*. He could be a fervent admirer of the Berliner Ensemble, Brecht and permanent companies and at the same time pursue a show-business, star-orientated policy. He could reconcile the apparently irreconcilable; and it was only when under attack that he took refuge in a sort of Socialist fundamentalism which transformed a choice into an ideological cause.

Tynan's passionate diversity, his romanticism and verve, was not to everyone's tastes, even those whose opinions he expressed with such apparent conviction. The left-wing looked on Tynan with suspicion as a radical chic butterfly, lounging around doing what he liked on a fat expense account (although it was really rather limited) and ignoring the sterner class struggles. Gaskill was the most 'committed' director of the management four, both in the narrow 'political' sense and in the fact that he had a clear idea as to how the company should be run. Gaskill provided a useful distinction between types of National productions—'red-gold' and 'green-brown', the spectacular, splendid productions (such as Dexter's of Peter Shaffer's *The Royal Hunt of the*

Sun) and the sombre, monochrome ones (such as Gaskill's of Brecht's *Mother Courage*).

Gaskill was inspired by Brecht. It was no coincidence that his first production for the National was of Farquhar's *The Recruiting Officer*, which Brecht had adapted into his own version, *Trumpets and Drums*, brought to London as part of the Berliner Ensemble's repertoire in 1955. Gaskill, typically, hated the fussy gestures and coy archaisms ('obleeged' for 'obliged') associated with early eighteenth-century comedy. He saw the play not just as a bawdy, light-hearted Restoration farce with roistering soldiers, gormless peasants and gullible gentry, but as a valuable portrait of its society. He believed that the stock Restoration style in fact obscured Farquhar's words, what they meant in their true, literal sense. He wanted to establish the 'realism' of the play — by which he did not mean stock naturalism, but a proper recognition by the cast of the motives involved. Were the peasants so easily tricked by the recruiting officer? If they were, then why? What did life offer them in their ordinary jobs? What were their class motives?

This meant that the actors had to consider how Farquhar's society worked before considering the normal questions of acting style. After the preliminary reading, he encouraged the actors to dispense with their books and simply improvise, using their own words but the basic conflicts of each scene. Tynan once asked Gaskill the purpose of the improvisation. He replied: 'To establish the sequence of emotions in the actors' minds' — but by emotions he did not mean 'emotionalism' (love, happiness, hatred, fear), but rather the primary needs and concerns of the characters which gave rise to these feelings.

Improvisation was not then a conventional part of rehearsing technique. Gaskill was working with actors such as Max Adrian (Justice Balance), Maggie Smith (Sylvia) and Olivier (Brazen), who were not accustomed to such methods. He started with them very simply — asking the cast to hand round imaginary objects and to swop lines of dialogue — drama-school exercises; and gradually they responded. He then (again following Brecht) asked them social questions, along the lines of 'Who owns whom?', so that a group approach to the problems and themes of *The Recruiting Officer* would emerge. He was very patient, an excellent teacher working with diligent (if sometimes startled) pupils; and the result was the first major success of the National's career at the Old Vic, the first 'hit' which had not been tried out at Chichester. *The Recruiting Officer* emerged as a fascinating social document, as well as a brilliantly funny comedy.

This example serves to illustrate what was Gaskill's **main dream for** the company: a co-ordinated acting team with no stars, working by democratic discussion towards a common goal; the better understanding of society. That was the purpose and function of their art. And Gaskill believed that this direction must eventually include an acceptance of Socialist principles and beliefs. He was therefore opposed to the policy of inviting guest stars and directors, anti Tynan's show-business, sceptical of Olivier's actor-managerial approach and worried about the 'spectrum of world drama' idea. By trying to do too much, by trying to embrace every genre and every style, the National would achieve too little. It would sacrifice its cohesion and concentration for a totally false comprehensiveness. Gaskill was the first of the management four to leave the National—to become George Devine's successor at the Royal Court—and when that episode of his life ended, he became a teacher, touring around the world lecturing to drama students, and then becoming associate director of a fringe company, Joint Stock. As a director, he was—and is—excellent, but in a deliberately limited style: his greatest impact, perhaps, is as a teacher, and as someone who practises what he preaches.

Dexter was the journeyman director of the four, the practical craftsman who could always be relied upon to produce a competent production. But he was also the one who could snatch up ideas and expand them with a brilliance and fluency unmatched by the others. The routine side of his work was shown by such productions as St Joan, Hobson's Choice and even Othello, for the outstanding feature of that smash-hit was Olivier's extraordinary performance, not Dexter's directing. These productions revealed how Dexter could provide a firm context for his actors, while encouraging them to reach personal heights of performance. His work could be unobtrusive.

But it was not always so. Before coming to the National, Dexter's reputation had been based largely upon his productions of Wesker's plays, particularly The Kitchen and Chips with Everything. These productions revealed one of Dexter's great strengths—his ability to organize a very complicated stage picture, with elaborate cross-movements among the actors and a delight in mime. He was the only one with a hit musical to his credit, Half A Sixpence. This particular talent was demonstrated by the astonishing appearance of The Royal Hunt of the Sun, the first new British play produced by the National.

Peter Shaffer's play was not one of Tynan's discoveries. Dexter found the script lying on Olivier's desk, where it had eventually dropped, having passed through Devine's hands at the Royal Court, and half the other script-readers' in London. Most thought that this epic would either be too costly to stage, with its large cast and many changes of set, or was, in fact, unstageable. Shaffer then was not a particularly well-known dramatist. His *Five-Finger Exercise* had received a respectable London run, but it was a conventional play, domesticated and well-made, set in a middle-class drawing-room with a bedroom above. Dexter was attracted to Shaffer's latest script by one laconic stage direction, noticed while leafing through the pages: 'They cross the Andes.'

The Royal Hunt of the Sun was a wonderful adventure story, but scarcely more than that. Shaffer had the capacity to make it seem more by drawing some anti-colonialist, anti-materialistic morals and by providing a sharp contrast between the cragged, sceptical soldier Pizarro (Colin Blakely) and the God-King of the Incas, Atahualpa (Robert Stephens). It was based on Prescott's *Conquest of Peru*, telling how a small band of Spanish *conquistadores*, led by Pizarro, conquered the vast Inca empire. This yarn presented all kinds of theatrical challenges. It had to be spectacular, but the spectacle could not be based upon naturalistic changes of set. You could not actually bring a model of the Andes onto the stage. The long trek across land, through the swamps, and up the freezing slopes of the mountains, before descending into the broad, well-cultivated plains of the Incas, had to be achieved by mime. The visual excitement of the play was realized in Michael Annals's set by one glowing sun, golden and large, symbolizing the Inca empire, which was then destroyed by removing the gold, leaving a hollow, darkened circle—an empty eye. Annals, whose sets for the National came later to be criticized for a *kitsch* ornateness, chose the simplest and most spectacular means to realize the glitter of the sun: he got hundreds of metal bottle tops, beat them flat and tacked them to the struts of the sun.

The set was thus rudimentary, but it did not leave this impression. Only Peter Brook among British directors (or Guthrie in his younger days) could have matched Dexter's capacity to create constantly exciting and changing images from so simple a picture. Dexter split his cast, making one half walk and behave like the rough European soldiers, and the other like the pastoral Indians. For most rehearsals, these teams were kept apart, so that they would actually feel the shock of difference when they were brought together in the later stages. He drew from Robert Stephens an extraordinary performance. Stephens, previously associated with rather smarmy, weak young men, confidence tricksters (and the Dauphin in *St Joan*), seemed to transform himself physically: he worked for ten weeks in the gymnasium on exercises which made him look slender and athletic. He moved with an animal alertness. Indeed,

Dexter tried to invent a world for him, that of the Peruvian Indians of whom very little is known. Marc Wilkinson, the National's resident composer, listened to a surviving lament from the modern Peruvians, discovered that they stressed such consonants as 'k', 'p' and 'b', and incorporated bird cries and howls into their singing—and from these fragments, constructed a language and a sound for them. Dexter brought all these different elements together, tried out the production at Chichester in July 1964 and transferred it to the Old Vic in December.

The success of *The Royal Hunt of the Sun* had many consequences. It was, for example, the first National production to match, and even perhaps excel, the epics then being staged by the R.S.C., a tradition which began there in 1961 with John Whiting's *The Devils*, continued with Peter Brook's production of Peter Weiss's *Marat/Sade* and arrived with symptoms of decadence at *US* and Peter Barnes's *The Bewitched*. It began a similar tradition at the National, which survived in a more controlled form, with Dexter's production of John Arden's *Armstrong's Last Goodnight* where a slightly less remote society was created, with its own language—that of medieval Scots—and with dialects of that language. It established the National's reputation for theatrical athleticism, for mime and visual effects, so that in time Claude Chagrin, the National's teacher of mime and movement, would rival in reputation Litz Pisk, who worked mainly with the R.S.C. It brought Robert Stephens, whose reputation from the Royal Court flowered at the National, to the front rank of the younger British actors; and above all, it provided the foundation for a settled partnership between Dexter and Shaffer. It was Shaffer who had the bright idea (borrowed from the Chinese) of staging a comedy, supposedly in pitch blackness but in fact on a well-lit stage—so that the audience could see the actors groping around blindly, missing each other by inches and trying to move furniture and hand out drinks at the same time. *Black Comedy* was just an idea when it was first scheduled for production at Chichester in 1966— the script was not completed until just before the opening night—but the confidence between the director and the writer was such that the production moved with meticulous speed and skill. Dexter, too, directed Shaffer's *Equus*, a major success at a time when the National needed it most, in 1973.

This valuable partnership between Shaffer and Dexter nevertheless illustrates what is sometimes held to be Dexter's chief weakness, his choice of scripts. Shaffer is a skilful 'middle-brow' dramatist; his views are often predictable, Sunday-supplement stuff, which he manages to make seem more profound than they are. In *Equus*, for example, he snatched up the familiar Laingian arguments about the dangers of an analyst tampering with the deep passions in a boy's soul—without examining them further; and Dexter was not the sort of director to demand intellectualism from his authors. Indeed, he was almost an anti-intellectual, another showman, which meant that he would tackle some scripts (John Osborne's *A Bond Honoured* and Adrian Mitchell's *Tyger* would be examples) which any other self-respecting director would have sent back to the authors, scribbled over with queries and comments demanding rewriting.

The balance of professional skills within the management team was thus admirable: each supplied a talent which the others lacked, and there was a comparable balance in life-styles and backgrounds. Olivier was, in his private life as well as in the company, assuming the role of a solid paterfamilias, delighting in his marriage and his young children. Tynan, who was divorced from his first wife, Elaine Dundy, in 1964, was a man-about-town, rather parading his liberation from puritan restraints. Gaskill and Dexter had their own forms of liberation, too, while the sexual gap (if that phrase can be used) in the management team, that of an 'indispensable woman', was filled by Joan Plowright.

There was also a variety of class backgrounds, Dexter and Olivier coming from the poorest families, though ones of very different social status. Dexter was the son of a Derby plumber, who left school when he was fourteen, and had difficulty in throwing off the feeling that the theatre was for other people, the wealthy middle classes. 'I am still more class-ridden than practically anybody I know,' he said in 1971. 'Still. It bothers me no end.' He always wanted to know how much each character in a play earned—in relationship to the other characters—before tackling a production. The knowledge focused his mind on the realities of the play. It was a more ingrained approach to class warfare than, say, Gaskill's ideological one.

When the National was in the process of establishing itself, the strength of these four men, working together for a common cause and battling through their differences of outlook, drove the company forward. After the National had been established, the tensions which resulted nearly undid their hard work, and would have done so, but for the remarkable tenacity and willpower of Olivier.

The balance of abilities within the management was partly reflected in the acting team, of whom 12 names were announced in August 1963, and an additional 23 in September. The aim was for a company of about 60, fewer than that planned by Granville-Barker in 1930; but the

Old Vic was smaller than the two theatres which Barker envisaged. Of the first 12, 4 actors were particularly associated with the Royal Court: Finlay, Stephens, Robert Lang and Joan Plowright; 2, Maggie Smith and Max Adrian, were best known for their work in intimate revues; 2, Diana Wynyard and Michael Redgrave, were established stars. Martin Boddey, Anthony Nicholls, Derek Jacobi and Olivier himself completed the original 12 which, despite the bias towards the Royal Court, nevertheless provided a reasonable cross-section of the various theatre traditions in Britain.

The programmes of the first four seasons reflected the blend of opinion within the management, a very stimulating and enjoyable collection, not biased towards literature or academic research, not cautious and concerned to defend its status, but buoyant and outward-looking. Tynan was particularly concerned that the National should not became a parochial institution, and by that he meant not mere nationalism, but also the parochialism of being 'contemporary', the temptation of following fashions. He was influenced, like everyone else concerned with building the National, by Granville-Barker, but not slavishly so. Granville-Barker's various categories for National repertoires can be seen as a dim shadow behind the actual selections, but without the dependence on Shakespeare. The National's programmes, too, were grouped into categories: 'new plays', 'classic revivals', 'recent plays worthy of revival' and 'plays from abroad' — and the stress within the opening seasons was on the last of these groups.

Four of the 9 plays in the opening season came from abroad, 2 (out of 6) in the second, 3 (out of 8) in the third and 3 (out of 4) in the fourth. These included 2 Chekhov plays (*Uncle Vanya* and *Three Sisters*), 2 by Strindberg (*Miss Julie* and *The Dance of Death*), 1 Ibsen (*The Master Builder*), 1 Brecht (*Mother Courage*), 1 Feydeau (*A Flea In Her Ear*) and several less familiar choices: Max Frisch's *Andorra* (a British première, with Tom Courtenay as its star), Sophocles' *Philoctetes* (whose contemporary relevance was rather overstressed in a horseplay production by Gaskill), Lope de Vega's *La Fianza Satisfecha* (mis-handled by Osborne as *A Bond Honoured*) and Ostrovsky's *The Storm*. It is scarcely surprising perhaps, that the company seemed most assured in those works which were already familiar to them and involved no complications of style. The Chekhov plays (both directed by Olivier) were triumphs, the *Uncle Vanya* ripening in the two Chichester summers until it reached a maturity of timing, ensemble playing, understanding and sensitivity on its arrival at the Old Vic; *The Master Builder* (directed by Peter Wood) was a solid production, both with Redgrave as Solness, and then

Olivier; and while *Miss Julie* was competent but disappointing, with Albert Finney too dominant for Maggie Smith's brittle Miss Julie, *The Dance of Death* featured Olivier at his incomparable best, a hard-faced, bullet-headed Captain, bluffing and torturing his way through a hell of a marriage.

With such productions, however, the National was not exactly absorbing fresh ideas from abroad, and bringing them to Britain, but rather developing those which it knew already. Gaskill's *Mother Courage* was a competent imitation of the Berliner Ensemble production, with Madge Ryan between the wagon shafts instead of Helene Weigel; but the true influence of Brecht was rather to be found in his classical revivals, *The Recruiting Officer* and (much less successfully) Marston's *The Dutch Courtesan*. But the National company did respond to two foreign styles, polished them and brought them into their repertoire of skills. The first came from the Comédie-Française with Jacques Charon, who drew a style and precision of farce-playing from the company, unseen from a British company and unlike the other farce tradition in Britain, that of the Aldwych farces, which depended more on character comedians. The second came through Franco Zeffirelli and the Neopolitan comedies. His production of *Much Ado* was exuberant yet not totally successful, but this Italian connection eventually led to a much better achievement, the National's version of Eduardo de Filippo's *Saturday, Sunday, Monday* in 1973.

There were four 'new plays' in the first four seasons, *The Royal Hunt of the Sun* and *Black Comedy*, *Armstrong's Last Goodnight* and Tom Stoppard's *Rosencrantz and Guildenstern Are Dead*, a genuine discovery, first seen by Ronald Bryden, the critic, in an undergraduate production at the Edinburgh Festival and directed by Derek Goldby for the National in 1967. Some critics suspected that this play was too clever by half, mere pastiche, toying around with the neat basic idea of concentrating on two characters lost in a whirl of events of which they knew nothing but the audience everything. It was almost another *Black Comedy*, but more sophisticated, doffing its hat to existentialism and the new-wave novels. Stoppard, however, has so many good ideas, which he can develop brilliantly and, as with Shaffer, he was not lost with other clever dramatists who failed to mature. *Jumpers* was another Stoppard success with the National, in 1972.

The 'new plays' may have been a small collection, but they were a notable bunch, far removed from mere experimentalism. The 'recent plays' section also included five productions: *St Joan* and *Hobson's Choice* (1963–4), *Hay Fever* (1964–5), Pinero's *Trelawny of the 'Wells'* and

O'Casey's *Juno and the Paycock* (1965–6). By the end of the first four years, at least one side of the National's reputation had been established beyond question: it was the most marvellous company for comedies. Each year had brought productions which were, in different ways, brilliantly funny; and the range of comedy styles was surely unmatched by any other company in the world. The actors excelled in the lyrical comedy of *Trelawny of the 'Wells'*, in the Gallic precision and toughness of *A Flea In Her Ear*, in the boisterous farce of *Black Comedy*, the 1920s 'sophistication' of *Hay Fever*, the Restoration comedies *The Recruiting Officer* and *Love For Love*, and in *Rosencrantz and Guildenstern Are Dead*; and it was this constant vein of liveliness and good humour which took away pomposity from the National's image.

And yet it was not best known for its comedies. One performance fixed the National's reputation in the public's mind—not even one production, for as a production it was less evenly successful than others in the National's repertory: Olivier's Othello, one of those astonishing, mind-riveting performances which become legendary long before their time is over. Olivier was frightened by the part. Tynan had to 'woo' him to tackle it. He was afraid of forgetting his lines, of the sheer physical challenges of the role which Shakespeare had written (Olivier was convinced) to prove that here was something which neither Burbage nor anyone else could play, with climax succeeding climax in an un-broken effort of energy, of the dangers of failure and the demands of success. Olivier thought he was too old for the part at fifty-seven, for the ideal Othello should be some ten years younger. His voice was thought to be too light. 'Larry's a natural tenor,' Orson Welles once confided to Tynan, 'and Othello's a natural baritone.' Olivier imposed strict training sessions upon himself, building up his strength and his vocal command over the lower registers in his voice. ' ... weeks of daily voice lessons ... throbbed through the plywood walls of the National Theatre's temporary offices,' recalled Tynan, and at the end of them Olivier had extended the bass register of his voice by some six full tones. 'Who could have believed', wrote Harold Hobson, 'that Sir Laurence could make his voice so deep and dark?'

The chief challenge, however, was that of conception. Olivier had acted in *Othello* before, as Iago to Richardson's Othello in a Guthrie production at the Old Vic in 1938. He had then evolved a complicated psychoanalytic interpretation, based on Professor Ernest Jones's idea that Iago's motiveless malignity stemmed from the fact that he was a suppressed homosexual. Now Olivier wasn't interested in such an idea. He wanted his Iago to be 'a solid, honest-to-God' N.C.O., seized by a racial rivalry and professional jealousy. The secret of the play lay in the fact that Othello was black. He had to be not just black in a West Indian, African or Moorish sense, but the distillation of blackness, what every prejudiced white man is supposed to fear, the energy and vitality of the Dark Continent—which has to be conquered, by fair means or foul. 'It's the only play in the whole of Shakespeare', Olivier once said, 'in which a man kills a woman, and if Shakespeare has an idea he goes all out for it. He knows very well that for a black man to kill a white woman is a very big thrill indeed ... '

And so Olivier went all out to provide an image of the black hero, moving like a panther on the balls of his feet, a challenge to white supremacy, whose downfall is brought about not just through jealousy, but through a self-deceiving pride that he is the greatest. Dexter encouraged the rest of the cast to see his Othello as a kind of Muhammed Ali, 'a pompous, word-spinning, arrogant, black general'. It was an astonishing feat of impersonation, one which involved a change of voice, gait, presence and mannerisms, which may have failed in one respect, by not being sufficiently moving emotionally, but otherwise could only be criticized on its premises, not its achievements. Jonathan Miller, for example, thought that Olivier was providing a Western cartoon of blackness. He was right, but that was Olivier's intention.

Olivier's Othello took everyone by surprise, even the cast at his first reading. It turned the box-office upside-down and threw Stephen Arlen's careful preparations, less carefully carried out, into turmoil. Applications for tickets arrived by the sackful. Queues stretched round the block for tickets, and there were stories that some foreign visitors had paid £5, not for tickets, but just for places in the queue. Attendance figures, which were high throughout the National's first seasons, topped 100 per cent for *Othello*: all the seats were occupied, and the standing room in the theatre was packed as well.

The National was thus faced with the sort of success which is almost an embarrassment. The Old Vic with its 880 seats immediately seemed too small. The members of the Vic–Wells Society complained that they could not get tickets, which were too highly priced in any case, and so Arlen was faced with a difficult choice. The traditional supporters of the Old Vic provided a solid public core around which audiences in future could be built. That was the theory—but practice had made it unnecessary. Throughout the first season audience attendance figures topped 86 per cent of capacity. What should Arlen do? Dispense with preferential treatment for the Vic–Wells members, thus risking the loss of an audience 'core' which might be useful in less happy times? Or retain the 'core', thus running the National into accusations of preferential treatment for stalwarts and marginally preventing it from being a totally 'public' theatre? The booking concessions were not large in themselves, but they had a symbolic importance. Was the National to cut its links with the 'poor people's' movement of which the Old Vic was so important a part? Audience survey figures at the end of the first year revealed that only 0·3 per cent of its public came from the 'manual workers'.

There was also the problem of the regions. *Othello*'s success led to demands that it should be seen more widely around the country. In fact, the National had from the start taken its regional responsibilities seriously. It had organized a spring tour, beginning at Newcastle-upon-Tyne in the last week of March, which included *Uncle Vanya, Hobson's Choice* (shortly after its première at the Old Vic) and a pre-London run of *Othello*. *Othello*, due to open at Newcastle, in fact did not join the repertoire until the second week, at the Alexandra Theatre, Birmingham. Olivier's strength had suffered from the strains of launching the National, and in February he caught a bad attack of 'flu 'which shook me like a dog shakes a rat'. His health was worrying everyone, and almost as soon as the *Othello* run started, his friends wondered how long he could continue even in repertoire (which did not require nightly performances), with so demanding a part on top of his other work. Since the run of *Othello* had to be limited—though it stayed in the repertoire for several years—how should the performances be divided? Were taxing tours the best way of using that energy? In fact, *Othello* received over the years 89 performances at the Old Vic, 17 at Chichester, 4 in the West End and 10 on British regional tours.

These were the troubles of success, Olivier's black man's burden. But there was also one quite unexpected, totally unpredictable benefit. Jennie Lee had become the Minister for the Arts (or, to give her the proper title, the Joint Under-Secretary at the Ministry of Education and Science with special responsibility towards the Arts) in Harold Wilson's government. One of her first tasks had been to contact Mme Furtseva, the Soviet Minister of Culture, with the intention of organizing a cultural exchange pact. The Cold War of the 1950s was slowly defrosting. Khrushchev seemed a more moderate man than Stalin; and the Labour Party was trying to re-establish comradely links with the Soviet Union. As part of Britain's side of the bargain, the National Theatre company was invited to visit Russia—in September 1965, for a short two-and-a-half-week season at the Kremlin Theatre, which was to be followed by a visit to West Berlin. The Kremlin Theatre was a new theatre, started just before Stalin's death and the National was the first foreign company to play there.

The tour was organized in a terrible hurry. The contracts had not even been signed by the time the company returned — an administrative lapse for which the British Council (who organized the tour) blamed the National. A new production, Congreve's *Love For Love*, was part of their programme, with *Hobson's Choice* and *Othello*. But the production which opened the season was *Othello*, the play widely known in Russia, with the actor who was also famous there, from war films mainly, Olivier. The response from the Moscow audiences was quite astonishing. The reception, wrote Felix Barker reporting for the *Evening News* on September 8th, 1965, from Moscow, 'makes enthusiasm a pale word':

As the curtain fell on the tragic figures of Desdemona and the Moor entwined in death's agony on the bed, the audience from the back of the theatre swept down the central gangway in a great human tide. They stood three-deep in the front of the stage, hurling flowers and clapping, many with their hands above their heads.

But two rows in front of me, I saw a woman in black — sitting while all around her were on their feet, crying 'Bravo'. What was the matter? Was she anti-Shakespeare, anti-British? A Russian critic perhaps? Then she turned slightly and I saw. Tears were running down her cheeks. She was too overwhelmed to get up.

Three hours before I had been stopped in the Red Square by young Russian girl students begging for a ticket. Only fear of the police, I suspect, prevented them from offering black-market prices. I had watched the extraordinary enthusiasm of an audience, who, even with tickets, fought and shoved their way through the single entrance as if their lives depended on being seated to hear Roderigo's first line.

The ovation on the first night lasted for well over ten minutes. Similar receptions took place every night, and for the final performance President Mikoyan led the applause. London critics in Moscow may have felt that the productions had suffered a little in the transfer, while Russian critics were at first taken aback, as everyone had been, by the sheer 'blackness' of Olivier's interpretation. Entering the stage barefooted, carrying a rose, was not, at first, thought to be dignified and serious. But the final result was not in question: it was a triumph for the company — and for Olivier personally, not just as an actor, but as an ambassador, whose few curtain words in Russian were welcomed with almost as much enthusiasm as the performance itself.

In Britain, as news of the National's success grabbed the headlines, the public started to look on the company with fresh appreciation. The Moscow visit demonstrated the value of having a company which could, in some way, represent Britain. It was breaking down international barriers of culture and thought. It was also waving the flag in a city supposedly hostile to the British. For theatre-lovers, the occasion could be compared to winning the World Cup. In the National's absence from the Old Vic, the Berliner Ensemble were holding the fort in Waterloo Road; and it would make a pleasant balance to record that they had had an equivalent reception in London. They did not, of course. The critical response was fairly warm, but the audiences were polite, rather than tumultuously enthusiastic. It is sometimes more comforting—as well as more blessed—to give than to receive; and the brief gift of the National company to Moscow raised its esteem in Britain—and indeed the self-esteem of the British—as no visit by a foreign company to London could have done. The National was behaving like a National. It was demonstrably justifying its existence.

12

A Monument to our Time

IF THE company were going to be the best in the world, it was quite obvious to everyone that it was going to need the best building—not a throwback to the 1930s in stone and glass, not a massive monument reeking of civic pride and national jingoism, but something which reflected the deeper values of the age, a humanism, a new seriousness, an awareness of how people actually live in towns and what actors really require on a stage. Nothing less than the best would be even suitable. Just as the National Theatre company pursued excellence through a process of balancing and discussing different views, so the South Bank Theatre and Opera House Board sought advice from every possible source of informed opinion.

This process continued through the 1960s, and even into the 1970s, after the site had finally been determined, the substructure laid and the superstructure begun. It soon became clear that the problems were not just architectural and theatrical ones, but economic as well, and political, and matters even less tangible, such as the question of appropriateness. The project would round off the South Bank arts complex and bring it to fruition; but the South Bank idea itself was almost a feature of old London, the London of post-war reconstruction, and in the intervening twenty years or so, London had changed. Inner London was slowly becoming depopulated, the outer suburbs were growing and so too were the new towns, within commuting distance.

This far from gradual change was reflected in new organizations and new businesses. On March 31st, 1965, for example, the old L.C.C. became the Greater London Council, whose authority now stretched to the outer suburbs; which meant that prosperous middle-class areas were brought in to balance the old disparity between the rich London (of, say, Kensington and Hampstead) and the poor (Kennington and Stepney). Since 1934, the Labour Party had fancied its chances at local elections to win (and retain) control of County Hall. It had become the 'natural party' of London's government. But in 1967, the G.L.C. elections returned the Conservatives to power, and their policy included the traditional one of protecting the ratepayer and cutting down on public expenditure. The National Theatre came under particularly close scrutiny.

Of equal significance was the way in which the physical landscape and 'feel' of London had changed: the new roads (such as the Hammersmith flyover) where the commuting cars would idle in jams at rush hour, the ring roads almost physically parcelling up one neighbourhood from the next, the parking meters, the one-way streets and the new pressure on office space in London, leading to tower blocks, property speculation and an end to 'mixed development' despite all good resolutions. Parts of London were now, by old standards, empty and desolate —particularly in the evenings and the weekends. The office workers would leave, while the few remaining residents would huddle in little conclaves. There should have been no housing problem in London: but there was. Indeed, it had scarcely improved since the war. Rows of serviceable houses, a little old perhaps, Victorian and fashionable only with the chic young marrieds, were scheduled for redevelopment, more often by councils than private developers, and they were left to rot while the ambitious plans passed from desk to desk. In the 1960s, prefabs—whose life-span after the war had been estimated at between five and ten years—were still being used for families, as well as for the National Theatre's administration.

All these factors had to be taken into account; London was being reconstructed, a process which often seemed desperately slow, particularly so for those enduring the many inconveniences, and sometimes savagely fast. Beyond the little world of London, the nation, too, was changing, in small and large ways, many of which affected the progress of the National directly, and all contributing again to a different 'feel' within the country. The National, for example, was affected by a change in the status of the Arts Council, which should have been a mere formality. In February 1965, the Labour government published a White Paper, *A Policy for the Arts*, whose main feature was the transfer of control over the Arts Council from the Treasury to the Department of Education and Science. Jennie Lee, as we have seen, was the under-secretary in this department with special responsibility for the arts. In one way, this was regarded as a long overdue recognition of the importance of the arts. At last the arts had someone in the government (if not in the Cabinet) to act as a parliamentary spokesman. Jennie Lee, apart from her standing within the Labour movement, was a close friend of the Prime Minister, and her support was invaluable. Over the next few years, the government was much more generous to the arts. In 1964–5, the Arts Council received £3,205,000, which rose to £5,700,000 (1966–7), £7,750,000 (1968–9), £9,300,000 (1970–1), £13,725,000 (1972–3) until by 1974 the Arts Council asked for, and received, over £25 million.

This rapid growth in government money to the arts had many consequences. It reflected, for example, the growing centralization of money in government hands, marking the decline of the private sector in the theatrical economy and a growing dependence on grants for survival. It meant the end of Sir William Emrys Williams's old emphasis upon 'partnership in patronage', with different independent sections of the economy each contributing to a common cause and, instead, a new reliance on government good-will. The National had always needed this government support, and therefore to some extent benefited. But sacrifices had to be made on the way. Lord Cottesloe, for example, had always rather liked the old system whereby, as chairman of the Arts Council, he could speak to the Treasury directly, putting in his requests and trying to persuade officials that they were necessary. He (and Chandos) were so used to the corridors of power that they knew exactly on what Civil Service peg to hang their hats. Now all such requests had to be siphoned through the Department of Education (and Jennie Lee), who would appeal to the Treasury on their behalfs. It seemed a slightly more cumbersome process, made worse by the fact that money for the National was subject to parliamentary consent.

The trouble was that nobody knew quite how much money would be available and when. In the absence of a realistic 'ceiling' figure, the South Bank Theatre and Opera House Board worked on the assumption that if they devised the best possible plans, the money would eventually be found from somewhere. It might require political manoeuvring, a succession of Acts, but in national (and international) terms, the sums involved were likely to be so small that no benevolent government was likely to refuse them. What nobody fully appreciated, perhaps, was the endless delays which this procedure would involve, the disappointments (most significantly, the cancellation of the Opera House) and the occasional hints of sharp practice. In the meantime, however, the South Bank Board tactfully ignored the £2·3 million (supplied by the government and the L.C.C.), which was all they *knew* would be available, and planned on another scale altogether, for the best possible building, in the best possible setting, in the best possible city, in the best of all possible worlds.

The first casualty in the pursuit of excellence was poor Brian O'Rorke, who had battled through the 1950s, attending endless boring committees, drafting designs which showed little chance of being built and generally sticking to his post beyond the call of duty. He was worn out, and even before the two boards were established in 1962, the National's supporters were worried about him. Devine thought him studious, competent but uninspired, while Olivier felt that O'Rorke was 'a fine architect and a really nice man', but his theatre 'lacked, well, some spirituality, shall we say?' Sir Kenneth Clark, whose support for the National had lasted even longer than O'Rorke's, dating right back to the early days of CEMA in the 1930s and who had tried at the very outbreak of war to establish the National quickly as a British rallying symbol, was a tactful chairman of the joint council's executive. He kept his options open, retained Devine and Olivier, and drifted back from his support for O'Rorke.

The appointment of the two new boards to replace the old joint council meant the chance to start afresh. Almost as soon as it had been established, the South Bank Theatre and Opera House Board decided to think again about the architectural plans, without ruling out the possibility that O'Rorke could be right for the job. The board's own position was a curious one. It had, for example, no funds of its own; and it was required to keep in touch with its two paymasters, the government and the L.C.C. The composition of the first board reflected its different requirements. The two arts organizations which it was intended to serve were strongly represented—with Chandos, Olivier, Norman Marshall and Prince Littler speaking for the theatre, and David McKenna and Norman Tucker for opera. The heads of the two main political parties in the L.C.C., Hayward and Sir Percy Rugg, were on the board; and so were two invaluable civil servants, Sir William Hart, C.M.G., the Clerk to the L.C.C. and 'an outstanding administrator', and Sir Leslie Rowan, K.C.B., C.V.O., whose particular task was to stay in touch with government. It was, Lord Cottesloe recalled, a 'strong board of true believers'; and the board's first task was to decide on the basic requirements for a National Theatre and Opera House, 'from which the architect or architects selected by the board would prepare designs and estimates'.

But how should the architect be chosen? The policy of the R.I.B.A. was to favour open competition: an attractive idea, for it ruled out any snide rumour that the 'architectural job of the century', as Sean Kenny flamboyantly called it, had gone to a friend of the chairman. But, in addition to the known problem of open competitions—that the best architects do not want to enter them—there was another problem: no clear specifications could be given because, frankly, the board did not know what it wanted. They might find themselves tempted by a paper design which, like the Sydney Opera House, would prove expensive and perhaps impractical in the actual building. Sir Robert Matthew, who was president of the R.I.B.A. and partly responsible for building the Royal Festival Hall, was a friend of Cottesloe, who himself had worked on a sub-committee in connection with the Festival Hall. Matthew advised Cottesloe to choose an architect not from an open competition, but from a short-list of possible architects, culled from applications. This was also, with some modifications, Olivier's view. Olivier saw the original dilemma as being the choice between an open competition (which might result in the architect having entire authority over the final design) or a selected eminent architect whose credentials, as far as theatre was concerned, would almost certainly be limited. The board had already decided in principle that the architect should be British, although he might have advisers from abroad; and the fact was that no theatre had been built in Britain of the scale required for the National Theatre.

And so Cottesloe and the board decided, with Olivier's support, that applications should be sought, which would then be scrutinized by a panel consisting of Sir Robert Matthew, P.R.I.B.A., F.R.I.B.A., Mr Hubert Bennett, F.R.I.B.A. (architect to the L.C.C.), Sir William Holford, P.R.I.B.A., F.R.I.B.A., John Piper (the painter and set designer) and Norman Marshall (the director and joint-chairman with Olivier of the National Theatre's building committee). They would compile a short-list of architects to be interviewed. In May 1963, the board publicly invited architects registered in Britain 'to submit evidence of their ability to design and supervise the construction' (of both the National Theatre and Opera House) 'with some indication of their understanding of and approach to the problems involved'.

There was a rush of applications, about 120, from which the advisory panel compiled a short-list of 20 names. These 20 architects were then given a provisional brief, a basis for discussion rather than a set of fixed specifications. It was for:

(1) A main or large theatre, seating about 1000, and adaptable, so as to offer two theatres: (a) an amphitheatre with an apron or peninsular stage (not a theatre-in-the-round), and (b) a proscenium arch stage.

(2) A small theatre, seating about 400, mainly for experimental purposes.

It was the simplest possible list of specifications, and the board were cautious not to rule out the possibility that an adaptable theatre, as suggested, might not work. They just wanted to know whether or not it could be satisfactorily built. The board's process of looking for an architect came in for some criticism. Forty-five architects signed a letter to the *Builder* complaining that there was not going to be an open competition, while others feared that the looseness of the specifications (and the duty laid upon the architect to co-operate with the board and the National Theatre's building committee) might result in a 'tame' theatre, a victim of compromises between contradictory tastes.

Throughout July and August, the names of possible architects were being tossed around in the press. Some cautious lobbying may have been going on, though some of those whose names were suggested had not even applied. Stalwarts were mentioned, such as Brian O'Rorke, and very eminent architects, such as Sir Hugh Casson and Sir Basil Spence; and architects particularly associated with the theatre, such as Sean Kenny, and Peter Moro, who had helped with the Festival Hall and designed the new Nottingham Playhouse, which opened in 1963. Some architects from abroad entered into informal partnerships with British ones. Philip Johnson, who was designing the Lincoln Center in New York, was an American contender. There was a determined challenge from Dr Werner Ruhnau, the architect of the Stadttheater at Gelsenkirchen, who gave an interview to the *Sunday Times* with space-age ideas:

> The new theatre that I'm dreaming about will be a mobile building with revolutionary technical equipment. And it'll stand in a climatised town. By that I mean a town in which the climate will be mechanically controlled — not by means of an artificial skin or sky, but by machinery that will correct the weather about the town. Then the dogs ... the human dogs, I mean ... will sniff around the town and recognise the theatre as the place where new and exciting things are being done, the place where it's dark in the day and light in the night, the place where you can colour the sky blue or red, or yellow, just as you please [*Sunday Times*, October 27th, 1963, interviewed by Vera Russell].

The board were not looking for that kind of imagination. But what were they looking for? They themselves did not precisely know, and their choice, when it was finally announced on November 22nd, 1963, came somewhat as a surprise. Denys Lasdun had not designed a theatre before. His firm, Denys Lasdun & Partners, was of a compact size, not over-large, and Lasdun thought that they had as much work as they could handle. But he was known, not widely but among the influential circles of the R.I.B.A., as one of the most brilliant architects in Britain; and in searching for the right men, Cottesloe (in consultation with the panel) had written around to various possible names, pointing out to them that the quest was still continuing and hinting that they might consider applying. Lasdun did so, subject to such considerations as when the plans were to be expected and the building to commence.

Why was he thought a 'possible'? He was perhaps considered to be of the right age, forty-nine, and with the right background: a Londoner, educated at Rugby, whose architectural studies began at the Architectural Association. As a young man, he had come closely into contact with the 'white architecture' of the 1930s, rooted in cubism and social concern, whose leading figure was Corbusier. Unlike Lutyens, whose early experience had been gleaned from building private houses in the country and who had then moved on to big civic and business buildings, Lasdun was attuned to the needs of a different age:

> Modern architecture in England dates itself from the '30s. Its characteristics derive from a different social attitude—housing, as distinct from the private house, the demands of education in school building. These were the requirements of a welfare state and architects had to respond. This is not only congenial to me, it is mandatory. I have to feel identified with the purpose of the building [*The Times*, March 24th, 1975, in an interview by Brian Connell. Copyright *The Times*, London].

Lasdun, however, had come to regard critically many features of the 'modern movement', and indeed was concerned to reassess fundamentally the nature of architectural aims. Corbusier's utopianism, for example, could lead to the superimposition of an architectural dream upon a landscape unsuitable for it, if by 'landscape' we mean not just land, but also the surrounding social landscape. A 'modern movement' building of the 1930s might be entirely functional, coherent in its principles of design, but still out of touch with the surrounding town or society; and it was this aspect of the movement which Lasdun found particularly distasteful. If the key feature of the modern movement lay in its choice of new materials, shapes and functionalism, Lasdun was concerned with landscapes and the practical usages of a building.

From such basic premises, Lasdun had evolved an attitude towards civic architecture which could be seen in such early buildings as the Hallfield School in Paddington (1951), the butterfly-plan housing blocks in Bethnal Green, the flats in St James's Place overlooking

Green Park (for which he was awarded the R.I.B.A. Bronze Medal in 1962), the Royal College of Physicians' headquarters in Regent's Park (which received another medal) and the University of East Anglia. The distinctive feature of his style was its creation of an urban landscape which would not dwarf its inhabitants but provide a comfortable, appropriate background for normal lives. 'I believe passionately', he once said, 'in a sense of belonging.'

On the crowded walls of his office in Queen Anne Street, near Portland Place, among the photographs and designs of buildings, one picture stands out by seeming not to be about 'architecture' at all. It is of the Piazza San Marco in Venice, but you cannot see the Doges' Palace, which Ruskin so praised, just, in the background, a section of the colonnade flanking the square. The foreground is of a group of people, gathering to watch or listen to something, with passers-by pausing to catch a word or so before drifting on. Lasdun held strong beliefs about the importance of city squares, broad walks, the dimensions of space within a city which should be so designed as to invite casual, and intimate, companionship. In that passion, he had inherited a certain classical concept of town life: piazzas were not a waste of good real estate—they were the communal heart of a town.

'Of all the interviewees,' recalled Olivier, 'Lasdun came by himself. It was a brilliant stroke. That man can talk divinely. Words poured out. Everyone else had cohorts of advisers. Then we asked him—we thought of this as a sort of partnership. He said that that, of course, is the essence of the matter. At that, he'd got it.'

Cottesloe thought that the selection of Lasdun was a minor 'miracle'. The interviewing committee meeting the selected twenty architects had sat for three solid days of interviews with architects who had brought along drawings and advisers. The committee itself was composed of some fifteen members, with Sir Robert Matthew in the chair, and it included representatives from the National Theatre and the Sadler's Wells Opera. The members were not agreed about what they wanted from the complex of buildings, nor were they individually certain. If Lasdun had not appeared, they could have argued almost indefinitely about other architects; and yet, without discussion and without dissent, everyone was convinced about Lasdun.

The key question at the interview was perhaps that of the adaptable theatre. Adaptable theatres are always politically attractive, because they cost less than building two separate theatres. But knowledgeable theatre architects realize that the two types of theatre are, in fact, incompatible. They call for different-shaped auditoria, different relationships between the audience and the stage, a different use of space. In a proscenium-arch theatre, the audience 'confronts' the stage: in an open-stage theatre, the audience 'embraces' it. Lasdun suspected that this was the case, but he could justifiably plead ignorance on the matter. He was prepared to listen, learn and try out alternatives. Cottesloe was reminded of one of Chandos's remarks, delivered at a school prize-giving: 'it is the hallmark of the educated man that he doesn't know all the answers'. 'We felt', said Cottesloe, 'that here was a man with whom we could work.' The interviewing panel knew that Lasdun would be sensitive to the river landscape: they found out that he was modest enough to listen to their suggestions. 'They wanted someone', Lasdun has said, 'who wouldn't make them feel uneasy if they said things that were ridiculous, and vice versa. We had to learn to work together, which is a very tender relationship, tender and tense.' As O'Rorke had done, Lasdun was prepared to sit through endless committee meetings.

It was a difficult, but intensely rewarding, partnership. In his designs, Lasdun worked from inside out, starting with the main auditorium and developing the building from that heart. Thus, his early meetings were mainly with the National Theatre's building committee, not with the County Hall planners or even with the South Bank Board. While designing the National Theatre, he was also working on plans for the Opera House: he would have refused to have taken only one of these buildings, because he wanted to relate them together to provide a total scheme for the South Bank. First of all, however, he wanted to understand the uses for which the buildings were planned. His first question to the building committee, meeting on January 9th, 1964, was a very basic one. 'Let us discuss', he said, 'the nature and the anatomy of the theatre ... '

It must have been like putting a stick into a crowded pond, and watching the minnows, previously lying still, dart away in all directions. On the building committee, Olivier and Marshall had brought together some of the most intelligent, imaginative and thoughtful men of the theatre, not just in Britain, but perhaps in the world. Brook was a member, the *enfant terrible* who had not been tamed by growing up, who would take an 'established' theatrical idea, turn it upside-down and shake the clichés from its crowded pockets. Hall was another, seeking a clarity and precision from the theatre which matched academic enlightenment. Michel St Denis, who had always insisted that new theatrical architecture must precede the kind of new dramatic styles for which he craved, sat near George Devine, his comrade from the

Old Vic theatre centre days and the builder *par excellence* of the new wave of British drama. The determined Gaskill was there, with Dexter; and Michael Elliott, perhaps the coolest mind on the building committee, very practical and impatient with dogma. Michael Benthall was a member, like Elliott a former director of the Old Vic; and two theatrical designers, both associated with the establishment of open-stage theatres, Roger Furse, who had worked with Olivier at Chichester, and Tanya Moiseiwitsch, a colleague of Tyrone Guthrie at Stratford, Ontario. Kenneth Tynan was often present, invited by Olivier to be an *ex officio* member—known to favour proscenium-arch, rather than open, stages, but eager to see both.

It was a marvellous collection of intelligences, with scarcely a common approach between them but simply with a common aim, to build the best possible theatre. Lasdun had to listen, abstract the essentials from what they were saying and discover the architectural solutions. They met regularly, on the first Wednesday of each month, and they talked about everything connected with the theatre, the seating arrangements, the shape of the stage, the plays to be staged, the problems of actors and the relationship between the theatre and the outside world. Elliott, for example, was in favour of tiering the audience, in circles and balconies, arguing that this was the only way by which more people could be brought into an auditorium without extending the distance of the last row of seats from the stage. This traditional argument could not, of course, be left unchallenged. Gaskill believed that tiered auditoria separate audiences into class groups—the richest people occupying the stalls and dress circles, the poor ones above. 'Though old theatres have charm,' he said, 'they are hierarchical'—to which Elliott could have retorted that the more people who can be seated sensibly in a theatre the better. By cutting out the circles, you simply are likely to restrict the numbers of people who see the productions, which cannot make a theatre more democratic. But was it a good idea to have a large auditorium, seating maybe 1,500 to 2,000? Did not the very size affect the necessary intimacy of a theatre, that almost tangible audience-actor relationship which was the theatre's greatest asset over the mass media? Furthermore, large auditoria bring pressures to bear upon the managements, who must behave cautiously. An audience of 900 at the Old Vic means a triumphant success, with 'House Full' notices outside the box-office; but a similar audience at Drury Lane means a flop, with the house more than half empty. Large theatres demand large popular shows—and was this what a National should provide?

All members of the building committee agreed that it was essential that every member of the audience at the National should be able to see and hear properly—which led to the acceptance of the principle, expressed by Peter Hall, that nobody should be seated further than about sixty feet from the stage, or rather, from the 'point of command'—which can roughly be interpreted as the stage's focal point. But spatial measurements of this sort were not enough. At Chichester the seats were all within a sixty-five-foot radius of the stage, but the building committee knew that this did not mean that all parts of the audience could see and hear equally well. Olivier in particular wanted 'as equal intensity as possible' around the auditorium at all times. He stressed 'intensity'. This meant that every member of the audience had to be, as far as possible, under the command of the actor's most potent weapon, his eyes, and to catch every nuance of the voice. Mere audibility was not good enough, and at Chichester, Olivier realized (even without Tynan telling him so) that his asides were not equally effective to all parts of the audience.

This emphasis on an 'equal intensity' finally decided Lasdun and the building committee against an adaptable theatre. It would have been possible to engineer a retractable forestage, a moveable proscenium arch and to design variable blocks of seating; but to provide 'equal intensity' for both types of stage, it would have been necessary to alter the whole shape of the room, its walls, ceilings and seating angles: an impossible task. But was it possible, without having an adaptable theatre, nevertheless to design one which would be equally suitable for those plays (Greek, Elizabethan and modern 'epic' drama) which seemed to require open staging and for those which needed a proscenium arch? A remark from Michel St Denis gave Lasdun a clue for a possible design. 'What I am dreaming about', said St Denis, 'is a space stage that would give the feeling of the audience and the actors being in the same room.'

At that, Lasdun doodled on a piece of paper. 'Really what you're all asking for', he said, 'is a room'—and he drew a square—'with a stage in the corner.' There was, he recalled, 'a sort of silence in the room, because it was very basic'—and he scribbled seats around it—and then 'somebody tried to take the drawing away from me, but I grabbed it back, because I knew we were on to something, but I knew it was simplistic and we had a long, long journey ahead of us before we found out what it was.' This basic pattern—for a stage set in one right-angle of a square room with seats banked around it—formed the nucleus for an idea which was known as Scheme A, shown to the building committee in March 1964.

Scheme A was a development from this doodle, which also bore in mind the needs of an adaptable theatre. It was not adaptable as such, but it was an attempt 'to encompass the greatest range possible between an "open" and a "closed" [i.e. proscenium-arch] solution'. There was no proscenium as such, but the ceiling was graded down, step by step, to a corner stage; and one of these 'steps' was where a proscenium would normally be. It therefore gave the feeling of a proscenium without actually having one: and above the stage was some limited flying capacity, normally excluded from an open stage. This plan was a step forward. Above all, the architects had defined the crucial architectural difference between open and closed stages. 'Closed' was defined as a single-direction stage, providing confrontation, and 'open' was one giving the possibility of viewing the action from more than one angle, thus emphasizing its three-dimensional quality.

Nobody was happy with Scheme A. It was a compromise between 'confrontation' and 'embracement', geometrically neat, but without flair. Nor did it satisfy searching criteria. The flying capacity was too limited, while the atmosphere within the auditorium was considered likely to be 'cold' and 'formal'. 'This', said Peter Brook, 'was what I dreaded'—in short, a Civil Service theatre. Lasdun, of course, would never have allowed Scheme A to be built. It was a deliberate 'Aunt Sally', a proposal put forward whose main purpose was to stimulate the arguments as to why it was not desirable. The knocking down of wrong ideas was part of the process of discovering the right solution.

The compromise theatre, like the adaptable one, had to go. A decision had to be taken. The theatre either had to have an 'open' stage, or a proscenium one, or the theatre complex had to contain both. By May 1964, it had been agreed with the South Bank Theatre and Opera House Board that two theatres were necessary, of which one would be a straightforward proscenium-arch theatre, seating about 700 people. In addition, Lasdun submitted plans for an uncompromising open-stage theatre, as Scheme B. Again, the shape of the auditorium was to be a square, with a stage in the corner, and with the audience facing it around a 90° arc. There was, however, no graded ceiling, and the flying capacity was limited. The scenery was envisaged primarily in terms of three-dimensional objects, trucked in from rear stages or dropped by spot-line flying. There would be no feeling that the audience and actors were 'in separate rooms'.

Scheme B was accepted much more wholeheartedly by the building committee. It provided the basis for future plans, and a model was shown at a press conference on May 26th, 1965. The directors on the

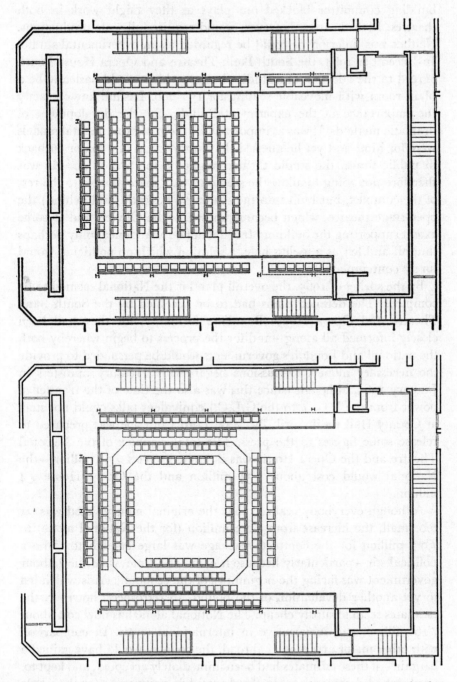

Figure 3   (a) and (b) Two plans for alternative seating arrangements in the Cottesloe Theatre

building committee blocked out plays as they might work in both theatres. Both theatres, however, would require full-scale productions. Neither was 'inferior' or could be regarded as an experimental studio. In December 1964, the South Bank Theatre and Opera House Board agreed to the addition of a studio theatre, which would basically be a plain room with moveable seating for 150–200. Lasdun knew exactly the importance of the experimental studio for the development of dramatic methods. It was as important for them as experimental models were for him; and yet he guessed that in the event of a major cutback in public funds, the studio theatre might be the first to go. He was therefore not going to allow the studio to be a mere annexe to the rest of the complex, but built into the structure, beneath (and behind) the open-stage theatre, which became known as the Olivier, and to some extent supporting the building. It could not be abandoned, only perhaps shut off and left as a useless hole, a solution which no politician would surely contemplate.

By the spring of 1965, the overall plan for the National seemed to be complete. The detailed plans had to be accepted by the South Bank Theatre and Opera House Board—a formality, for they had been closely informed all along—and for the process to begin whereby both the national and London's governments would be persuaded to provide the necessary money. Discussions began with Treasury ministers in January 1965, although (since this was also the time of the transfer of power from the L.C.C. to the G.L.C.) equivalent talks could not start at County Hall until April. By May, Lord Cottesloe was prepared to release some figures to the press. The total complex of the National Theatre and the Opera House was estimated to cost £9½ million—the National would cost about £5½ million and the Opera House £4 million.

Although everybody realized that the original money voted was far too small, the increase from £2·3 million (for the National alone) to £9·5 million for the complete package was large enough to cause a political stir—particularly because it came at a time when the Labour government was facing the beginnings of the economic crisis which led to yet another devaluation of the pound. In retrospect, however, the estimates seem absurdly cheap. The National alone has now cost about £16 million, still inexpensive in international terms. In comparison with other major arts centres abroad, the country would have gained a bargain—if these estimates had been immediately accepted, and kept to. Lasdun had designed a marvellously satisfying city-scape for the whole area between Hungerford Bridge and County Hall. Cottesloe called it, with a justifiable pride which some mistook as propaganda, a model for 'the finest architectural group in London, the Royal Naval College with the Queen's House at Greenwich always excepted'.

Lasdun had incorporated the tower block of the Shell Building into his design, previously considered an intractable eyesore, and had managed to persuade the Shell authorities to modify their rights concerning a strip of land between their block and the river. This land was now the 'valley' between the Opera House and the National Theatre, but in the model it was occupied by a sequence of small piazzas, each overlooking the river, which graded upwards towards the main theatres, and their fly towers. The appearance was of foothills leading with natural and rhythmic logic to the mountains behind.

Although the Opera House from the early days of discussions about the South Bank had been considered a necessary part of the development there was no formal government commitment for it, unlike the National. Beset with economic crises, the Labour government in the mid-1960s wanted to cut down on all public expenditure to which it was not already committed. Goodman, now a lord, had succeeded Cottesloe as chairman of the Arts Council in May 1965, and he was apprehensive that the new Opera House might conflict with the interests of Covent Garden. Opera companies are notoriously expensive to run: Covent Garden was by far the largest single item then on the Arts Council's bill. The decision about the South Bank Opera House was dumped on his desk during his first few months of office, and it was an agonizing question. Should the Arts Council join in trying to persuade the government to build it? Despite the troubles, Jennie Lee was a powerful voice in the Cabinet, not inhibited by being nominally Anthony Crosland's 'inferior' at the Department of Education. Goodman came to the conclusion that the Opera House was unnecessary — for there were two other theatres in London (the Coliseum and the Palace) which could house Sadler's Wells. For the National, however, he was prepared to fight. 'I have to say that in my heart of hearts,' he once admitted in a private conversation, 'I was never absolutely sure we would not have been as well served by Drury Lane or the Haymarket ... but Denys Lasdun had designed a marvellous building. It may be liked or not liked, but because the designs were there, we would have been cowardly not to build it.'

Political opposition to the proposed Opera House grew during 1965 and the early months of 1966, until in March Cottesloe was forced to announce that, while government permission had been received to build the National, a decision on the Opera House was to be deferred for a year. Privately, although the lobbying went on, the Opera House supporters (of whom Stephen Arlen was particularly vocal) feared that the Opera House would be shelved indefinitely, and thus the Lasdun plan for the overall riverside panorama was ruined.

It was a cruel blow. Furthermore, in the months of waiting, the impetus which had led to the formulation of the plans was petering away into doubts and worries. The building committee did not meet with Lasdun for a year, from January 1965 to March 1966, and in the meantime fears were forming about Scheme B. Tynan, for example, was privately objecting to the open-stage plans, putting forward those arguments which he had already expressed with considerable force from the start; but the building committee, in planning 'mock' productions on the model for Scheme B, had come across various problems. There was, for example, a 'no-man's land' behind the main acting area; and the stage seemed too large in relationship to the auditorium. The seating plan was considered too rigidly formal. They were all curable faults, but the building committee was worried that Lasdun might not listen to them. The long absence meant a loss of confidence in their special relationship. They drafted a list of complaints, very formally, which could have meant the end to the whole project as planned. Peter Hall, for example, was having doubts about the 'point of command' on the open stage. The actor had to be able to 'contact' each section of the audience without turning his head—and this requirement in itself seemed to conflict with the three-dimensional nature of the open stage. Brook was also worried. His view was that the auditorium suffered from being designed in too mathematically perfect a way. The theatre was an 'imprecise' art, depending on a kind of community growth, with compromises and fellow-feeling somehow providing, perhaps accidentally, the circumstances in which drama could thrive.

This composite list of complaints was handed to Lasdun in April 1966. He read them, and offered a new plan, Scheme C, which was considered by everyone, the building committee and the architects, to be 'dull', although it did meet with some of the objections to Scheme B. There was, for example, now improved flying capacity. In the meantime, from June to December 1966, the more straightforward designs for the proscenium theatre were approved. It would seat 900 people, rather more than the building committee had wanted, altered under some pressure from Lord Goodman and others who believed that the lower seating capacity (of 800) would leave the theatre particularly uneconomic to run, and have a stage opening of between 40 and 57 feet,

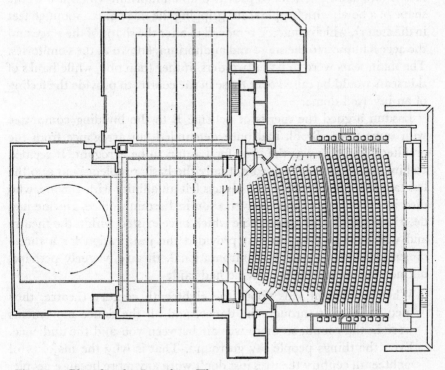

Figure 4 Plan for the Lyttelton Theatre

with a height of 24 feet. The seats were all within 70 feet of the stage
(not 60, which Hall had indicated as the optimum distance) and the
seating plan contained certain features, such as cheaper 'ripple' seats
in the front rows of the stalls. There was one balcony, very non-
hierarchical. The South Bank Board accepted this detailed design for
the proscenium-arch theatre 'enthusiastically' in December 1966.

But the problems remained with the open stage. Gradually, however,
Lasdun and Peter Softley were working towards a solution which started
to arouse their enthusiasm; more than enthusiasm perhaps, a conviction
that this was the way in which the theatre should work. They had been
experimenting with modifications to Scheme B, involving a smaller
stage (35 feet in diameter) and a single tier of seating banked around.
This scheme was shown to the building committee as Scheme D, but it
was not the one which aroused Lasdun's enthusiasm. He had realized
that what was wanted was a relaxed 'armchair' effect for the auditorium, retaining the basic dynamics and structure of Scheme B, but
providing a less angular and more organic effect, 'pure geometry of the

most subtle kind'. Scheme E provided an auditorium which was in the shape of a bowl, with 'ripple seats' gripping the stage area (about 36 feet in diameter), which could be removed to alter the shape of the stage and the access tunnels to the stage and auditorium, known as the vomitories. The main seats were to be in two tiers, rather than one, while banks of side seats would be raised over those in the centre, to provide the feeling of an inverted dome.

Lasdun argued the merits of Scheme E to the building committee with some force. Brook had once demanded 'an arrogance from the architect' and this was the time for Lasdun to be arrogant. It seemed to him that Scheme E solved not only the basic problems, but also the less tangible ones. Lasdun had always felt an affinity with Devine, who died in 1966. In a private conversation in Lasdun's office, Devine had described the kind of atmosphere which once existed within the theatre and was hard to recapture. It provided the justification for a three-dimensional, as opposed to confrontational, theatre, vaguely perhaps, but not just theoretically. Devine had said:

> When we taught kids about the eighteenth century theatre, they used to learn it through the dance, and all the dance movements were in the round, so there was air between you and the audience. Even the things people say go round. That is why the majority of eighteenth century theatres just don't work any more because people, except rather sophisticated people, don't want this kind of elaboration, which is why the director is such an important dramatist, although he is not particularly popular, because there is this harsh direct thing all the time. It's an angular attitude to the situation.

These words stuck in Lasdun's mind, and it seemed to him that Scheme E managed to provide that community feeling within the theatre. The physical shape promoted the comradely spirit.

The building committee pondered and declared themselves delighted. Olivier stated to the South Bank Theatre Board:

> This auditorium and stage answers everything we have asked for in terms of an 'open' solution. It has perfect sight-lines; and an acting area of the right size; the possibility of having enthusiastic members of the audience close to the stage; the possibility of modifying the configuration of the seating against the stage to amplify the thrust or take a more bland view. It will have a marvellous atmosphere.

The board were equally happy.

Denys Lasdun & Partners, as architects, were concerned with the design of the building; the design of the stage equipment, and most of

NATIONAL THEATRE PRODUCTIONS: 23 (*above*) Peter Shaffer's *The Royal Hunt of the Sun*, 1964
24 (*below left*) Sir Laurence Olivier and Maggie Smith in *Othello*, 1964 25 (*below right*) Diana
Rigg and Alec McCowen in Molière's *The Misanthrope*, 1973

26 *Left to right:* Lord Cottesloe, Lord Goodman and the Rt Hon. Baroness Lee

27 Sir Laurence Olivier looking through the window of the temporary offices of the National Theatre in Aquinas Street

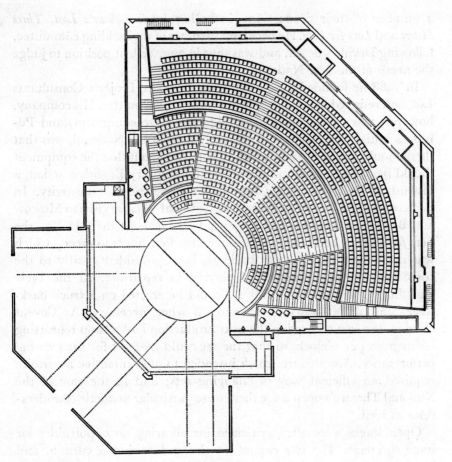

Figure 5   Plan for the Olivier Theatre

those technical facilities concerned with putting on plays were outside their brief and were the responsibility of another firm, Theatre Projects Consultants Ltd (as they became known), who occupied a comparable role towards the stage equipment contractors as Lasdun did to McAlpine's, who were later chosen as the building contractors. They too were 'architects', rather than builders or suppliers of equipment.

Richard Pilbrow, a lighting designer, had originally founded Theatre Projects Ltd in 1957, a firm primarily concerned with the design of lighting and sound equipment. The company gradually expanded into the fields of a producing management in London, whose shows included *Fiddler on the Roof* and *Cabaret*, while it also advised and designed equipment for various new repertory theatres in Britain. Pilbrow himself became the lighting director for the National Theatre; and he had lit a number of their productions, including *Love's Labour's Lost*, *Three Sisters* and *Love for Love*. He became a member of the building committee, following Devine's death, and was thus in an excellent position to judge the needs of the new National.

In 1968 he founded a new company, Theatre Projects Consultants Ltd, and resigned as a member of the building committee. His company, however, was commissioned to design the stage equipment, and Pilbrow's initial view, formed in the early days of the National, was that there should not be too much technical trickery, but that the equipment should be plain, simple and practical. It was a very English reaction, a distrust of elaborate technology and a preference for austerity. In September 1965, however, during the National Theatre visits to Moscow and Berlin, his opinions had somewhat changed. At the Old Vic, the *Love for Love* set had taken twenty-five men four hours to erect — which was not only a cumbersome business, but also added greatly to the costs and the inconvenience of playing in repertoire. At the Freie Volksbühne in East Berlin, the set could be erected on a truck backstage, and simply wheeled on and off when necessary. At Covent Garden, the cast rehearsing the next production had to stop rehearsing on stage at one o'clock, so that the set could be built for the evening performance. Any theatre which intended to offer intensive repertoire required an efficient way of changing sets; and in the case of the National Theatre's open stage there were particular aesthetic considerations as well.

Open stages were often criticized for allowing no opportunity for stage spectacle. The sets cannot be changed behind a curtain, and blackouts can rarely be so absolutely black that scenery can be assembled to surprise an audience. Since it was necessary for economic and practical reasons to have a system for changing sets rapidly in repertoire, it looked desirable to go further so that sets could be rapidly changed on an open stage during performances. This could mean simply trucking full sets on from side stages, but there were practical limits to this system, among them the capacity of the side stages. Pilbrow was attracted to a kind of stage already in use at the Burgtheater in Vienna. This contained a large revolving stage (behind a proscenium arch) which had in it four large rectangular elevators. It was possible to sink two of these lifts, to receive a set from a lower stage level, which thus meant that you could have side and back stages containing built sets, beneath the stage as well, and so double the capacity for scene changes. In addition, the revolve would swing round, so that there would be no awkward time-gap while sets were trundled on.

Pilbrow analysed the Burgtheater stage carefully: he wrote a pamphlet on it. He noticed that it had certain problems which could be particularly difficult to overcome on the National Theatre's open stage. The fact that the elevators were rectangular meant that the set could not fill the semicircular area of one half of the revolve: carpets might overlap, and there might be no way of quickly getting rid of an odd downstage chair. Pilbrow therefore proposed that instead of having rectangular elevators within the floor of the revolve, the revolve instead should be split in half, with both semicircles being lifts which could be raised and lowered to receive sets. This split-revolve should be placed inside an outer drum-revolve, whose purpose would be to turn one semicircular set around on the stage, so that it could face the audience at different angles, while the second half of the split-revolve could sink to a lower level perhaps and swing round independently of the drum-revolve to receive the next set.

It was a complicated modification, but there seemed no reason why it should not work. Pilbrow also wanted to discover a satisfactory method of flying scenery for an open stage. The scenery was likely to be three-dimensional, which ruled out ordinary fly-bars—straight pipes hung above the stage on which flats and other two-dimensional pieces of scenery could be hung—and suggested a system known as spot-line flying. Under this system, instead of raising and lowering fly-bars, there is a grid above the stage, consisting of a number of tracks. Along these tracks run individual pulleys and hoists, like small cranes on a building site. Lines sliding through these pulleys hook on to parts of the set, which can thus be raised and lowered.

> We began to search around the world for all available methods of achieving this [i.e. spot-line flying] satisfactorily. Finally, we discovered that there were no truly satisfactory systems then existing and new developments had to be initiated to meet the criteria we had set ourselves. These criteria included a system that was absolutely safe, that could move scenery at least as rapidly and sensitively as a human being was able to do in conventional circumstances and was capable of taking the required estimated loads and position them with great accuracy [Richard Pilbrow, 'Innovations' in *Architectural Review*, January 1977].

Pilbrow also felt that there should be some way of handling scenery with the simple touch control of a lightboard: all that humping and heaving in a technological age was expensive and old-fashioned. And so, gradually, Pilbrow was drawn away from the tried and simple mechanisms of traditional British theatres towards innovatory techniques.

Meanwhile, with the basic architectural design more or less settled, there remained the question of relating the internal theatres to the outward appearance of the National Theatre complex — and to the riverside and the town. The inspiration for the external theatre remained similar to that shown in 1965 — a sequence of overhanging terraces receding rhythmically from the riverside, leading to the brooding fly-tower of the Olivier Theatre and the lesser fly-tower of the proscenium-arch theatre, the Lyttelton, which balanced it. These terraces served a double purpose. They enabled the audiences to wander out from the foyers to overlook the river, thus linking the internal building to the spaces of the surrounding city. They also provided what Lasdun termed the 'fourth' theatre — which meant both the external panorama of city life, and places where street theatre and other forms of open-air entertainment could take place. Within the foyers too, spaces had been planned to serve a variety of purposes — as interval meeting places for audiences, forums for poetry readings and informal music sessions.

The key question, however, was still the site. If the Opera House was not going to be built, half the landscape in the 1965 plans would go. The National Theatre would be the unbalanced half of an incomplete design. The government in 1966 was still reluctant to commit itself, and the G.L.C. was even more reluctant to go ahead without full government support. After a year's indecision, the G.L.C. decided to make alternative plans, without the Opera House.

In February 1967, the G.L.C. wrote to the South Bank Theatre and Opera House Board with the suggestion of an alternative site. They thought that, in the absence of an Opera House, the National Theatre should be relocated to a site next to Waterloo Bridge (downstream), on a derelict patch, euphemistically known as Prince's Meadow. This would enable the G.L.C. to develop the site in front of the Shell Building for new council offices — if necessary; but its chief advantage was that the National Theatre would no longer seem part of an aesthetically incomplete pattern. It would relate to Waterloo Bridge instead of a bare patch where the Opera House ought to have been. There were other advantages too. Prince's Meadow had better access from Waterloo roundabout, and a more dramatic view over the river. The site was also a little larger, although it would require some additional support to the river wall. The changed site would not require vast changes in the National's basic design; but the angle of the building would have to be altered. Instead of the main foyer and the building being angled downstream, the entrance would be directed towards Waterloo Bridge, hence angled upstream. The upper terraces would have a walkway leading directly on to the bridge, while the rear side of the building, above the entrance for cars, would hold the offices for the National, each with spectacular views down the river.

The South Bank Theatre and Opera House Board considered the idea and discussed it with Lasdun, who made some suggestions. They agreed eventually and, by September 1967, formal planning permission was sought to build the National Theatre on the Prince's Meadow site. The board also reluctantly dropped the Opera House from its title. It was now officially to be known by its familiar shortened form, the South Bank Theatre Board. The very deep, and even bitter, regrets which lay in the wake of the decision not to build the Opera House, were at least tempered with the thought that at last the site had been chosen—and was not likely to be chosen again—and that the design for the National Theatre had received approval (even acclaim) all round. It was only necessary now to build the thing.

If the board were under the impression, however, that there would be an easy ride from now on, they would have been much mistaken— for there were wrangles ahead with the government (who in 1968, faced by a worsening economic situation in the country, nearly cancelled the whole project), and with the G.L.C. (for some members of the newly elected Tory majority wanted to abandon the project and, when they decided that such drastic action was unwise, suggested cuts in the scheme which had to be fought, line by line, brick by brick), and with inflation, and with the contractors, and with the labour force on the site—and even with Parliament, for new Acts had to be brought before the Commons to enable extra money to be raised. The most tiresome struggles, in a sense, were still ahead—and it required the combined determinations of Cottesloe, Chandos, Goodman, Jennie Lee and Olivier to drive the project forward, even at what seemed a desperately slow pace.

To encourage them, however, they had a scheme for a building which might well become, in Devine's phrase, 'a monument to our time'. What characterized this 'monument' was not its technical complexity nor the innovatory nature of the Olivier Theatre, but its humanism. Hall once summarized its basic premise: 'What never varies in architecture', he said, 'is the scale of the human body.' The complex had been designed with this human scale in mind. It influenced the size of the auditoria, with its strict concentration on proper sight-lines, intimacy and good acoustics. The two boards, and the building committee, from Chandos and Cottesloe to Gaskill and Brook, had stressed endlessly that the theatres should not be too large, simply for economic reasons. Nobody wanted vast mausoleums to drama on the South Bank; nobody, that is, who worked on the project. Lasdun had extended this premise to apply to the surroundings of the complex, so that the terraces, foyers and paths would also be of a human scale. The ceilings would be low in the foyer, the carpeting warm and friendly, the tiles in a blue brick which would glow with age. In contrast, the reinforced concrete blocks from which the structure would be built would be deliberately roughened with the lines of their wooden casts, to take away the harshness of plain concrete. The concrete itself was chosen to whiten, not darken, with age; and in time, Lasdun hoped that the building would seem to grow out of the river, slightly stained with lichens. 'The majesty of the river', he said at the start, 'was what I believe will influence me most'—but this majesty was to be tamed to provide an area where people could live naturally, enjoy themselves without being overawed or intimidated. They would seem to 'belong' to the theatre, as the theatre belonged to them, and both would 'belong' to the side of the tidied-up Thames, to London, and the country beyond.

In his essay 'The Soul of Man under Socialism', Oscar Wilde wrote that 'a map of the world that does not include Utopia is not worth even glancing at'; but a map which only shows Utopia is a waste of parchment. Lasdun's theatre seemed to combine ideals with practicality. Appropriateness was all—appropriateness to its situation, to its art form and to the people who would inhabit it. There were aspects of it which were innovatory and experimental, however, which still needed to be tested in practice. It was also a building on a scale bigger than anything which British theatre contractors had so far attempted. Their competence had to be tested. Furthermore, ideas of appropriateness change. Though the scale of the human body might be a constant factor, as Hall pointed out, what is considered appropriate to house those bodies does alter. Reinhardt's sense of proportion was not the same as Grotowski's; and the ancient Greeks (as Lasdun knew well) built superbly appropriate theatres for their times, seating 20,000 and more. Sixty years before, it would have seemed highly inappropriate to spend so much money on the theatre and so little on the company for which it was being built. The grant to the National itself could have been considered disproportionately large in comparison with the grants to other theatres. Appropriateness was not just an ideal, it could be a rhetorical weapon easy to turn against those who were wielding it.

13

Four Green Bottles

From the start, the National Theatre Company had been under-capitalized. The South Bank Theatre Board knew that this was so, so did the management team, the administration and the company itself. If they didn't know at first, then they just had to look around at the row of Nissen huts, first in Duchy Street, then in Aquinas Street, and the general atmosphere of hand-to-mouth improvising which pervaded their temporary headquarters, to realize the truth. Chandos and Olivier may have hoped that the Dunkirk spirit would see them through, for the government grant of £130,000 to establish the company and carry it through the opening year was £20,000 less than Granville Barker had deemed necessary in 1903.

It couldn't be helped. Chandos was relieved to get the company going at all, following the split with Stratford. But the difference between running two theatres (with the one at Stratford potentially profitable) on £230,000 and one small, unprofitable theatre on £130,000 with a still unformed company, was considerable. Before the National had opened its box-office, £117,000 of this grant had been spent, leaving £13,000 for the rest of the year. A loan from the S.M.N.T. trust helped them, together with some touring grants from the Arts Council (£10,000) — but the National still ended its first year showing a substantial deficit, £22,500, with much of its original capital investment still unpaid and, in a sense, unsecured — except by the thought that no country would surely allow its National Theatre to founder, or at any rate not so quickly.

By the second year, the situation was much more serious. The deficit had swollen to £139,000, which was enough to cause press complaints that Chandos had too free a way with overdrafts. By the end of the 1965–6 financial year, the running deficit was nearly £¼ million, a small sum by current National standards, but then quite critical. Fortunately, Jennie Lee had arrived and the National was riding along on the crest of a wave. In February 1966, Jennie Lee announced to the Commons that the government intended to spend £2¾ million more on the arts, an increase of a third in the Arts Council's budget, and part of this sum was earmarked to wipe off, in progressive stages, the National's deficit.

That was the good news. But it brought with it a nagging little doubt, no more than a small cloud on the horizon. Was the National always going to be bailed out like that? What about other, less privileged companies? During the middle to late 1960s, when more money was regularly being injected into the theatre, potentially jealous rivals were kept quiet and pacified. If the National were getting more, so were they. If the time came, however, when government support for the National might mean sacrificing other companies, then of course the rows would begin. There was also the question of status. If the National's position at the top of the theatrical ladder were to be preserved, whether its productions justified it or not, by the mere size of its subsidies, then its rivals would also be envious. Peter Hall was one of the first to realize the implications of such decisions. He had received a polite but firm warning from the Treasury. In 1962, Hall had argued that the Royal Shakespeare Company too was operating, and would continue to do so, on 'a National Theatre level'. The Treasury replied:

> If this statement means no more than that their productions will in due course have to compete with those of the National Theatre, there can be no quarrel with it. I am bound to put formally on record, however, and to ask you to tell the Royal Shakespeare Theatre authorities that the Treasury would not be able to accept any wider implications which might be held to flow from any such assumption.

The 'wider implications', of course, referred to the possibility of grants to the R.S.C. on a National Theatre level. 'The civil service English', commented Hall, 'masks an iron hand.'

During its early years, however, the National was in debt, and nobody knew quite where the money was going to come from to keep it going. It could not be raised through the box-office at the Old Vic, for the full-house takings per performance only amounted to about £700. A week of full houses would barely pay the staff and the company, leaving nothing to finance further productions. A commercial management could have considered one of two alternatives. The seat prices could have been raised or the National could have taken over a larger, possibly a West End, theatre for one of their hit productions. These solutions were both difficult for the National. To raise the seat prices would have led to the charge that the National, a publicly subsidized theatre, was simply catering to the rich middle classes. It would have antagonized the Old Vickers and may have been self-defeating in that the very high attendance figures (around 85 per cent) could have dropped. The second idea—to take over a larger theatre—required complicated forward planning, to avoid breaking up the National Theatre company, which was already in danger of being fragmented by the tours and the seasons at Chichester. Eventually, a short ten-week season was arranged with H. M. Tennent Ltd at the Queen's Theatre, which began on August 4th, 1966, and included three 'hits': *A Flea In Her Ear*, *Trelawny of the 'Wells'* and *Love for Love*. This season was the first of several National excursions into the West End, but it did not solve the immediate problem of the deficit. It provided (on this occasion) a little more pocket-money, but there were some (Lord Goodman among them) who wondered what the National was doing in the West End? It was not extending a range of audience—those who came to the Queen's could have come to the Old Vic—and was the mere marketing of a National production to favoured Londoners and tourists a policy which should occupy a high place on the National's list of priorities?

The only other solution was to economize. But how and where? It was an article of faith that the productions themselves should not suffer. Therefore, the production costs were not cut. They remained roughly on a par with those of the R.S.C.: the budgets were estimated at between £7,500 and £16,000, the lower and upper limits, which were by no means excessive. In Europe, state theatres frequently budgeted for production costs of £80,000 or more, which was also the price of staging a large musical in the West End. Nevertheless, as the deficit increased, rumours of production extravagance spread in the press. It was pointed out that Michael Redgrave's five costume changes in *Hamlet* cost £100 a time. 'Someone's going to take a cut in his salary for this,' murmured an actor rather publicly, as he tapped the solid oak scenery built for *The Recruiting Officer*. John Dexter had ordered some contact lenses to change the eye colourings of Maggie Smith and Robert Stephens in *A Bond Honoured*, an effect barely visible from the front rows. Kenny's 'Revolt' was considered an unnecessary luxury, particularly when it didn't work. And so on. Actual poverty magnified the little details of occasional extravagance.

The economies were elsewhere. The size of the company never reached the intended numbers of about 75 or more, starting at about 40 and rising to about 60, with guest stars. The number of new productions dropped, from 9 in the first year, to 6 in the second, 8 in the third year, 4 in the fourth. The highest annual output (from 1963–4) was little more than a fifth of that suggested by Granville Barker for two theatres, and also less than that originally envisaged by Tynan and Olivier. Several interesting plans for productions had to be dropped — Granville Barker's *The Voysey Inheritance* (later produced by the Royal Court) and Alan Sillitoe's translation of *Fuente Ovejuna* by Lope de Vega (eventually presented by an amateur company at the Theatre Workshop, Stratford, East London) among them. These omissions, however, may not have been solely due to careful housekeeping.

From the public's point of view, this drop in output was not particularly important. The National's repertoire during these years contained enough successes to keep the Old Vic, and probably several other theatres if they had been available, going with pride and every evidence of its far-ranging ambitions. Inside the company, however, frustrations were mounting. Gaskill, for example, directed nothing during his last year as associate director on the National, 1965–6. There was not room within the budget for productions which directors just wanted to do, for experiment's sake perhaps; and the pressures of success shouldered out initiative. Indeed, in retrospect, it is surprising that the National could be as adventurous as it was. Actors and actresses too were not given the parts which had been informally offered to them; and there were rumours of favouritism — which always exist in the theatre but which can be damaging to the company spirit.

Loyalty was particularly important, because so many of the most talented (and best-known) members of the team were receiving salaries far below their normal commercial rates. Low wages were another aspect of the National's economies. Tynan received £46 a week, with expenses; and Virginia Fairweather, the press officer, £40. Even in the late 1960s and early 1970s, there were complaints about the low sums paid to visiting (British) directors. Blakemore and Miller pointed out to Olivier that the sums offered to them for directing National productions were ludicrously low — £500 a time, working out at about £30 a week. They had to subsidize their work for the National from other sources, a situation which Olivier appreciated all too well, for he was doing the same. He subsidized himself by taking on films, which he was not entirely happy about, and commercials on television — in the United States, for he thought it inappropriate that the National's Director should appear in television commercials in Britain. If one encouraging side to this state of affairs was that nobody went to the National just for the money, the discouraging aspect was that nobody would want to battle through the inevitable frustrations to hold on to a good job. The stability of the company depended upon patriotism and happiness within the team.

It was probably easier for the younger and less well-known actors and actresses within the company to feel this dedication. To be chosen for the National was a great honour. It meant that they would be working with the finest actors in the world and some excellent directors. Their opportunities outside the National were less tempting; and the chances inside the company were excellent. Louise Purnell, for example, had originally been picked as a dancer. She was chosen then as an understudy in *Hay Fever*, took over when the actress who was playing the part fell ill, and subsequently was picked for a leading role in Olivier's production of *The Crucible*. The early days at the National made the names of many previously 'unknown' young professionals — Edward Petherbridge, Ronald Pickup, Derek Jacobi, John Stride, Colin Blakely, Robert Lang, as well as Maggie Smith, Robert Stephens and Frank Finlay, who were better known than the others but whose work at the National elevated them to the rank of stars. Among the 'middle' range of actors, the National gave the opportunity to play parts other than those for which they had previously been known. If Stephens's performance as Atahualpa was the prime example, there were also the chances offered to such known but underrated actors as Anthony Hopkins (who eventually played Coriolanus and Macbeth, having started by just walking on in *Love For Love*), Denis Quilley (a one-time singer, who became a stalwart for the National), Jim Dale, Jeremy Brett and John Moffatt.

The situation was much more difficult for established actors, stars, either visiting or in residence. It was not just, or even primarily, the question of money. The problem was really that they were being squeezed on both sides in an unloving fashion. 'Beneath' them was a solid core of talented young men and women, who had worked together in several productions, gathering confidence and skill all the time. They were encouraged by at least one of the associate directors, Gaskill, to think of themselves as a democratically organized permanent company, and thus to question (if not to resent) big names. Above them, however, was Olivier, who could be very generous with younger men, but apprehensive about possible rivals. Of the visiting 'stars' to the National, Redgrave and Finney stayed the longest, each for about a year; and Finney was Olivier's first choice as his successor. Gielgud came in to play Orgon in Guthrie's production of *Tartuffe* and Oedipus in Peter Brook's production of Seneca's play. That was in 1968, and despite the success of *Oedipus*, he did not return until Peter Hall's *The Tempest*—in March 1974. Edward Woodward, Christopher Plummer and Paul Scofield all came and went. Edith Evans and Celia Johnson paid equally short visits, although they at least can have felt no rivalry with Olivier.

The dilemma of the 'stars' was afterwards used as an argument for doing without a practising theatre man at the head of the National, but choosing an *Intendant* as Director. But within the company, it developed into another kind of conflict—about whether the National should have 'stars' at all. Tynan was in favour of them—and Gaskill against; and this led to one of the minor rows which helped to precipitate the first management crisis of Olivier's regime. The quarrel stemmed from discussions about the 1966–7 season and Gaskill's fear that Tynan was having too much influence over Olivier:

> Ken suddenly started to talk about the need for more stars. I objected and said to Larry: 'I can understand that you have to rely on Ken's advice about the choice of plays. But I don't think in any circumstances he should be allowed to dictate the choice of actors. That's not his business as literary manager.' It developed into a big row and I'm afraid that I got very angry. Larry left the room and went upstairs. He re-appeared about half-an-hour later and said, 'I have to tell you that I must have Ken involved in all these discussions.' It was at that point that I knew it was no good going on, I couldn't work in that kind of set-up [Gourlay, *op. cit.*, pp. 176–7].

This was an issue in which many conflicting minor principles were involved. Gaskill may have feared the 'special relationship' between Tynan and Olivier, if it existed; but equally Olivier wanted to ensure that all major management discussions were 'open' to his closest associates. Otherwise, little rival cliques would have formed. Furthermore, Gaskill's insistence on a fully democratic, organic company could sometimes be irritating. Sometimes the ideal actor did not exist within the company to tackle a particular part; and sometimes practical box-office considerations intervened, which perhaps (from Gaskill's view) should not have interfered with casting, but in practice did and had to. Gaskill's ideals were sometimes rather frightening in their purity. It was surely right to insist on a steady growth in company expertise; but at one company meeting, apparently, an actor stood up and asserted that Gaskill had told them that it was not necessary to be 'ready' for a first night—if their acting performances had not matured to that stage. In some Continental state companies, productions could be held together for a year or more in rehearsal until everyone was totally satisfied with the result—but the National was not working with that size of grant, nor indeed would have wanted to do so, for perfectionism can lead to sterile, unlively productions.

On the other hand, it was true that Tynan did sometimes interfere tactlessly and unwisely. George Devine, the least quarrelsome man by nature, had objected to Tynan's intervention in his production of Beckett's *Play* during the first season. Devine had invited Beckett to the closing stages of the rehearsals, and Beckett had made suggestions. Tynan disagreed with them, thought that Beckett's influence was damaging the production, and said so forcibly. Devine wanted Tynan removed from the theatre.

Gaskill had left by the autumn of 1966, although the first flush of his enthusiasm had grown paler for some months before that. If he distrusted Tynan, he also never felt entirely at ease with Olivier, whom he may have seen as someone who did not entirely fit into his egalitarian vision. Olivier entered into the improvisation sessions for *The Recruiting Officer* courteously and freely, but nobody could pretend that he was just another member of the company. 'Perhaps,' Gaskill said,

I should have approached him differently—in a straightforward technical way. But because, among other things, he was playing a supporting part [Brazen], I had an idea that he should feel the sense of the ensemble—the way we were working and improvising. I think he understood what I was after, though he never quite caught it [Gourlay, *op. cit.*, p. 172].

Equally, in later years, Gaskill discovered that sometimes he needed to work with actors and actresses of special knowledge and talents— which was one reason why he returned to the National to direct *The Beaux' Stratagem*.

Dexter left six months later. He had a row with Olivier during the early rehearsals of the all-male *As You Like It* in March 1967. It was an important production for Dexter. He had spent more than a year planning for it. Its inspiration came from an essay by Jan Kott, in which Kott argued that the humour and clarity of the comedy emerged through sexual ambivalence, which in Shakespeare's case would have been emphasized through his boy actors.

Rosalind plays Ganymede playing Rosalind. She plays her own self marrying Orlando ... The astounding poetry of these scenes has never yet been fully revealed. As if the contemporary theatre did not possess an appropriate instrument ... [Jan Kott, 'Shakespeare's Bitter Arcadia' in *Shakespeare Our Contemporary*, p. 219].

Dexter wanted to find that instrument. It was to be a production which would reflect the new mood of swinging London. He brought in Donovan, the folk singer, to write some songs. When eventually Clifford Williams took over from Dexter, Ronald Pickup, a Dexter choice for Rosalind, played the part looking surprisingly like Twiggy. Everything seemed prepared — when Olivier seemed to get cold feet. He may have thought that Dexter was indulging himself by directing a drag show. Whatever the reason, Dexter found out that schedules had been changed, with *Rosencrantz and Guildenstern Are Dead* replacing his production.

It should not have been an important quarrel, and in the long run perhaps it was not. Dexter and Olivier parted 'on good terms', and when the National was in deep trouble in 1971, Dexter returned. He directed Olivier again, in *The Party* (1974), and they retained a respect for each other. At the time, however, Dexter's departure, so soon after Gaskill, was a major blow. 'If you have a Dexter,' commented Tynan, 'he's wholly irreplaceable.' That was true for several reasons. Unlike Gaskill, Dexter was a pragmatist. The two directors, close friends, balanced each other. Dexter had few rule-of-thumb methods in his approach to productions. 'I have no formula,' he once said. 'You read a play, you like it, you decide to do it, and you find a way of doing it ... it's a private process.' He was, however, prepared to be firm with his actors, including Olivier; for he knew that in the last analysis they relied upon a directorial detachment and incisiveness. Gaskill's approach, relying on discussion, improvisation and group understanding, was an excellent one — up to a point, but it sometimes left productions unpolished and, in a sense, unfinished, for the company process was continuing. Dexter could be an awkward customer, brusque, rude, highly intelligent and sometimes dismissive; but the company relied upon him to know what he wanted and that trust was rarely broken.

The *As You Like It* quarrel was really the outcome of a series of battles between two forceful men, who respected each other but were prepared to fight for their points of view. Their relationship may have been fractious at times, but it was a civilized, usually unmalicious tension. Dexter regarded Olivier as part-Garrick, part-Kean — the gentleman actor and the roaring boy. One side, in production, had to be roughed up, the other calmed down. Their working relationship had been established during *Othello*, and in particular, in Cardiff, the last stage of the pre-London regional tour. Michael Redgrave came down to see the performance, which was taking about fifteen minutes longer than it should have done. Redgrave and Dexter talked about the production in the bar afterwards, and Redgrave suggested that Dexter needed to be tough. 'What you ought to have', he said, 'is a good row with Larry.' Dexter went on the stage and said to the company, 'Ladies and gentlemen, you are letting this play run away with you. You are all being indulgent, all of you, from Sir Laurence downwards.' Olivier was about to leave the stage when he heard this. He said, 'John, I'd like to talk to you in my dressing room.' When Dexter went to see him, Olivier said, 'If you ever talk to me like that again, in front of my company, I'll have your guts for garters.' Dexter retorted with similar force, and they had a massive row, which could be heard through the thin walls of the dressing rooms, and echoed round the rest of the cast. The day after the storm, however, dawned clear, mild and calm. In the hotel, afterwards, Olivier suddenly smiled: 'I think this merits a champagne.' His respect for Dexter increased, and his responsiveness during rehearsals was enhanced. Dexter curbed some of Olivier's slight faults—the temptation, for example, to make too much of his entrances and exits—and as the sturdy Glaswegian Trotskyite in Griffiths's *The Party* Olivier rewarded Dexter with one of his finest, subtlest and most restrained performances.

Dexter may have been one National Theatre director to stand up to Olivier, but equally Olivier felt the need to curb Dexter. Dexter's faults as a director were that he could let his enthusiasms run away with him, providing showy, spectacular productions without much inner content. *Tyger* was perhaps the chief example, in July 1971, but the set for *The Party* was needlessly flamboyant as well. The quarrel over *As You Like It* most probably stemmed from Olivier's fear that Dexter too was becoming self-indulgent, letting himself go at the expense of the text. But, unlike the early days at the National, these two men had now worked together for four years. Dexter had become a world-famous director, really rather keen to try out his talents elsewhere. He was earning between £40 and £50 a week at the National, which did not seem enough for a man in his forties who had no savings behind him, and who could have earned six times that amount elsewhere. He wanted to direct films, operas, work on Broadway with other companies and other actors. Olivier, too, felt that their relationship was likely to turn sour if unduly prolonged.

The loss of Dexter, however, meant that only two of the original four company pillars were left standing; and one of those remaining was showing signs of having been through a major battle. Tynan did not resign from the National company after the *Soldiers* controversy, but his status was damaged, as was that of the National itself in public eyes, and the open battle which resulted was more fundamental to the National's survival than any other had been. It raised so many issues, among them the role of the National Theatre Board, the relationship between the National and the public at large, the extent to which the 'public interest' could be represented by the Board, the dangers of government inter-ference or, more particularly, establishment interests, the extent to which the artistic policy of the National could or should conflict with such interests, the freedom of artists versus the interests of the state, and also perhaps an example of how this 'freedom' might be abused. It was the classic dispute, deriving from seeds of trouble deeply embedded in the whole institution of a National—which, some argued, Tynan's presence nourished. The controversy reached its climax only a month after Dexter's departure, in April 1967.

Tynan had been in trouble with the National Theatre Board before. He disliked Chandos, whom he saw as a typical establishment Tory, very tense and British over matters like sex. Chandos regarded Tynan as a wayward left-wing anarchist, dangerous because his loyalties were suspect and lacking in moral fibre: too clever by half. The first local difficulty had cropped up over Wedekind's *Spring Awakening*, a play about the right and wrong ways to educate adolescents, particularly sexually, which was later performed both by the Royal Court and the National (in 1974). It is an early classic of German Expressionist drama, for which no defence is needed as a play, but in the early 1960s it was still banned by the censor. The Royal Court turned itself into a club theatre for its production. Tynan wanted the National to stage it, with the cuts demanded by the Lord Chamberlain, which meant the omis-sion of one scene; but the board took the view that the standards of the National should be 'above' those of the censor.

Tynan accepted that decision. He turned his attention to the censor instead, providing more useful ammunition in the battle to abolish stage censorship, which was won in 1968. The National Theatre Board established a drama sub-committee, consisting of Sir Kenneth Clark, Hugh Beaumont, Sir Ashley Clarke and Derek Salberg, which served a double purpose. Its role was partly to suggest plays to the company management, and Tynan in particular; but it also provided a kind of *cordon sanitaire* between Tynan and the board. As Tynan grew in con-fidence, this committee became increasingly unnecessary and had dwindled into virtual non-existence before *Soldiers* came on the scene.

Tynan was widely regarded as a 'controversial' figure who needed such protection. Mr Cordle, the Conservative M.P. for Bournemouth East and Christchurch, had asked in the Commons (June 1964) whether he was 'a fit and suitable person to hold such an influential and important position' in view of his 'part in making kitchen sinks, lavatories, drugs, homosexuality and crime standard ingredients for success in the West End?' Tynan's name was a red rag against which the old bulls of the right-wing establishment were always charging, often to find that it had been neatly flicked away at the last moment.

Tynan had consistently maintained that 'no theatre could sanely flourish unless there was an umbilical cord between what was happening on the stage and what was happening in the world outside': a reasonable and indeed non-controversial view, for even Chandos would not have wished the National to stage a programme of purely escapist or 'art' drama. What that umbilical cord should be, of course, was another matter. In the spring of 1966, Tynan was considering various kinds of documentary drama, the Theatre of Fact. Clancy Sigal and Roger Smith were approached to write something about the Cuban missile crisis. There were also plans for a documentary about the General Strike of 1926. 'One of [the] functions of a national theatre', Tynan insisted, 'should be to create a place where the gigantic historical issues, as the Greeks and Shakespeare understood them, could be raised.' Such parallels were totally convincing, as far as they went, but it could be argued that Shakespeare and the Greeks usually acted as apologists for their societies, where Tynan (and the Theatre of Fact movement) intended to be critical. In 1966, for example, Brook had directed a Theatre of Fact play, *US*, an indictment of the United States's involvement in Vietnam, where an actress called for napalm in Hampstead to bring home to the British people the horrors of the war. Could a National have staged such a play? It caused a lot of trouble for Hall and the R.S.C. If the National did so, what would the word National mean—for its stance was directly opposed to that of the British government? Would a government continue to finance a company expressing opinions in open conflict with its own?

Officially, the answer would probably have been a qualified 'yes'. But the qualifications were important. Neither the government nor the National Theatre Board wanted to interfere with the company's artistic policy, but, as Chandos pointed out,

the Board should give the artistic director the greatest independence possible—and, I repeat, possible—in a modern society. This cannot be absolute because certain questions arise which bring wider considerations into play. Now suppose you had a satire of the present government [Labour] — well, only a Board can decide if it's harmlessly amusing ... or concerted propaganda to win a few Conservative votes [*Sunday Times*, April 30th, 1967].

Tynan, however, believed that the freedom of the artistic director should be absolute; and he fought the issue over *Soldiers*. *Soldiers* was an earnest play about an important theme: whether, in times of war, soldiers were justified in using the massacre of civilian populations in order to demoralize and defeat their enemies. Is 'all fair' in war? Rolf Hochhuth, the German historian-dramatist, drew his examples from the Second World War, choosing a man, Churchill, and a cause, whose aims he supported. Hochhuth was not anti-Churchill. But he did portray Churchill and his advisers, among them Lord Cherwell, as being deliberate accomplices in the mass-murder caused by the blanket bombing of Dresden and in the 'assassination' of General Sikorski, who died in a 1943 air crash. Hochhuth insisted that his view of events was supported by documentary evidence, some of which was locked up in a Swiss bank, untouched and untouchable for fifty years.

Tynan was ecstatic about *Soldiers*: 'This is the most *imposing* new script I have ever read!' Chandos, who had, after all, served in Churchill's war cabinet and should have known what was going on if anyone at the National did, was equally vehement in opposition: 'The play is a grotesque calumny on a great statesman. It's too ridiculous; the poor old Prof. [Lord Cherwell] is made out a sort of Mephistopheles and the Paymaster General is shown running the country.'

The row boiled up on April 25th, 1967. Tynan was summoned before the board. He was asked whether he had consulted any historians of contemporary history to find out whether they supported Hochhuth's thesis. Tynan replied that he had — and that the result was 'very much an open verdict'. Chandos asked him whether he had consulted Jack Wheeler-Bennett. Tynan said, 'No.' 'Did you consult Hugh Trevor-Roper?' 'Yes.' The impression was left in the minds of some members of the board that Trevor-Roper, a Professor of History at Oxford, was 'open-minded' about the possibility of Churchill's conniving in Sikorski's death. Trevor-Roper, however, had told Tynan that he regarded the idea as 'absurd', having 'neither evidence nor probability to support it'. Tynan was accused (and vigorously defended himself against the charge) of distorting the opinions of others to support his case before the board. Tynan retorted that he had said truthfully that he had consulted Trevor-Roper but he had not implied that Trevor-Roper was 'open-minded', whatever the board had inferred.

Disregarding this misunderstanding, however, it was clear that basic issues were involved. Tynan resented in principle any 'interference' from the board on matters which he considered to be of artistic policy. In a sense, he was trying to have it both ways—for the Theatre of Fact movement was usually justified by social and political rather than narrowly 'artistic' reasons. Tynan hated the word art.

'I serve the National Theatre,' he proclaimed, 'not the National Theatre Board'—and he found support in the Commons, by lobbying Labour M.P.s. Ben Whitaker stood up for him. Nor was the board totally unsympathetic. Hugh Willatt, for example, who became secretary general of the Arts Council, expressed the dilemma succinctly:

> It is essential for the lay board to recognise that the theatre must be run by professionals ... but as more and more theatres are partly supported by public money, the Governors become trustees of the public interest. The problem has not yet been solved [*Sunday Times*, April 30th, 1967].

In the National's case, however, this problem was particularly acute, because it received more public money than other theatres, was regarded as the pinnacle of British theatre and, in a sense, representative of national culture. 'If we put on this play,' said Chandos, 'some poor Italian gentleman might say, "Ha ha, so that's what went on in England during the war." If somebody chooses to put it on at some theatre club in Hampstead, that's a different matter ... ' 'I'd die for free speech,' he added, 'but remember the foreigners.' There was also a political dimension, other than those mentioned. The National Theatre Board and the South Bank Theatre Board were currently negotiating for more money from the new Conservative G.L.C., and a play which seriously and perhaps unfairly criticized a national hero might well have damaged their chances. 'Getting a National Theatre going has been forty years' work,' said Chandos, 'I wouldn't like Tynan to ruin it in two weeks.'

It was a bitter affair. Chandos wanted Tynan to go, and taunted him because he stayed. Defying Chandos, Tynan was determined to remain, joining the 'resistance' movement (as he put it) inside the National rather than fighting the organization from outside. That war parallel impressed nobody. Olivier publicly supported Tynan—he could be very loyal—but privately he didn't like the play and thought that Tynan was being rather naïve. 'My choice', Olivier said, 'when I joined the National Theatre was cloudy but simple. Do we have a National Theatre with a *faute de mieux* ambivalent contract between its Director and its board, or do we not have a National Theatre at all?' He did not believe that a government could or ever would appoint a National Theatre Director—and then leave him to get on with the job without a board or any interference. He recalled a Jean-Louis Barrault anecdote. When Barrault was the director of the Théâtre de France, the former Salle Luxembourg, France's second 'National', he wanted to stage Genet's *The Screens*, a play highly critical of what was then French policy in Algeria. He thought it wise to ask permission from the French Minister of Culture, then André Malraux, a personal friend. 'Of course, my dear fellow,' Malraux replied, and Barrault went ahead. The next year, he wanted to bring back the production, and again Malraux agreed. But when Barrault asked again the following year, Malraux hesitated and refused: 'You see, it's election year.' And so when Tynan proclaimed to the press that 'no paternalistic boards sit in judgment over the Comédie-Française, the Théâtre de France or the Théâtre National Populaire,' he was factually accurate—but, as Olivier knew all too well, this did not prevent them from feeling political pressures.

Soldiers was later produced with mixed success independently of the National, in Dublin and London. Many critics wondered why Tynan had chosen to make this of all plays the pretext for a fight. Or had he done so? Might this have been another example (similar to the all-male *As You Like It*) where simmering tensions required—and found—a catalyst? But the consequences of the row were profound. It was, for example, generally agreed that the board should not interfere with artistic policy. This convention before *Soldiers* received more formal acknowledgment afterwards. But this meant that boards became more cautious about the appointment of artistic directors—not only at the National but in reps around the country. They did not want to appoint someone who could embarrass them. Furthermore, good boards can act as valuable influences on artistic directors. The history of the reps suggests that those theatres thrive where there is a firm 'supportive' relationship between the boards and their artistic directors—and dwindle away when there is not. By robbing the board of its overall responsibilities in one important area—indeed, the most important—there was a danger that inferior, less enthusiastic and effective boards would be chosen.

Tynan's status at the National never fully recovered from the *Soldiers* affair. He took on more journalism and other work (including the formulation of *Oh! Calcutta!*) outside the National. Two years later, he took a prolonged and overdue holiday, for more than six months, returning to find that the name of his job had been changed. He was not the National's Literary Manager any longer, but a Literary Consultant, working with Derek Granger, the former head of plays at London Weekend Television, as another Literary Consultant. Nor was the board unscathed. The press publicity and the Parliamentary Questions had been bad for it. The papers, for example, picked out the fact that the board's members were all rather old. The average age was sixty. Although Chandos was confirmed as chairman of the board in October 1967, for a further three years, the composition of the board started to change—with John Mortimer replacing Henry Moore, Leslie Freeman (a G.L.C. alderman) taking over from Victor Mishcon, and Alfred Francis, that tough old codger, moving into the seat occupied previously by Sir Douglas Logan, the principal of University College, London. Hugh Beaumont and Hugh Willatt retired in August 1968, to be replaced by Professor Raymond Carr, George Geddes, Victor Mishcon (on the rebound), Professor Terence Spencer and Leopold de Rothschild. Although some of these retirements would have occurred in any case, the National Theatre Board had a very different appearance within eighteen months of the *Soldiers* controversy.

1966–7 had already been a year of disasters for the National—but worse was to come. Olivier's health was deteriorating. Nobody at first knew why. He looked ill, his face was drawn and he was often clearly in pain. It was assumed that the pressure of running the National was becoming too much for him—particularly after the rows and after losing two valuable colleagues. Somehow, on the stage, the physical strains were not noticeable. He pulled himself together with a great effort of will and seemed a man twenty years younger. Olivier's will-power was incredible—and could be dangerous. During the bout of 'flu which prevented him from appearing in the first scheduled performances of *Othello* on the regional tour, he had been lying in bed in Brighton. It was winter, and his temperature had just reached normal. He suddenly started to worry in case his muscles were becoming flabby in bed. He got up, dressed in a track suit and went for a training run along the front—and simply collapsed, too weak to move. He had to be brought home by a friendly tradesman.

He always took elaborate care to keep himself fit: running, gymnasium sessions, vocal and breathing exercises. But he also expended an almost unnatural amount of concentrated energy on stage. 'If Paul Scofield played Othello,' Dexter once said, 'it would be all right. He could play Othello or Lear nine times a week ... But Larry can only play it twice a week because he puts so much emotional intensity into it.' The performances of *Othello* indeed drained Olivier's stamina: they made him realize that he was growing old. Tynan, Joan Plowright and others who watched Olivier night after night would comment on his 'tigerish' or 'lionish' quality, that animal energy which sometimes seemed ferocious but could soften into an almost feminine sensuality.

That marvellous vigour, the flow of life which had helped so much to bring the National into existence and had sustained it, the very soul and energy of the place, was suddenly threatened. In June 1967, the news was released that Olivier was undergoing treatment for a tumour on the prostate gland—which proved malignant. He was suffering from cancer. He was given the choice of a conventional operation, which would have removed the growth without necessarily doing anything more than delaying the spread—or a new treatment, hyperbarbic oxygen radiotherapy, which would mean regular visits to hospital for a few weeks, to be placed in a hermetically sealed chamber, in near freezing temperatures and bombarded with X-rays. He chose the latter treatment. The National announced that Olivier would not act again for the season, but there were fears that he might not act again at all.

But Olivier's determination was not to be thwarted. In the first few days of the treatment, he continued taking rehearsals for the *Three Sisters*, due to open on July 3rd. He attended St Thomas's Hospital as an out-patient. He then caught a mild attack of pneumonia—and was forced to take a holiday. It was expected to be a long one, but it wasn't. Olivier really felt that he could not leave the National. Who could take over from him? Gaskill and Dexter had gone, and Tynan was in all sorts of trouble with the board. It was necessary to groom successors, but in the meantime Olivier simply continued, carrying the full burden without complaint. His sheer doggedness was heroic. He gave up playing Othello, but carried on with *The Dance of Death*. In February 1968, on another regional tour, in Edinburgh, he collapsed in pain. He had been playing Edgar in Strindberg's play, and the doctors diagnosed appendicitis. He was flown back overnight to London where he had an emergency operation. This operation revealed the welcome fact that the cancer treatment had been totally successful. There was no trace of the tumour, no signs of a spreading malignancy.

He was still a sick man, however, and his illness cast a shadow over the next few years. He concealed his condition as best he could, particularly from the company, would talk about it off-handedly as if it did not matter. But, in August 1970, following a mild attack of pleurisy, he suffered a thrombosis, which blew up one leg like a balloon. He still went on: conserving his energies as best he could, taking regular exercise, listening to his doctors and sometimes being a good patient, travelling up to London by the Brighton Belle most mornings and down again at night, a businessman commuter, whose morning paper concealed the scripts he was studying. Although he wanted to spend as much time as possible with his young and growing family, and although acting had ceased to be an attractive profession, administration an effort, and directing a strain, he was determined to bring the National to its new home on the South Bank. He would not let that burden fall, which he had carried so long, before he had delivered it safely to its destination.

Quite apart from the ordinary stress which she must have felt during these years, Joan Plowright had one vivid memory which haunted her. She had been one of George Devine's pupils—and later a colleague and close friend. When Devine died in 1966, she was among those who had gathered by his bedside at St George's Hospital. She believed that it was partly the struggle to establish and maintain the English Stage Company at the Royal Court which brought about the exhaustion causing Devine's death. The infant ideal had grown up to become a tyrant over his life. He had wanted to go, but there seemed nobody around who could replace him, until ill-health, age and tiredness forced him to leave—by which time it was too late to save his life. In the hospital bed, Devine had been shrivelled, prematurely old and half-paralysed. He had beckoned Joan Plowright behind the screen protecting his bed. He laid one hand on her arm: 'Don't let it do to him, what it's done to me.' The trouble was that Olivier was even more determined than Devine had been and the National was of greater weight than the English Stage Company. How do you stop Sisyphus half-way up the hill?

14

Lean Seasons

CHANGES were needed. That was clear. After the optimism of the first four years, the company was in trouble, while the South Bank Theatre Board, having dropped the opera house under instructions from above, were now battling with a Tory G.L.C. The National Theatre Board found themselves saddled with the reputation of being the interfering fuddy-duddies whom they had employed Tynan to be anti; and the government had not yet introduced the Bill into Parliament which would allow more public money to be released to build the theatre. As the weeks of 1968 slipped by, it seemed as if a different kind of effort were now needed. The days of high ideals and ambitious planning were past. What was needed now was, in a sense, more bureaucracy, patient effort in small rooms sorting through difficult problems one by one, diplomacy and a little blackmail. It was time for 'men of affairs' to take charge.

The troubles with the G.L.C. lasted for about a year, from March 1967, when the Tories came to power, to the following February, when Desmond Plummer, the Conservative leader, announced that 'at last the National Theatre project can go ahead'. It could have been a much longer dispute than it was, for the Conservatives had promised cuts in public spending and the National was a prime target. They also distrusted the South Bank Theatre Board's estimates. The board had stated that the National would cost about £7½ million, of which the G.L.C. would have to find half; but Leslie Freeman, the new chairman of the general purposes committee of the G.L.C., feared that the costs might rise to as much as £12½ million. These figures were not as absurdly incompatible as they might appear. The £7½ million was based upon the current 1967 prices, whereas the £12½ million was a figure derived from what was then considered to be a thoroughly pessimistic view of inflationary trends within the economy.

The basic choice before the G.L.C. was either to withdraw support from the National altogether or to cut back the project to more moderate proportions. The first course of action was considered rather drastic, in view of the two-party support for the National over so many years, and so the haggling took place over possible cuts. The restaurant could be removed, saving £190,000. The studio theatre could be blocked up. The underground car park could be modified. Richard Pilbrow had submitted three estimates on the stage equipment—one fairly elaborate, the second technically well-equipped but without frills, and the third providing little more than the basic equipment to be found in most theatres. Even the power-flying under the third system was severely restricted; and thus it would have led to increases in stage staff at the National. In initial costs, however, the third system was cheapest; and therefore chosen. There were other proposals for saving the burden on tax- and rate-payers. Plummer, for example, received an offer from a property developer, who was prepared to build the National free of charge to anyone but himself, in return for the free use of another site on which he could erect 500,000 square feet of office space. That sort of bargaining smacked too much of the market place, and Plummer turned it down haughtily.

The G.L.C., therefore, took another tack. It insisted that it would only pay £3¾ million towards the cost of the National; that is, exactly half the estimated 1967 figure. Sir Reginald Goodwin, the leader of the Labour opposition, insisted that this was an inflexible approach; but the Conservatives intended it to be just that. They knew that the costs of the National were bound to rise above these estimates, and that only £100,000 had been allowed in these figures for inflation. The Conservatives were determined that the G.L.C. should not bear any part of the additional costs.

Here the political Catch-22 came into play again, as it had done before in the National's history—for what would any council do, or any government, with a half-completed building on the South Bank? However strongly the G.L.C. worded its refusal to spend more than £3¾ million, once the building had begun (and the estimated £7½ million spent), it would have to be finished. The money would have to be found from somewhere. Plummer knew this as well as Cottesloe and Chandos. The real value of such statements would come with the subsequent bargaining. The G.L.C. could point to its statement, to persuade that government to provide the rest of the money from central funds; while if the Labour Party subsequently regained control of the G.L.C. and voted more money to complete the National, the Conservatives could claim to have protected the rate-payers more diligently.

The same principle could be adapted for use in Parliament. Once a plausible amount had been voted through, time would take care of rising costs. Jennie Lee welcomed Desmond Plummer's February statement and prepared one of her own for March. On March 21st, Dr David Kerr asked when the building of the National would begin, and Miss Lee replied that it would do so very soon. The government proposed to introduce legislation which would enable it to match the G.L.C. pound for pound. It too would supply £3¾ million, 'but no more', and the South Bank Theatre Board had an additional £100,000 in trust funds (from the S.M.N.T. fundraising) in case they ran out of public money. Mr Strauss (Labour, Vauxhall) popped the awkward question, which Miss Lee deflected with great charm:

> What is to happen, supposing because of rising costs, the final expenditure comes to more than is anticipated?
> MISS LEE: If with £7,500,000 and an additional £100,000, we cannot build a splendid theatre, then we all ought to jump in the Thames. (Laughter and cheers.)

It did and they didn't.

The necessary legislation was mentioned in the Queen's Speech (October 1968) and subsequently passed through its various Commons stages, until by March 1969 it was in force. There was no opposition to it. Its wording was simple. It was simply an amendment of the National Theatre Act, 1949, authorizing the Secretary of State to make contributions 'not exceeding £3,750,000' to the cost of building and equipping the National. But the situation behind the Bill was far less straightforward.

There are two kinds of contracts normally sought with builders. The first is a 'fixed-price' contract, which puts the onus for covering rising costs upon the builder. Fixed-price contracts are usually between 10 and 15 per cent above the estimated cost for the job, to allow for delays, shortages and inflation. At the lower of these two figures, which no contractor was likely to accept, the cost of the National through a fixed-price contract would have been about £8¼ million. In fact, it would have been nearer £9½ million, for no builder would have agreed in 1969 to a contract based on the estimated figures from 1966–7; and, in view of the uncertain economic situation, not to mention the potentially booming property market, he would have been foolish to have considered less than a 15 per cent margin. He might not have considered even that, in view of the building's experimental nature.

The second type of contract operates on a sliding scale, with the onus for covering rising costs resting upon the employer. The employer and the contractor agree upon a basic price for the job, which in this case could have been the 1967 estimates, but there would be clauses in the contract allowing the contractor to pass on any rises in the cost of materials, labour and services (such as a general rise in electricity prices) to the employer. 'Sliding' contracts are invariably cheaper at first glance than fixed-price contracts, for they do not contain the 10 to 15 per cent margin left for inflation. Whether they work out cheaper in the long run is a matter entirely of guesswork. If inflation in building costs rises above the 15 per cent margin, then the employer who has opted for a sliding contract loses money. If it does not, then he has saved some.

Both contracts have advantages and disadvantages. The builder with a fixed-price contract has a real incentive to complete the job quickly, because the longer the delays, the more chance there is that the inflation margin will be absorbed in rising costs. If he completes the task within the original estimate, then the inflation margin becomes pure profit. The employer, however, might complain (particularly if he represents public bodies like the G.L.C. and the government) that the builder is profiteering. With a fixed-price contract, the employer might be annoyed, but he would have little chance of redress. With a sliding contract, the employer would be protected against profiteering by builders, although the builder would have no financial incentive to get on with his job. Under both types of contract, however, it is perfectly clear who is to bear the additional costs of a job, should they arise.

Unfortunately, however, politicians sometimes like to leave little grey areas of doubt within which they can manoeuvre. By putting a ceiling on their contributions, at £$3\frac{3}{4}$ million, the government and the G.L.C. were apparently expecting that a fixed-price contract could be struck within this total figure. It may have been an absurd hope, but there it was: both bodies had insisted that no further money would be available—and that meant a fixed-price contract. The South Bank Theatre Board, however, was advised by the Treasury that sliding contracts would be in order; and indeed they were absolutely necessary, for any fixed-price contract must have been above the sums allocated. The South Bank Theatre Board's Annual Report for 1968–9 records the sliding contract struck with the main contractors, Sir Robert McAlpine & Sons Ltd, very innocently. It was only, at this stage, for the substructure: 'The practicability of having a fixed-price contract for the substructure was considered, but it was found that such a contract could only be at a figure which in all probability would not be to the advantage of the Board.' It would also have been well above the amount allocated for the substructure within the total £7,600,000; and the board not only had to take 'proper precautions' to stay within this amount, but to be seen to be doing so.

And so the situation arose whereby the contracts apparently envisaged by the government and the G.L.C. were 'fixed-price'—for the simple reason that they had both declared that no more money would be available for the project—whereas the contracts actually reached with the builders were 'sliding'. To get the lowest tender within the ceiling figure in any case meant pruning details of the project and trying to streamline various procedures; and the Treasury insisted that no additions should be made to the original specifications without their specific approval.

In retrospect too, it cannot have been entirely to the South Bank Theatre Board's advantage that the sum within which the contracts were to be reached was known before the tenders were invited. The £7½ million, give or take £100,000, had received parliamentary discussion, therefore press coverage. The contractors knew the amount available, although the divisions of this amount were not known. Their tenders were therefore likely to reflect the probable allocations. Instead of the usual situation, where the employers do not divulge private estimates before inviting tenders, the contractors were in the useful position of being able to guess at these estimates.

In April 1969, a month after the National Theatre Bill passed through the Commons, the contracts were put out to tender, to a limited number of contractors. Open tenders were not invited, because it was considered that there were only a few building firms who could have undertaken the job. The contracts were in two stages—the substructure and the superstructure—because the detailed requirements of the building had not yet been fixed, another uncertainty affecting the costs. McAlpine, which had allowed the National Theatre to use its Nissen huts as temporary offices, won the contract because its figures tallied most closely with those of the South Bank Theatre Board; and it was assumed that the contractor who worked on the substructure would be in the best position to tackle the superstructure as well. The two-stage contract simply allowed the South Bank Theatre Board to have second thoughts about the contractor if the substructure was not satisfactorily tackled.

The contract for the substructure was signed on December 1st, 1969; but it was just a formality. Work had already started on the site and there had been another foundation ceremony, undoubtedly the last.

The foundation stone was not needed, and it was thought more tactful not to bother the Queen. On November 3rd, a windy autumn day and Jennie Lee's birthday, there was a Ceremonial Cement Pouring. A huge hole had been dug in the ground of Prince's Meadow; and a brontosaurian cement-mixer perched precariously by the edge. About eighty people stood around shivering, to catch the symbolic moment, the most privileged ones with spades. Olivier could not be there. He was filming *Three Sisters* (from the National's stage production); but he sent a telegram: *'How grateful my profession will be for what will ensue from this day's work.'* Cottesloe, Chandos, Desmond Plummer, Selwyn Lloyd and Jennie Lee stood by, as the cement-mixer rattled and churned before disgorging the rough-and-ready mixture down a long wooden chute into the hole provided, V.I.P. shovels patting it into place. Speeches were made, congratulatory remarks exchanged, and the first hard blocks of the new National started to stiffen into shape.

Meanwhile, another kind of strengthening process had been going on, with a human support system being poured into the holes left by the 1966–7 troubles. The South Bank Theatre Board was reconstructed in 1967–8. A new board was necessary for two reasons—first, because several members were present on the board because of their connections with opera in general and Sadler's Wells in particular; and second, because the original terms of office held by all the board members (with the exception of Sir William Fiske) were due to end in August 1968. Normally, perhaps, most members of the board might have expected their tenures to be confirmed, and extended for a further three to five years—if only to see the job through. Cottesloe was retained as chairman, Richard Lynex as secretary, and Chandos and Olivier stayed to represent the National Theatre Board. All the other members, however, left—including Sir Isaac Hayward, Prince Littler, Norman Marshall, David McKenna, Norman Tucker and Sir Percy Rugg—and in their place Jennie Lee, whose job as Minister of State in the Department of Education and Science included such dispensations of offices, brought in more 'men of affairs'.

These were men who knew how governments, the Civil Service and industry worked, knew whom to ring and their first names, and who would not, like mere artists, dither around in a crisis not knowing quite what to do. Jennie Lee trusted them to force the National towards its fruition. Lord Goodman, the chairman of the Arts Council, was one of the new members, with Sir Joseph Lockwood, the chairman of Electric and Musical Industries (E.M.I.). Lockwood had originally won his reputation by building flour-mills: highly automated affairs, where grain-ships unloaded their holds directly on to conveyor belts which carried the raw wheat, with the minimum of handling, through every stage to the flourbags. There were also two civil servants from the Department of Education and Science — J. A. Hudson and W. D. Lacey (who was also an architect) and H. F. Rossetti, another civil servant and an assessor. Plummer represented the Conservatives on the G.L.C., and Sir Reginald Goodwin the Labour Party, with Leslie Freeman also from County Hall. There were thus three G.L.C. representatives and three from the government; while the chief casualties on the board were those with a practical knowledge of the arts — Littler, McKenna, Tucker and Marshall. The value of Goodman and Lockwood was particularly shown by the way in which they could cut through what might otherwise have been interminable delays, say, in the supply of materials, such as steel, and parts, such as electric motors.

The changes on the National Theatre Board showed a less systematic pattern, but were equally drastic. Of the nine-man committee which had stared across the table at Tynan during the *Soldiers* controversy, six left within the year, for various reasons: an untimely death (Sir Maurice Pariser), expiration of terms of office and (in the case of Hugh Willatt) promotion to the post of secretary general of the Arts Council. J. B. Priestley left the drama committee, complaining that this body was merely expected to rubber-stamp other people's decisions and talked about money all the time. The new appointments, however, which included academics (Raymond Carr and Terence Spencer), theatre professionals (Alfred Francis and John Mortimer Q.C., the playwright), G.L.C. representatives and an industrialist, did not alter the balance of the board, only the actual members — some of whom (Hugh Beaumont and Victor Mishcon, for example) were later re-appointed.

Continuity within the National Theatre Board was more important to maintain than in the South Bank Theatre Board, whose work would be over when the theatre was built. The National Theatre Board, however, was likely to be around for the duration of the National Theatre company itself; and it was important that methods of procedure should be established whereby the board and the company could work happily together. In 1967–8, for example, the board found itself faced with an unfamiliar, but not unwelcome, problem. For the first time in its short history, the National Theatre company had shown a reasonable profit, of £52,400. In the previous year, the current account had just broken even.

This profit was partly due to the substantial increases in the Arts

Council grant to the National, which had jumped up from £130,000 (1964-5), to £187,866 (1965-6), to £200,000 (1966-7), and £240,000 (1967-8). These grants were not expected to meet the running deficit of the company, with which the board had been burdened from the company's formation, which amounted to £241,994 in 1965-6, but was reduced by annual special grants of about £80,000 a year. By 1967-8, the deficit stood at a mere £81,994.

In a sense, the National Theatre Board, the Arts Council and the government were trying to discover what the right level of subsidy should be for the National; but the profit in 1967-8 had also been the result of National Theatre economies, the dropping of a production so that the general level of activity had reached its lowest point ever (only four productions) and the scheduling of more performances of *Othello* (until Olivier's illness intervened) to make up the balance. Attendances at the Old Vic were still remarkably high (86 per cent capacity), and the National Theatre company had also undertaken a profitable six-week tour of Canada (coinciding with Expo 67), with Olivier leading the team.

But what could a non-profit-distributing company do with a profit? The National Theatre Board were worried lest the Arts Council should think that the grants were too high, thus cutting back in the following years. The board wanted to impress upon the Council that the profit was due to exceptional factors—the lower activity, the high box-office figures—and they had a perfectly valid case. They could not count on such circumstances. But there was still the question of what to do with the surplus. The Arts Council could not be a party to a situation whereby an individual company accumulates its annual grants, getting richer year by year. This money was needed by other theatres. And so, for the time being, the surplus was retained by the National Theatre Board until they could discover, in consultation with the Arts Council, on a proper way to get rid of it. They eventually decided to put it into another new theatre, a converted building just down the road from the Old Vic. It became known as the Young Vic, although it had comparatively little in common with the Young Vic of the years after the war.

But the chief question which worried everyone was that of Olivier's successor. Finney, Olivier's first choice, lacked experience in running a company and, in any case, was turning his attention to films. Olivier's other suggestions, of Richard Attenborough or Joan Plowright, were not taken seriously by the board; and the opinion was formed that he was only putting up these names to prove his own indispensability. But

Olivier had a vision of a National devoted primarily to the actors' art, which partly accounts for his choice of names. They were all well-established actors who could get on with people in the profession; and although his choice of Joan Plowright might have seemed too maritally dutiful, he also may have thought of Helene Weigel, who carried on running the Berliner Ensemble after Brecht's death. Olivier, too, wanted to establish a company comparable with the Ensemble, forming its own traditions, which would be perpetuated by his successor.

On the National Theatre Board, there were differing views. Alfred Francis, thinking of an *Intendant*, suggested J. W. Lambert, the arts editor of the *Sunday Times* and chairman of the Arts Council's drama panel. Lambert, he argued, had no personal ambitions to direct or act; but he knew a lot about the theatre and would be able to pick the right people for the different jobs. He would be able to see the operation as a whole. He would not say, 'We need more money from the bar so that I can stage *Tamburlaine* with real gilt on the chariots.' But the board wanted a 'name', a theatre professional who could also adminis-trate, and someone not too controversial who might land them in another *Soldiers* row; and with these assumptions the choice narrowed around the name of Peter Hall, who was then in the process of leaving Stratford, having helped to appoint his successor, Trevor Nunn.

But Hall would not work as Olivier's second-in-command, and Olivier was still the National's director. Hall could not be groomed to take over. Within the company, there were others who were either regarded (or considered themselves) as possible successors. Robert Stephens was one. He was appointed associate director for 1967–8 and given his first opportunity to direct a play, one of a *Triple Bill* of comedies, in June 1968. It was not a particularly successful experiment. Plowright, too, took a hand in organizing and directing. She had been irritated by the lack of women dramatists, as well as plays with exciting parts for actresses. After a somewhat disastrous excursion into new-wave drama in 1968 (Natalia Ginzburg's *The Advertisement*), in which she had played a lonely, wronged woman in a Rome apartment, Plowright set about commissioning the plays which seemed to be lacking. She chose four leading women novelists (Sheena Mackay, Margaret Drabble, Gillian Freeman and Maureen Duffy) and asked them to write plays for an experimental season at the Jeannetta Cochrane—of which only Duffy's *Rites* was considered worth transferring to the Old Vic, in a double bill with a shortened version of John Spurling's *MacRune's Guevara*.

The *Triple Bill*, organized by Stephens, and *An Evasion of Women*, organized by Plowright, were two attempts to bring new life to the National Theatre management and company, as well as performing the expected function of such seasons—of discovering new playwrights and trying out young directors. Victor Spinetti, Robert Lang and Derek Jacobi were given their chances as directors within these seasons—as well as Stephens and Plowright. For the 1967–8 programme at the Old Vic, three well-established, highly experienced British directors— Guthrie, Brook and Clifford Williams—came for brief visits, without bringing more than weekend suitcases. None of them looked like staying, or would probably have wanted to do so. Guthrie was considered too old to settle down, Brook too mercurial to do so, while Williams was also an associate director of the R.S.C., on loan to the National. Williams's first production at the Old Vic was the all-male *As You Like It* which Dexter should have directed. He also tackled, in 1969, Shaw's *Back To Methuselah*, that sprawling monument to the temptations of prophecy which some also regard as a monumental bore. Guthrie's *Tartuffe* suffered from that stiltedness which often accompanies British productions and translations of Molière's plays; while his *Volpone*, with Colin Blakely as the wealthy fox trying out his 'friends' by feigning mortal illness, fell between the two stools which Jonson so deceptively provides—of fantastical satire and straightforward storytelling. Brook's *Oedipus* was a box-office success, startling, lively and accused by some critics of untidiness. Seneca's play had previously been considered mere closet drama, but Ted Hughes had translated it into tough, perhaps over-tough, sinewy English. Brook used the play as a springboard to present a society gripped by an emotional and sexual compulsion, with a huge golden phallus as its central symbol, the cast charlestoning around with every appearance of abandon, with Gielgud and Worth (as Oedipus and Jocasta) providing a centre of austere acting to the orgiastic whole. The critical and box-office success of the season, however, was Olivier's *Three Sisters* which, like his *Uncle Vanya*, was a clear, firm and sensitive production of a great play, only lacking the range of intuitively brilliant performances which had made the National's first Chekhov production so memorable.

More directors were tried out during the 1968–9 season. Michael Elliott was approached to join the National's team. Donald MacKechnie came to assist other directors (Olivier, Plowright and Williams), without establishing his public identity in his own right. Geoffrey Reeves and Michael Langham came for brief stays. Charles Wood had wanted Reeves to direct his ambitious and difficult play, *H*, about General Havelock, the colonizing British soldier in India at the time of the

Indian Mutiny, who believed that it was possible to be a Christian and a professional soldier at the same time. The play ironically proves the opposite. It was written in that terse, idiomatic half-humorous, half-grim dialogue which characterizes Wood's work. It was also an epic play, ranging from the massacres of the Indian Mutiny to the evacuation of Lucknow; and, like many epics, it lacked an inner coherence to help the director. Reeves tackled it bravely, but the result could not compare with the former National epics. Langham's stay was short and rather unhappy. Congreve's *The Way of the World* is not the easiest of plays to direct. Its brittle, highly stylized wit can leave the cast looking like a row of formal tulips, bright flowers on particularly skinny stalks. But the National had had several successes with Restoration comedy before — with *The Recruiting Officer* and *Love for Love* the chief examples — and the company seemed especially equipped for Congreve. Maggie Smith and Geraldine McEwan were part of the team, witty and stylized actresses *par excellence*.

But Langham did not apparently get on too well with the company, which in any case had lost the comradely spirit of former years. Personal problems started to become hard to handle. The break-up of Robert Stephens's first marriage and his subsequent marriage to Maggie Smith produced stresses within the group — which indirectly led to Geraldine McEwan being selected to play Millamant in *The Way of the World*. Since Smith had joined the National originally as an actress who could be groomed to succeed Edith Evans as the chief exponent of high comedy, and Millamant was exactly the part which she had been expected to play, its loss was a blow — and not only missing such a role, but the manner in which she received the news. Maggie Smith had escaped down to Brighton for a few days, recovering (at Olivier's invitation) from the emotional pressures of London. When she returned, she found a brief directorial note, saying sorry but the company could not wait and that McEwan had been selected as Millamant. Maggie Smith sent off a rude telegram in exchange.

Such incidents, which happen in any company, were felt particularly keenly by members of the National — for a variety of reasons. For two years, they had been subject to a number of directors, each with a different approach, which can be unsettling if there is no consistent policy behind their selection. Furthermore, several members of the company — Smith, Blakely and Finlay among them — had risen through the ranks to become stars in their own right; and therefore other opportunities, more superficially tempting than those at the National, were now open to them. They started to drift away. Lastly, the sense of fellowship, of working in a common cause, had declined, and many felt the loss of this friendship acutely. Dexter, away from the National, longed for the early days, which could not be brought back. He wanted just to sit down with Olivier, Gaskill and Plowright to plan future productions; but he had gone his own way and the old rapport was lacking.

And so, Langham's *The Way of the World* was a disappointing production, a conventional one with slightly ragged performances, and another possible associate director bit the dust. The 1969–70 season was much more promising, with the arrival of Michael Blakemore and Jonathan Miller to direct their first National productions and the brief return of Gaskill to direct a brilliant *The Beaux' Stratagem*. By now, however, the National's internal problems were starting to be reflected in falling attendance figures and increasingly caustic critical remarks. John Dexter was asked (by Joan Plowright) to return, and he accepted, becoming an associate director with Blakemore, Paul Scofield and Frank Dunlop for the following year, 1970–1. But 1970 also saw the effective loss of the one man who, arriving in 1967 to lift some of the burden from Olivier's shoulders, had actually managed to do so: Frank Dunlop.

Dunlop had been appointed Associate Director (with Robert Stephens) in the autumn of 1967, but by January his title had been changed to Administrative Director, two words which could mean almost anything. They could have meant that he would simply administer the entire operations of the National, allowing others to go on with the directing of productions. But there was already a general manager, George Rowbottom, who left the National in April 1968 to go to the Nottingham Playhouse — a conscientious man but prone (as who would not be, under the circumstances?) to worry. He was replaced by Anthony Easterbrook, from Sadler's Wells, cool, decisive and reliable. Dunlop's job was really to fill the gaps left by Gaskill and Dexter, without (as a newcomer) having that status which would have allowed him to formulate artistic policy. Policy was left in the hands of Olivier and Tynan, although Dunlop became more assertive as the months went by. His job was largely to sort out the mass of detail, part administrative problems, part those of artistic policy, which was accumulating at Aquinas Street. He would also be a house director, capable, like Dexter, of tackling straightforward productions (such as Maugham's *Home and Beauty*) and of dazzling audiences with lively inventive pieces, such as *The White Devil* (November 1969) or his version of Molière's *Les Fourberies de Scapin*, which, as *Scapino*, opened the Young Vic. He was to be the professional dogsbody, kept initially on the Tynan–Olivier leash; but he had his own reasons for going to the National, in addition to his general desire to be of use. He wanted to establish a young people's theatre, as part of the National Theatre organization.

He seemed admirably suited to this general role. He had had a varied theatrical career, which had not quite raised him to the front rank of British directors. He had studied English literature at University College, London, and served in the R.A.F., before joining the Old Vic centre after the war. He had thus studied with St Denis and Byam Shaw, although he was particularly attracted to Devine's Young People's Theatre. Like the others (such as Joan Plowright and Michael Elliott) who had gone through that tough, demanding school, Dunlop combined a far-ranging knowledge of different aspects of theatre with a sense of theatrical purpose. He thought he knew what the game was about. In the early 1950s he had started a small group in Manchester, the Piccolo Theatre, before going to the Bristol Old Vic as assistant director. He had then gone freelance, writing and directing *Les Frères Jacques*, which received a brief run at the Adelphi. He ran the Théâtre de la Poche for a year in Brussels, which began a long association with Belgian theatres. He received a rare invitation to direct *Pantagleize* for the Belgian national theatre in 1970—exceptional because the dramatist who wrote the play was Michel de Ghelderode, Belgium's leading modern (though scarcely 'contemporary', for he was a twentieth-century mediaevalist) dramatist. The Théâtre National de Belgique brought this production to the Old Vic during its 1970 visit.

But the achievement for which Dunlop was best known in Britain was his work towards the establishment of the new Nottingham Playhouse in the early 1960s. He had run the company in the years just before and just after the opening of its new theatre, from 1961 to 1964, achieving remarkable results from what was originally just one regional company among many. He had built up the Playhouse company, which suggested that he was a good administrator. But Dunlop was no diplomat. A non-pompous man himself, he could be scathing of pomposity in others, and he was too ambitious to want to bask in someone else's glories. He also had firm ideas as to the kind of theatre he wanted to see—bright, colourful, young and energetic, popular rather than stately or formal. He had started a company in 1966 called Pop Theatre.

From one angle, Dunlop's work could be considered as lacking in *gravitas*—from another, as lacking in 'commitment'. He was not impressed by radical chic, and he was not going to time-serve for state art.

His first production was impressively competent, Brecht's version of Marlowe's *Edward II*, where he stepped between two pitfalls, excessive Brechtiana and costume rhetoric. The result was a firm, tough, sensible evening in the theatre. *Home and Beauty* illustrated the other side of Dunlop's work, perhaps the best-known, as a lighthearted director of comedy, sometimes striving to be too funny. Both these productions were staged in 1968, and without them (and Olivier's *Love's Labour's Lost*), the year would have seemed lean indeed.

Dunlop directed three further main productions for the National at the Old Vic — *MacRune's Guevara*, *The White Devil* (November 1969) and *The Captain of Köpenick*, each successful, each arriving at the right time for the National. Paul Scofield played the title role in Zuckmayer's marvellous comedy about a down-and-out who dons a uniform and immediately becomes a man of substance; and Dunlop proved through his production of *The Captain of Köpenick* that he, like Dexter, could construct with true inventiveness the right vehicle for a star actor. He kept the production moving quickly around Scofield, but left him room to establish the details of the miraculous transformation. It was one of Scofield's finest performances, and almost certainly his funniest. *The White Devil* was a sumptuous production of the Jacobean tragedy, with sun-baked white walls framing the stage, athleticism from the actors (trained gymnastically by Claude Chagrin), rich costumes and performances (from Edward Woodward's Flamineo, Derek Godfrey's Bracciano and Geraldine McEwan's Vittoria) to match.

No other director from these uncertain three years could point to productions which, in all-round competence, equalled those of Dunlop. He had proved his usefulness almost as conclusively as Dexter had done in the early years. But Dunlop was not happy. He felt excluded from the National's inner councils, and thought that the old guard were treating him too lightly as a mere snapper-up of trifles. He had battled with Tynan and Olivier over *MacRune's Guevara* — and, in effect, lost, for it was a sad, truncated version of the play which eventually arrived at the Old Vic. John Spurling had written a rich comedy, closer in style to Tom Stoppard (and perhaps to David Halliwell's 'multi-viewpoint' drama) than to other British dramatists. He had cleverly contrasted three different views of a historical situation, the revolutionary career of Che Guevara. The dramatist supposedly writing the play is one Edward Hotel, a great admirer of an unsuccessful Scottish artist, MacRune, a Marxist who lived and died in a small room obsessed by his hero, Guevara. MacRune had covered the walls with sketches, graffiti and odd enigmatic tributes to Guevara's life; and Hotel, after MacRune's death, comes to live in that room. Hotel decides to re-create the majesty of MacRune's obsessions in the form of a play. Unfortunately, however, Hotel is not a Marxist: he is, if anything, a solid supporter of established governments. And so his interpretation of MacRune's obsession with Guevara's life bears little relationship either to the revolutionary's career or to MacRune's opinions. History, in short, is known only through the multifariousness of prejudice, which was Spurling's point.

It was a pioneering play, using a number of different genre parodies and attacking radical chic. It was the first play which Dunlop had decided on his own to direct. But it did not please Tynan, who apparently stopped Dunlop in the corridor one day, to remind him that Guevara was regarded as a hero by millions of people and that this play might well offend them. Dunlop, remembering the row over *Soldiers*, found that remark very amusing, and said so, which did not please Tynan either. Tynan, who evidently suspected right-wing infiltration into the National, also took Spurling aside to remonstrate with him about the true dimensions of the class struggle, using Vietnam as an example.

There was indeed a very minor left-wing rumpus over *MacRune's Guevara*. Someone shouted out 'Where's the real Che?' during a scene called the Three Judases; but the chief effect of this was not to support Tynan's opinions unduly but to prick Olivier's anxieties. Olivier had been kind to Spurling during the early rehearsals—'avuncular and feudally friendly', to use Spurling's slightly acid phrase. But between the opening at the Jeannetta Cochrane, where the play received excellent reviews, and the stint at the Old Vic, his worries increased. They were not political ones, although Tynan may have encouraged his doubts: he just thought that the mixture of styles and arguments was slightly non-serious. He was afraid that the audience might be bored by a jolly student romp. And, therefore, on the night of the Old Vic's dress rehearsal, he called Dunlop and Spurling together—and told them to cut the play to its bare story-line. ' ... having failed entirely to understand the purpose of the play's structure,' Spurling thought,

> he was behaving exactly like any commercial impresario one's ever met, who always believes that, even at the last moment, by drastic cutting and rewriting, some sort of viable vehicle for the actors will be got on the road just in time for the patrons. It does not seem to occur to this type of impresario (it certainly didn't weigh with Olivier if it did occur to him) that such drastic alterations the night before might play merry hell with the actors.

Little local difficulties like that encourage nobody's determination to stay. There can be rows on principles which leave opponents the best of friends; but minor irritations can be very destructive. Dunlop was pressing for an opportunity to start his young people's theatre. The surplus from the 1967-8 season had given the National Theatre Board the opportunity to develop another side to the National's work which they were eager to seize. After all, the new National building was now starting to take shape on the South Bank site. The contract for the superstructure had been awarded (to McAlpine) in September 1970, and because one company was tackling both stages of the job, the work on the superstructure could start while the substructure was being finished. The scheduled opening date was set for 1973.

But when the National company moved into its new theatre, it would have to find productions for three auditoria; and therefore it seemed sensible to gain experience in running two theatres before that happened. The Young Vic was only a quick conversion, a kind of Road-to-Damascus theatre, and rather ugly to look at. A long coffee bar ran parallel to the road; but inside there was room for a small studio and a much larger open-stage auditorium, with banks of benches around. It cost a mere £110,000, receiving an Arts Council 'Housing the Arts' supplementary grant to add to the 1967-8 surplus. The fact that it was an 'open-stage' theatre was another factor in its favour, for the National had long since lost its special relationship with Chichester.

The Young Vic opened in August 1970, with Dunlop in charge. It was the ideal place for him to try out his young people's theatre scheme, and the first season illustrated what to expect. *Scapino* was a lively *commedia dell'arte* romp, rather like the kind of pop versions of classic plays which Joseph Papp was trying out in Central Park, New York. Indeed, *Scapino*, which was brought back into the repertoire for season after season, was a great hit in the United States. To prove, however, that Dunlop was not just a 'fun' director, the first season included weightier works, tackled in an equally direct style – *Waiting for Godot*, Yeats's *Oedipus*, *The Soldier's Tale* and *The Taming of the Shrew*.

The intention was that the Old and Young Vics should use the same company. Jim Dale, who played Scapino, also played in Arrabal's *The Architect and the Emperor of Assyria*; while Dunlop, though in charge of the Young Vic, would also direct at the Old. Young directors (such as Roland Joffé) could be tried out at the Young Vic, as they had been at the Jeannetta Cochrane season. Splitting the company like that, however, proved awkward to arrange, and in any case Dunlop wanted independence. The two theatres drifted apart, and while Dunlop was still listed as an associate director for the National for the 1970-1 season, it was announced in January 1971 that he would concentrate almost exclusively upon the Young Vic.

For a few brief weeks in the autumn of 1970, the National was running three theatres, an operation which matched in scale (although it was far more cumbersome) its anticipated programmes at the new building. The Cambridge Theatre had been taken over for a thirty-week season, which started in June with a transfer from the Old Vic of Jonathan Miller's *The Merchant of Venice*; and Olivier's Shylock duly pulled in the crowds. Other Old Vic productions transferred to complete the repertoire, and although the joint seasons lost money—the total deficit for the year was £61,413, for which the Arts Council provided a supplementary grant to balance the books—the attendance figures were reasonably high: 73 per cent at the Old Vic and 70 per cent at the Cambridge, a satisfactory total for what was basically an attempt to expand the company's level of operation to meet the demands to come.

The attendance figures would have been much higher but for Olivier's thrombosis in August, which forced him to rest, take a holiday and cancel his performances for the Cambridge season. Unlike the traumatic days of 1967, when Olivier's illness had taken the company by surprise, his latest sickness was an eventuality with which the company had learned to cope. There was the described reshuffling of the team, with Dexter and Blakemore joining Scofield and Dunlop as associate directors; and, in February 1971, Patrick Donnell joined the company as administrative director. He was an old friend of the Oliviers, who had worked as an administrator with the R.S.C. and on several Arts Council committees. He had no ambitions to be either a director or an actor. His job was simply to see that the organization ran smoothly, that budgets were observed and politicians kept informed and satisfied.

On paper, the team looked a strong one; and, as Olivier recovered more rapidly than anyone dared hope, the National heaved a corporate sigh of relief. The storms had been weathered fairly well. The ship had rolled around at times, but had not actually sprung too many leaks. Although attendance figures had fallen slightly and some recent reviews had been far from flattering, the overall image of the National had not been too badly damaged. Who worried too much about *The Advertisement*, or Anthony Quayle's production of *The Idiot*, while *Rosencrantz and Guildenstern Are Dead*, *The Dance of Death* and (more recently) *The National Health* were harvesting bouquets like a flower festival?

Furthermore, there were the discoveries—particularly of Miller and Blakemore. While Miller's production of *The Merchant of Venice* was not received with general critical approval, it was clear that here was a director of exceptional talents. He had first become known as a brilliant member of the *Beyond the Fringe* team, a soloist mime and mimic, with the associative vocabulary of a polymath. He could relate with dazzling ease different areas of thought—from medicine (he was a qualified doctor) to philosophy, ethics, art, changing patterns of culture and, of course, the theatre. But his great ability was to look at familiar plays afresh and with casual ease, cut through the crusts of other remembered performances to the bones of the play beneath. It was a typical Miller idea to look at *The Merchant of Venice*, that well-worn play, and recognize that it was a comedy about money and commerce. He therefore chose what seemed to him its most appropriate period, the late nineteenth century, with Shylock as a Rothschild in the making.

Blakemore had started as an actor, working at the Birmingham Rep and the Shakespeare Memorial Theatre in the 1950s; and he retained a particular sympathy with the problems of actors. He was a supportive director, never interfering unduly with the natural development of an actor's conception of his part, but providing a clear image of the whole production, while working through the problems of rehearsals. Miller, a highly instinctive man, could be lazy in working out details of productions, particularly those which bored him. Blakemore was a controlled professional, who may have lacked Miller's insights but could be relied upon to provide competent, imaginative productions. He joined the Glasgow Citizens' Theatre in the mid-1960s, becoming a co-director; and two of his Glasgow productions had made their marks in London—Brecht's *Arturo Ui* and Peter Nichols's first successful stage play, *A Day in the Death of Joe Egg*.

Nichols also provided Blakemore with his first National production, *The National Health*, a telling black comedy about the health service, in which Jim Dale played a narrator-orderly and almost a figure of Death. The reality of hospital life—the gloomy barrack-room ward, the patients moved nearer to the door as the likelihood of their deaths approached—was contrasted with the fictional image of hospitals—with pretty, nubile nurses, handsome doctors and brilliant surgical successes in operating theatres. *The National Health* was a difficult play to direct, but it was a triumphant success, lively, forceful, funny and apt. It confounded Olivier's expectations, who had prophesied disaster; and it proved that Blakemore, a mild man, was capable of standing up to Olivier. He had a row with him, similar in scale to the rows between Dexter and Olivier, and earned his respect in the process.

The general outlook for the National, as it approached the 1971 season, therefore looked good. There were many minor problems to overcome. The Cambridge season had tailed away after Olivier's departure from it, although Ingmar Bergman's production of *Hedda Gabler* (with Maggie Smith as Hedda) kept the pot simmering—unlike the rather clumsy *Cyrano* whose Gallic literary romanticism never quite manages to find an English translation to do justice to it. Ronald Eyre's production of *Mrs Warren's Profession* was sensible, if rather dull; but *The Architect and the Emperor of Assyria* was an experiment which went wrong. Victor Garcia, the Spanish director, best known in London for his striking production of Lorca's *Yerma* (staged on a huge trampoline), had been invited to direct Arrabal's play, which seemed to require stylistic brilliance. Unfortunately, Garcia's kind of brilliance, featuring an enormous fork-lift truck as its main prop, and encouraging an indolent athleticism from the two actors concerned, left an impression of campness. It had poor reviews and comparatively small audiences. Arrabal, too, disliked it.

These were, nevertheless, small setbacks. There were reliable productions to come—*The Captain of Köpenick*, which should surely bring audiences back, and Dexter's production of Heywood's *A Woman Killed With Kindness*. Dexter would rally the company—and he did. The Heywood tragedy was one of the best ensemble productions seen at the National for years. For those members of the public who preferred stars to ensembles, Christopher Plummer had been booked for coming productions, adding a film-star's glitter to a company which (with Woodward, Scofield and Dale) was already sparkling brightly.

And so, when in the spring of 1971 caustic articles began to appear in the press about the National's 'decline'—'Panned, Pampered and Half-Empty' was one headline in the *Daily Mail*—various spokesmen for the National (Olivier, Tynan and Dexter among them) felt justified in brushing them aside. The press had got it wrong again. What they should have seen were signs of a resurgence at the National. The bad days were almost over. The major problems had been solved. In any case, the National had not been too bad, even in its lean seasons. The successes had outnumbered the failures—just. At any rate, matters would be different from now on.

With this new optimism against a background of criticism, the National was determined to prove itself. There are two very human reactions to minor—and major—crises. One is to play safe—to become cautious and introverted, determined not to gamble. The other is the exact opposite—to 'double up', to tempt the fates and bully one's way out of danger. The National took the second course and it nearly wrecked the company.

15

Long Day's Journey

MEANWHILE, back on the ranch by Waterloo Bridge, matters were also 'continuing satisfactorily'. The 1969–70 and 1970–1 Annual Reports of the South Bank Theatre Board had both been thoroughly optimistic. In the first year, 120,000 cubic yards of earth had been excavated, to be replaced by 34,000 cubic yards of concrete. To forestall an expected steel shortage, the board had authorized bulk-buying of steel, thus cutting a corner which could have led to delays and an inflation in costs. By the beginning of 1971, the substructure was virtually complete, and work on the superstructure had reached a point from where, at a distance of a year and a half, one could contemplate the prospect of a topping-out ceremony. The new theatre was still expected to open its doors in 1973. The years had been ones of 'substantial progress'.

The troubles started to crop up in the late spring and early summer of 1971. 'Construction work', declared the 1971–2 Annual Report,

> has been delayed by the labour trouble which has affected the whole building industry. Short-time working on the National Theatre site in early summer was followed by a complete shut-down. Every effort is being made to push forward again, but the effects of the strike will be felt for some weeks to come. It is now expected that the structural fabric on the main part of the building will be completed early in 1973.

Which meant that the building would probably not open until 1974.

If we leave aside the petty grievances which could be irritating and lead to short stoppages, but were not fundamental, the 'labour troubles' of 1971 were caused by the complex problems surrounding the boom in the property market which had begun in the 1960s, had led to fortunes being won and lost, and was now approaching its peak of the early 1970s. A new member of the National Theatre Board knew all about such problems: Sir Max Rayne. Rayne, appointed to the board in August 1970, was an industrialist and a property developer—a man of great charm, very businesslike and efficient, whose conduct at meetings was very cut-and-dried, unlike Chandos, who when the mood took him, could ramble on delightfully in French. Rayne had become the chairman of London Merchant Securities in 1960, a holding company primarily, with world-wide interests in firms whose products ranged from lead acid batteries to cosmetics. The total value of the turnover of this company in 1972 was £56·9 million, and it employed 5,486 people. Through this company—and as a director of the New River Company Ltd—Rayne had an interest in various building and development companies. He became a patron of the arts in 1966, as a governor of the Royal Ballet School and the Yehudi Menuhin School; and then became the chairman of London Festival Ballet in 1967. He contributed to the Arts Council's Theatre Enquiry Report, and was a friend of Lord Goodman, who decided that he was one of those 'men of affairs' which the National needed.

Rayne was not however on the South Bank Theatre Board initially, otherwise he might have warned them not to be optimistic. They were heading for trouble. The property boom had led, inevitably, to a labour shortage, which again inevitably would lead to rises in labour costs. The collective bargainers of the building unions would not read in the papers about the profits being made from property development—and then just sit back, taking no notice. The shortage of labour provided them with the classic bargaining weapon: unless employers gave them more, the workers would go elsewhere. In this situation, employers with fixed-price contracts were the fortunate ones. The contractors would have to bear the rising costs of labour. Rayne himself had taken gambles on having fixed-price contracts, against the advice of some of his colleagues. Employers with sliding contracts, however, were in trouble—particularly those like the South Bank Theatre Board, who could not easily extend their overdrafts at the bank, hoping to recoup their losses later. The South Bank Theatre Board's funds had been fixed by Parliament and the G.L.C.: it would be a long and arduous business, first, to persuade the government that the National Theatre Bill, so recently passed, needed to be changed yet again and, second, to find time in the Commons programme to get the necessary legislation through.

Thus, the anomalies caused by the political tactics of 1969 backfired rather unfortunately in 1971–2. At a time when it was particularly important for employers to be 'flexible', the South Bank Theatre Board had their hands tied, and it was of no comfort to realize that their own fingers had helped to loop the worst knots. In vain Cottesloe must have regretted the passing of the good old days when, as chairman of the Arts Council, he had been able to approach the Treasury directly, face to (many) faces. The procedure for getting more money for the National was much more complicated, and in the meantime the South Bank Theatre Board could only plough on until the money ran out, trying to persuade the contractors that the additional money would eventually be provided—and perhaps appealing to their patriotic instincts. When the labour troubles on the site were over, there was still the problem of labour shortage; and only bold contractors could ignore the better offers from elsewhere to devote their resources to the South Bank. The sub-contractors providing the theatre's stage equipment were also comparatively small firms, who had competed vigorously to offer the lowest tenders for what they regarded as prestige work. They had under-rated in some respects not only the costs of their jobs, but also the technical expertise which would be required to design the new equipment. They had been tempted to gamble in the first place, and having done so, were now in a sense being asked to increase their stakes. Although most of the sub-contractors were prepared to give the South Bank Theatre Board their full support, it only needed one sub-contractor in a vital section to divert a few trained men elsewhere, for delays to occur—which would pluck on further frustrating halts—until a chain-reaction would set in, blocking up the entire system, until the most loyal sub-contractor wondered what he was doing keeping his men around the National Theatre site when there was more profitable work to do elsewhere.

Thus the construction work, which had begun so promisingly, slowed down, stopped, shuddered to a start again and continued on a slow, bumpy path. By 1972, it had become clear that more money would be needed from the government, now Conservative, with Lord Eccles as Minister for the Arts. Eccles responded promptly. In a written reply on August 9th, 1972, he said that legislation would be introduced to raise the total sum to £9·8 million, with the government providing an additional £1·95 million and the G.L.C. £350,000. 'We are advised', said Lord Cottesloe, 'that we cannot expect more.' This sum was enough, however, to meet inflation and also to restore some equipment (such as power-flying) lost in previous cut-backs. The National Theatre and Museums of London Bill became law by February 1973; but scarcely had it done so before there were rumours of a new crisis. In 1973, the OPEC countries raised their oil prices and transformed overnight the economic picture of countries like Britain, heavily dependent on over-seas oil. All energy prices were affected, which in turn meant that the National would cost even more to build (and to maintain, once built) — and the South Bank Theatre Board was back in its old situation, facing steeply rising inflation, which it was obliged contractually to meet, and with pegged funds, to eke out as best it could.

These recurring problems required the closest co-operation possible between the two boards, between the boards and the company, and between everybody at the National and every politician who had ever ventured a word of support. It was the time to close ranks. Lord Chandos's last term of office came to an end in August 1971. He was now nearly eighty, not in the best of health and his political and business colleagues had by now mainly retired, or died. He was made a life president of the National Theatre although, sadly, his subsequent life was not to be a long one — he died on January 21st, 1972, four years before the theatre which carried his family name opened. Sir Max Rayne succeeded him as chairman of the National Theatre Board. In many ways, he was in a much better position to rally the forces; a generation younger, in touch with the business world, in good if not close contact with the government and the G.L.C. — a widely respected and liked man.

But his task was not easy, for apart from the troubles facing the South Bank Theatre Board, the National Theatre company was going through the worst crisis of its life, caused mainly by a disastrous excursion into the West End — the New Theatre season. The logic behind the season was perfectly sensible. Just as in the previous year, the National had been trying to prepare for the task of running the three theatres in the new building by taking on a West End theatre to accompany the Old and Young Vics, so in the summer of 1971 the National had extended its operations to the New Theatre in St Martin's Lane (now the Albery). Unlike the Cambridge season, however, the stage at the New was intended not primarily to market productions first staged at the Old Vic, but to present a completely fresh repertoire of plays on a more long-term basis — the situation which they would have to face in the new building. It meant doubling the output of productions, increasing the company to match and taking the chance that the improved box-office returns would meet the rising costs of production.

The New had been Olivier's 'lucky' theatre. It was here that the great Old Vic seasons of the mid-1940s had been presented, after the Vic itself had been bombed. It had seen Olivier's Richard III, his Hotspur and Shallow, his Oedipus. The season was designed to catch the summer tourist trade in London – by starting on June 15th – and, from that springboard, to leap hopefully into the warm waters of the autumn, surviving through the colder ones of winter until the spring sun shone again. The New was about the right size for the National's second theatre, not much larger than the Old Vic, comparable in seating capacity with the larger theatre in the new building on the South Bank. It was the ideal testing ground.

The statistics tell part of the story. The season had to close after thirty-nine weeks. The audience attendance figures averaged 63 per cent, not a shamefully low figure, but nearly 20 per cent below the figures now considered 'usual' for the Old Vic, which continued to hover around the 80 to 85 per cent mark, and also considerably below the break-even box-office target of about 73 per cent. The season, which could have made money, contributed substantially to the £80,791 deficit with which the National ended the year; and the board had to face the fact that there had also been a considerable loss on the previous year's operations. The National was living well above its means. There-fore, economies had to be made. Its acting company was cut back within two years from seventy-five members to forty, at a time when it should have been expanding to meet the demands of its new building. Indeed, the most profitable side of the National's organization had become the Young Vic, which was playing to 72 per cent capacity, going on tour on its own account – to Zurich, Berlin, Edinburgh and Madrid, winning the Theatre Critics Award in Madrid for the Best Foreign Company performance in Spain during 1971.

These figures hint at, but do not fully express, the real problems caused by the season. The first casualty was that new-found confidence with which the 1971–2 season had begun. Those star attractions, Scofield and Plummer, both left – Scofield discreetly after completing his year as associate director, with the general cutbacks, Plummer more publicly following a singularly unnecessary row over *Coriolanus*. They went for different reasons. Scofield had not been at ease with the company: Olivier's mantle weighed heavily on his shoulders, and he wanted to wear one of his own. The problems of organizing two seasons from the National company had meant frequent cast changes in *The Captain of Köpenick*, a production which his performance held together. His role as the apparently tolerant husband in Pirandello's *The Rules of the Game*, which opened the New season, was less demanding, but also less exciting, until the tense last act.

Scofield had also been offered Coriolanus, but backed away from the part – which was then offered to Christopher Plummer. Plummer did not fit easily into the National team. He was accustomed to a certain kind of star treatment. The East German directors from the Berliner Ensemble, Wekwerth and Tenschert, had been invited over to direct *Coriolanus*, with Plummer's approval; but on the first day's rehearsal, he decided that he could not work for them and demanded that they be replaced—or he would go. The problem was put to the company, who decided that the directors should stay. Coriolanus was eventually played by Anthony Hopkins, but the production was not a National success. The East Germans were more accustomed to Brecht's interpretation of the play: Brecht had been on the side of the plebeians, and Wekwerth and Tenschert were puzzled by the thought that Shakespeare might have felt differently. They produced a compromise—Shakespeare's play, but made to seem as much like Brecht as possible.

Plummer was saddled with the real play selection mistake of the New season, Giraudoux's *Amphitryon 38*, which Olivier directed, playing Jupiter, the god outwitted by the resourcefulness of a mere human's love, provided by Geraldine McEwan's Alcmène. It was a very faded piece of 1939 French literary charm, and Plummer was neither particularly successful nor happy in it. He left the company, and other actors drifted away: Jacobi, Petherbridge, even Robert Stephens. It may have been time for them to go, but if the National had genuinely seemed to be accelerating towards the climactic opening of the new theatre (still scheduled, in 1971, for 1973) they would scarcely have wanted to do so.

Loss of confidence among the actors only reflected the serious doubts about the artistic direction of the company—which spread beyond the bounds of the National. Occasional flops were all right; they were expected. The National like the Royal Court could claim the right to fail—but it was not a right which could be claimed too often without the public questioning what their money was subsidizing. Nor did just the fact of failures matter—it was the tone and quality of them. *Tyger*, the musical written for the New by Adrian Mitchell and Mike Westbrook, was an example. Dexter directed it, and it could have been exciting, a treatment of William Blake's life which related Blake's visions as a Romantic radical with today. In fact, Mitchell's script was considered polemical, one-sided and banal, and Westbrook's music rather noisy. 'One's worst enemy', commented Goodman, 'should not write musicals about Blake'—particularly not, perhaps, by attempting to assert that everything that lives is holy, to rock music which suggests the contrary. *Tyger* was a kind of literary *Hair*: and it caught the tail-end of a flower-power fashion, and tripped over it. Some rather influential friends of the National thought that it was singularly ill-bred of the National to imitate the worst excesses of the commercial theatre while thumping out an anti-establishment message. That was not the way to boost grants.

The last play in the New Theatre season, *Danton's Death*, Büchner's classic early nineteenth-century epic which influenced Brecht and many other German Expressionist writers, was probably the only one to merit selection in any National programme—for *The Rules of the Game*, a sturdy play, is one of Pirandello's less remarkable works and the game is duelling for love in Sicily, hardly a burning theme for Britain in the 1970s. Jonathan Miller directed *Danton's Death*, in a translation by John Wells. It was reasonably successful, but by that time the season had been lost; and the post-mortems had begun. Who was to blame? Basically nobody—and that was the problem. Nobody had thought through the opportunities of the season, and decided what the National could and should do. Kenneth Tynan, who had returned from his long sabbatical in 1969, had for years argued for *Danton's Death*—and he strongly supported *Tyger* as well. But he was sharing the literary consultancy post with Derek Granger; and neither felt happy with the arrangement. Tynan blamed Granger for various failures, *Cyrano* among them. Olivier had wanted the Giraudoux play, while *The Rules of the Game* was a stock choice, to bring Pirandello into the National repertoire without having to bother about his more complex masterpieces.

The press attacks began again—not just in the *Daily Mail*, but in *The Times*, the *Guardian* and the Sunday papers as well. Robert Brustein, the American critic visiting the *Observer*, saw many symptoms of theatrical decadence in London's theatre, citing the National as the main culprit. Dexter's production of Goldsmith's *The Good-Natured Man* did little to help the situation, apart from filling in a gap in British drama—eighteenth-century comedy, surprisingly neglected by the National. The National had reached a low point indeed—when the old warrior buckled on his greasepaint again.

The part of James Tyrone in Eugene O'Neill's *Long Day's Journey Into Night* was Olivier's last major role at the National. This is not to underrate his performance as Tagg in Trevor Griffiths's *The Party* nor his delightful vignette as the hat-mutilating grandfather in *Saturday, Sunday, Monday*—but these were comparatively secondary characters, given a scene or two, then left. Tyrone was a part comparable in size and range to his Othello or Edgar in *The Dance of Death*; and *Long Day's Journey Into Night*, directed by Michael Blakemore, was one of those National productions which justify all the hopes and the years of labour. Brustein thought that Olivier lacked the tragic dimension in his portrayal, a frequent complaint of Olivier's acting, but on this occasion it was easy to feel that Olivier's objectivity, his marvellous touches of comedy and unstressed pathos, held pain at a distance—not because he did not know it was there, but because it could have overwhelmed if it came too near. There was something tragically apt that he should have played that part at that time, unknowingly perhaps, certainly not fully aware of what was happening around him, and yet perhaps sensing betrayal in the air. Tyrone was a once-famous actor whose life and career had turned sour. O'Neill based his portrait on his father, James O'Neill, a romantic nineteenth-century star who toured the United States with his own company, until years of hoofing and swashbuckling and dodging creditors had left him mean, suspicious and dependent on drink. Olivier was not that man, he was not even remotely like him; but he understood him with an intuitive insight which etched deep lines on the minds of those who were lucky enough to see his performance.

In retrospect, however, it was the context of his Tyrone which was so tellingly sad for, without Olivier's full knowledge, steps were being taken to replace him as director of the National. Just before Rayne's assumption of duties as chairman of the National Theatre Board, in that month's hiatus when Chandos was clearing out his papers and Rayne was briefing himself, Lord Goodman had spoken to Peter Hall. Ten days before, in July 1971, Hall had decided not to go ahead with his post as Director of Productions at Covent Garden. He had been working there for a year, on the understanding that he would be a co-director of Covent Garden with Colin Davis from September 1971. But Hall had not been happy there. He disliked the inelasticity of opera programmes, the necessity to plan so far in advance that all the excitement seemed to go before the productions began rehearsals, the hampering traditions of grand opera. He even said that too much money was being spent on an élitist art form. And so, before his appointment fully came into effect—there had been a probation period—Hall offered his resignation, deciding to go freelance. There was, he insisted, no connection between his leaving Covent Garden and his appointment at the National—although he must have guessed that following the National's lean years and Olivier's illness, the time would probably be coming when the board would look for a new director.

When Goodman spoke to him, Hall responded cautiously. He was not going to be Olivier's assistant, and he did not want to be another associate director. And he did not want to take over without Olivier's approval. He did not want a row which would rock the National boat again. He asked to speak to Olivier. The board asked him not to. It would have been unfortunate for Olivier to hear in a roundabout way that the question had even been discussed about his going or that there had been private discussions about his successor. Indeed, the question of Hall's succession and Olivier's departure had not even been discussed at board meetings. Alfred Francis knew nothing about the matter until it was a *fait accompli*. Hall just had to avoid seeing Olivier, for he was instructed not to talk to him about the question which concerned them both and yet silence in the future might have been misconstrued as duplicity. When he saw *Long Day's Journey Into Night*, Hall could not go backstage to congratulate Olivier.

And yet was all this Machiavellian tact really necessary? For when Rayne had taken over as chairman, Olivier had immediately gone to see him, to offer his resignation—which Rayne had refused. Indeed, he reassured Olivier. He told him that his services to the National were invaluable. The board did not want to lose him. And so Olivier carried on, while discussions about his successor continued behind his back. In defence of the board, it must be added that, first, they had not yet made up their minds that he should go, and second, several of them were convinced that he wanted to stay until the opening of the new theatre, whatever he might have said to Rayne.

These discussions took place in the late summer of 1971, July and August. Olivier did not hear about them until the following March, and in the meantime he was playing James Tyrone. Irving Wardle described his performance in *The Times* in a review which, written within a couple of hours of the final curtain, captured the immediate impression more exactly than perhaps a longer-considered piece could have done.

... a performance of intense technical and personal fascination. Personal in the sense that James Tyrone was an actor with the kind of career which Olivier spent his life in avoiding: a strong young talent destroyed by years of imprisonment in profitable type-casting. We see Tyrone at a stage where he is all too aware of this; and the dejection that settles on Olivier's frame from the start—his body hunched and his mouth cracked into a small crooked line—expresses a sense of defeat that encompasses his whole life and not merely his family. There are touches of the old ham: as where he smugly intones a few of Prospero's lines and turns to his son in naked appeal for applause; and where Olivier pulls out a pair of his own incomparable physical tricks in staging two contrasted descents from a table. But what marks out his performance most from the others is its breadth; all the components of the man are there simultaneously—the tight-wad, the old pro, the distracted husband, the ragged Irish boy—and there is a sense not only that O'Neill is showing off the different sides of the character, but that Olivier is consciously manipulating them for his advantage [*The Times*, December 22nd, 1971].

Olivier's last major role at the National could have been chosen more self-consciously. It might have been, say, Prospero, or King Lear (a part which had been pencilled in for several National programmes) or even perhaps Nathan Detroit, in Loesser's musical *Guys and Dolls*. *Guys and Dolls*, which the National had planned to do, was one of the casualties of the New season. Patrick Donnell had argued that, in view of the deficit, the National simply couldn't afford to take the risks with a major musical. But it might have appealed to Olivier to end his National career lightheartedly, with people saying, 'He's funny', rather than too sombrely; it was a trait in his character which took even his friends sometimes by surprise—that determination to deflate tension, which he felt acutely. At a memorial gathering at the Coliseum, following the death of his old colleague, Stephen Arlen, he had gone on the stage and sung comic songs, almost in the style of Archie Rice the music-hall ham, before continuing with a tribute. That was on March 4th, 1972, and at the end of the following week Rayne told him of the board's decision.

Rayne had for some time been trying to tell Olivier, but it had not been easy to arrange a suitable meeting. They were both busy men. After the run of *Long Day's Journey Into Night*, Olivier had gone to Italy filming, and Rayne waited until his return. They met on March 11th, and it was a polite, formal meeting, hedged with several qualifications. Hall had insisted that there were two pre-conditions before he would accept the job—first, that Olivier himself should approve; and, second, that the board should consider (and accept) Hall's view of the necessary policy changes at the National. The board also added that they wanted Olivier to lead the company into its new building—and therefore they wanted him to remain in charge with Hall as co-director, until 1974, the expected date of opening.

On the surface, and judging from public statements, all was sweetness and light. 'I gave [Olivier] an account of our thinking,' Rayne stated afterwards to the press,

234

saying we hoped he would continue his association with us as an actor, and told him we had plans to perpetuate his association with the National Theatre, including his appointment as Life President. I also said that in our view the outstanding candidate for the succession was Mr Peter Hall, but we did not wish to go ahead with the idea unless he was wholeheartedly in favour of it.

The choice came as 'a surprise' to Olivier, but he 'expressed unqualified pleasure, as he still does'. The subsequent meetings between Hall and Olivier were equally friendly, as Hall has recalled. Olivier sent him a telegram: 'Dear boy, how wonderful!' and subsequently promised him his full support.

Beneath this surface, however, there was acrimony. Olivier had not been properly consulted and, when he was finally told, he was sworn to secrecy so that he could not tell his closest colleagues, such as Tynan, who were also involved. In the only comparable example, from Stratford in 1968, Peter Hall himself had nominated his successor, Trevor Nunn, a choice approved by the board of someone who had 'grown up' with the company. Olivier probably felt that the lack of consultation reflected upon his status at the National, and also that of his closest colleagues, whom he would certainly have asked for advice. Indeed, at the beginning of March, Joan Plowright had told him that she thought that Hall was being considered—and Olivier had smiled at her, warning her not to listen to rumours.

The company only heard the news on April 9th, following a press leak from a member of the board to the *Observer*. Tynan, who was in Paris, flew back immediately to London, complaining bitterly. On Tuesday, April 11th, Olivier met the company, all sixty of them, in a sad, confused gathering which lasted for about fifteen minutes. He told them that he, not Hall, would lead them into the new theatre, that he had no intention of resigning immediately and that he had not exactly been 'stabbed in the back'. Two questions were raised which Olivier found impossible to answer. 'Is it true that Hall will be coming in in December?' and 'Why did the board not consider us fit to be consulted?' Tynan afterwards called the board's decision 'reckless' and demanded that Rayne should consult the 'artistic executive' (of Dexter, Blakemore, Dunlop, Olivier, Donnell and himself) before coming to a decision. 'We do not hold the same view', Tynan said, 'about who should be appointed, but we do agree that a theatrical organization is an organic thing, and must develop by evolution rather than imposition.'

Once more, therefore, as in the case of *Soldiers*, Tynan was questioning the status and function of the board, and, by implication the way in which state-organized and -financed theatres should be run. The board certainly had the legal right to appoint Hall without consulting the artistic executive — but two questions were raised by Tynan's remarks. Was this 'right' a just and proper one? And was their method of handling this 'right' wise and tactful? Tynan's view was straightforward; and if the artistic executive had retained the full confidence of the board, undoubtedly they would have been consulted. The danger, however, of consulting an artistic executive which, for one reason or another, has lost that confidence, or its sense of direction, is that the board and the company together become involved in a self-perpetuating disaster. A failed leadership might recommend as its successors those who would continue to pursue or in some way justify the previous policies. On the other hand, people who have done the job, usually know more about its nature than those appointed as public trustees by the Minister for the Arts. It is the classic dilemma of all state-supported theatres, particularly acute in the case of the National, which had been foreseen since the days of Irving, Arnold and Granville Barker.

Nor was it quite true, however, to suggest that members of the company had not been consulted at all. Delicate and confidential conversations had been held with the comparatively detached and 'fringe' members, such as John Wells, during the preceding months. The board's decision was a snub to the artistic executive — and was seen as such. Nor did the board appreciate perhaps the rivalry between the National and the R.S.C. — one thought to be the creation of true stage professionals, the other of bright university boys with degrees, 'show-biz' versus 'art'. The withdrawal of Stratford from the proposed scheme in 1961–2 still rankled in some memories; and at the time, *Private Eye*, the satirical magazine, had displayed a prophetic cartoon, showing Lord Southbank (Olivier as Duncan) being stabbed by Hall's Macbeth, who would take over his kingdom. Tynan feared that, instead of having one National Theatre made in Hall's image, there would now be two. He even felt that there might be a merger between the two companies — with Hall, now in charge, as its architect, not wrecker.

And, of course, everybody felt his or her job at stake. In vain might Hall protest that Olivier 'is a man I love and respect, and it will be my job to help him and the company next year, and not rush around destroying it'. Everyone knew that Hall's style of management would be different from Olivier's, that some posts would cease to exist, others would change and that this new broom would sweep thoroughly. Olivier, however, would stay in charge until the opening of the new theatre. That had been decided. The opening date was only twenty months away, in 1974. If, however, the building were delayed, for one reason or another, Olivier would be in an awkward position — for his treatment had indicated that he had lost the confidence of the board. Would he, under those circumstances, retain the confidence of the company, particularly if they were looking towards the future and what Hall might do?

Ironically, the National had now entered a glorious spell, the Indian summer of Olivier's regime. *Long Day's Journey* marked the turn of the tide. The next production was of Stoppard's *Jumpers*, directed by Peter Wood, perhaps his funniest play, an excursion into logical positivism, with Michael Hordern as the rambling philosopher, his arms deeply tucked into the pockets of his baggy cardigan. Two other productions from the 1972-3 season were outstanding — Blakemore's of the Hecht/MacArthur comedy about the press, *The Front Page* and Dexter's of Molière's *The Misanthrope*, translated by Tony Harrison. The following year, 1973-4, brought Dexter's production of Shaffer's *Equus*, Zeffirelli's of *Saturday, Sunday, Monday* and, in a small, austere mobile production, Jonathan Miller's best production for the National, *Measure For Measure*, set in the Vienna of the 1920s. Surrounding these highlights was a wealth of competent, intelligent and strong productions — Miller's *The School For Scandal*, Blakemore's *Macbeth* and *The Cherry Orchard*, Dexter's of Griffiths's *The Party* and Olivier's of Priestley's *Eden End*. There were some disappointments — Roland Joffé's *The Bacchae* — which did not matter because the overall standard was high.

What was strangely impressive was the unity and purpose of the company. There was no great dependence on stars, nor any self-conscious efforts to discover a company style. It was the period when sturdy professional actors, disliking cant and theory, came into their own: Denis Quilley in a succession of roles — Hildy Johnson, ace reporter, in *The Front Page*, Lopakhin in *The Cherry Orchard*, the lecturer socialist in *The Party*; Alec McCowen with two supremely subtle and delicate performances in *Equus* and *The Misanthrope*; Diana Rigg's Celimène; Joan Plowright in *Saturday, Sunday, Monday* and *Eden End*; and so on. It was not an experimental period in the National's history. No great gambles were taken, except in details — Blakemore's surprising end to *The Cherry Orchard*, where the whole set swung round to reveal Fiers, trapped in his little cupboard, or the sheer daring of Harrison's *The Misanthrope*, setting the play in the Paris of de Gaulle, and matching the wit of Molière's couplets with those of his own. It was, rather, a flowering time, with no great plans in the offing, no axes to grind, no difficult rivalries. The company just seemed to relax and get on with their jobs, taking failure with equanimity, and success.

Transfers came without the company balance suffering. *Saturday, Sunday, Monday* had a successful West End run. The 1973–4 season wiped off the National's deficit from the previous year, and provided a continuing log of productions for the future. The regions were served by the inexpensive touring productions, which sometimes improved on those in the main theatre. Dexter's production of *The Party* was staged in a very elaborate set by John Napier, which contrasted rather jarringly with the concentrated arguments about the nature of Socialism, and whether revolution was possible in Britain, provided by the text. David Hare's mobile version was more simply staged and therefore more effective.

If the National could have entered its new building in 1974, as planned, it would have done so with the best company and the best overall range of productions in its history. Its actors would have included Frank Finlay (who returned for *Saturday, Sunday, Monday* and *The Party*), McCowen, Rigg, Plowright, Quilley and Olivier; and its directors would have been Dexter, Blakemore, Miller and Olivier. Hall, too, whose first National production was *The Tempest* (which opened its previews in late February 1974), had brought Gielgud back to the company to play Prospero and had lined up Harold Pinter as a director for the future. The combination of Hall and Olivier, if it had ever been possible for them to run the company genuinely together, would have provided an exceptionally strong team—their talents so exactly balanced, their faults, virtues and even their different ranges of chosen colleagues would have slotted together, a match of dissimilarities.

But as the building was still not ready and nobody quite knew when it would be completed, Olivier decided not to carry on. He announced this at a news conference on March 13th, 1973. It was a quiet occasion. Olivier looked fit and well, in a dark brown suit with thin stripes, very much the businessman, though not one about to retire. He was approaching his sixty-sixth birthday. By his side, Hall looked even younger than forty-two, his round face wreathed in smiles, paying tributes to Olivier in his quiet, very sincere voice. Tynan, more silent than usual, seemed withdrawn and tense, though sporting a black shirt and a bright tie. The battles over the years had left their marks: his hair was turning grey and he had developed trouble with his lungs, which left him short of breath. He had no very definite plans, but he wanted to settle down to write some books. He was asked why he was leaving the National. He replied quietly, 'Sir Laurence asked me to join. He was always my host, and I was his guest. And I think that it is only fitting that I should go when he does.' Privately, he knew—as Hall did—that there would be no place for him when Hall took over.

Miller, Blakemore and Pinter did not come. Farewell ceremonies over canapés in the Old Vic's circle bar may not have appealed to them. Olivier gave the only firm news to the surrounding journalists—that he was going. He deflected awkward questions with professional charm. What were the National's plans for the future? They would be announced in due course. What about those television commercials in the United States? Would they be shown in Britain? No comment. Finally, B. A. Young, the doyen of theatre critics (from the *Financial Times*) thanked Olivier for his courtesy and help to them over the years; and the assembled critics and reporters drifted away. Hall's regime was about to begin. Olivier's was almost over.

What had been achieved by his (nearly) ten years at the National? What had distinguished his reign? Well, he had got the place going, very convincingly, and often against great odds. He had kept the company together through continual difficulties, some of which were of his own making, but most of which were not. The first few years had been harassed by lack of money, the latter ones by uncertainties over the building, and throughout his health had been suspect, partly because of the way in which he would unreasonably drive himself to exhaustion when others would have relaxed. Time and again, when the company was facing difficulties, he would rescue them, like a tough actor-manager of the old school, with performances which nobody else could match. Irving would have saluted him from the shades of the Lyceum, and one reason, as Robert Cushman has pointed out, why British theatre-goers should be grateful to the National is that it kept Olivier in one place, London, working so hard for so long.

How did the results at the National compare with the aims at the start? Did it provide a 'spectrum of world drama'? Of course not. One can point to whole areas left untouched, not just of world drama but of European drama (no Corneille, no Racine in his time, no Schiller, no Lorca, very few contemporary dramatists from the Continent)—and not just of European drama, but of British too (only Marlowe before Shakespeare, only Goldsmith and Sheridan from the eighteenth century). The 'spectrum' had been filtered through several selective prisms. Nevertheless, the National in his time was probably less parochial than any other British theatre has been, before or since, and for that fact, credit must go to Tynan the architect of the non-parochial policy, and to Olivier for listening to him.

Did the National provide 'the best of everything'? Obviously not — but it retained an awareness of the best, even in its lean years. It never became a complacent, Civil Service or bureaucratic theatre. The contradictions of its policies — 'stars' versus a 'permanent company', for example — derived from a knowledge of how good different approaches could be. They wanted to try them all, and in some seasons seemed to reconcile the incompatible. If *Othello* was the perfect example of a star-orientated production, then *Uncle Vanya* and *The Recruiting Officer* were superb ensemble productions. Olivier's handling of his company was criticized, rightly, from both angles. His presence deterred major actors of his own generation from joining the National, and those who came often regretted it. Equally, one could hardly expect the democratic ensemble such as Gaskill envisaged to gather around an actor-manager like Olivier. Nevertheless, there were very few occasions during Olivier's regime when one felt that the acting company was simply unable to tackle the tasks which it had been set. They may have been the wrong tasks, or poor productions, but the failures were of judgment, not of talent. If Olivier lacked that generosity sometimes to tolerate rivals, he could show the utmost patience with comparatively inexperienced actors and directors, much younger than himself, without his great technical range, encouraging them more by example than words and by simply making himself available.

Guthrie thought that when Olivier went to the National he was wasting himself. He would have to neglect the thing that he did really well, acting, for managing and administrating, which others could do equally well, or better. This may have been true — but Olivier brought a particular quality to running the National. To use an ugly word associated with notepaper and handkerchiefs, he 'personalized' it. From the public's point of view, his performances represented the National at its most unique, if not always its best; and he also embodied a kind of nationalism — whose origins could have been traced back not just to the Vic seasons during the 1940s, nor to *Lady Hamilton, Pride and Prejudice* and the other popular 'classic' films which made his name a household word, but to the way in which his personality retained an Edwardian flavour, even when adjusting to the demands of new worlds. This antique style was not dandyism, but a sense of dignity; not jingoism, but an unforced patriotism; not personal honour exactly, but a strong feeling for duty; the capacity to worry in silence and the determination to show himself a man when trouble struck; the separation of his private, from his public, self; the standing up quite suddenly for causes when nobody knew he cared — either trivial ones, against the opening of Shakespeare's tomb, or the kippers struck from the breakfast menu of the Brighton Belle, or more controversial ones, such as his championship of Edward Bond's *Saved* which brought prosecution against the Royal Court; his loyalty to—and cynicism about—friends; his way of shouldering aside accusations of heroism, his curious detachment, his stage virility and even his mistakes. The more Olivier seemed to adjust to circumstances, the more, it seemed, the public identified with him, for they were doing the same. But he also represented the limits to adjustment: he would go so far, but no further. He may have been wrong about the stands he took, but his fear of making a fool of himself and 'letting the side down' by bringing the National into disrepute was also very British.

Within the company, too, his role was a particularly personal one. He was not a natural leader, but he knew what was meant by leadership, and acted the part accordingly. He once described his job as that of being a kind of archbishop—by which he may have meant father confessor, sympathizer, wise old man and spiritual adviser. He probably could have been all these things, from time to time, but there was a strong vein of egoism unsuitable for archbishops. This selfishness, however, made him more, rather than less, endearing in the eyes of some, because it prevented him from being too inhumanly remote. He could be cantankerous, unreasonable, domineering, over-forceful and often demanding a protectiveness from others which he was unwilling to give himself. But he was there, as a father figure should be, and reliable, and prepared to set an example, and sufficiently humble to recognize his limitations. He had favourites in his family, but those who were not rarely had reason to fear him. But he liked to keep rivals away. He had strong territorial instincts.

Olivier also provided a centre of established excellence, around which other talents could grow, although they did not always want to stay. And he himself seemed to grow, for he lost some of that determination to prove himself at every gesture, at each flicker of an eyelid, which had made his earlier performances at the National sometimes seem too studied. He pulled in honours at the National without seeming to fish for them— Honorary D.Litts from Birmingham and Edinburgh Universities, Best Actor awards from the Variety Club of Great Britain and the *Evening Standard*, a special Tony Award from the United States, a Gold Medallion from the Swedish Academy, the Sonning Prize (never before given to a mere actor), his portrait hung with the greats in the Garrick Club, and, of course, his life peerage, in the June 1970 Birthday Honours List. He dithered a bit before accepting it. It was as if, like many

Britons of the time, he associated such honours with unfair wealth and privilege. When he accepted it, he had trouble in finding the right title, eventually choosing Baron Olivier of Brighton, In The County of Sussex.

The National under Olivier was prevented from being just a state theatre. That perhaps was his greatest achievement. If it did represent the hierarchical height of a state-supported system, receiving more money than other theatres and greater prestige, it was not resented for doing so—partly because everyone was aware of the struggle to establish it, partly because Olivier's headquarters in the Nissen huts in Aquinas Street scarcely suggested the ultimate in privilege; and partly because there seemed an appropriateness to the status. Olivier was our greatest actor. The National seemed the least we could give him.

16

The New Broom

THE new National Theatre building was 'topped' out on May 2nd, 1973. It was another small ceremony, a bookmark in history, indicating that the external fabric had been completed, although the work inside (of decorating, fitting and installing the complicated new machinery) had scarcely begun. Altogether elsewhere, 100 miles away, one large component of that machinery, the drum-revolve for the Olivier stage, was rising up outside the Mole-Richardson works at Thetford in Norfolk, looking rather like an empty gas-holder.

It was a cold spring day. The Thames was wrinkled with small waves as the invited guests, some eighty of them, climbed to the roof of the scenery store, and then to the top of the amphitheatre. A privileged handful clambered higher still, up the wooden steps to the top platform; where a dignified crane greeted them, bowing at right-angles, a court dignitary from a technological age. In a somewhat less dignified gesture, it lowered and disgorged the last bucket of concrete into place. A piper played 'The Battle's O'er'.

Speeches were made. Olivier praised Lasdun: 'God, and now we, know that Denys Lasdun knows his business.' Lasdun, suddenly shy, looked down at his feet. From the roof, there was a tourists' brochure picture across and along the river, to Westminster Abbey and the Houses of Parliament, to the Old Scotland Yard building by one of the forgotten possible sites for the National. The 135 years of the National struggle were recalled. Cottesloe, after a short, to-the-point speech, gave one or two perfunctory pats to the wet concrete; and then, as if this was what he had wanted to do all his life, smoothed away at the last dollop in the last hole. Applause. A boatload of tourists drifted down the river, with the guide's description of London's sights booming across. The National was now one of those sights.

In his speech, Olivier warned everybody that the owners would be sacrificed to the Gods unless they fed the builders; and so, ceremony over, they all trooped back down to the foyers, which had been cleared of rubbish. Trestle tables had been laid out for celebration purposes. The guests and workers kept mainly in separate groups, though some tried to circulate. Two of the builders produced mouth-organs: some danced, mainly Irish jigs. Above the building, a laurel branch had been nailed, a traditional symbol of good luck, warding off evil spirits. After what the National had already been through, this charm seemed a little belated. Now that the National had been so firmly constructed on such a public site, now that its presence (in Irving's words) rested upon 'a very secure basis', what further threats, short of earthquakes and wars, could assail it?

The building itself now provided the National supporters with an unanswerable argument against its opponents. It was there. It was no longer a cause, but a fact of life. What was necessary now was to prepare for the eventual move and, thereafter, to sustain and justify its presence. That was the first, and perhaps crucial, difference between Olivier's and Hall's regimes. For the ten years of Olivier's time, a company was seeking an institution: for the first four years of Hall's, an institution was seeking a company and a way of operating.

Hall responded to the challenge with great enthusiasm. He loved the promise of the new building:

> It's the best theatre complex in the world that I have seen—there's everything you could possibly desire from the first idea to the opening night—you can store, make and rehearse everything under one roof [from an interview with Philippa Toomey, *The Times*, March 14th, 1973. Copyright *The Times*, London].

His five-year contract had begun on January 1st, 1973, which was intended to give him time, first to run the company for a year in harness with Olivier, second to build up a company and a stock of productions for the eventual move, and lastly, to run the new theatre for three or four years, over the humps and ruts of novelty, and into the smoother road ahead. Privately, he said to friends that he did not want to move into the building until the last nut and fuse were in place. Reputations can be ruined by new theatres which do not quite work as intended.

The company which he was now helping to run had gone through a period of high success. The 1972–3 season had almost wiped out the deficit from previous years, which had been £140,284 at the end of the 1971–2 year, and was now only £10,220. The National Theatre had walked away with the annual *Plays and Players* awards, compiled from a poll of London's theatre critics. It had received the Best Actor and

Best Actress Awards for 1972 (Olivier and Constance Cummings in *Long Day's Journey Into Night*), the Best Director Award (Blakemore for *The Front Page*), the Best New Play (*Jumpers* by Tom Stoppard), while Denis Quilley had received the Best Supporting Actor Award for his work at the National. If Blakemore's achievements had brought him to the front rank of British directors, Jonathan Miller was regarded by many critics as the best directorial prospect in Britain, with an immense fund of energy and originality, burning a hole in the pocket of his mind, which he was longing to lavish on the new theatre. What Hall was about to receive was no tired and dispirited group, torn by the controversies surrounding Olivier's replacement. Conflicts certainly existed, resentments too, but they took their place within a buoyant atmosphere.

But the question as to what would happen when the National entered its new building dominated everything. Hall did not lack advice, public and private. Michael Billington, the *Guardian* theatre critic, wanted Hall to 'reform—indeed revolutionize—the whole concept of repertory planning' in Britain. He hoped that Hall would get away from the 'mythical sense of balance' in programme planning (for every tragedy, a comedy) in order to provide repertoires in which each play 'casts a stimulating new light on those around it'. He also put forward a much more contentious argument: that the new National Theatre company should have 'some shared idea of the kind of society they believe in', a sense of social vision, which was an unlikely idea, given the diversity of opinion in Britain, and which might have led to the charge that the National was being propagandist. Billington, however, felt that such a vision was necessary if the company was to develop a common purpose. Large companies, of 100 actors or more, cannot simply be run on the basis of personal friendships, team spirit and salary structure.

Whether the National Theatre company would eventually acquire a social vision or not, the National Theatre management certainly had to be aware of the social context in which the new theatre would come into being; and this surrounding atmosphere contained germs of many disputes. The new scale and size of the National's operations would mean, for example, that it would absorb an increasing proportion of the Arts Council's money. One myth about new theatres, thoroughly exploded by 1973, is that they are (or should be) cheaper to run than old ones. In certain limited aspects, that might be so. Richard Pilbrow pointed out (in the *Stage*, January 3rd, 1974) that technology had transformed backstage jobs, lessening the dependence on sheer muscle-power and a large labour force:

It has long been accepted that the lighting operator's role has changed from the days of the hand-operated grand master board. Now in the very largest theatres, the flyman's role will change from being a haulier of ropes to being what is virtually a computer operator.

This might not mean a reduction of the total labour force at the National, because obviously there would be many more productions to handle. That fact points to one reason why new theatres are rarely cheaper to run. The aura of modernity leads to higher expectations. The new National was also one of those self-contained buildings, with controlled heating, lighting and air-conditioning, designed for an age before the fuel crisis. This meant a large maintenance staff. There is also a historical difference between the highly cost-effective nineteenth-century theatres with large auditoria and comparatively small public service areas, such as bars and foyers. In the new National, there were large foyers, as if to stress that going to the theatre meant more than just seeing plays; and these areas also had to be maintained and cared for. The output of productions would mean an enlarged front-of-house and publicity staff; and all these factors combined suggested that the new National would require larger subsidies rather than smaller ones—in any terms, 'real' and 'relative'.

In 1972–3, for example, the National Theatre received £398,637 from the Arts Council (excluding touring grants), out of a drama budget spent on theatres in England and Wales of £3,048,660—or, roughly, an eighth of the whole. By the financial year which ended in March 1976, a year which finished with the opening of the Lyttelton Theatre and therefore could not be taken as typical of full-scale new-theatre operations (although it included some of the expenses of the move), the National Theatre company received £1,931,500 from the Arts Council, out of a drama budget of £7,216,500—or more than a quarter of the whole. The National Theatre could claim that no money was actually being taken from other theatres to pay for its increased operations; but at the same time, the gap in privilege (as gauged by grants) was clearly widening—between the National and the R.S.C. (which was in grave financial trouble), and between those two national companies and the rest of the subsidized theatre system, consisting of sixty-one theatres and ninety-eight other organizations.

This state of affairs was made more difficult by soaring inflation (which affected every theatre, but the National more than most), by building delays and technical troubles, and by a growing feeling within the theatrical profession that much money had been spent on buildings,

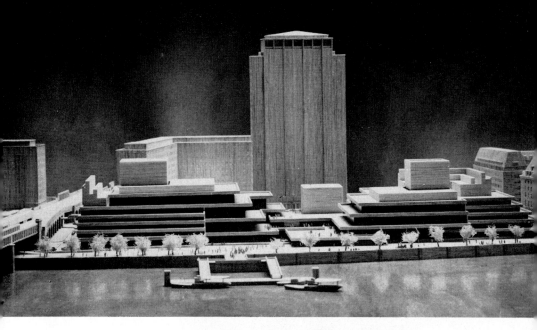

28 Model of the South Bank
National Theatre and
Opera House, June 1965,
designed by
Denys Lasdun

29 Discarded models for
a National Theatre
complex in Denys Lasdun
and Partners' offices

30 Model for the re-sited
National Theatre in
its eventual location
by Waterloo Bridge,
by Denys Lasdun

Left:
31 Lord Olivier filling in the last hole on the roof of the new National Theatre at the 'topping out' ceremony, May 2nd, 1973

Below:
32 The interior of the Cottesloe Theatre

Above right:
33 The interior of the Olivier Theatre under construction, showing the drum revolve

Below right:
34 The auditorium of the Cottesloe Theatre

35 The auditorium of the Olivier Theatre
36 The auditorium of the Lyttelton Theatre

but too little on improving the lot of actors and actresses. In December 1972, Equity published a report which pointed out some stark facts. Despite all the new theatres, two-thirds of Equity members were out of work at any given time, a proportion which had scarcely declined since 1966. The median earnings of those employed (a figure obtained by excluding the very high amounts received by stars, and then finding the average wage of the rest) had scarcely risen in eight years. The average wages of Equity members in 1971 were just under £20 a week for men and just under £12 a week for women—roughly £16 and £18 respectively less than the average gross weekly earnings for all working people, as provided by the statistics of the Department of Education.

This report eventually led to a campaign for 'living wages'; and, in May 1973, the National Theatre negotiated new minimum salaries for its actors, which raised the lowest wage from £18 a week (with 50p performance fees) to £25 a week (with £1·50 performance fees). The stage staff at the National, however, had a better deal than its actors and actresses. A stage manager's minimum wage was £47 a week, his deputy's £37 and an assistant stage manager's £30. Under the spartan circumstances at the Old Vic and Aquinas Street, under the pressure and excitement of creating, and belonging to, a National company, the company might be prepared to accept these low basic rates; but how would they feel in the new building, surrounded by evidence of state munificence which had somehow neglected their interests?

Building up a company to enter the new building would, at some stage, mean a fresh look at the conditions of employment—and not just the money, but the delicate balance required between security and 'freedom'. Actors pinned down to long contracts might get frustrated, particularly if their earning capacity (perhaps boosted by successful appearances at the National) had greatly increased, and they had been offered tempting roles elsewhere; but, equally, short or *ad hoc* contracts, lasting for a production or so, would damage the company's continuity and weaken the sense of personal security. There was also the matter of stars, who might not want to join the company, except to play particular roles in named productions. A National without stars might be thought not to represent the best of British theatre; but a National over-attracted to the star system would be operating almost like a commercial company.

The general relationship between the new National and London's other commercial and subsidized theatres also required thought, for the arrival of a large complex containing three auditoria can be compared to the building of a multiple store in a shopping area, previously reserved for smaller, well-established businesses. The other traders were likely to scream 'Unfair competition', particularly since some of their money was helping to boost a new, mammoth rival. The high proportion of Arts Council money spent on the National inevitably would mean pressure, expressed through the Arts Council's drama panel, that more money in future should be spent on regional theatres and that London's other subsidized theatres should have a lower priority. This might mean that it would be politically inconvenient to subsidize the Old Vic after the National had left, which proved in fact to be the case, and if the National ran 'new plays' seasons effectively, what would become of the Royal Court? It could be argued that the National's presence would help to streamline the tasks performed by other theatres, but this view was not likely to be accepted by companies suffering in the streamlining process.

The commercial sector of London's theatre scene was about to face a particularly tough time. Apart from the continuing burden of V.A.T., from which all theatres suffered, there was simply less money left in private hands to pay for the theatre through the box-office. Various measures to help commercial theatres (such as the Theatre Investment Fund) were slow in coming to fruition. Although in London tourists kept the West End alive and breathing, the commercial theatre was generally in decline, particularly in the regions and among those managements which had formally received touring shows. The old powerful touring circuits had broken up in the late 1950s and early 1960s; and the Arts Council was now trying to implement the touring grid proposals set out in their document *The Theatre Today in England and Wales*, which envisaged that there should be a new network of between twelve and eighteen touring theatres, a sharp decline from the days when there had been more than 100 of them. Thus the situation envisaged by Granville Barker, whereby the National should be a protected area within a predominantly commercial system, was no longer the case. The National was now the head of a state-subsidized system: it had been placed there by several government acts and maintained by grants.

Within a commercial system, for all its faults, there is always some fluidity. Companies rise and fall. One theatre gains pre-eminence, and then another. The National was in the curious position of not being able to rise or fall in this way at all. Its status had been fixed by its title and its building. The National was thus in danger of becoming an adjunct to the corporate state; and while this metamorphosis might seem to some like that of a grub to a butterfly, it might appear to others more like a change from a frog to a fossil. Hall's task was one which reflected the recurring dilemma of Socialism. In trying to build, from central government action, a fairer and more democratic society, it is too easy to land up with the exact opposite. Just as nationalization, aiming to take an industry out of the hands of a privileged few, ends up with one board instead of fifteen, with a chairman who is a political appointment, so Hall found himself eventually in the unpleasant position of being a man with no rivals, only friends and enemies.

The problem facing all state-subsidized theatre systems is a classic one, that of 'values'. How can a small group of men and women, however enlightened, however representative of different aspects of the theatrical profession, decide what talents in the country require support (and by how much) and which do not? It is obviously an impossible task, but one which the Arts Council had to tackle as best it could. In Britain, the time-honoured solution was to invoke the 'arms-length' principle — whereby governments are supposed not to interfere with the choices of the Arts Council (apart from determining the total size of the Arts Council's grant) while the Arts Council tries not to interfere unduly with theatre boards, which in turn give as much freedom as possible to their artistic directors. In effect, this usually means that institutions are supported (rather than people) — in the hope that the talents will come along in time, to fill and justify the institutions.

At a certain point, however, the arms-length principle can become a polite phrase for another practice altogether, of washing one's hands of the 'values' problem, for it is almost impossible to disassociate patronage from preferences. There have to be some reasons why one theatre is favoured rather than another. When artistic considerations fly out of the window, political ones batter down the door. Future historians will probably note ironically the sheer number of reports, committees, investigating teams, party manifestos and other time- and money-consuming bits of action which surfaced through the first five or six years of the 1970s, all somehow arriving at the conclusion that more money was needed for the arts from somewhere to do justice to everyone. A different kind of salesmanship emerged. It was not necessary now just to sell a production to the public, but to sell a theatrical institution to the Arts Council and, beyond them, to the government. One had to justify the theatre as a Necessary and Vital Part of the Life of a Community.

On the South Bank, there was a particular problem, in that it was hard to show that a community life actually existed, for the whole area from County Hall to London Weekend Television headquarters had been so relentlessly dedicated to the arts and other social services (such as car parks and G.L.C. offices) that the former small businesses and rows of tenement houses had gone altogether. It was almost necessary to create a sense of community life so that the National could be part of it, for otherwise Lasdun's terraces and walkways would have remained untenanted, as desolate as the roundabout near Waterloo Station, or the windswept archways supporting Hungerford Bridge, where, among the damp and derelict vaults, the artist Feliks Topolski was in the continual process of creating a giant mural for our times.

By the autumn of 1973, the South Bank Theatre Board felt confident enough about the building's progress to give a new and fairly firm date for its opening:

> ... it is the aim and hope of the Board that the building shall be complete before the autumn of 1974 and that, after time has been allowed for ensuring that the building is fully operative, the official opening can take place in the first half of 1975 [*South Bank Theatre Board Annual Report* 1972–3, brought up to the date of its publication on November 30th, 1973].

Confidence, perhaps, is not quite the best word to describe the mixture of feelings which accompanied that simple statement. The exact date for the opening was still provisional, April 23rd, 1975: but the board thought (and Rayne and Hall agreed with them) that if a date were announced, the contractors would double (or quadruple) their efforts to meet the target. Hall had agreed with the general proposition that the only way to get the builders out was to start to move the company in. It was felt that the situation was similar to any family trying to get into a new house: until you actually start sitting in one of the rooms, making coffee on primus stoves, the builders and decorators do not realize the urgency. The contractors themselves, of course, might tell a different story—about clients becoming so impatient that they hover around and get in the way. This domestic parallel (often mentioned) was a little too simple for comfort—for while it may be possible to hurry builders along who are grappling with comparatively simple tasks, the contractors for the theatre were sometimes installing highly complicated and experimental equipment, where more haste could very easily mean less speed.

Having changed his mind about waiting until the building was ready, as soon as the South Bank Theatre Board gave him the green light Hall revved up the National Theatre engine, ran through his gears from bottom (nearly) to top and got ready to race to the smooth motorway ahead. Unlike Olivier, always reticent about public statements, Hall was fully aware of their importance and thus gave many interviews; and, again unlike Olivier, he expressed a vision for the company which ranged far beyond the particular programmes which they were likely to present—offering a picture of the role that he intended the National to play within the whole theatrical system (both in London and the regions) and its future significance for society at large. His views were expressed through interviews, press statements and in the underlying reorganization of the company; and altogether they provided a radical departure from, and a dramatic extension of, the policies previously envisaged for the National.

Hall did not want, for example, the sheer size and status of the company to tempt it towards the *rigor mortis* of a bureaucracy:

> Change is the essence of the theatre, of any dialogue with the public. But one thing is constant for me: a belief that the theatre is a living element of our community, altering its nature according to the responses it receives, and modifying those responses by its work ...

> You almost always disturb people when your theatre is alive, because art always challenges preconceptions. As a nation, we are usually sceptical of dogma, whatever its political complexion. So the need to ask questions in our theatre is strong. It's a small part of our democracy ...

> The theatre is essentially ephemeral, uncertain, unfixed ... Theatre erupts all over the place, in pubs, basements and unused shops [Interview with Helen Dawson, *Observer* Magazine, September 16th, 1973].

Hall did not therefore intend that the National should be just a company with a particular kind of repertoire, filling a certain gap in Britain's theatrical life; but a *place* (where theatre could 'erupt') and a *process*, a dialogue with the public where the 'right' questions ought to be asked. For this reason, he wanted the doors of the National to be open all day every day 'to the fringe, to musicians, to poets, to the young with their experiments from here or the other side of the world; not in the interests of comprehensiveness or trendiness, but because this is the way to keep the National Theatre's own work alive. It must be, in a very real sense, the nation's theatre ... '

This sounded fine, though also, for some tastes, too vague, too much concerned with presenting an acceptable public image and reminiscent of the enthusiasms of the late 1960s. Theatre can erupt, but much of it is highly premeditated; it can ask awkward questions, but often does not; it can be part of a democracy but also of totalitarian societies. And so on. Furthermore, by stressing that the theatre is essentially ephemeral, Hall seemed to be diverting attention away from the fact that while the activity may change and be short-lived, the institution which he was about to run was not. Such statements also reflected the growing importance of fringe theatres – and perhaps of the fresh interest in access TV or chat-ins on radio programmes. Was this the way of demonstrating that state institutions like the National or the B.B.C. could be perfectly democratic and open to the public at large? Were such demonstrations merely cosmetic? In another interview, this time with Tynan on the B.B.C.'s 'Arena' programme (October 30th, 1975), Hall said that 'the theatre is society's debate with itself, at flashpoint' – but unfortunately, to have a flashpoint theatre, you really need a powder-keg society; and in such societies, alas, as in Belfast, the debate can rarely be contained within a theatre.

One of Hall's first, and most distinctive, appointments was of someone who could arrange this flow of surrounding events, Michael Kustow. Kustow had been part of Hall's R.S.C. team, editing the house magazine, *Flourish*. His personality shared some of Hall's *chutzpah*, his openness and bounce. Kustow was also likely to be useful to the National in other ways. He had just completed (in November 1973) a book about Roger Planchon, the French actor-dramatist-director, whose work at Villeurbanne, near Lyons, led to his appointment as a joint-director of the Théâtre National Populaire (T.N.P.). Kustow's knowledge of European theatre meant that he could be put in charge with Molly Daubeny of visiting companies; and the T.N.P. was the first foreign company to arrive at the new National, in autumn 1976.

The nucleus for this surrounding activity was to be provided by the company; and Hall had clear ideas as to how the National Theatre company should be run and what type of work it should undertake. At a conference organized by the Council of Regional Theatres (CORT) in November 1973, he outlined his plans. The Olivier was to be the permanent home for the National Theatre company, while the Lyttelton would provide a place for visiting regional and foreign companies, as well as seasons for new writing and for programmes based around certain themes. One such subject might be German Expressionist drama:

German Expressionist drama is totally unknown in this country. It's just something we pay lip service to. I would think twice about doing a Toller play or a Kaiser play in the Olivier repertoire, but if I was going to do three of them together for a short season in the Lyttelton, called German Expressionist Drama, with a few films at the National Film Theatre of German Expressionism, some pictures in the foyers and a few talks about German Expressionism, one could get something going [Interview with Robert Cushman, *Plays and Players*, August 1974].

The Cottesloe would feature small-scale work (Hall disliked the word experimental) from the National Theatre company and visitors.

Outlines are outlines, and experience has the untidy habit of twisting them out of shape; but there are some interesting features in Hall's verbal sketch for the new National. Granville Barker's old idea, for example, that two auditoria would lead to a fuller use of a permanent company, had either been dropped or considered so obvious that it had been omitted. The National Theatre company, which would consist of about 100 actors, would occupy the Olivier continually — 'I am not going to have, and I say this absolutely categorically, I'm not going to have guest visits in the Olivier' (interview with Robert Cushman) — and sometimes play in the Cottesloe; but there was no stress on a full and economic use of the permanent company, by arranging the repertoires so that, say, a large-cast play in the Olivier would balance with a small-cast one in the Lyttelton. Nor were there indications that Hall considered that the shapes of the two stages and auditoria at the Olivier and the Lyttelton would, in a sense, dictate the choice of plays to be performed there. He was evidently keeping his mind open on this question, so open, in fact, that *Blithe Spirit* (which most directors would assume to be a proscenium-arch play) was at first scheduled for the Olivier, while the example quoted in the Cushman interview — of German Expressionist drama for the Lyttelton — seemed another curious choice, in that the scenic scope, the free-flowing narration and the symbolism of that genre would appear likely to benefit from the Olivier.

Hall was concerned that the necessary size of the National Theatre company might prove too large for a proper company spirit. 'Forty is about the maximum,' he said (in an interview with John Higgins, published in *The Times* on June 29th, 1974), 'and 30 is the ideal.' He therefore proposed to split the company into groups, each working with a certain degree of independence. An example of that system came during the 1974–5 season, while the company was still at the Old Vic. One team tackled Wedekind's *Spring Awakening*, *The Tempest* and, on tour, *Romeo and Juliet*, a less successful mobile production. Thus, Jenny

Agutter played Thea and Miranda, while Beryl Reid took the parts of Mrs Bergman and the Nurse. A second team (including Gemma Jones, Benjamin Whitrow and Gawn Grainger) appeared in John Hopkins's *Next of Kin* and Beaumarchais' *The Marriage of Figaro*; while a third could be regarded as *The Front Page* company, which went to Sydney, Australia, for a ten-week season in April 1974, and returned to rehearse and open A. E. Ellis's *Grand Manoeuvres* in the autumn.

By dividing the company into teams, Hall was not only trying to keep the units small and unwieldy, but also allowing sections of the company to detach themselves from the main group in order to tour.

[This system] also gives us flexibility in our own movements. A National Theatre should be what its title says, a theatre for the whole country. And that is the way it must be. We can easily and at short notice send one of our groups out of town, or abroad, without up-setting the stockpile of productions we have available in London. But as we send out, so we want to receive back, at the Lyttelton and the Cottesloe [Interview with John Higgins, *The Times*, June 29th, 1974. Copyright *The Times*, London].

Hall thus seemed to be bearing in mind the needs of the regions, and such tours might either be arranged on their own account or as part of a swop arrangement with regional theatres. This policy appeared to extend quite dramatically, into a long-term and systematic commit-ment, the practice which had been followed during Olivier's regime whereby regional companies would visit the Old Vic while the National company was on tour. There were snags, however, in the way of such an extension. For regional companies to visit the Lyttelton on a regular basis, there would have to be detailed forward-planning, which was always hard for regional companies to undertake. They often did not know the size of their annual grants until a week or so before the begin-ning of their financial year, in March. The National, too, was subject to such uncertainties; while the technical capacities of the new stages presented the National Theatre management with an awkward touring dilemma. No regional theatre could adequately match the facilities at even the Lyttelton Theatre; and so what should Hall do? Should he pursue the policy of a normal touring management, designing his pro-ductions for all the regional theatres on the schedule, taking the lowest common denominator (the smallest stage, the least adequate flying capacity) to govern the scale of the productions—thus neglecting the opportunities of his new theatre? Or should he plan for the new theatre, and modify (scaling downwards) his productions for tours—thus running into the charge that the regions were only seeing inferior brands of National Theatre productions? Or should he concentrate on the cheap Mobile Productions? Or take the drastic step of trying to persuade the Arts Council or the local authorities to adapt the touring theatres to meet the National's needs?

During the 1974–5 season, the National Theatre company undertook no fewer than forty-one weeks of touring, but even without the additional problems which would be caused by the new theatre they ran into many of these difficulties. Two Mobile Productions, of *The Party* and *Romeo and Juliet*, revealed the best and the worst of low-cost touring—one neater and more telling than the Old Vic production, and the other clumsy and ill-rehearsed. For Peter Hall's production of *The Tempest* to visit the Bristol Hippodrome it was necessary to book that theatre for an extra week in order to install the flying equipment used at the Old Vic—a very expensive addition to the costs of an eight-performance run. In return, the Old Vic received the Nottingham Playhouse production of Trevor Griffiths's *The Comedians*, which afterwards went to the Wyndham's Theatre under joint National Theatre and Nottingham Playhouse management.

In order to provide actors with that difficult mixture of freedom and security, Hall proposed a system whereby actors should have roughly eight months at the National, then eight in the outside world, returning to play a further eight months, perhaps with the same team. In that way, productions could be brought back with similar, if not identical, casts. Actors would not be burdened with long contracts, and the structure of individual teams could be preserved. It was never possible, however, to issue formal contracts along these lines, as a matter of course. It was a pattern of work which could be accepted (or not) by mutual agreement with the individual actors concerned.

Behind such a scheme was the attempt to maintain the freshness of the acting groups. Hall also wanted to break away from the 'idea of Granville-Barker and Shaw, who saw the National Theatre as an adjunct of further education, as a kind of library with a repertory of forty plays, which you took down from the shelf in rotation'. Hall believed that it was only possible to maintain a repertory of about six plays in a state of sparkling readiness, but that these productions should be excellent indeed, containing high-definition performances. This was another important departure from the original scheme for the National as it had developed—for the great justification for the National had always been that it would provide a repertoire of classical and outstanding modern plays, played by a permanent company in the sole

theatre in London designed expressly for that purpose. Hall was proposing a smaller repertory but one which aspired towards a higher level
of achievement. He may have been influenced by two factors, first,
that there were now many repertory companies in Britain whereas in
Granville Barker and Shaw's days there were not, and, second, that
Britain lacked directors' theatres, rather than reps. To emphasize a
few productions, rather than a whole library of them, gave greater
scope to the outstanding skills of individual directors.

Hall's policy was summarized in a press statement issued on May 13th,
1974, at his first press conference as sole Director. It contained 'three
central considerations'. The National Theatre was to be:

(1) ... a unique facility for the public, open round-the-clock as a
centre in one of the most superb riverside positions in the world.
To encourage this, a great variety of offerings will be constantly on
show, including Sundays. As well as productions in the main
auditoriums, there will be lunchtime, late-night and other performances on the terraces and in the foyers. And these, plus the
bars, restaurants, buffets and any special exhibitions, will be open
to the public all day, every day.

(2) ... a unique facility for the British theatre as a whole, not just
as a home for the National Theatre company staging only work
which represents the tastes of its Director and his associates. It should
as well, regularly provide a temporary home for other companies or
groups—regional, foreign, alternative theatre—who have something they would like to show in the National Theatre environment.

(3) ... work of the National Theatre company should be taken
regularly to the regions, and also seen abroad as often as can be
managed, possibly on an exchange basis.

At the same press conference, Hall announced details of the forthcoming
programme. He forecast the arrivals (and returns) of Gielgud, Sir Ralph
Richardson, Ashcroft, Finney, Diana Rigg, Blakely and Finlay to the
National Theatre company; and described the bank of new productions
which would open at the Old Vic during the course of the year, prior
to transferring to the new theatre when it was ready. There were seven
of them, to join an existing repertoire of *The Tempest*, Priestley's *Eden
End* and John Hopkins's *Next of Kin*. Bill Bryden, a young Scottish
writer and dramatist, who had worked with Gaskill at the Royal Court,
was to direct *Spring Awakening*, Miller would tackle *The Marriage of
Figaro*, Peter Nichols's new play *The Freeway* and Etherege's *She Would
If She Could*, and Blakemore would direct *Grand Manoeuvres*, another

new play. Hall would direct Richardson in *John Gabriel Borkman*, and Schlesinger a star-studded cast in *Heartbreak House*.

It was an impressive programme—and an even more authoritative conference, for Hall had outlined his plans with clarity and a kind of buoyant confidence, which was infectious. It seemed as if the National's hour had found its man. In the meantime, and behind the scenes, the National's management team was being changed and restructured. Above all, the management style was altering its 'personality' and daily 'methods'. Patrick Donnell was in a good position to assess the strengths and weaknesses of both Directors, Olivier and Hall, for he had worked with them both—with Olivier on tour in Australia and at the National, with Hall at the R.S.C. and, latterly, concentrating on the Barbican project. When the proposed new theatre for the R.S.C. at the Barbican development site near St Paul's Cathedral was temporarily shelved, he had come to the National, at Olivier's request. Donnell thus knew both men well; and for the first two years of Hall's management he was the main connecting link between the old regime and the new.

Some differences were obvious. Olivier was an actor, first and foremost. He learnt how to manage a theatre almost as an extension of that job. He therefore relied heavily on Donnell as his administrative director, who in turn had the services of Anthony Easterbrook as general manager. Hall, primarily a director, also loved administrating. Although he had once sworn (on leaving the R.S.C.) that he would never run a large, permanent company again, he actually seemed to enjoy the round of meetings, the full diary and the daily directorial chores. Under his leadership there was likely to be no detectable split between the artistic and the administrative sides of the organization. Hall held the strings of command firmly in his hands.

Olivier, apparently secretive, could be very frank: Hall, apparently open, could play his cards close to his chest. Whereas Olivier, particularly when first nights approached in which he was appearing, invited protectiveness from those around him, Hall was sometimes like a Tigger whom others wanted to unbounce. With Olivier, Donnell (like others) could quarrel as an equal. He had done so, over the proposed production of *Guys and Dolls* which Donnell had judged prohibitively expensive. There had been a row, patched up over drinks, which left no hard feelings. It was less easy to confront Hall, although Donnell had done so once at the R.S.C.—when Donnell objected to applying cost restrictions on productions from other directors which did not seem to apply to Hall's. At the National, under Hall, Donnell's status was less, as an assistant director, Administration, and often Hall would seem to back away from an open conflict. To that extent, Donnell's relationship with Hall was more impersonal, however friendly it may have seemed on the surface. It was difficult to challenge Hall, to say exactly what one felt, knowing that any initial acrimony would blow away. There was no acrimony, but at the same time, frankness was lost. Donnell felt that if Hall's mind was made up, Hall would eventually get his way.

This meant that those who held strong feelings about how the National should be run which were contrary to Hall's might feel frustrated; and initially, in the changeover between the two managements, there were bound to be differences of opinion.

On another level too, impersonality intervened, for whereas Olivier knew the names even of minor members of his staff and would chat to them as he passed through the foyers, or as he sat in the canteen, Hall was less instantly approachable. He could be charming, but he lacked the gift to pass the time of day companionably. Miller and Blakemore also noticed this trait in Hall's character, and it could have important consequences. Telling decisions in running a theatre can often be taken quite casually, in response to an immediate crisis, where a quick word with the director can be vital in restoring confidence or in gleaning a second opinion.

On the other hand, Hall was concerned to establish a system for consultation and decision-taking which was more broadly based than the inner cabinet which had surrounded Olivier – and more apparently 'democratic'. Hall developed the planning committee which had existed under Olivier into a more far-ranging and representative body. 'All members of the Planning Committee', stated the press release from Hall's first press conference, 'have a voice in all decision-making, with the director as final authority.' The collective nature of the National Theatre management was afterwards stressed in National Theatre programmes and playlists, although Hall was not one to pretend that a higher form of democratic life had somehow evolved through the planning committee. He was the committee's chairman, appointed its members and was prepared to take the final decisions.

In any case, a truly collective leadership would have been difficult or impossible to achieve, given the nature of the planning committee, which represented under Hall so many different skills and interests, and consisted of full- and part-time members. The committee, announced in May 1974, contained eight part-timers: Blakemore, John Russell Brown (heading the script department), Dexter, Kustow, Miller, Olivier, Harold Pinter and John Schlesinger. But they were not all equally 'part-time'. Dexter quickly left, after he had been appointed Director of Productions at the Metropolitan Opera House, New York. Schlesinger was primarily a film director, who spent much of the year in the United States, while Olivier (following his formal resignation in October 1973) was doing his best to retreat into the background.

The situations of Miller and Blakemore were different. They were symbols of continuity with the previous management, directors of proven excellence, and both were prepared to commit themselves fully to the National. 'Blakemore and I', said Miller, 'were prepared to work our guts out for the National. What the new theatre would require would be a constant outpouring of work and energy, no introverted ponderings about the Nature of Art; just straight dog-work, leaving at quarter-past nine in the morning and battling straight through the day.' There were suggestions floating around that each should be given official or unofficial charge of a team within the overall company, although this idea never reached the stage of formal agreement. They received salaries of about £6,500 a year, and were prepared to forgo other opportunities for the National's sake. Even in this brief comment from Miller, however, it is possible to detect a different approach to the National from that expressed by Hall, for Miller wanted an outpouring of work from the National Theatre company. Hall envisaged a limited number of high-definition productions, surrounded by a welter of other activities.

Before the new theatre came into operation, however, the chances of Blakemore and Miller were likely to be limited, which may have been why they were listed as part-time. The same argument could apply to Kustow, who became listed as a full-time associate director in 1976. The appointment of John Russell Brown revealed a striking departure from Tynan's days as literary manager. Whereas Tynan had been a potential showman, with cosmopolitan flamboyance, some practical knowledge in commercial theatre and a theatrical knowledge so far-ranging that it bordered on one-upmanship, Brown was a tall, sympathetic, cheerful literary don from Sussex University. His best-known book, *Free Shakespeare*, was a retort to both the over-academic approach to Shakespeare and the over-directorial one. He believed that actors should be given their heads, to respond directly to the texts and their instincts; and he hit against those who believed that there was one correct way of directing Shakespeare, or who thought that his texts could be twisted to any topicality. He was an excellent and scrupulous editor of texts; but his practical experience in the theatre was limited, particularly in that sort of theatre which helps to pay for itself by attracting audiences. Some critics came to feel that his liberal tolerance was in itself a kind of academic conditioning.

The full-time National Theatre employees on the planning committee were Donnell, Easterbrook, John Goodwin (publicity and publications), John Bury (design), Michael Hallifax (company manager) and Hall. That was the team announced in May 1974; and it was intended that two actors should eventually join the planning committee, although none had done so, even by the date of the Olivier's opening, in autumn 1976. Every other side of the National's operation by that time seemed to be represented, including catering and music; and the absence of actors from the management team was another significant difference in emphasis from Olivier's time—for Olivier had always thought of the National as an actors' theatre.

By 1975, however, the composition of the planning committee had radically changed. Members associated with the previous administration had left—Dexter, Olivier, Donnell, Easterbrook and Miller—leaving Blakemore as the sole connecting link. They had left for various reasons, but their departures altered the balance on the planning committee. Other sides to the organization came to be represented. Simon Relph joined as technical administrator, Douglas Gosling as the financial administrator (and also succeeded Kenneth Rae as secretary to the National Theatre Board), Peter Stevens (who joined the National Theatre company as Hall's personal assistant and became general administrator, taking over from Donnell) and Lord Birkett, whom Hall appointed to be in charge of 'packaging' productions, including such commercial off-cuts as video-cassette recordings, films and records.

Because several associate directors were part-timers, and not always regular in their attendance at the fortnightly meetings, the balance on the planning committee tilted towards the administrators. As the planning committee evolved, other characteristic features of Hall's management selection emerged. Whereas Olivier had chosen as his closest associates three men (Dexter, Gaskill and Tynan) whose talents he greatly admired but with whose backgrounds he felt no natural affinity, who were not initially personal friends but almost counteracting forces, compensating for weaknesses in himself which Olivier had recognized, Hall seemed to select (by accident or design) planning committee members who were either personal friends, or long-standing associates or those whose presence in the management team was unlikely to provide a strong challenge to his leadership.

Although Hall once said that he liked to surround himself with men of strong individuality, the evolution of the planning committee suggests that he did not go out of his way to seek the test of rivals. Goodwin, Bury, Kustow and Pinter were old associates from the R.S.C. days; Birkett had been a university friend. Brown and Stevens were unlikely appointments to their jobs, elevated there at Hall's wishes; which is not to suggest that they were unsuitable, but that they were comparatively unknown in the theatre world of London. Stevens had a reputation in the regions for opening new theatres (such as University Theatre in Newcastle) against the odds. There is nothing unusual in a director wishing to surround himself by those on whom he feels most reliance; but it did mean that those who did not belong within that circle felt somewhat isolated and in danger of always being in a minority of the planning committee. Furthermore, three of Hall's appointments had little practical experience in the theatre, although they adjusted to their jobs quickly. The backgrounds of Birkett, Relph and Gosling were mainly in the film industry, like Schlesinger's, who, however, enjoyed theatre directing as well and had had practical experience of it. The film men brought to the National a new awareness of large-scale planning and marketing of National Theatre productions; but there were other consequences. Relph, for example, was initially more used to film crews, rather than stage-hands, and the practices of a different union (A.C.T.T. rather than N.A.T.T.K.E.).

Because the Planning Committee was concerned with how the whole National Theatre operation was to be run, it was really necessary to have another committee which would concern itself with artistic policy. Hall arranged for monthly gatherings of his associate directors, at first in his flat at the Barbican, and then in the new National Theatre offices, where they could all float ideas which appealed to them, however remote from immediate practicalities. And so that company members as a whole should not feel remote from the management, Hall arranged for regular gatherings, shout-ins, for the actors.

Olivier had encouraged a family atmosphere within his company, with himself as paterfamilias. Hall's age (apart from any other factor) and personality prevented that sort of informality from continuing. Instead, he devised a management system which seemed to combine openness and the opportunity for democratic debate with good order and definite lines of command. It was usually possible to get a quick decision from Peter Hall; and a number of members of the company found Hall's approach refreshing and businesslike. His private telephone number was widely known and so, if his schedule during the day was crowded, it was usually possible to phone him at home in the early morning. Hall's energy in itself was a considerable asset to the

National Theatre: he was prepared to tackle all kinds of jobs with equal enthusiasm.

The tests of the system which he had devised, however, would come in the way in which it handled major policy crises, disagreements among his associates and, more importantly, the planning of continually effective repertoires. It is easy to map out on paper democratic machinery which will work if there are no difficulties—much less easy to anticipate the problems. And Hall did not have long to wait before the first crisis struck.

17

Cobwebs

1974 was a vintage year for British crises. Leading the list of several dozen brands of crises came inflation, which throughout the year exceeded a rate of more than 20 per cent, that symbolic figure chosen by analysts to mark the point where democratic institutions were liable to break down. It had been fuelled by a sharp rise in the price of oil and it burnt up the plans for industrial expansion, which had been one main strut of the Conservative government's policy for the country. One answer to inflation, an effective incomes policy, seemed to have been ruled out by Heath's failure to establish a wage-negotiating system for the country, with effective limits on cross-the-board wage rises. In trying to lay down the ground rules for such a negotiating system, Heath came into conflict with the miners—which resulted in the three-day working weeks of February and March, and the eventual fall of the Conservative government. In the ensuing election, the Labour Party was returned as the largest single party in Parliament, though without an overall majority in the House of Commons and a bare third of the votes in the country. Another election (which eventually took place in the autumn) was on the horizon, almost as soon as the votes from the first one had been counted.

The country was in a mess, which was one reason why it was such a pleasant interlude for journalists to be taken during the summer on guided tours around the new National. Some were taken down the Thames on a pleasure-boat in May, where they saw the building from unusual midstream angles and listened to Hall's optimistic forecasts as to what the new National would be like—'a facility for the whole nation's theatre'. On July 8th, parties of journalists were taken around the building itself, wearing green plastic helmets as protection in case something fell. The guides gave encouraging news:

According to the latest information from the South Bank Board ... the date of their handover [of the building] to the National Theatre

Board for furnishing and commissioning will enable public performances to be given in April, 1975, or very soon afterwards. Should
the present situation improve, the National Theatre themselves are
geared to open public performances at any time from February
onwards [press release, May 13th, 1974].

Unannounced, but in everybody's minds at the National, were the
plans for the official opening. It was going to be a big-blast, multi-
theatre event, with short productions in each auditorium, and the
audience would move between them, catching a show at the Cottesloe,
before moving on to the Olivier: a celebration, a massive party, rather
than a series of Gala performances.

On site, however, the building looked very far from completion in
July. Sections were almost ready, some dressing rooms, parts of the
scene dock and workshops; and these were duly admired. The sound
'petals' in the Olivier were slowly being hoisted into position. The
Cottesloe looked like an empty studio. The Lyttelton, closest to completion, still looked like an empty car park. Outsiders, however, could
not guess how much of the remaining work was a matter for quick
fitting or of more substantial labour. The wires leading from walls
could have been quickly connected to boxes of tricks assembled elsewhere, or they could have required the installation of difficult on-site
equipment.

Journalists were generally of the opinion that the building might be
ready by April 1975, but only just, and there was something about the
known schedule which seemed a bit optimistic. 'Originally,' Richard
Pilbrow of Theatre Projects Consultants Ltd wrote in the Stage on
October 28th, 1976, 'it had been planned to include a full six months'
minimum to test ... all equipment and facilities before rehearsals
began.' And that was the kind of time-scale envisaged in the 1972–3
South Bank Theatre Board report. But for a six months' testing period
to begin in time for an April opening, and allowing only six weeks for
rehearsal in the new building, the equipment would have to be installed
by, say, mid-September: a bare two months away. That seemed very
unlikely. Even by cutting the six-month testing period to four months,
which was one suggestion, the schedule seemed implausible.

Why was it necessary to have so long just for testing? If the stage
equipment had been made properly by the sub-contractors, and the
specifications were right, why couldn't the stuff be installed, leaving a
few weeks to get rid of the snags? Were Theatre Projects being unduly
apprehensive about the quality of British workmanship? The answer is

no, for even if every item of equipment had been designed perfectly and built perfectly, six months or so would still have been needed to make the place work as planned. The reason lay in the nature of the control system which Richard Brett of Theatre Projects had designed to handle the revolves and the spot-line flying of the Olivier stage, and the fly-bar lines in the Lyttelton. It was a sophisticated system, with many innovatory features and, bearing in mind Pilbrow's original criterion that, say, the spot-line flying had to be capable of moving scenery 'at least as rapidly and sensitively as a human being', it had to work with an exceptionally high degree of precision.

If we simply consider the Olivier revolve, the problem is clear. It consisted of two large moving components, the outer drum-revolve and the inner split-revolve; and these had to synchronize exactly. The split-stages had to lock into position on the drum-revolve, when they were in the right place; and the drum-revolve had to have the capacity to turn very slowly or very quickly, according to the demands of the production. The drum-revolve was driven by a number of electric motors, attached to wheels on its base and, since no two electric motors functioned identically, it was necessary to compensate for the fractional variations which might occur if one motor were going faster than another.

The spot-line flying also needed careful adjustment. The electric motors had to be capable of placing the individual scenery hooks at exactly the right point on the grid above the stage, and lower the lines from the pulleys at an exact speed, predetermined but (like the revolve) capable of an almost infinite number of variations; and it had to be possible to synchronize the points together. If a three-dimensional set were hung on, say, three lines, leading from three pulleys on the grid, then obviously the lines would have to descend at an even rate, because otherwise the set would tilt in the air. The pulleys also had to be in exactly the right place in relation to one another, because otherwise the set would split apart or sag in the middle. The lines had to be capable of taking various loads, from light to very heavy; and for spot-line flying it was not possible to use a counterweight system — that is, a method which places weights on one end of a line in order to balance the scenery load on the other. The motors themselves had to adjust to the weight of the set and the pull required.

Because the questions of speed, timing and precision were so important, Brett had devised a system whereby the motors were to be controlled and driven not in the conventional way (by D.C. motors), but by what was known as a cyclo-convertor system. Cyclo-convertors controlled the electric motors by changing the frequency of the current. They were not experimental pieces of equipment in themselves, but they had not been used before in this theatrical context. Several of the sub-contractors, whose equipment was going to be controlled by cyclo-convertors, were not too sure how they worked and were a little suspicious of them. Each cyclo-convertor was like having an ideally obedient stage-hand, in that it could control a tug on a line, or the moving of a point, exactly as a stage-hand would have done. The sixteen cyclo-convertors in the Lyttelton theatre were equivalent to sixteen stage-hands. The Olivier stage had thirty-five cyclo-convertors.

The cyclo-convertors had to be tuned, somewhat as radios are tuned, so that they could relate to the electric motors—which was one reason for the six-month testing period. They also had to be attached to computers, which could store the information required for changing a set. Computers—as every bank employee, or client, knows—take time to programme; which was another reason for the delay. The plain mechanics of the stages were not too complicated. Anthony Easter-brook, on a visit to the Mole-Richardson works at Thetford in 1973, had seen the drum-revolve rotating; and when it was installed in 1974 the drum-revolve and the inner split-revolve had also worked in this simple way. There had been an unfortunate accident, it is true, when a leaky roof led to flooding at the base of the revolve; but this was not a vital matter, only an annoying hindrance.

The real problems were likely to crop up during the testing period, when everything had to synchronize exactly. The control computer for the revolve had to be programmed to cover every desirable merry-go-round revolution, from one taking hours to one of a few seconds which might have thrown the actors, giddy and reeling, off-balance if not off-stage. Another computer looked after the spot-line flying, which if it were properly handled, should achieve a kind of aerial ballet, as the different parts of the total set slid smoothly into place. The two computers could be linked together, so that the revolve sets and the flown scenery also synchronized; and it is scarcely surprising perhaps to learn that the firm which developed and built the control system, Evershed Power Optics, also specialized in parts for guided missiles.

Evershed Power Optics, however, could not begin to test and programme their control system until every other item of equipment had been properly installed and was functioning as it should. They were expecting to come into the theatre on September 7th. On July 16th, however, there was some serious news discussed at the building progress sub-committee meeting at the offices of Sir Max Rayne, at 100 George

Street. This committee, sometimes known as the ginger group, had been set up in the previous months, at the instigation of Rayne and with the full co-operation of the South Bank Theatre Board, to investigate the delays to the building, to keep the National Theatre Board closely in touch and to try to get the problems quickly solved as they cropped up. It brought the contractors, sub-contractors and consultants together when needed, and it contained representatives from both boards, and from the National Theatre, such as Peter Stevens. Hall was an *ex officio* member.

The news in July was that there was a serious shortage of electricians on site; and that the basic work of installing the main wiring for the Olivier theatre had been disastrously delayed. Indeed there was now only about one week to do several months' work. Until the wiring was completed, the equipment could not be properly installed, and therefore Evershed Power Optics could not begin testing. The chances of opening in April 1975 now looked extremely remote.

Despite the ginger group and this meeting, the significance of the delays to the electrical installation had not been fully appreciated by the South Bank Theatre Board or the National Theatre, which went on planning for the April opening. There was a meeting of the planning committee on July 26th, discussing arrangements for the South Bank; and another, of the associate directors, on August 1st, to discuss repertoire. On August 16th, Donnell had lunch with John Vernon to talk about the B.B.C. coverage of the opening ceremony; and, in the meantime, Kenneth Rae had contacted Martin Charteris, the Queen's private secretary, with the plans for the royal opening. The invitation was still at an informal stage, a matter of pencilling in the engagement for April 23rd, 1975; and the official invitation was to follow in due course, to Balmoral, where the Queen was staying. It was never sent.

Donnell discovered the bad news by accident. In mid-August he had interviewed a possible recruit as box-office manager, David Jackson from Covent Garden, who had looked over the plans for the National Theatre box-office in the new building. He had not liked the way in which the box-office was designed, and said so to Donnell. Donnell decided to walk over from his office in Aquinas Street; and on the way, he met Richard Pilbrow, who told him about the shortage of electricians. The electricians could not cope with the problems immediately arising; and a backlog of work was piling up. Donnell investigated and agreed with Pilbrow that the proposed schedule simply could not be met.

Immediately, Donnell returned to Aquinas Street, and held back the official invitation to the Queen, until the situation could be examined more thoroughly. On September 30th, the National Theatre called for an emergency meeting with the contractors and sub-contractors, with Rayne and Hall asking point-blank questions of them, which could be minuted, documented and thus produced in evidence against the contractors, should they fail to meet their commitments. When would their work be finished? How advanced were their schedules? One by one, they hesitated, qualified their remarks with important reservations, until they all gradually realized that the April deadline was impossible. Indeed, nobody could say for certain when the building would be finished. The target date had turned out to be mere speculation once more, as the others had been, spring 1973 and spring 1974.

That was dreadful. Everybody's plans were ruined, including Hall's. The National Theatre machine, accelerating to top gear, had to be slammed into reverse. Donnell had to arrange for more than 100 letters to be written, cancelling, altering or postponing contracts and agreements. Famous actors had to be told, 'Sorry, but can you come back next year — or some time?' Anthony Easterbrook had planned to place some National Theatre maintenance staff, particularly electricians, into the new building, under Douglas Cornellisen, so that they could learn about the building while it was being fitted. Cornellisen, a senior stage manager in Olivier's time, was in the process of learning his new job, as head of the maintenance staff.

Nothing could be more damaging for someone like Hall, who had arrived at the National with the reputation of being a brilliant administrator, than to find his grand scheme destroyed by circumstances beyond his control. His long-term policy had to give way before quick decisions, pragmatically taken; and such choices are inevitably challengeable. Only one production of the announced 1974-5 programme was cancelled — that of Etherege's *She Would If She Could* which was to have been directed by Miller — but *Grand Manoeuvres*, which had received bad reviews and poor box-office attendance, was quickly withdrawn. That meant the disbandment of one of the three teams, which naturally disturbed Blakemore, although he did not oppose the decision.

Miller and Blakemore were thus the two associate directors whose work was affected most directly by the cut-back. Neither had had good seasons at the National. Miller's *The Marriage of Figaro* had been a curiously uncertain production, neither funny nor hard-hitting enough to represent early revolutionary drama, which Beaumarchais' comedy is usually considered to be. Miller's other main production, *The Freeway*, was an allegory about Britain in the future written by Peter Nichols, who took a choked-up highway as his main symbol. There were cartoon characters and some amusing lines; but it was an obvious, rather clumsy play, and Miller's production failed to find the form, missing from the script, which could have helped the production to work. *Grand Manoeuvres*, a documentary about the Dreyfus affair, was also disappointing, a mixture of fact and invective, of caricature and documentary realism.

In all, it had been a disappointing season, both for them, and for other directors. Hopkins's *Next of Kin* was an efficient family drama, which Pinter directed without his usual flair; while Bryden's production of *Spring Awakening* was also tidy rather than imaginative, set on an open set carrying overtones of a Brecht–Gaskill austerity, but not of Wedekind's flamboyance. Hall's *The Tempest*, with John Gielgud as Prospero, employed the techniques of Jacobean masques to convey the fantasy of Shakespeare's island; but it had been intended to open the new theatre, and on the Old Vic stage the impact of its stage mechanics was considerably lessened. Hall's production of *John Gabriel Borkman* began beautifully, in a gloomy nineteenth-century drawing room, with a high ceiling resounding with the footsteps of Borkman pacing above. Richardson played Borkman as someone whose grand visions had lost touch with reality, leaving him a doddering old ham. Sometimes the comedian in Richardson seemed at war with the tragedian, a tension suitable for Ibsen's character, although it was hard to believe that Gunhild and Ella, those forceful sisters, would allow their lives to be swallowed up by love and resentment over him, particularly when played by such commanding actresses as Wendy Hiller and Peggy Ashcroft.

It was only at the end of the 1974–5 season that the National Theatre could claim its first undoubted successes, of Shaw's *Heartbreak House* and Pinter's *No Man's Land*, which opened in February and April 1975. By that time, however, some of the psychological damage, partly caused by the building delays, was starting to have its effects. Naturally, morale in the company was low: to have the new theatre snatched away from them was frustrating in itself. Miller understandably disliked having productions withdrawn from him: 'It was like an artist being given a state pension on the understanding that he should only paint two canvases a year.' Blakemore and he had been given the most difficult assignments of the year, and they had failed; but Miller believed that too great an emphasis was now being placed on outward success—so that failures in difficult productions were penalized. What made the situation harder for Miller to bear was the thought that his extremely successful Mobile *Measure for Measure* was brought to the Old Vic for only six performances; and that his season at Greenwich, of *Ghosts*, *The Seagull* and *Hamlet*, all produced on a shoestring and bringing out as a season the family preoccupations within these three plays, had been so much more artistically successful than his work at the National.

Between Hall and Miller, there were also strong personality conflicts. Hall's manner was too plush for some tastes, including Miller's, too redolent of Madison Avenue. This style, which sometimes seemed particularly out of place in the tatty, hand-to-mouth existence at Aquinas Street, caused some friendly and not so friendly amusement, so that when, for example, Hall appeared in an advertisement for Sanderson's wallpaper casually checking a score at a piano, 'Very Peter Hall, Very Sanderson', the cutting could be found on half the green-room notice boards in London. It seemed to typify the kind of mod elegance which, it was maliciously suggested, Hall mistook for High Art. Nor did Hall's image within some parts of the theatre profession improve when he took on another prominent (though scarcely time-consuming) job outside the National Theatre, as the presenter of London Weekend Television's arts programme, 'Aquarius', at a salary rumoured to be in the region of £16,000. It seemed impossible even for a man of Hall's energy to direct plays *and* administer the National *and* present a weekly television programme.

In Miller's case, however, amusement at Hall's style quickly became a positive dislike of the man. A brilliant mimic, a compulsive talker, with a patrician disdain for discretion and even normal politeness, Miller would wander up and down the corridors of the Aquinas Street huts, telling the latest Hall-isms with relish. Miller had an ingrained distaste for large organizations and, following the withdrawal of *She Would If She Could*, he had an increasing uncertainty about his future. It was an uncomfortable situation for both men. Miller started to develop a nervous allergy to the National, which left swellings on his face. The allergy disappeared when, early in 1975, he resigned. Hall's position was also difficult. The authority which Olivier could command —of age, experience and long-standing reputation—was necessarily denied to Hall, who was subject to the enmity between equals which occur within a generation. If Dexter, Gaskill or Blakemore quarrelled with Olivier, the thought perhaps lingered at the backs of their minds that even Olivier could not go on for ever. Hall's age, in his early forties, was such that he lacked this kind of double-edged protection.

As 1974 turned into 1975, however, it was not Hall's personality which was a telling factor, but his curious fate. A web had been constructed around him, of ill-luck and bad judgment, in which he had become entangled; and his situation was not less worthy of sympathy because there may have been strands in that web which he had helped to spin. Hall might talk about the country being in the midst of a 'nervous breakdown' and about his hope that the National would become a 'reviving symbol'; but such comments did not really explain the nature of that breakdown—nor were they intended to do so.

It was tempting for the press and others to blame the building delays on the contractors, or the laziness of British workers; and there was some truth to the criticism. But the contractors had had considerable problems, which got worse not better as the months dragged by in 1974. In international terms, the delays over a national theatre were not unknown—or even unusual. The Sydney Opera House had problems as well. The British contractors were tackling unfamiliar work on insufficient money. They had accepted contracts at 1969 figures with certain sliding clauses for limited inflation; and the total price for the project had been fixed by Parliament.

Under normal circumstances, the contractors and sub-contractors could probably have survived slight losses or insufficient profits on their National contracts and cheerfully looked to the future, where their 1974 industrious labours could have reaped gains, perhaps in 1978. But 1974 was not a normal year, and when the blizzard of inflation hit them, they had little protection. All the contractors and sub-contractors were in financial difficulty, in some cases facing bankruptcy and liquidation. To protect their own interests, they had to pull workmen away from the site, for this was the only way in which they could survive. Mole-Richardson was the subsidiary of a much larger group, British Electric Traction Company, but it was uncertain whether the parent company would support them; and they were losing a lot of money on building the drum-revolve, in excess of £300,000.

In retrospect, therefore, it may seem that Parliament should have been blamed, for setting ceiling prices in the first place, which were then to be so blatantly overtaken by events. But without ceiling prices the various pieces of National Theatre legislation would have been unlikely to have passed through Parliament at all; and only acute observers of the Middle East scene could have foreseen the steep rise in oil prices.

Perhaps the whole problem of the building delays should have been handled more philosophically. The South Bank Theatre Board should have been more sceptical about the promises of the contractors, realizing the complexity of their tasks, and they should not perhaps have given a tentative green light to Hall in 1973 as a way of getting rid of the builders. The National Theatre Board, too, might have been more dubious about the hopes of the South Bank Theatre Board. Perhaps the presence of the two boards, a historical accident dating from the days when the total development of the South Bank had been envisaged, complicated matters. Chandos and Olivier, the original representatives of the National Theatre Board on the South Bank Theatre Board's executive, had had little experience of building projects on this scale — although Rayne had. Rayne was continually sorting out the difficulties of the building, trying to make sure that vital missing parts were delivered, on time, from various quarters of the world.

Hall too could have been more cautious. In an interview with John Higgins (*The Times*, June 29th, 1974), he said that he had never believed in the old saw about not running before you can walk; but in this case, some judicious walking, testing out the ground carefully, would have been wiser. Instead of trying to unfold an elaborate scheme for the National, with promises to everyone all round, the regions, the fringe theatres, a sick nation and aspiring directors, he could have concentrated on building up a much smaller company, aiming for a sense of purpose, quality of performances and productions, for stylistic variety and solid achievement. If he had established the company at the Old Vic as a truly integrated team, with a strong artistic leadership, he could have built on this nucleus at a later date. He could have guessed that there would be problems with the stages: there nearly always are — particularly with technically elaborate ones. He could thus have tried out productions which required comparatively little scenery. He had even forecast that this should be done. 'With the cost of raw materials and roaring inflation,' he said in an interview with Robert Cushman (*Plays and Players*, August 1974), 'we are going to be driven, and in my view should be driven, into discovering ways of doing theatre with people in space and with light.' Exactly so: and Hall was later at pains to stress that the technical equipment at the new National was not just there for mere display — but to help the repertoire system. But in the cause of scenically rudimentary theatre, Hall did not set a good example. His own productions — of *The Tempest*, *John Gabriel Borkman* and *No Man's Land* — were comparatively elaborate scenically.

Getting caught in such confusions, and muddling through, seemed to be the real English disease of 1974, not laziness or inefficiency solely, but feeling trapped in a maze of related problems, for which nobody was exactly to blame nor entirely free from fault, with opportunities all round to blame others, and with historical imperatives acting as a safety net for those who, having accidentally caught the buck as it passed, toppled over with the weight of it. What was happening at the

National seemed to reflect the situation elsewhere in the country. The pound was being propped up by foreign loans, at disastrous rates of interest, thus adding fuel to inflation; and the subsidized theatre, being a 'labour-intensive' industry, was particularly badly hit.

Throughout the country, major reps, many with smart new theatres built in the reckless 1960s, requiring large staffs to run them, were forced to cut back on their plans. The situation was described in the *Financial Times* on November 16th, 1974, as 'A Tragedy Playing All Over Theatreland'. Reps had to discontinue their theatre-in-education programmes; while one newly built theatre (erected at a cost of £350,000 and opened by Princess Margaret) was left with a running grant of only £3,000 to last the year, scarcely enough to pay its artistic director, who, as it turned out, had had no experience of running shows commercially. Although the Arts Council, after much private bargaining with Hugh Jenkins, the Labour Minister for the Arts, managed to arrive at an acceptable compromise between the money needed and the money which, it was felt, the country could afford, the total Arts Council grant for 1975–6 (originally £25,000,000, although it was raised to over £27,000,000 during the year) still meant that few subsidized theatres in the country could do more than the minimum necessary to stay open.

During this period, when as Cottesloe said in the House of Lords, 'the world in which we live, balanced as we are between severe inflation and hyper-inflation — inflation out of all control — is for nearly all of us alarming', the costs of building the National Theatre (and the anticipated ones of maintaining it) came to be regarded within the theatrical profession as a continual drain on precious resources. The building costs already had escalated above £10½ million; and this was the time when yet another National Theatre Bill was introduced into Parliament.

Its purpose was simple — to remove the ceiling price for the National from the hands of Parliament — but it could scarcely have come at a more tactless moment. Hugh Jenkins, M.P., presented it before the House of Commons during the Second Reading on November 7th, 1974.

The House will recall that there have already been three Acts of Parliament on the National Theatre — in 1949, 1968 and 1973. These raised the limit of the Government's financial contribution respectively from £1 million in 1949 to £3·75 million and then to £5·7 million in 1973. The GLC has likewise raised the original contribution by the LCC from £1·3 million to its present authorised level of £4·68 million. A smaller contribution from the Shakespeare Memorial Trust took the total resources available in 1973 to £10·55 million.

... It was clear earlier this year that the 1973 figure of £10·55 million would be overspent. The Government and the GLC, therefore, entered into urgent negotiations for a solution to these problems.

The solution was all too simple:

> The purpose of the Bill is to remove the statutory ceiling on the Government's contribution to the project so that, in agreement with the GLC, the National Theatre building can now be completed as quickly as possible. This should not, however, be read as a resignation by the Government and the GLC from continued control over the costs of the project ... It will be noted from lines 11 and 12 of the Bill that no contribution by the Government can be made without the consent of the Treasury. We have specified that additional resources can be used only for completing already approved work. There can therefore be no question of new requirements being added to the various contracts simply because the statutory ceiling on expenditure is being removed.

Jenkins also indicated that the excess costs were not likely to be less than £2 million. Norman St John Stevas, the opposition spokesman for the arts, supported the Bill, which was accordingly passed.

This staunch display of cross-party unity did nothing, however, to calm the anxieties which were being expressed elsewhere. Indeed it may have increased them, for it seemed as if the National Theatre Bill had unwittingly sounded a horn, summoning ghostly and embryonic Adam Smiths from distant corners of the theatrical nation. If the costs of the National Theatre were not subject to public debate in Parliament, then was it not possible that centralized government would pursue a project recklessly on which it had set its heart, at the expense of other theatres in the country? Speakers in the debate, including Stevas and Jenkins, were at pains to point out that this was not so; but without public debate, how could anyone be *sure*? Although the costs of building the National were not part of the Arts Council's budget, of course, it did seem as though the 'arms-length' principle, separating government from the dispensation of grant-aid to the arts, was shrinking to the width of a cuticle.

The National Theatre Bill may have been needed, it may have been (as Cottesloe thought) long overdue, it may have prevented the ridiculous situation from occurring whereby other Bills with new ceiling-prices in them would have to be passed every six months or so as inflationary pressures mounted, it may have met the worries of contractors anxious that their bills would not be paid, and it may have been hedged around with every obstacle to extravagance; but, at a time when every council with a half-built theatre, hospital or school was having to face unprecedentedly severe money rationing, when favourite projects were being shelved all around the country, the South Bank Theatre Board alone seemed to have direct access to the Treasury coffers. And even they did not know how deeply they would have to dip.

18

The Malcontents

DURING the Second Reading of the National Theatre Bill, Hugh Jenkins, M.P., had some harsh words to say about the growing number of critics of the National Theatre project. So did Norman St John Stevas, M.P.:

> STEVAS: The gnats—I mean, the rats—the rats are gnawing.
> MR PATRICK CORMACK, Staffordshire, South-West: The gnats are gnawing, too.
> STEVAS: When I mentioned 'gnats', I was thinking of the *New Statesman*, which is a sort of gnat—a gadfly. It is extraordinary that there should be this carping, although I am not surprised at the *New Statesman*. It is a paper that has always acted as a jackal, and it is now at the heels of artistic progress. I agreed with the Minister when he termed that leading article headed 'The National Theatre Tragedy' a disgrace, because that is what it was. It was a disgrace that it was written, and it would be a calamity if anyone were taken in by it [Second Reading: National Theatre Bill: November 7th, 1974].

A 'gnat', a 'rat', a 'gadfly', a 'jackal', a 'disgrace', a 'calamity': the staunch political supporters of the National were not going to be conciliatory towards those who disagreed with them. There was a marked change in parliamentary tone from, say, the thoughtful, civilized debates of 1913 and 1949. Some of the arguments, too, had a somewhat specious ring. It was sad to hear a former Minister for the Arts glibly associating the arrival of a new theatre with 'artistic progress'. Art, if it 'progresses' at all, does not develop just like that.

It was also disconcerting to hear the arguments of the then Minister, Hugh Jenkins, who seemed to believe that more money for the National would mean more money to the arts all round:

By putting more money in at the top, one gradually raises the proportion of State and municipal help at all levels.

At a time of an expanding economy, with inflation well under control, such a view might have carried more weight. As it was, Jenkins seemed to be carried away by the need to defend the National at all costs. A rather simplistic interpretation of what he was saying would lead one to believe that by building another Buckingham Palace you could raise the standards of council houses throughout the country. Jenkins expressed his views further in an *Evening Standard* interview, which appeared on the same day as the debate on the Second Reading:

> Our theatre generally is of enormous prestige value to our country ...
> We once had a great reputation as a sporting nation, but we don't
> have that now. What we do have is an international reputation in
> the world of the arts. For drama, music, ballet, opera. The National
> Theatre ought to become the symbol of our achievements in the
> theatre.

Without apparently realizing it, Jenkins had touched upon one of the chief fears felt by the National's critics — that the National was about to become another, expensive, prestige project. Since the end of the Second World War, Britain had faced recurring economic crises, loss of empire, loss of overseas markets, loss of money, loss in the value of the pound and, worst of all, continual losses of pride and self-esteem; and successive governments had responded to what they regarded as unpatriotic despondency by undertaking grandiose prestige projects — Bluestreak, T.S.R.2, the independent nuclear deterrent and Concorde. We seemed to have got into the habit of waving flags, instead of picking up shovels. If that little acre by Waterloo Bridge was expected to hold up another banner for a Brighter Britain, how long could the National last? Was it not likely to join the other dusty, tattered, patriotic flags, rotting away in museums?

The leading article to which Stevas, Jenkins and Cormack had referred appeared in the *New Statesman* on October 25th, 1974. Its opening paragraph stated:

> The new National Theatre is nearly finished, and already it seems
> as cumbersome as a Dreadnought; expensive to build and maintain;
> demanding a crew of hundreds; dubiously relevant to the later 20th
> century. People are not so much excited as worried, and rightly so.

It ended:

> The mania for grand glass-and-concrete, unchallenged in the early

1960s, has begun to look naïve, if not actually damaging, to the cause of good theatre. It is time we cured ourselves of it. The public may by now have no option but to pay for the reckless ambition of the finance-house cognoscenti on the National's board; but such men must never be allowed to have their heads again.

This article, too, had its elements of specious argument, as the last sentence reveals, for it obviously had not been wicked financiers who had encouraged the country to indulge in reckless extravagance, but predominantly left-wing administrators in government and County Hall, with Fabian enthusiasts and artistic philanthropists, a point made by Hall in his reply, published in the *New Statesman* a fortnight later:

> The radicals of the theatre have fought for nearly 150 years for a national theatre building worthy of our place in drama. But ironically it is some of today's radicals, who seem most worried by the arrival of the building. Bernard Shaw and Granville-Barker must be laughing wrily in their Fabian heaven.

By this time, however, the battle lines were becoming too firmly drawn, the opponents entrenched, ducking down behind the barricades to avoid arguments and bullets, raising their heads to snipe at random. The new National Theatre was not going to be just a useless concrete-and-glass monstrosity: it was a perfectly serviceable theatre complex, of a type which London certainly needed and, in international terms, cheap—even at the latest estimated figures of between £14 and £16 million. Compared to the Sydney Opera House (reported to have cost £75 million), it was a bargain.

Within this atmosphere, there were also signs that genuine fears and grievances were being misunderstood and that soluble problems were becoming insoluble. Stevas, for example, who in the Second Reading of the National Theatre Bill, wanted to 'discount ... the jealousy that there is, and what I may call—I hope without offence—the sheer theatrical bitchiness ... which is being directed against the National Theatre Board', seemed to share Jenkins's opinion that theatre managers around the country were simply afraid that their grants would be docked to pay for the National. That may have been one fear, although the real worry was that grants would not rise to meet the demands of inflation and that the National would absorb too much of the national resources of money, talent and skill.

At a CORT conference (held in Newcastle on November 22nd and

37 Peter Hall, director of the National Theatre

38 Sir Ralph Richardson lighting the rocket for the opening production at the Olivier Theatre

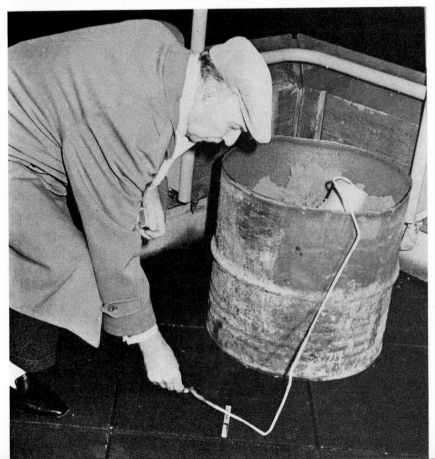

39 Sir Ralph Richardson as Hirst (*left*) and Sir John Gielgud as Spooner (*right*), in Pinter's *No Man's Land*

40 *Hamlet*, with Albert Finney in the title role

41 Kite-flying on the terraces; one of many spontaneous activities

42 H.M. Queen Elizabeth at the opening of the National Theatre on
October 25th, 1976, with Lord Cottesloe and the Duke of Edinburgh

43 The main foyer of the Lyttelton Theatre

24th) André Morell, then Equity's president, stated that public spending on the arts could be doubled and still leave Britain behind 'the rest of civilised Europe'; while Hazel Vincent-Wallace, the chairman of a CORT working party and the founder-director of Leatherhead's Thorndike Theatre, pointed out that six out of twenty-six regional theatres studied, faced immediate closure, while the others were drastically curtailing their work. David Forder, from Colchester's Mercury Theatre, described a situation among regional reps where 'play safe and play small' had become the rule, leading to diminishing and ageing audiences. The debate in the country was thus about priorities in arts subsidies, not blind opposition to the National, and although Stevas was fully aware of the needs of regional theatres (as his article, 'Double Our Money' in the *Sunday Times* on November 17th, 1976, indicated), his answer to the charge that politicians had got their priorities wrong was less than convincing. Whatever else might be sacrificed in the cause of national austerity, it would not be the new National; and if money was available to support the National, could it not have been used more profitably, in artistic and economic terms, elsewhere in the system?

Stevas proposed a way of protecting the National from the gnawing of the gnats:

> Why not make the special grant for the big four — namely, Covent Garden, the National Opera, the Royal Shakespeare Company and the English National Theatre — a separate grant-in-aid, payable through the Arts Council, but as a separate accounting matter? In that way the Minister would effectively allay the fears of those who think that the Arts Council will pay for these big projects at their expense. [Second Reading, National Theatre Bill, November 7th, 1974]?

George Strauss (Labour M.P. for Vauxhall) pounced on this suggestion with the sturdy common sense which he had shown in other National Theatre debates: 'It would appear to be an obvious trick to make other recipients of Arts Council money believe that they are not in competition with the major recipients.' Indeed it would. Furthermore, it would have removed deliberations about the National's money from the Arts Council's drama panel, the advisory body which was supposed to consider the relative priorities to be given via grants to different parts of the theatre system. Stevas's proposal thus touched upon another sore area — the growing feeling within the drama panel that the National was becoming a matter outside their sphere of influence. Such a situation had cropped up before, with Covent Garden, though not so significantly, for there was not a large number of other opera companies in Britain (as there were theatres) whose needs also had to be considered. A working party report, commissioned by the Arts Council from a firm of management consultants, Peat, Marwick, Mitchell & Company, in March 1975 and completed in June/July 1976, described the unique situation of the National among subsidized organizations. Its board was appointed by the government and could therefore be said to have a responsibility direct to the government; and yet it was financed through the Arts Council. It was possible therefore that a conflict could emerge between the aims of the government-appointed board and the ability of the Council to finance those aims; and in that situation, whose voice would win the argument? It was a matter of principle. If the Arts Council felt that its power to decide how money allocated to the arts in Britain should be spent, was being whittled away, then its role and authority would be held in question.

Stevas's suggestion received little support from the government or from the National Theatre; but there were other ways of trying to present the money given to the National in terms which seemed less blatantly privileged. Rayne, for example, favoured the view that the cost of maintaining the theatre building (estimated during the National Theatre Bill debate as £1·15 million) should be separated from the grant given to the company (estimated at £1·35 million). He felt that the building and its maintenance could be subsidized through the Department of the Environment or perhaps the G.L.C.; and in that way, the disparity between the grants given to the National Theatre and those given to other subsidized companies would seem less marked. But the same argument applied to a number of other new theatres in the country, where maintenance costs also seemed out of proportion to the production costs of its plays, or, indeed, to the revenue expected through the box-offices. 'Have you seen the *window-cleaning* bills at the new Birmingham Rep?' one director said in despair.

As the battle developed, however, it proved to be not solely about money, but about other resources too, such as trained manpower, and about the National Theatre's 'accountability'. In August and September 1974, Oscar Lewenstein, the artistic director of the Royal Court, approached a number of other directors, in the regions and in London, to canvas their views. A letter was drafted which was eventually published in *The Times* on October 15th, 1974; and signed by fourteen artistic directors, representing a wide cross-section of theatre opinion: Lindsay Anderson, Peter Cheeseman, Michael Croft (of the National Youth Theatre), Frank Dunlop, Michael Elliott, Richard Eyre, Howard

Gibbins (from the Bush fringe theatre), John Harrison (from Leeds), Ewan Hooper, Peter James, Joan Littlewood, Charles Marowitz and Toby Robertson. They offered general support to Hall and the National Theatre, but went on to describe some of the 'serious dangers' which might arise 'from the occupation by the National of so elaborate and prestigious a complex', arguing that 'the National's name, and its huge initial ambitions, cannot exempt it from the same obligations to economize as the rest of us':

> Perhaps an even more important danger is the drain ... on resources other than financial. For example, to staff the three auditoria, the National Theatre is said to be seeking 140 skilled technicians. It is doubtful whether there are many more than that number working in all the theatres of the country. From our own experience we can attest that the National has been busy for some time already, endeavouring to attract technicians with offers of salaries far in excess of anything these theatres can afford to pay. The implications of this are unhealthy.

Before this letter was sent, Hall had seen a copy. He wrote to Oscar Lewenstein, expressing his concern and suggesting that it should be redrafted in such a way that he could sign it as well. If, for example, the letter had simply been about the low level of theatre subsidies and about the general difficulties which the profession faced, then Hall would readily have added his name. Lewenstein, however, argued that the letter raised issues where there was a genuine conflict of interests, and that therefore it was not appropriate for Hall to sign it. The National Theatre management also challenged some statements in Lewenstein's letter, particularly insisting that they had not been wooing technicians with high salaries and in any case, did not require that number. On October 17th, 1974, Hall replied in *The Times* to Lewenstein's letter:

> I would be as appalled as Mr. Lewenstein if the demands of the building were met by sacrificing other theatres ... the NT does not need anything like 140 skilled technicians. Half of that number, of which some will be those already at the Old Vic, is enough ... The salary we are offering is comparable to the take-home pay for similar employment now.

This, unfortunately, was an area where facts had mostly to give way before 'guesstimates'; for even the phrase 'skilled technicians' was capable of many interpretations. The National might not be exactly wooing technicians—indeed they were not—but if the conditions and rates of pay were favourable, if the National were regarded as the summit of the technicians' profession, then they would come of their own accord, thus still leaving other theatres in awkward positions. It was still far from certain what the new rates of pay would be, say, for stagehands working in the new National, and how many of these could be trained for their somewhat changed jobs from a basis in Old Vic experience, how many would be recruited for their special skills or for jobs not required at the Old Vic.

In August 1976, following a short strike, a new long-term agreement was thrashed out with N.A.T.T.K.E., providing its members at the National with a guaranteed minimum wage of £88 for a fifty-hour week, which included ten hours' overtime. In the preceding months, the technical difficulties with the building meant that the amounts spent on overtime had fluctuated wildly. The new agreement was intended to stabilize the situation, and it also provided the National with some important concessions from the union concerning flexibility. Under one long-standing tradition, for example, stage crews were not expected to work on any other jobs in a theatre, while a production in which they were involved was going on. This was an admirable rule in most theatres, but at the National it could lead to wasted labour—while the stage-hands loitered around with little to do.

These rates of pay were roughly on a par with those in West End theatres and at the R.S.C., although the opportunities for overtime (certainly during the early months) were better at the National, and when the building was fully operational it was expected that the general conditions of work would improve. These rates, however, were higher than those in regional and the smaller subsidized theatres; and it was these disparities, of course, which worried the signatories to Lewenstein's letter.

The number of skilled technicians was also hard to determine. If one meant everybody in the National Theatre company concerned with the business of putting on productions, as opposed to appearing in them or marketing them or servicing the building, the entire backstage team in short, then there were about 223 of them, each with different skills. The total National Theatre company, after the National had moved, numbered about 500 members, of which 100 were actors and actresses. There were 75 members on the production staff (a heading which includes carpenters, painters, prop-makers, designers, lighting designers, metalworkers and wigmakers), 111 on the stage staff (the electricians, stage-hands, sound engineers, dressers and prop-men) and 37 production supervisors (such as Simon Relph). All of these were rated as 'skilled' by Peter Stevens and Simon Relph; although whether they were all in short supply, or would have all been counted under Lewenstein's or Hall's use of the phrase 'skilled technicians', was another matter.

With the general proposition of Lewenstein's letter, however, there could really be no argument—for the National obviously would absorb more skilled technicians than the Old Vic had done; and the same argument applied not only to technicians, but leading actors as well, dramatists and directors. The question really was one of degree. Would the National pursue its interests to the extent of damaging other theatres and managements, or would it show a deliberate restraint? Would the National generate as much new talent as it absorbed from other sources, or would it simply act as a kind of predator? Hall had given firm assurances that he did not want or intend that other theatres' interests should be sacrificed—that he was 'appalled' by the very idea; and there, for the time being, the matter rested.

Thus, the situation which the National Theatre faced in its winter of discontent, 1975, was one which required considerable tact, coupled with frankness, a determination to curb all forms of over-expenditure and a readiness to cut back even on cherished ventures. The priorities expressed through its policies were all-important. And yet, it was really rather hard to maintain a sense of balance and perspective in the depressing circumstances which surrounded them. Just wandering around the building was enough to dampen the spirits. The progress seemed so slow. Small groups of workers would settle down comfortably over their tea-breaks, which seemed to grow longer day by day; and if you asked them what they were supposed to be doing, they might answer candidly, 'Waiting'—waiting for something to be delivered, or which had been delivered but to the wrong part of the building, or for an electrician to turn up.

Could the South Bank Theatre Board, or McAlpine, have driven them along faster? Perhaps—but the days of hard, or even energetic, taskmasters were over. The risks of a confrontation with a union or its members on site were too great. They could have brought the place to a complete standstill, as had happened before, in 1971. It was a matter, as Cottesloe realized, of team spirit; and so the South Bank Theatre Board chose to control their impatience, to bear criticisms from the press and elsewhere with fortitude, to trouble-shoot (through the building progress sub-committee) immediate problems—and to encourage the men, gently.

The board's job, however, was a particularly difficult one, because simple logic suggested that it was no longer in the interests of some sub-contractors to finish the job quickly. That was another side-effect from the National Theatre Bill. The situation in the building industry had changed since 1971. The property boom had collapsed. Once the National Theatre work was over, other jobs would be harder to find. Ironically, when the property boom was over (once a source of delays because of labour and material shortage), it left an excess of labour, thus leading perhaps to further delays—for by removing the ceiling price from the public approval and debate of Parliament, contractors could assume that eventually money to complete their jobs would be found. Unfortunately, though, the Treasury and the Department of Education and Science took their responsibilities so seriously that it proved extremely hard for contractors to get additional money as and when they wanted it. Their paymasters, not unreasonably, insisted that the terms of their original contracts should be fulfilled, within such provisions for inflation covered by the 'sliding' clauses, which in turn were governed by rough rules for calculating inflationary rates laid down by the National Economic Development Office. The contractors and particularly the sub-contractors, however, often complained that the sliding clauses did not take account of the particular difficulties at the National Theatre.

In the meantime, the company was kicking its heels in Aquinas Street and at the Old Vic. After a poor season, in addition to all the other troubles, what was most needed was some tangible signs of success. These fortunately came in the spring. John Schlesinger's production of *Heartbreak House* was the most evenly successful event which the National had staged since Hall took over. It had a superb cast, with Colin Blakely as Captain Shotover, Eileen Atkins as Hesione Hushabye, Kate Nelligan as Ellie Dunn, Paul Rogers as Boss Mangan and Anna Massey as Ariadne Utterword, while the set by Michael Annals was a wonderful folly of a house, half-ship, half-country-mansion, with port-hole windows, winding stairs to upper rooms and a little cubbyhole for Shotover to experiment in. Hard-hearted critics, just a few of them, argued that the production was a little too good for the play, for Shaw had included some passages of dismally banal writing. In the sombre close to the first part, for example, Schlesinger made these lines sound like a chorus from Greek tragedy:

> SHOTOVER I built a house for my daughters, and opened
> the doors thereof,
> That men might come for their choosing, and their

> betters spring from their love,
> But one of them married a numskull;
> HECTOR   the other a liar wed;
> MRS HUSHABYE And now she must lie beside him, even as she
> made her bed.

More significantly perhaps, it felt as if Schlesinger were taking Shaw's 1920 mock-Chekhovian parable (where Britain's Ship of State is about to be overcome by another holocaust) as a prophetic statement about the present. If that were the intention, it surely misfired, for there is something majestically imprecise about *Heartbreak House*, an expression of gloomy foreboding which derived from the First World War and whose relevance to the problems facing Britain lies mainly in its pessimistic tone.

Heartbreak House, though an undoubted success, seemed to presage further National Theatre productions reverentially undertaken of rather second-rate plays—such as those of W. S. Gilbert's *Engaged*, Ben Travers's *Plunder* and Noël Coward's *Blithe Spirit*; and there were some who wondered whether the cast might not be a bit too 'starry', not just for the play, but for the development of the company. In the Peat, Marwick, Mitchell & Company report for the Arts Council, it was revealed that the National Theatre management had allowed for up to five additional actors per play, to supplement the basic company, estimated now at about fifty, which would eventually operate the Olivier and Cottesloe Theatres. The estimated size of the basic company was thus only half what had originally been envisaged by Peter Hall; but nevertheless if the provision for five additional actors had been used by the directors of National Theatre productions consistently, it might well have led to a weakening of the company spirit. There are often under five really good parts in a play, and if the company felt that these were going to 'outsiders', then their own opportunities would seem markedly less attractive.

Again, only time would tell how such a provision would be used; but *Heartbreak House* raised doubts about whether the National would provide a strong permanent company, as opposed to star-studded occasions. By April, however, the National Theatre could claim a genuine triumph, as representative of the kind of production to be expected from Hall's National as *Othello* and *The Recruiting Officer* had been of Olivier's. Harold Pinter had not originally wanted his play *No Man's Land* to be staged at the Old Vic. It was a play which required stillness and none of the distractions which so often occurred at the

Old Vic, with police cars and ambulances whining down Waterloo Road. Hall, who directed, shared Pinter's love of precise effects, which could be more easily achieved at the Lyttelton; nevertheless, the demands of the National were such that such reservations had to be set aside.

The characteristics of Hall–Pinter evenings in the theatre had been established during the mid-1960s, at the Aldwych Theatre under the R.S.C. – with *The Homecoming, Landscape* and *Silence,* and *Old Times*: the exactly timed pauses, the careful dimming of the lights, the sense of unspecified threats, the 'menace'. On this occasion, however, this almost too familiar atmosphere surrounded two quite outstanding performances, by Sir John Gielgud as Spooner and Sir Ralph Richardson as Hirst, both elderly public-school literati, who may have known each other previously. Spooner was a snob, dependent, poor, slightly camp, a heath-wanderer, bar-fly and little magazine man, a part which Gielgud invested with such detail, from the yellow hair to the contemplative cigarette and open shoes, that it must surely rank with his finest portraits. Hirst (particularly through the eyes of someone like Spooner) was a great man, successful and surrounded by the signs of opulence, such as a full drinks cabinet and an elegant pad, with high surrounding windows. Both, however, live a kind of limbo existence, with another world of different values, encroaching resentments and danger lurking outside. Two working-class, aggressor-menials, Foster and Briggs, hover around Hirst like expectant wolves. The no-man's land of the title describes all too aptly the bleak mud-patch of memories, habits and irrelevant emotions in which Spooner and Hirst are caught, with the gunfire in the distance, too far away to catch the bullets and explosions directly, but with lambs'-tails of flak puffing ominous dust near by. *No Man's Land* (like *Heartbreak House,* though more perceptively) could have been conceived as a parable for Britain; although it could also be criticized on the grounds that the public-school limbo was somewhat of a cliché.

With *Heartbreak House* and *No Man's Land* in the repertoire, with *John Gabriel Borkman* and a revival of *The Misanthrope* to back them up, and Peggy Ashcroft's superb (almost) solo performance in Samuel Beckett's *Happy Days* transferring to the Old Vic from its original role as a touring production, the National Theatre season in the summer of 1975 was a worthy and substantial one, to rank with the better seasons of Olivier's time. When, after forty performances, *No Man's Land* transferred to the West End for a commercial run and *Heartbreak House* went on a short regional tour, Blakemore's firm production of *Engaged* came into the repertoire, a slight play whose presence could be justified on historical grounds, for it anticipated the Edwardian genre of satirical comedies. Dexter came back to direct *Phaedra Britannica*, another Tony Harrison adaptation of a classic French play, which unfortunately did not quite match the success of *The Misanthrope*.

In the summer of 1975, the National Theatre company seemed to be back on good form; and there were encouraging signs from other directions. Although nobody still knew precisely when the building would be finished, at least enough of it was ready to begin preparing for the move from Aquinas Street and the Old Vic. The 'testing period' would have to take place with the company in occupation, and the elaborate devices to control the Olivier revolve and the flying system would not be completed; but there would be stages and seats, 'bare boards and a passion', and Hall was prepared to rely upon these simple necessities. Every month that the new National remained unopened and unoccupied added to costs all round, for, leaving aside the loss of box-office revenue from the larger complex, the Old Vic had to be kept as a temporary home.

Any thought of a Grand Opening, however, was put firmly from the mind. There would be no 'big-blast' this time, only a crab-wise sidle into the new theatre, occupying the Lyttelton first, and then the Olivier and the Cottesloe, which were due to be ready in June 1976. The National Theatre company would not attempt to launch new productions for the opening. The productions for the Lyttelton would all be tried out first at the Old Vic during the autumn and winter, before transferring in the spring. A fixed opening date for the Lyttelton was announced at the end of September 1975. It would be March 16th, 1976, with a final performance at the Old Vic on February 28th, a Lilian Baylis commemorative evening, *Tribute To The Lady*.

In the meantime, preparations could continue for such National Theatre activities at the new National as did not rely upon elaborate technical equipment. Michael Kustow and John Russell Brown had both been involved in trying out new plays and fringe events, while the National Theatre company was at the Old Vic. In 1974, the Young Vic had been used for lunchtime productions, then the I.C.A. theatre was pressed into service, and then, in November 1975, the Young Vic studio. One impressive new play was seen during these seasons, Barry Collins's *Judgement* (directed by Hall), about a Russian officer driven, with his comrades, to cannibalism. It featured an exceptionally good solo performance from Colin Blakely; and although *Judgement* was not a première—it had been seen before at the Bristol Old Vic with Peter

O'Toole—its production indicated the company's readiness to explore the area of new plays by unknown writers. Others who received productions during these seasons included such young dramatists as Alan Drury and Richard Crane.

There was, however, another major snag to the move—shortage of money, or at least of the sums which the National Theatre company thought that it would require. Hugh Jenkins, M.P., had indicated in the National Theatre Bill Second Reading that the National would require grants of about £2·5 million in its new theatre; but the economic situation, coupled with the publicity given to the National's finances during the 1974–5 winter, demanded austerity. During the 1975–6 season, the grants known to be available to the National amounted to £2·2 million, consisting of a basic Arts Council grant of £900,000, a G.L.C. grant of £300,000 and a supplementary grant of £1 million to cover the loss of the Old Vic, the costs of the move and special non-recurring equipment costs.

Jenkins's anticipated figures were, of course, for a full year's running in the new building; and the National did not begin to move in until September 1975, with the productions not transferring until the end of the financial year, March 1976. But the general rate of inflation had to be taken into account, and the costs of the move were likely to be considerable. Productions had to be prepared for the new theatre, while box-office income was only coming from the Old Vic. Productions designed for the Old Vic would not automatically fit on to the Lyttelton and Olivier stages.

Economies therefore, had once more to be made, twisting Hall's original scheme still further out of shape. The nature of these cuts would indicate the priorities given by the National Theatre management to different aspects of its work; and, once more, these priorities were challengeable. The National's critics, for example, complained on occasions that the company had been planned on too large and vague a scale, that many actors were under-employed, that the top management was too highly paid (bearing in mind the low rewards elsewhere in the theatre) and that certain productions were over-elaborate, in staging and in their use of 'star' (or, at any rate, very well-known) actors. Such criticisms were usually matters of degree and emphasis, rather than attacks absolute; and, as such, they could be dismissed rather too easily (in a manner which might anger the critics) and, in consequence, they sometimes took on a personal note, focusing on the style and behaviour of Hall himself.

Hall's own salary, for example, caused unfavourable comment, even though it was not known. His income from all sources (including 'Aquarius') was rumoured to be in the region of £60,000 a year. This figure had been arrived at rather simplistically, by totting up a presumed salary of between £22,500 and £25,000 from the National, £16,000 from 'Aquarius', roughly £10,000 in various forms of National Theatre benefits (such as company cars and help with his flat at the Barbican), and roughly £10,000 from directing work outside the National (such as Glyndebourne productions) and from directorial percentages gained when certain productions, such as *No Man's Land*, transferred to the West End.

Such attacks were two-pronged. They were levelled against the high amount which Hall was supposed to be earning and also against the fact that Hall's salary, paid for out of public funds, was not disclosed. The Prime Minister's salary, for example, was a matter for public knowledge. Why not Hall's (and other directors' in a similar position)? At this time, there were many campaigns to ensure that the business interests of M.P.s were registered, together with any income which they might have from sources other than their parliamentary salaries — which were known. Disclosure of the income of public figures, direct and indirect, earned and unearned, was almost a theme for the times. If there was to be any kind of general incomes policy for the country, which many advocated as one method of combating inflation, it was desirable that high incomes in the public sector should be known (and increases restricted) as well as low ones. Justice, in this case, could not be done unless it was also seen to be done; and the National Theatre itself was involved in complicated union negotiations.

For the theatre profession, this argument had a particular edge, in that average wage levels were extremely low and even well-established directors were known to receive as little as £200 to £250 for productions in repertory theatres. In the commercial theatre, it had long been accepted that certain star actors and directors could claim very high rewards for their work; but star appeal often is a quickly fading asset, and an actor who had earned a small fortune one year, could find himself bankrupt five years later. One expectation aroused by the arrival of state subsidies within the theatre economy was that the old boom-or-bust pattern would be broken. Actors and directors would forgo their chances of immediate bonanzas, in return for greater security and regular income. The excessive disparities between the lucky stars and the less lucky would be slowly whittled away.

If, however, it were felt that the subsidy system was working another way, heightening the contrast between the rich and the poor rather than toning it down, rewarding the successful with longer contracts backed by public money without having regard for those less fortunate, there was likely to be considerable resentment within the theatre profession. Hall's life-style, with its appearance of opulence, had aroused comment, sometimes envious, sometimes merely amused; but there was no way of clarifying the central question concerning disparities of income in the public sector of the theatre unless Hall's salary from the National were known. And it was not.

The Arts Council's position was basically that the onus for disclosure of such matters as top salaries lay with the boards of subsidized companies themselves, in accordance with the requirements of the Companies Act (1927). In this Act, employees of a company, earning more than £10,000 in total emoluments, were required to have their incomes registered in the company's public accounts, within a salary band of £2,500. Thus, the National Theatre's accounts for 1974–5 revealed that one employee (presumably Hall) received total emoluments of between £20,000 and £22,500 during the 53 weeks of 1973–4. In the following year's accounts, however, this figure was stated to be incorrect. The 1974–5 accounts revealed that two employees received emoluments of between £10,000 and £12,500; although these would not have included Hall. Hall had a service contract with the National Theatre Board as a self-employed person, which meant that his income did not have to be declared within the National Theatre's accounts. Hall, of course, was in a position to make public his income from the National Theatre, should he have chosen to do so; but, in an interview with Terry Coleman (*Guardian*, July 8th, 1977), Hall said that he had nothing to hide but that he thought that a man's income and his sex-life were his own affair.

Hall's many supporters regarded all this talk of Hall's salary to be positive proof of a malicious campaign being waged against him. Hugh Jenkins talked about the 'new philistinism' of those who seized on rumours about Hall's salary as a means of attacking the National. Behind such attacks, however, lay two much wider issues, the 'accountability' of the National and the priorities chosen by the National Theatre management when faced by the need to economize. Were, for example, the demands of the Companies Act (designed for companies large and small, whether in receipt of public money or not) sufficiently stringent to meet the public concern as to how its money was being spent? Was the Arts Council itself a strong enough body to control the way in which the National's money was being spent, not in detail, of course, but in broad policy outlines? Should it even try to do so? The Peat, Marwick, Mitchell & Company report indicated some areas where there could be strong policy disagreements between the Arts Council and the National Theatre, particularly if the National Theatre had to trim its budgets within strict financial limits. The National Theatre, for example, might cut its touring programme before reducing the cost of sets; or cut down its experimental programme; or employ less well-known (and therefore cheaper) actors instead of choosing plays with smaller casts. The working party who compiled this report did not advise that the Arts Council's officers (or a representative) should be part of the detailed decision-making machinery of the National. That had been a suggestion in the Granville Barker/Archer proposals, with the inclusion of a Reading Committee Man to protect the public interests. But they did indicate that conflicts could occur which might damage both the National and the Arts Council.

One such quarrel had indeed already happened, for, in economizing to meet the costs of the move, the National had cut back sharply on its touring commitments—from forty-one weeks in the 1974–5 season, to only four in the 1975–6 one. This must have been a hard decision for the management to take, for it went flatly against Hall's previously de-clared policy and his known wish to increase touring; and it also laid the National wide open to the charge that taxpayers around the country were being denied an opportunity to see the company which they were subsidizing. The Arts Council had established a joint working party, from members of the drama panel and the touring committee, which met during the summer and autumn of 1975, to consider the problems of drama touring in Britain and, in particular, the trials of those theatres which had no resident company but which relied upon touring companies of various kinds to fill their programmes.

These had been particularly badly hit in recent years, partly because (unlike the repertory theatres) they rarely received direct running grants from the Arts Council and also because the old touring networks, so important a feature of the theatre system in the past, had largely broken up. Individual theatres now booked visiting touring companies mainly on an *ad hoc* basis, from whatever was available at the time. Most of these companies were small-scale commercial ones, although some were directly subsidized through the Arts Council's DALTA (Dramatic and Lyric Theatres Association) scheme.

There was a marked shortage of the right kind of touring produc-tions and the working party thought that the National should do more to fill the gaps. Indeed, they felt that a point had been reached when the gap between the National Theatre's commitment to touring and the demand in the regions to see the National's 'prestigious productions' was such that the Arts Council should take action, making touring a condition of the National's receipt of subsidies. They were commenting on evidence received from Lord Birkett, who had indicated that it was unlikely that the National Theatre would be able to provide any substantial amount of touring in the immediate future and that, indeed, touring from the Olivier, the theatre's main auditorium and home of the company itself, would not normally be possible because of the 'unique physical nature of the stage' and of the productions designed for it. The Lyttelton was the only auditorium from which tours could be sent to proscenium theatres; and in order to do this, while simultaneously occupying the Lyttelton, two and a half companies would be required. Their Arts Council grant was not of a size to permit that; and the consequent problems of cross-casting would make touring extremely difficult.

In a subsequent letter, Birkett pointed out that touring had always been one of the National's aims, but that the gradual whittling away of their budget meant that it could no longer be undertaken as planned. It was hoped that productions from the Lyttelton could provide something like ten or twelve weeks of touring a year; but even those decisions had to be delayed, because austerity prevented forward planning on such matters. They would tour, if they had the money to do so, and since they had not, touring was, at best, a good intention dependent on circumstances.

Why did the working party, under its chairman Michael Denison, reject this view so firmly? It is hard to tell, for someone who was not present at their meetings. The underlying feeling probably was that if the National had had a genuine will to tour it would have found a way. Commercial managements in the past had found touring useful and profitable: Sir Barry Jackson, who had subsidized the Birmingham Rep out of his own pocket, once ran seven companies stemming from the Rep, three touring. Certain phrases in Birkett's letter may have raised their suspicions, particularly the somewhat disingenuous remarks about 'the question of dates' and 'leaving decisions late'. If such National productions as *No Man's Land* or, more significantly, *Equus*, could transfer to the West End so easily, why could they not also tour? The National could have argued that a commercial run of *No Man's Land* would have brought money to the company, whereas a touring production would not; but, in principle, should the commercial exploitation of a production take precedence over touring?

The working party apparently believed that touring should rank second in the National Theatre's priorities, below their South Bank work, but above West End transfers and foreign tours. In an article published in the *Sunday Times* on June 13th, 1976, Hall defended the National Theatre against the charge that they were unwilling to tour. On the contrary, he said, they were 'determined' to do so. Hall blamed the Arts Council for not sufficiently encouraging touring: 'touring is never central to their discussions. It is an after-thought, a hoped-for use of spare capacity, which is usually not there'. Economies had forced the National Theatre to maintain a smaller company than they had intended, which could not be 'divided for home and away fixtures at the same time'.

This short article, however, included two telling sentences:

> When the National Theatre goes outside London, audiences see our plays exactly as they are seen on the South Bank. It is the same cast, the same production, because our repertoire system can allow us to send plays to the regions during their London run.

Hall had evidently decided against 'second-string' — which is not necessarily 'second-rate' — touring; and that policy, despite the repertoire system, could limit widespread touring. He seemed to have set his face against the cheap touring of the Mobile Productions, which could fit up anywhere; and there were not many theatres in the country where the staging facilities were equivalent to those at the Lyttelton, so that they could receive *identical* productions. To insist that regions received the same casts as the London production also meant that whole groups of actors could be tied down because one member might be needed on the South Bank. Hall's intention sounded wholly admirable, but in practice it was likely to lead to an inflexible approach towards touring.

These two Arts Council working party reports — on touring and from Peat, Marwick, Mitchell & Company on the estimated budgets for the National — were internal discussion documents, relating to the Council's dealings with the National Theatre. Both revealed a degree of anxiety concerning the National's affairs which could not have been guessed from the public statements of support, expressed by Roy Shaw, who had been appointed the new secretary-general of the Arts Council in 1975, and others. Both reports were limited in their scope and, of course, the touring report was not confined to the National's role but included other companies as well. In the case of the report from Peat, Marwick, Mitchell & Company, the terms of reference were simply to examine the National's estimates of expenditure and income, and the basis on which these had been reached. This report therefore did not even attempt to relate the budgets to the artistic policy. The committee could comment on the proposed costs, say, of *Blithe Spirit*, without passing any opinion as to whether that play should have been included in the repertoire at all. Furthermore, since nobody still knew when the building would be operating fully, it had to comment upon plans which were still fluid and liable to change. Nevertheless the committee warned against 'the inherent danger with any "new" organisation of this size that there will be a proliferation of departments', and against the tendency to include too much overtime in the estimates (for 'budgeted overtime soon becomes necessary overtime'), and against the anomalies whereby 'a second dayman is likely to earn twice as much as some actors'. Throughout their report there ran a nagging doubt that the Arts Council was not really in a position to finance the National Theatre as the National had hoped, nor to control this vast new state beast as the Council would have liked.

The National Theatre commented on the Report in a subsequent letter, in which they pointed out that the National had to be regarded differently from other theatres. It could not be run by a small, dedicated staff, prepared to 'starve to death' if necessary, so that the show could go on. It was an 'industrial/commercial complex' and not a theatre in the normal sense of the word; and this meant that some of its staff simply worked there for money. High wages therefore were not the result of a whimsical demand from the Director, but a condition of survival; and this fact would become even more obvious when the theatre unions tightened their grip on the National's machine. That must have put the Arts Council in a delicate moral dilemma. Should they support the small dedicated theatres where the staffs were starving, or the large mercenary ones where many people worked solely for money? The phrase, 'an industrial/commercial complex' contrasted sharply with the ideals expressed about the National throughout its history—and, indeed, with the vision presented by Hall when he took over from Olivier.

Was it really inevitable that the National's size meant that a battalion of wage slaves was required to support a small, artistic High Command? Even with 500 employees, the National was still only on a par with small-to-medium (non-theatrical) companies. It was not British Rail or Sir Joseph Lockwood's E.M.I. Had that old theatrical spirit totally gone, whereby everyone felt personally involved in the success of productions, from the head cutter to Jimmy Hannah, the stage doorman? Was that comradeliness mere sentimentality? Or were the National's problems caused not by size alone, but by size and complexity, whereby there had to be many different small teams, each relating to the whole enterprise, which could only be brought together within a firm, if bureaucratic, structure? Was the National trying to do too many things, and hampered by too many difficulties, thus leading to the 'proliferation of departments'? Was it slowly being nailed on the cross of too high expectations?

Behind the many criticisms of the National Theatre was the feeling that power, wealth and influence in the theatre as a whole was being centralized, through the subsidy system, into one over-large organization. Even within the National Theatre, sceptical observers noticed an absence of those who, in former days, had the status and confidence to stand up to the Director. It was like having a weak Cabinet and a strong Prime Minister. Two widely respected and knowledgeable members of the planning committee had left: Patrick Donnell and Anthony Easterbrook. Donnell had been given a twelve-month leave of absence at the end of 1974, following the delay of the building's opening, and on his return he found that his place was being in effect filled by Peter Stevens and Lord Birkett. He asked to be relieved from the remaining years of his contract, a request which was granted. Easterbrook, who had battled on for nearly six years as general manager and probably knew more about the overall complexities of the building and its potential running problems than any other man, had been sacked by Hall as part of the general reorganization of the National Theatre's management at the end of 1974.

This left Blakemore as the sole remaining member of Olivier's regime, still holding his place as an associate director on the planning committee. Blakemore, a discreet man, would not be drawn into making public statements, which might be interpreted as critical of the management: whatever his private feelings may have been, he stayed loyally within the organization through the months of the move. Without knowing the inner story of the workings of Hall's cabinet, it was hard for the malcontents to know where exactly to place the blame, or if indeed it was necessary to blame anyone. Was the National such a monster? Was it wasteful and profligate? Or was it a victim of circumstances? Would the circumstances change, to allow the National to fulfil the role in the theatre system which had been planned for it? It was too soon to tell. The building had to open, it had to run for months —perhaps years, before any clear opinions could be formed. But, in the meantime rumours persisted, doubts came to the surface and then sank into silence; and the gnats roared.

19

Moving In

DOUGLAS CORNELISSEN was the first National Theatre employee to move his office into the new building—in June 1975. His official title was Building Services Manager; and he was basically in charge of the maintenance staff. He had tried to move in once before, in 1974, because Anthony Easterbrook had thought it necessary that the National Theatre maintenance men should know exactly how the building worked—where the cables ran, and the pipes, and what could go wrong. Cornelissen studied the building in detail; he learned a new range of skills.

The next office to move was that of Richard York, the South Bank liaison manager, on September 1st. His job was to supervise the transfer of the whole company from the Old Vic and Aquinas Street, to allocate offices and to examine (and solve, if possible) the problems which cropped up during the move. One such difficulty quickly emerged. There was no space in the building which could be allocated as a staff room for the cleaners and the security guards. There were only enough lockers for the catering staff. The workers in the paint-shop had a tiny cubbyhole, half the size of a normal office, in which they could change; and no showers to wash off the colours and dirt. York's job was made more complicated by the fact that the building had not yet officially been handed over by the South Bank Theatre Board to the National Theatre Board. Alterations to the building could not be authorized through York or the National Theatre Board at all. Minor problems could be sorted out either on site informally or, slightly more formally, at the fortnightly site meetings. But for work which required additional expenditure, an elaborate process had to be under-taken—whereby, say, a National Theatre technician reported a prob-lem to Simon Relph, who would inform Peter Stevens. Stevens would bring the matter to the attention of the National Theatre Board, prob-ably through Hall or the Planning Committee, and the Board would inform the South Bank Theatre Board. The South Bank Theatre Board, if the sums were small, would then instruct its contractors and sub-contractors; but if the sums were large—as in the case of adding a room for the maintenance staff—the Department of Education and Science had to be approached, and through them, the Treasury. Denys Lasdun and Peter Softley had drawn up plans for the additional staff room, but the National Theatre still had to wait for several months before they heard the answer to their request from the Department of Education and Science. It was turned down.

That was just one problem; and if it seems incredible that the needs of a whole department had been thus overlooked, it was just one of the unforeseen consequences of raising the whole scale of the National Theatre operations to the demands of the new building. The engineering staff for the building, about twenty men, had no changing rooms: the provisions for them, based on the experience at the Old Vic, included offices for the chief engineer and the deputy engineer. That, at first, was all. The specifications, laid down in 1965, had not allowed fully for the sheer numbers of people who would have to be employed. A few cleaners, mostly part-timers, could cope with the Old Vic. Now a staff of nearly eighty was required for building maintenance, divided into different departments, and consisting of full- and part-time employees. Those numbers could not be tucked away into odd corners. York had to find temporary space for them.

While York was moving in, other heads of departments were preparing to do so as well: Simon Relph, Martin McCullum (the production manager for the Lyttelton) and John Bury. Then, by the end of September, all the offices at Aquinas Street were shifted over, the filing cabinets and papers, the charms, potted plants and favourite coffee mugs were packed up and carried over to the still empty offices and corridors of the new building. It was not necessary to hire vast pantechnicons from outside contractors. The National Theatre vans did the job, while the staff humped and loaded. Some lights started to flicker in the evenings, and the hulk of concrete sprouted into life. There was a new spirit of cheerfulness: something was happening at last. The Aquinas Street huts looked increasingly deserted, bits of paper still scattered on the floor, once-crowded notice-boards now just pock-marked with drawing pins and fluttering with forlorn scraps.

On November 17th and 18th, 1975, Hall briefly switched rehearsals for his production of *Hamlet* (opening at the Old Vic on December 10th) to the Lyttelton, to try out the stage. Daniel Thorndike, Sybil Thorndike's nephew, spoke the first historic words: 'Who's there?', the opening line of *Hamlet*. First impressions were excellent. The acoustics at the Lyttelton, later a source of criticism, seemed fine. You could clear your throat on stage, and be heard from the back rows without the cough resounding. The comparatively short distance between the stage and the back rows meant that the problems of projection were easier to overcome. Albert Finney, playing Hamlet, remembered what it was like to star in *Billy Liar* at the Cambridge Theatre: 'It was so deep that it felt like putting your arm into a sack and being unable to reach the bottom. Timing was impossible. You played it for the stalls or the upper circle, but not both.' In the Lyttelton, the back row was at a distance equivalent to the front row of the dress circle in many theatres. All the seats were good ones, although the rows were rather wide. The problems of actors were thus easier to solve. You didn't have to strain to punch an effect across: you could relax.

What the Lyttelton lacked was something which it had scarcely had the opportunity to acquire: its individual atmosphere. Theatres sometimes seem to mature like violins. A tradition of acting grows up, so that actors know how to achieve a particular impression here which would be inappropriate there. Olivier, for example, always seemed to know exactly how to handle the Old Vic. He could build his performance to the size and the scale of the theatre, tilting his head upwards to the dress circle and galleries, catching the lights as he did so. The Lyttelton, for all its intimacy, still seemed an impersonal theatre. The light-coloured concrete walls gave that impression, as well as sometimes reflecting too much light from the stage, while the seat rows faced the stage too square-on, as if the confrontational aspect of proscenium-arch theatres had been taken over-literally.

Hamlet was one of three productions premièred at the Old Vic during the autumn and winter and destined to move to the Lyttelton. The others were Ben Travers's *Plunder* (directed by Blakemore) and John Osborne's new play, *Watch It Come Down* (directed by Bill Bryden). Hall's productions of *Happy Days* and *John Gabriel Borkman* would join the repertoire, shortly afterwards; and then, in June 1976, *Blithe Spirit* (directed by Harold Pinter) and in July David Hare's production of Howard Brenton's new play, *Weapons of Happiness*, the first two productions to be premièred at the Lyttelton.

This programme revealed the way in which schedules had to be changed according to the problems of the building; for in the National Theatre estimates, submitted to the Peat, Marwick, Mitchell & Company report, a quite different order had been envisaged. In these estimates, for a full year's running at the National, the Olivier and

Cottesloe Theatres had been included, with the result that the annual programme looked like this:

OLIVIER THEATRE:
Hamlet, Playboy of the Western World, Tamburlaine, Blithe Spirit, Tales from the Vienna Woods, Il Campiello, Agamemnon and *Julius Caesar.*
LYTTELTON THEATRE:
Weapons of Happiness, Jumpers, Bedroom Farce, Play D, Play E.
COTTESLOE THEATRE:
Troilus and Cressida, The Taming of the Shrew, Force of Habit, Modern Play 1, Modern Play 2, Modern Play 3, A. N. Other.

The changing of schedules was mainly caused by delays to the Olivier Theatre, which was going to open in June but actually opened in October while the completion of the Cottesloe was held over until the following year. The delays had many consequences for the company.

Chief among these was the way in which productions had to be rehearsed and planned for the new building, and then held back. A kind of log-jam of productions waiting to move built up at the Old Vic, which added to the costs of the move. The income from the box-offices at the Olivier and Cottesloe Theatres was not available, thus increasing the National's estimated deficits. There were psychological consequences too. All actors, if they are good at their jobs, love to act — to be seen on the stage. The delays to the building meant that casts were kept hanging around. Between March and August, about 111 actors were seen at the Lyttelton Theatre in about 184 performances, of 9 separate productions. If the company had been functioning normally, one might have expected each actor to give 3 or 4 performances a week, thus appearing in roughly half of the performances. In fact, the average number of performances given by National Theatre actors at the Lyttelton Theatre during the first six months was about 30, or less than a sixth of the total. These figures are somewhat misleading for several reasons. To compensate for the non-opening of the Cottesloe, a season was arranged at the Young Vic from June to September, which included *Troilus and Cressida,* Mrozek's *Emigrés,* Gawn Grainger's *Four To One* and several visiting fringe companies, including Hull Truck. In July, *Hamlet, The Playboy of the Western World* and *Blithe Spirit* visited Birmingham (with *Blithe Spirit* going on to Oxford) in a short regional tour. Furthermore, some actors in the total came in simply for individual productions, and were not part of the resident company. Nevertheless there was a considerable amount of spare acting capacity at the National, which was only partly absorbed by unduly prolonged rehearsals for *Tamburlaine*. There were other actors too, who did not appear at the National at all during these six months but had expected to do so. They had to wait; and boredom can be very unsettling.

Hall's *Hamlet* was expected to be the cornerstone of the opening season at the Lyttelton. It had been premièred at the Old Vic on December 10th, and (like the *Hamlet* which opened the National Theatre's career in 1963) it received mixed reviews. Hall had directed *Hamlet* before, at the R.S.C. with David Warner, an interesting and influential production which showed the Prince as a mixed-up young man, a prototype student for the 1960s. In this production, however, Hall had clearly been determined not to impose a directorial interpretation on the play. This production did not cut the text; and it concentrated on none of the three main levels of meaning in *Hamlet*: Denmark's social discontent, the family relationships, or Hamlet's communing with his conscience. Finney was an energetic Hamlet, more of a soldier than a glass of fashion; and he sometimes seemed to stress the bitterness of the part at the expense of its other aspects. Michael Billington of the *Guardian* and Robert Cushman of the *Observer* praised Finney's performance (and the production) highly; whereas Irving Wardle echoed the feelings of some other critics when he described it as a 'ponderous cultural event'.

There were, however, two particularly telling aspects to this *Hamlet* — one negative, one positive. The production did not seem designed to use the company in a particularly integrated way. The performances lacked intimacy. There were operatic touches, the courtiers who spoke in unison. The groupings were static and some actors, including such stars as Angela Lansbury and Roland Culver, seemed miscast — or if not miscast, directed in such a way that their individual qualities did not emerge. Even the normal friendship between Hamlet and Horatio was played down in this production — partly because Philip Locke's Horatio (a performance for which he won an award from *Plays and Players* as the best actor in a supporting role) was a generation older than Hamlet.

It seemed clear, however, from this production that Hall was already thinking about how best to use the Olivier stage. The most striking feature of the set was its stage floor, designed like a kind of compass, with an inner circle divided into segments with lines radiating outwards. At the back was a plain wall, with an arch. It was as if Hall were already trying to find ways to bring out what one architectural critic, Mark Girouard, called the 'cosmic' quality of the Olivier Theatre:

It is as though the theatre were a burning glass, through which sections of the world were being concentrated on to the section of light above which one is suspended ...

When the lights are down, the black-painted side-walls act, in effect, as a void in contrast to the enclosing structure of the white concrete. And the shell is literally cracked apart overhead and shattered into many fragments at the back of the auditorium. This cracking and shattering is used for the purposes of stage lighting and acoustics, but its effect is also visual and aesthetic ... [Mark Girouard, 'Cosmic Connections' in *Architectural Review*, January 1977].

The set for *Hamlet*, designed by John Bury, narrowed the focus of the stage through its use of an inner circle, but at the same time extended the dimensions of the stage outwards, into the auditorium, by the simple use of radial lines. The lighting heightened this concentration on a small focal point.

Hamlet, however, intended for the Olivier, was actually staged at the Old Vic and the Lyttelton, although features of its design seemed to influence *Tamburlaine*, which did open at the Olivier. *Hamlet*'s visual effectiveness, therefore, could not be properly judged at the opening performances. The other productions premièred during the winter were also somewhat disappointing. *Watch It Come Down* proved to be another Osborne talk-play about marital pain and the decadence of Britain, set among fairly rich people living in a converted railway station, with a tacked-on bit of melodrama as an ending: one death, a suicide and a shoot-up (with a wounding) in the last ten minutes, provoking some ribaldry on the first night. *Plunder*, certainly a likeable 1920s farce, was very lightweight, most efficiently staged by Michael Blakemore, although it was scarcely a play to test his talents. The most memorable features of these productions came with individual performances, from Frank Finlay (in both plays), Jill Bennett and Dinsdale Landen.

As a group, the new productions did not sustain the promise of the National Theatre productions of the spring and summer of 1975; but they were competent and had their supporters. They provided a reasonable programme for the Lyttelton's opening, which was not going to be the official opening of the National Theatre as a whole. They were in a sense paving the way; but there were those who wondered whether Hall himself was not laying too many stones. Four out of the first seven productions at the Lyttelton were his, and they included all the 'heavies' — *Happy Days*, *John Gabriel Borkman*, *Hamlet* and *No Man's Land*. His fellow directors seem to have been left with rather thankless tasks; and if Olivier had starred in as many productions during his first season, he would have been accused of hogging the limelight. The choice of these productions revealed the comparative failure of other works which had been tried out during the previous months; but the uncut *Hamlet* had originally been Blakemore's idea. He wanted to direct it at the Cottesloe, when it opened, possibly with Albert Finney. Finney was fired by the idea of playing Hamlet, and wanted to start work on it almost immediately, in 1975, at a time not convenient for Blakemore, who was planning to direct *Engaged* for television. Hall accordingly approached Blakemore to ask him whether he could take over the production. Such arrangements are normal, and in this case amicable; but the opening programme did point to a lack of breadth and variety in the National's artistic leadership, not a good omen at a time when the opening of all three theatres was so near.

In the meantime, farewells had to be said—to the Old Vic, and to everything which that theatre had represented for the National Theatre movement. There were really two such occasions, one accidental and the other more formal. One Sunday night in February, members of the National Theatre company took part in a charity performance, to raise money for the widow of a company actor, Jimmy Mellor, who had died of bowel cancer. It had not been organized by the National Theatre, but by a special committee on which Gillian Diamond, the National Theatre casting director, sat. It was not subject to the pressures of a big occasion, and therefore it seemed to express a genuine sense of loss, not only at Mellor's death, but also at the departure from the Old Vic.

The last National performance at the Old Vic was held on February 28th, 1976, and took the form of a documentary, *Tribute To The Lady*, directed by Val May. The lady in question was Lilian Baylis, played by Peggy Ashcroft, dumpy and bustling, with pebble glasses and her M.A. gown pulled over her shoulders like a shawl to keep her reputation warm. Baylis's old office, just off-stage in the old days, was now the set itself: with its roll-top desk, its telephone by which she used to pray as if ringing up God, its gas-ring and frying pan. Ashcroft relished the part. She snatched up the contorted vowels which made Baylis sound prim and common simultaneously, and delivered with barbed naïveté those remarks by which that simple, saintly woman cut through all opposition. 'Such a *sweet* little Goneril,' she remarked of one unfortunate actress. She also had a special warning for Hugh Jenkins, M.P. and Denis Healey, M.P., the Chancellor of the Exchequer, who were sitting in the dress circle. She warned them to guard the future of the

Old Vic; and said, 'All art is a bond between the rich and the poor.'
In her time, the Old Vic had provided such a bond. It brought West
End audiences across the river to watch with the locals productions at
prices which even the very poor could afford. Would the new poor be
able to afford the prices at the new National?

To give 1976 audiences a taste of the meals which Baylis had helped
to provide, Gielgud and Richardson were there. Gielgud seemed to
have been given the hardest job, of coming on stage to a Palladium-
type introduction from Finney, to a spotlight and over-expectant
applause, and then to provide a convincing morsel from *Hamlet*, his
legendary success from the 1929 Old Vic season. Gielgud chose the
'O, what a rogue and peasant slave' speech; and this slight, elderly,
balding man just nipped the bridge of his nose, to gather concentration,
with the fingers of his right hand. Then, as if from a spring of controlled
emotion, the speech poured out, passionate, trembling with self-disgust
and youthfulness, each syllable perfectly modulated, a combination of
a lifetime's devotion to his art and of a tradition in acting which
stretched back to Ellen Terry, his great-aunt, and Frank Benson,
almost to the origins of the National Theatre movement and the aura
surrounding Irving's Lyceum.

Richardson did not attempt to match him. Instead he played the
great English eccentric, wandering on to the stage, chatting very
casually with the audience, dotting his remarks with throwaway
reminiscences ('Harcourt Williams—never ate much—used to sit there,
scoffing Bemax'), before handing out pieces of *Antony and Cleopatra* to
Finney and Gawn Grainger like hymn sheets. His clowning drew the
pomposity from an occasion which might otherwise have suffered from
the Gala disease of glitter and solemnity. Instead the tone was one of
friendly nostalgia. Sybil Thorndike, frail and white-haired, was wheeled
into the foyer as the TV cameras rolled, her eyes still alert, responding
to the sight of old friends and to those new ones, whom she may not
have recognized but who certainly recognized her. It was one of her
last public appearances, for she died in the early summer; and it was
spent watching Susan Fleetwood playing her younger self, recalling the
first impressions of Baylis.

Afterwards there was a party which ran on until six in the morning,
leaving champagne glasses on the stage of the old temperance house,
and a few tears in the eyes of Jimmy Hannah, the National's stage door-
keeper. Hannah, a normally cheerful ex-pro, had appeared with Will
Hay and George Formby in pre-war films, but he had never made the
grade, because, he said, of his Glasgow accent. And so he turned to

looking after the stars instead, keeping out those fans, allowing friends in and casting a sharp eye on those who went in and out of the Old Vic's stage door. He rarely saw a performance. He couldn't be spared from his cubbyhole.

At the beginning of the following week, March 1st, he too moved his belongings to the new stage door, which was certainly not a cubbyhole. It was a rectangular reception area, with long glass windows, facing the new foyer. Two assistants sat with him there, manning the switchboards which stretched out in front of them, while, behind, the familiar honey-comb of slots, with alphabet letters, were already receiving messages for company members—memos, telegrams, *billets doux*, letters of con-gratulation and commiseration.

The doors to the inner building had not yet been fixed; but within a couple of weeks they were hung, and seemed, to an unknowing ob-server, to work by magic. Inside the building, there was an electric eye, so that members of the company going out would find that the door opened for them automatically. People going in, however, would also find that the doors opened for them; and there was no electric eye in the foyer. Nor did the doors open by floor pressure. The floors, like those of the main entrance foyer, were of dark blue-red brick. How then did the doors function with such sensitivity to the visitors' needs? The answer was simple. Hannah was pressing a button from behind his glass partition. If he knew your business, he would let you through. There was, however, a snag. If you were standing on the mat by the doors, while somebody was approaching from the inside, the doors would have swung open, knocking you sideways and flat. The tech-nicians had come up with an answer. If you stood on the mat, the doors would not open at all—thus preventing anyone from coming out of the building. Hannah found a solution, with Sellotape and lined school-book paper. A notice was stuck on the door, 'Keep off mat, when door is shut'. It worked efficiently, but later another solution was found. The doors were propped open.

Once inside these doors, you passed by the general notice-boards with playbills, Equity and N.A.T.T.K.E. notices and lists of Industrial Regulations, to the lifts, which took you to the offices. Each had mar-vellous views. You could stand for hours watching the downstream panorama of London; or fiddling with the internal telephone system, saying 'Sorry' politely and asking for someone else. You could go to the staff canteen, also with wonderful views, and a better-than-average selection of canteen cooking; or into the green room, with its bar and comfortable, not plush, armchairs. The long corridors looked a little like the warrens of the B.B.C., but you couldn't get lost in them, because, sooner or later, you would arrive at a picture window, where you could get your bearings by the sun. It was, in short, a very pleasant civic building, delightful to work in, if you weren't constantly running up against the technical problems of the stages; and it also felt, during those early weeks, like an enormous toy.

The stages still provided all kinds of snags; some of which could have been solved easily within a six-month testing period, if the demands of the National Theatre had allowed that period to happen, and others which were caused by unforeseen mechanical difficulties. The Lyttelton stage, with its comparatively straightforward design and equipment, should not have provided any major problems—and indeed it did not, although minor troubles can give major headaches to an incoming company. There were two main areas of problems at the Lyttelton: the low, neat revolve, designed to Theatre Projects's specifications and built by Hall Stage Equipment Ltd, 'bounced'—and Hall Stage were worried about the flying system as well. Theatre Projects were also concerned about the flying, which had not been installed according to their plans.

The Lyttelton stage had been designed to be fully 'trapped', with sections of the floor which could be raised and lowered at will. It seemed sensible therefore to specify that the revolve should be trapped as well; and to ensure that there was no high step up on to the revolve, which might have hampered the loading of scenery, the revolve had been designed so that it stood only about eight inches from the floor. Unfortunately, these two specifications taken together led to trouble. It would have been easy to build a low revolve if the struts holding its surface could have been designed like bicycle spokes, radiating outwards from the centre; but because the floor was trapped, the struts had to be designed like a grid, with wide gaps to allow actors to climb up through the traps. As a result there had to be long struts, about twelve feet in length, with comparatively few supports to them. This meant that there was a tendency for them to 'give'. Theatre Projects had allowed for a 'give' of a quarter of an inch, when the revolve was fully loaded. Hall Stage had built such a stage, or so they argued, but the give was noticeable even when not fully loaded. The stage surface bounced when the actors were walking across the revolve; and eventually the revolve had to be strengthened by adding another eight inches to its height. In the meantime, the National Theatre company had to find another revolve, for two productions in the opening programme required one. It was constructed quickly along the lines of a portable revolve which they had used on tour.

The Lyttelton stage possessed an ordinary counter-weighted flying system, the only difference from traditional theatres being that the lines were not designed to be operated manually as a matter of course, but by small electric motors, which were linked up, through cyclo-convertors, to a computer-like 'calculator'. This, when programmed, would have controlled the system, leading to a comfortable situation whereby one man could have controlled all the fly-lines. But before Evershed Power Optics could install the control system, the mechanics of the flying system had to work properly; and again there were bones of contention between Hall Stage and Theatre Projects, this time concerning the braking system.

The problems with the Olivier stage were much more complicated and dragged on all summer. Again, the difficulties occurred with the flying and the revolve; but in this case, the spot-line flying could not be operated manually and the drum-revolve was not a small piece of equipment which could be replaced by a portable revolve. It was the stage itself. The hydraulics operating the split-stages took a long time to install, thus preventing Evershed Power Optics from fitting up their control system; but an unexpected difficulty emerged with the wheels. The drum-revolve had to work with great accuracy: it had to stop exactly in line with the tracks which ran from the side-stages on to the revolve, because if these tracks were fractionally out of true, the scenery simply could not be wheeled on to the stage. The drum-revolve could stop within half an inch of the required place, but that was not good enough. Nor, at first, could anyone discover what was going wrong. Eventually, it was found that the polyurethane wheels (chosen because metal wheels would have been too noisy) were slightly depressed with the weight of the drum-revolve, so that as they went round a kind of ripple effect developed on the surface of the wheels. When they were stopped at the correct point, the slightly distorted shape of the wheels caused them to slip backwards.

There was no snag quite like that to hamper the spot-line flying. The principle and design for both the flying and the control system was sound, though innovatory. But it was necessary to tune the cyclo-convertors, programme the computers and ensure that the National Theatre staff were fully trained. Without the testing period, all this work had to be delayed, and eventually the flying had to be handled on a stand-by control system, which meant by-passing the computers alto-gether and plugging the motors directly into the cycle-convertor drives.

Was all this gadgetry really necessary? In one sense, obviously not, for good theatre, as Hall pointed out, can 'erupt' anywhere, in the small black box of a fringe club, without flying or even wing-space. At the same time, to design a National Theatre tempts one inevitably to seek the latest technological equipment at one's disposal. To do otherwise would not only seem timid, but might result in a reactionary-looking theatre, outsmarted by the mechanical marvels elsewhere. The National Theatre was a project far more ambitious and experimental than any which had been attempted before by British theatre contractors: it was their laboratory—to try out new ideas. German civic theatre builders might have been able to provide a theatre of similar scale with greater efficiency and speed; but it would not have been cheaper—indeed it would have cost far more—nor would it have been tailor-made to the requirements of the theatre professionals on the building committee. Whole sections of the technological work operated perfectly. The lighting-control system, designed by Theatre Projects, was almost equally innovatory, in that it could shift patches and areas of light and colour in a manner more flexible and accurate than previous systems. The sound system worked first time as well. The experience gained from building the National was invaluable both for contractors and consultants. Shortly after it opened, Theatre Projects Consultants Ltd won a major contract to advise the Ministry of Culture in Iran, while Mole-Richardson won another contract in Yugoslavia as the result of their work at the National.

That was no comfort, of course, to Simon Relph, who had to cope with the stage problems as they cropped up, almost daily, in some crisis or other—nor to the acting company, who had other problems on their mind, such as acting. Bearing in mind the stage difficulties, the opening repertoire was ambitious, although it included no new productions. Five productions were seen in the opening week at the Lyttelton, which meant five changes of set on an unfamiliar stage, whose equipment was not working properly. On Monday, March 8th, which began the week of previews to critics and invited audiences, there were two productions, of *Happy Days* in the afternoon, and *Plunder*, a complicated three-set play, in the evening. More overtime—and additional stage-hands—had to compensate for what was lacking in equipment at the Lyttelton, thus forcing up the costs of the shows.

Meanwhile, the front-of-house organization had to be planned: the side-shows in the 'fourth' theatre of the foyers and terraces, the restaurant and catering, the pricing policy for the theatre and the almost innumerable small jobs connected with looking after the public—the cloakrooms, programmes and publicity arrangements, the contacts with hotels and booking agencies. Naturally, too much had to be done at the last moment, even after all the delays to the building. Has any theatre opened, except in a frantic rush? Michael Kustow organized quickly a photographic exhibition about the National's history; and also directed a local documentary, written for the occasion about that story, and read by National Theatre actors in the unfinished restaurant. He also booked the music groups: and laid plans on how to bring the terraces to life by such activities as kite-flying.

February and March were frantic months. There was the whole question of how to launch this new place into the awareness of the general public. Sheer curiosity might attract audiences at the beginning, but what would happen when that wore off? What if the first season were less than successful? Would they still come? There were also specific new schemes to sell, such as the ticket voucher system.

One problem, unique to the National, was this—what do you do about varying the seat prices in a theatre if all the seats are (or at least claim to be) equally good? Do you sell them all at the same price, which would seem logical? That might mean, however, that the average seat price was rather high, excluding sections of the population in a manner unbecoming to a National Theatre. Do you then offer concessions to certain groups of people (such as students and old-age pensioners) which might be class divisive, or do you offer a certain number of cheap seats? You can't offer too many cheap seats because (given that all the seats are equally good) only blatant snobs presumably would want to buy the more expensive ones? How, in short, do you run an egalitarian theatre in a non-egalitarian society? Peter Stevens thought of a solution. The seats should be sold primarily on a voucher system basis, which entitled those who bought vouchers to seats in the theatre, but not *specific* seats. If you wanted to sit in a particular place, say, in the eighth row, you had to pay an additional reservation fee. When the Lyttelton Theatre opened, the vouchers cost £2·35 and the reservation fee £2·00. Together a reserved seat would cost £4·35, which was roughly equivalent to the price of a best stall in the West End; and the principle behind the system lay in the hope that the minority of comparatively rich theatre-goers would choose to subsidize the majority, thus keeping the basic voucher price comparatively low. It was intended for people who did not wish to go through the system of exchanging vouchers at the theatre in return for specific seat tickets on the night. In addition, a certain number of tickets were held back at each performance to be sold for £1 each; and half of the £1 seats were bookable in advance, while the other half had to be sold on the day of the performance.

It was not a complicated system, but it was an unfamiliar one, which therefore provoked some complaints. Apart from the inconvenience of exchanging vouchers, some felt that the basic voucher price was too high. It was hard for a family of four, even with a slightly higher than average income, to afford the ten pounds or so which a visit to the National would require; and the £1 seats were not always available, without queuing, and even then you could be unlucky. The days of cheap seats in the gods were gone.

Nevertheless, the audiences, as they drifted in, seemed to like the theatre, although builders' vans were just around the corner and the catering arrangements were sparse indeed in the opening months. However formidable a lump of concrete the National Theatre had seemed when empty, it was a friendly building when occupied, warm and quickly springing to life. The foyers, with their low ceilings, odd corners, window seats and concealed lighting, managed to combine space with intimacy—and there was a theatrical flair to them. One architectural critic pointed out a comparison between the grey concrete pillars and Gordon Craig's set design for *Hamlet*, also with plain pillars.

When there were only a few people around, the foyers never looked depressingly empty, because of their scale. When, during intervals, the foyers were full, the place rarely seemed overcrowded. There were places for reading and browsing. You could buy newspapers and theatre periodicals at the bookstall, as well as books. In that awkward time gap between the ending of office hours and the start of performances, the foyer musicians would play, sometimes giving an impression of human *muzac* but adding liveliness to the surroundings. Even at the first preview, when the place should have looked uncomfortably new, it was relaxing enough for one couple to sit on the carpeted floor, leaning up against a pillar, chatting through the hubbub.

Through the long, hot months of May and June, the terraces were discovered, where you could sit outside and watch the river drift by. In the world outside, disasters were happening, worse even than the crises Relph was facing. The pound plummeted to a record low level on the day of the first preview, although the events were not directly connected. Harold Wilson resigned as Prime Minister on Tuesday, March 16th, the day of the official opening at the Lyttelton Theatre, thus thoughtfully providing a topic of conversation for an audience of celebrities and V.I.P.s during the interval. But the Thames still floated past; and a rare species of crab was found near Hammersmith Bridge. It was the sort of building which, in a very English way, used nature to pull calamity and political upheavals into perspective. The record heat of the summer added an Edwardian touch. Alfred Lyttelton would have approved of that summer.

As people walked down from Waterloo Bridge, or across the raised path to the first level of the National, they brought with them the bustle of the town. The forbidding notices which had protected the National site for so long were, one by one, taken down, so that cars could drive up, leaving their passengers by the corner box-office. People were starting to take over 'their' theatre: and in time, the long struggle to bring the National Theatre into existence would be forgotten. It would become part of the accepted landscape of London; and the concrete would whiten and stain with age and use, as the National's career itself would develop, brightened by its successes, coloured by its failures, scandals and trials.

20

The Challenge of the National

THE week of previews and the official first night (of *Hamlet*) at the Lyttelton had run, if not smoothly, at least without too many mishaps noticeable to the audiences. On Wednesday, March 17th, there was a meeting of the associate directors, gathering not (as before) in Peter Hall's Barbican flat, but in the boardroom attached to the executive offices in the National: a large impressive room, with a stained blackwood boardroom table. The meeting started at about 6.00, was scheduled to adjourn briefly at 8.30—so that the directors could meet some of the invited guests during the interval of *John Gabriel Borkman*— and the discussions would continue afterwards, perhaps for several hours. Michael Blakemore had asked for some space on the agenda, though nobody else at the meeting quite knew why.

Blakemore had been concerned for some time at the way in which the National was being run, and, in particular, about the role of the associate directors, who were supposed to 'share in all decision-making', as publicized through the National Theatre programmes and publicity. His basic argument was that this was not so—that policy-making decisions had been taken which by-passed the associate directors and the planning committee, that certain policies had been approved in general principle but had received unexpected interpretations in practice, and that some policy decisions which associate directors had opposed 'albeit in a muted fashion' had nevertheless been implemented. His case was not that the decisions were necessarily wrong—although he gave several examples of decisions to which he was personally opposed—but that it was wrong to implicate the associate directors in decisions over which they had had little or no influence. He did not necessarily disagree with the idea of a strong executive, but only with the pretence (as he saw it) that decisions were collectively taken when they were not:

At the moment [he said] this committee is sometimes a rubber stamp, sometimes a way of insuring that the risk of an ill-advised decision is spread, but hardly ever an effective, decision-making body. Let the three-man executive [of Peter Hall, Peter Stevens and Lord Birkett] run the organisation with a free hand. By all means, let this committee continue as a think-tank. By all means let each one of us accept responsibility for those areas over which the individual has real control ... By all means let us continue our meetings and our dinners, to be briefed by Peter on what has been decided and to share with him through discussions the immense problems of running the organisation. But let us call ourselves what we are, not a planning committee but an advisory committee. And let us re-name ourselves tonight.

Blakemore illustrated his general argument with various examples, some of which contained confidential and indeed contentious matter. He therefore typed out his statement, to prevent misunderstandings, and handed out copies to the associate directors; but to ensure that there were no leaks to the press, he kept these copies in his own hands before the meeting, so that he took personal responsibility for them. At several points during his statement, he stressed that 'my goodwill to the National and to Peter is intact'. He described Peter Hall as 'a man of unique energy, ability and persuasion', whose interests were best served not just by the loyalty of his associate directors, but by their 'watchfulness and scrupulously argued differences' as well. He delayed making his statement until after the problems of moving in had been tackled.

He divided his statement into three sections, each showing how the committees had failed effectively to influence policy decisions. In the first section, he was concerned with the way in which the opinions of the associate directors had been overlooked, and he cited alterations in the planning of repertoires. In the case of *Grand Manoeuvres*, his own production, the decision to drop it from the repertoire was taken within two days from the opening night, following hostile reviews from the daily papers, and without consulting the associate directors, two of whom had not even seen the production. As a consequence, a team of actors who had worked together so successfully in *The Front Page* and provided continuity with Olivier's regime, was broken up. A similar case involved Jonathan Miller, whose three projected productions for 1975 (*The Importance of Being Earnest, She Would If She Could* and a revival of *Measure for Measure*) were all cancelled, thus leaving him with little option but to resign. These instances all pointed to the thought that the National Theatre executive was placing too high a premium on success, as gauged by press reviews; but Blakemore's argument was not that 'these decisions were necessarily wrong ... only that the associates did not have the least influence on them. Yet they were at the very heart of what we call planning.'

The second section concerned the way in which associate directors had agreed to a policy decision in principle, but not necessarily to the way in which it was applied in practice; and Blakemore gave examples which, because they involved money, he acknowledged to be 'delicate'. The first concerned the differentials paid to the various levels of National Theatre actors, some of whose salaries had been greatly increased.

> This matter was first raised by Peter at an afternoon planning meeting, and we all murmured our assent to his general contention that actors in the subsidised theatre were under-paid and that this should be corrected.

But Blakemore was disturbed by the fact that this general principle had been interpreted in such a way that the differentials between the lowest and highest paid members of the company had increased:

> In the previous regime, the differential between the lowest and highest salary was very approximately one to three; that is, the highest paid actor received three times the salary of the lowest. This does not take account of performance fees which in fact swung the balance rather more in favour of the leading actors, but it does give us a mode of comparison. Since the new increases, the differential is in the order of one to ten. Whilst the lowest salary remains exactly where it was in the forties, the highest is now £500 and this for only one or two performances a week. Per performance this is a much higher salary than 10% of the gross of most West End theatres.

The consequences of such a decision were, according to Blakemore, far-reaching:

> What we have done is to jettison a tradition that has not only sustained the idea of the National Theatre over the years, but has actually made it possible. From Granville Barker and Devine at the Court, to Lilian Baylis, Guthrie and Olivier at the Vic, not to mention the work at Stratford, some sacrifice of potential earning capacity has long been accepted as the price for doing uncompromised work, even perhaps as a guarantee of seriousness. This is a very English, puritan, and perhaps philistine tradition, but it had life in it, and

until recently was widely understood and accepted by the profession. When John Gielgud joined the National in the sixties, it was for a salary of £67, a ludicrous figure, but one which he was prepared to accept ...

He could have added (although he did not) that wide pay differentials are not thought generally to be good for the morale of permanent companies, for they prevent the feeling that all actors are in the same boat, the production. Some have more to lose or gain than others; and high wages for leading actors usually suggest the operation of the star system.

Blakemore's second example in this category concerned the royalties from West End transfers:

At another afternoon meeting, Peter proposed that in the case of such transfers, the artistic personnel should be entitled to their full commercial reward. Again we assented. So far there has only been one transfer to the West End, *No Man's Land*, so any discussion of the way this policy works out in practice must centre on this single instance. I think we know the background to *No Man's Land*; Harold offered it to the National on the condition that after a certain number of weeks at the Vic it move to the West End. Being himself an associate of this organisation, there was perhaps some conflict of interests here, but I think that we would all concede that, as the play's author, Harold's first loyalty was to its best exposure. As Artistic Director, however, Peter's first loyalty was clearly to the welfare of the National Theatre, and the *No Man's Land* situation was pushing him towards the creation of two far-reaching precedents, both theoretically endorsed by us. The first was that it was acceptable for a member of this organisation to draw two salaries from it at the same time for the same job of work. The second was that a playwright, or any theatrical figure with sufficient muscle, could make the offer of his services conditional on a West End transfer ... This matter of royalties on top of salary raises innumerable questions ...

Indeed it did, for behind Blakemore's rather stern remarks on the *No Man's Land* transfer — which was not of course the only National Theatre transfer to the West End, but the first one of a new play in Peter Hall's regime — lay the possibility that future associate directors might decide on programme policies at the National in the light of possible West End transfers. Thus, the National would become a means whereby productions could be rehearsed and staged on public money, and then exploited commercially, to the benefit of the directors. Blakemore appreciated that Harold Pinter had not wanted *No Man's Land* to be staged at all at the Old Vic: he had written the play with the new National in mind. The Old Vic season (of some forty performances) had thus been a concession on Pinter's part to the needs of the National. But Blakemore was concerned that the precedent of *No Man's Land* would be cited, for less scrupulous reasons, by future artistic directors.

The third category concerned matters over which there had been some opposition from the associate directors, although mildly expressed, and which nevertheless had been implemented. Blakemore cited the appointment of Michael Birkett (whom he called 'a friend and valued colleague'), whose services were not considered particularly necessary by the associates initially, and the acceptance by Peter Hall of the 'Aquarius' job, which might leave the mistaken impression in the public mind that Hall was neglecting the National by taking on a second highly paid job. The crux of Blakemore's argument, however, lay throughout the paper in his belief that various committees were not effectively controlling the policy of the National, and probably would never be able to do so, whoever was in charge:

> My previous experience suggested that the policy of a theatre is dictated less by statements of intent, no matter how complex or considered, than by those day-to-day crises that arrive on someone's desk at eleven in the morning demanding a solution by three in the afternoon. The policy of any theatre is most truly the accumulation of these daily decisions—decisions which reveal priorities, create precedents and eventually map out a discernible course. Alas, it is precisely in this area that no committee can possibly participate.

Blakemore's statement was not particularly well received by his fellow associates. He could scarcely have expected that they would do so, for some were being directly criticized. Some factual errors were pointed out. Blakemore had suggested that 'Aquarius' took up about one and a half days of Hall's time, whereas Hall insisted that it was only Tuesday afternoons, a few hours or so. The question of salary differentials was disputed, in that it was suggested that Blakemore based his case on a couple of highly atypical examples. The Peat, Marwick, Mitchell & Company report pointed out that two or three artists received weekly earnings (without performance fees) of £500, although most actors received between £45 and £250 with performance fees ranging from £3 to £30. The 'normal' differentials within the company would be roughly 1 to 5; but, of course, Blakemore could have argued that the very presence of one highly paid actor taking a star role within a company production was enough to weaken the company spirit. It was pointed out that the decision to withdraw *Grand Manoeuvres* had not been taken so precipitately—but *after* the Sunday reviews had appeared, and *after* checking that the advance bookings were low, and *because* it would result in substantial cost-savings at a time when economies were particularly needed, and *with* Blakemore's full agreement. Blakemore conceded these points; but insisted that, none the less, a production which had received the support of every associate director, except one, had been withdrawn without reference to the committee.

A more substantial matter was whether the *No Man's Land* transfer had created a precedent, as Blakemore claimed, or whether it was the continuation of a well-established practice. In one sense, it was clearly the latter, for managements of subsidized theatres had almost invariably drawn income from the proceeds of West End transfers: and that had applied as much to National Theatre productions as to those of Guildford's Yvonne Arnaud Theatre. Blakemore claimed, however, that 'in the past, the work of the National Theatre has been widely exploited both in the West End and abroad, but never before have those participating in the rewards continued on full salary here'. Among subsidized repertory theatres, there were also unofficial codes of conduct, amounting almost to a concept of fair play. A director on £50 or £60 a week, such as Michael Rudman at Hampstead Theatre Club, who was lucky enough to find that one of his productions was bought for the West End, could regard such a transfer as a reward for working for years on a low salary. Any director, however, who solely aimed for West End transfers, and thus distorted the repertoire of his company in order to make a bid for a bonanza, was liable to be looked on with disfavour by his fellow directors in other companies. Blakemore's point concerned a nebulous area where the subsidized theatre overlapped with the commercial, where feelings were likely to run high and where the conventions were by no means clear-cut. Whether his views were right or not, it was certainly a matter for serious discussion among the associate directors.

There were other smaller points of disputed detail; and the question arose as to whether the inaccuracies damaged the substance of Blakemore's argument. Hall later insisted that they did, whereas Blakemore said that they did not. How did the fellow associates react? Schlesinger was not present at that meeting, but Pinter, Bury, Brown, Harrison

Birtwistle, Bryden, Stevens, Kustow and Birkett were there, as well as Hall. At the end of the meeting, Kustow asked whether any of the associates wanted to take the paper away for further consideration. Pinter at one point during the discussion had asked for a chance to think about Blakemore's statement at greater length, but Hall had indicated that he did not really want the papers to leave the boardroom although, realizing that this might suggest that he distrusted the discretion of the associate directors, he quickly withdrew that spoken doubt. Kustow's question was, in a sense, a leading one—for the associate director who took the statement away would, by that act, be implying that Blakemore's arguments had substance to them and, in the event of leaks to the press, the associates with copies might be suspected. One by one, as in some slow, blackballing ceremony, the associates laid their copies before Blakemore, Bryden seeming to hesitate a little before finally placing his copy as well across the black table. Blakemore was left with the complete pile of his photocopied statements.

There the matter might have rested, for Blakemore had pledged his support for Hall and was prepared to work within the National Theatre company. His statement had not been minuted. But a bizarre incident intervened, a mere misunderstanding, no doubt, which led to Blakemore's resignation in May.

Blakemore's contract was being renegotiated with the National. It was almost a routine matter for him, and indeed for other associate directors. There had been one meeting in July 1975 between Terence Owen, Blakemore's agent, and the National, through Peter Stevens. The new contract, if it had been agreed, would have begun in April 1976; and its intention, according to Blakemore and Owen, would have been to have raised Blakemore's salary from the National to a figure of around £9,500 a year. Instead of being on a fixed salary, however, Blakemore would have been on a retainer of about £20 a week, and paid additional fees (of roughly £2,500 to £3,000) for each production. With three National Theatre productions a year, Blakemore's salary would have shown an increase of about £1,000 over his previous fixed salary.

The dispute basically concerned whether these three productions were guaranteed or whether they were dependent upon the circumstances being right, both on the National's side and on Blakemore's. Blakemore and Owen insisted that the productions would have to be guaranteed, because otherwise there was no advantage to them in changing the terms of the contract which already existed. Hall and Stevens evidently thought that the three productions would have to be conditionally offered, bearing other factors in mind. In a letter to

Blakemore, replying to his resignation, Hall pointed out that Blakemore could have received a gross National Theatre income of £9,500, if he did three principal productions a year. The key word here is 'if'. If the National were not in a position to offer Blakemore three productions a year—a possibility not seriously contemplated in July 1975 when everyone assumed that the three theatres in the building would be fully operational by 1976—or if Blakemore's prior commitments were such that he could not quickly adapt to the National's needs, then his National Theatre income would, at worst, be reduced to £20 a week. That 'if' placed Blakemore in a dilemma. With three guaranteed productions a year, he could have afforded to neglect work outside the National or to have organized that work around his National commitments. Without the guarantee, he would have to take on outside productions, thus making it more difficult for him to take on National productions as and when required.

Under normal circumstances, this disagreement could have been sorted out amicably enough. Blakemore and Owen saw no troubles ahead; and Blakemore, following the trials of moving in, went off for a few weeks to France, to read scripts and think about future productions. He was therefore surprised when his April cheque from the National did not arrive and to hear from his agent that apparently written instructions had been left by Peter Stevens to the effect that no payments should be made to Blakemore until further notice. Owen accordingly phoned up Stevens, but could not actually speak to him for nearly six days, from the evening of Wednesday, May 5th, to the morning of Monday, May 10th. In the meantime, however, Stevens had left instructions that Blakemore should be paid six months' salary at the retainer fee of £20 a week.

If this fee had been accepted without question, then it might have implied that Blakemore was accepting a contract which did not include guaranteed productions; but in any case, Blakemore was incensed that Stevens had not contacted his agent more quickly. He interpreted the incident as a snub, not unconnected with the reading of his statement to the associate directors in March. Accordingly, he sent in his resignation on May 11th, which Hall received with regret. Blakemore, too, did not want the parting to be accompanied with enmity, and he was prepared, if asked, to work with the National on a freelance basis, an offer which Hall was evidently willing to consider. In a further letter sent on May 13th, Hall expressed his regret that Blakemore was leaving and hoped that he would continue occasionally to direct plays for the National Theatre. One production which Blakemore was scheduled to direct, was *The Madras House*; and he was prepared, indeed eager, to continue with that task.

The atmosphere surrounding Blakemore at the National was clearly unhappy, however. Another small incident serves as illustration. Blakemore was usually extremely reticent at talking to journalists. Indeed one had spoken to Blakemore around the time of his paper to the associates, and had put forward arguments similar to those expressed in that statement. Blakemore, on that occasion, had defended Hall and the National with considerable vigour. On April 12th, however, a rather critical article, written by a friend of Blakemore's, had appeared in the *Evening Standard*; and it was assumed by many members of the National's management that Blakemore had supplied the information on which that article was based. Blakemore denied that this was so, and in particular insisted that 'the confidentiality of the paper I read at the Associates' Meeting on March 17th was, and has remained, absolute'. Nevertheless, the suspicions remained and when, on May 19th, a fairly bland comment from Blakemore about his resignation appeared in the *Evening Standard*, the response from the National was extremely sharp. Blakemore had said that his departure had been 'fairly amicable':

> I've been there for five years and it is time to move on. I hope to go back to do free-lance work at the National. There have been areas of differences over policy, but amicable differences ... I'm full of admiration for the way Peter Hall copes. He has a job of back-breaking magnitude [*Evening Standard*, May 19th, 1976].

These remarks, however, preceded the official press statement about his resignation by a few days; and at an Associates' Dinner held on Wednesday, May 26th, in Blakemore's absence, it was agreed that Blakemore should be scheduled to direct Granville Barker's play *The Madras House*, with the proviso that if any adverse comment appeared in the press originating from Blakemore, the offer should be withdrawn. When Blakemore read the notes of this meeting, which thus cast doubt on his reliability and integrity, he decided not to direct *The Madras House*; and severed his associations with the National Theatre altogether.

The loss of Blakemore, as was realized inside the National and among the observers on the outside, had serious consequences. Primarily, it meant that Hall had lost his most experienced stage director at a time when it was particularly important that the artistic leadership at the National should be strengthened, rather than weakened. Apart from Hall, only Bryden was now left as a permanent staff director among the associates, who could be relied upon to put aside all other commitments to concentrate on productions for those three theatres which, in the not too distant future, would have to be filled. Pinter and Schlesinger could be trusted to provide occasional productions, but not for the constant output required.

There was also a less easily defined gap, that mixture of imagination and experience required to cope with the problems likely to be faced in the still unfinished building. Hall needed to be surrounded by people who would not be flummoxed by technical troubles, but would use their inventiveness to get round them. Blakemore could have been one such director; and although his record at the National had not been outstandingly impressive since Hall took over, he was still remembered as the man who staged *The National Health, Long Day's Journey Into Night* and *The Front Page*.

And the Olivier Theatre, like a great sailing ship drifting into view whose holds might contain almost anything, riches and risks alike, was approaching completion. Nobody knew, however, exactly when it would be completed. The opening date was still officially placed in June; but that calendar event was clung to, as a kind of talisman, in the belief that if the National Theatre let go of it, the eighteen months' delay which had already occurred would drift on indefinitely. In March, all the signs pointed to further postponements. Seventeen weeks before the opening of the Lyttelton, for example, it had been possible to hold a successful dress rehearsal on the Lyttelton stage. Nineteen weeks before the proposed opening of the Olivier, it was clear that there could be no such rehearsals for some weeks on the Olivier stage. It was clear that the spot-line flying and the drum-revolve would not be working properly by June; and that, of course, Evershed Power Optics would not be able to install the control system — and that the most that anybody could expect would be a rudimentary stage with rudimentary equipment. But still the pressure to open had to be maintained, although the official opening was put back to July, allowing a month's rehearsal on the Olivier stage; and when that basic schedule was confirmed by the National Theatre Board in March, Theatre Projects Consultants Ltd sent an urgent memo to all its employees and the sub-contractors, bidding them to achieve the impossible — and by 'impossible', they meant just that.

The National Theatre company had to have a production suitable for the opening, and *Tamburlaine* was chosen, with Hall as its director. The first readings took place on April 20th, 1976, when some fifty actors assembled in Rehearsal Room 2. A full account of the long, six-month rehearsal period for *Tamburlaine* has been written by John Heilpern (*Observer* Colour Magazine, December 19th, 1976). Heilpern, a journalist with some theatrical experience gleaned from working with Peter Brook, was allowed to be Hall's assistant director, sitting in on rehearsals, and watching the evolution of a production which, at one point, Hall declared to be the most difficult of his career. Originally, the rehearsal period had been planned to last for ten weeks, but after three weeks of blocking out scenes, the July opening was postponed by a month, to August 24th—and then, after two weeks' rehearsal in the Olivier in July, it was postponed again. On August 23rd, the final opening date was announced: October 4th; but even then there were snags which threatened to delay it, although they did not. In August, there was a strike of stage-hands, and within a week of the opening Albert Finney, tackling the long and difficult part of Tamburlaine, fell ill from bronchitis.

Apart from these problems, there was the play itself, acknowledged to be one of the most awkward classics in English dramatic literature. Its literary significance is partly that it is a forerunner for Shakespearian history plays, Jacobean revenge tragedy and a school of playwriting with which most English theatregoers are all too familiar; and precisely because it anticipated so much of what was to come, *Tamburlaine* is hard to accept on its own terms. When listening to the verse, one is reminded of Shakespeare but misses the Shakespearian subtleties of meaning; its story is a sequence of bloodthirsty episodes, about the rise of a shepherd who became a tyrannical emperor—and his death. It is one of the most difficult plays to hold a company's attention over a long period—because there is only one really good part in it, that of Tamburlaine. For that reason alone, it was an almost recklessly ambitious choice for the opening production.

Heilpern has described how the actors discovered that their techniques, 'rooted in naturalism and Shakespeare', were 'too private' for Marlowe; how they had to summon up the *chutzpah* to deliver the speeches directly and rhetorically to the audience; how Hall began to realize that the strength of the play, its inner structure, lay in its use of symmetry, with the figure three (three emblematic colours, three physicians, three clear divisions to Parts 1 and 2) assuming a greater importance as the rehearsals progressed; how after months of rehearsals, with the actors feeling stale, Hall took them out on to the terraces, where they played to passing audiences, in the hot summer afternoons and evenings, against the background roar of the traffic; and how, at the last minute, Hall turned the *chutzpah* into an almost Churchillian statement of defiance against the National's critics and, in a sense, their fate. According to Heilpern, Hall's instructions to the actors, just before the opening performance, contained these words:

> If you think we're in the shit, you're *right*. There's no way we can live up to the opening of the Olivier. They'll be expecting a miracle. But what we can do is put two fingers in the air to all the National's critics and say to them, 'This is what we are! This is what we can do! And to hell with you!'

Heilpern does not mention, however, the plans to take over the Roundhouse for *Tamburlaine*, because the Olivier was not ready, although these plans had to be abandoned as too expensive. Nor, more significantly, why *Tamburlaine* was chosen in the first place. The temptations to do *Tamburlaine* are obvious—a marvellously panoramic play, ideal for an open stage and one which had not received a production in London for twenty-five years, since Guthrie's version at the Old Vic with Donald Wolfit, which had drastically shortened the play. The logistics of *Tamburlaine*, however, were worrying, bearing in mind the likely delays to the building. It would keep a large number of actors pinned to the South Bank, prevented from touring or from taking more rewarding parts than Marlowe had given them; and so was likely to prove a costly production as well.

The costs of running the National were now escalating alarmingly above the estimates. Every month that the Olivier theatre remained unopened meant the loss of £100,000 in box-office revenue. This cannot be regarded as a total loss, because, of course, actors were not being paid performance fees and further productions with their necessary expenses had to be delayed. These losses were, however, serious, as were those caused by the heavy repertoire on an unfinished stage at the Lyttelton. The repertoire was simplified during the summer, from five separate productions a week to four, three and sometimes two, but still the resident stage crews had to work long hours of overtime; and labour had to be drafted in to haul scenery around which, if all the equipment had worked, could have been handled by a few stage-hands. It was calculated that the costs of additional labour hours amounted to £120,000.

By the autumn, the situation had become quite critical. The estimated deficit was £1,009,272, after taking all other factors into account: the £1·9 million already 'intimated as being available' from the Arts Council, the £350,000 G.L.C. subsidy, a touring guarantee of £25,500 and the balance of £207,426 available out of the 1975–6 rolling guarantee. The National Theatre attributed £691,860 of the deficit to delays in the completion of the South Bank building, and £317,412 to the 'shortfall in normal revenue funding'. It was simply hard to know or even to guess where the Arts Council could find that amount of money, even if they had the will and the political muscle to do so. It could scarcely have been a worse time to ask for more money from the government, who were in the process of negotiating foreign loans to bolster the falling value of the pound; and Healey had made it clear to the Arts Council that their Treasury grant, in real terms, was to be decreased in years to come, not increased.

There were other reasons why the climate of opinion was unfavourable for the National to request so much additional money. Although the opening season at the Lyttelton had been favourably received, as a whole, and attendance figures had been maintained at an extremely high level (about 90 per cent of capacity), the new productions had raised doubts. *Blithe Spirit*, directed by Pinter, was an excellent production in itself, but should the National want to tackle this light and trivial comedy, which had bashed around the reps for so many years? It was not a choice comparable to *Hay Fever* — in that Coward was not around to direct it and it was not part of an attempt to burnish the reputation of a writer who had recently been neglected. On the contrary, it caught on to the end of a fashion — for there had been many Coward revivals since *Hay Fever*. Howard Brenton's *Weapons of Happiness* was a brave new play, which examined in Marxist terms (though, it must be added, simplistically) a strike in a small factory, as seen through the eyes of a tired ex-revolutionary, Josef Frank (Frank Finlay) who had suffered under Stalinist tyranny. Although *Weapons of Happiness* was an honourable choice, and eventually won for Brenton the Best New Play award from the *Evening Standard*, it was not really the kind of unchallengeable success which the National needed. As if to remind audiences of the successes of former days, *Jumpers* was revived at the Lyttelton. Rather cruelly, too, Jonathan Miller's production of *Three Sisters*, originally staged at Guildford on three weeks' rehearsal and with production expenses totalling £3,000, came to the West End; and won for him the *Plays and Players* Best Director award for 1976.

Nor was the National's cause helped by the publication in September of three articles (written by Max Hastings) in the *Evening Standard*, which revealed, among other matters, the contents in summary of the Peat, Marwick, Mitchell & Company report. The estimates in that report were already out of date. *Tamburlaine*, for example, had been calculated to cost £36,000 simply for sets and costumes, which was roughly in line with the general principle that productions at the Olivier should be allocated between £20,000 and £30,000 for such production expenses. *Tamburlaine*, being a long play—indeed two plays, with the chance for spectacle, had been granted a little more money; whereas *Blithe Spirit* (at £20,500) and *Il Campiello* (at £26,500) had been given a little less. But it was now common knowledge that *Tamburlaine*'s production costs had risen, partly because of the long delays, considerably above that figure, to more than £50,000; while the long rehearsal period had added greatly to the bill for paying actors.

What was as worrying (although it received less publicity) was that the National no longer seemed to be in a position where it was generating new talent and new ideas. This was partly the consequence of the narrowing artistic leadership. Hall was, of course, aware of this problem but it was not one which could be easily solved—particularly without the use of the Cottesloe Theatre. Although the sums to be spent on the Cottesloe were trivial in comparison with those allocated to the main stages, and although the simple 'black box' theatre, with its variable fourth wall and elevators beneath the floor which could transform its shape, was a theatre which tempted most directors who saw it, its completion had been delayed for lack of money and because the contractors' efforts had been directed elsewhere. Ideally, the Cottesloe could have been used to try out new actors, writers and directors on inexpensive productions; but it was not available. The Young Vic was taken over for a three-month season during the summer; and Hall used this opportunity to groom his assistant director for *Hamlet*, Elijah Moshinsky, to take a more responsible role within the National Theatre organization. Moshinsky directed *Troilus and Cressida* at the Young Vic, a moderate production, and Thomas Bernhard's *The Force of Habit* at the Lyttelton in November, unfortunately an outright failure.

Since, if only temporarily, the National Theatre was not in the happy situation of having a constant flow of new ideas and talents coming from within the company, it was tempting for them to look elsewhere. Nor was this at all inconsistent with Hall's general vision for the National. He had always said that the National should provide a facility for the nation's theatre, and should be a shop-window for British talents, without laying down any restrictive definitions as to what kind of talents. He wanted to include a wide range of genres in the repertoire; and under normal circumstances, the talents brought in from outside the National would have been matched by those generated from within. However, if the National were thought to be 'poaching' from outside managements, commercial or subsidized, then clearly that would cause much resentment; and some plans for the National which became known in the troubled autumn raised such apprehensions.

The least contentious example concerned the commissioning of a new play from Alan Ayckbourn, whose highly successful comedies had previously been staged in the West End by the impresario Michael Codron. Codron raised no objection to the idea that the National should produce Ayckbourn's *Bedroom Farce* (premièred at Scarborough), and it was a tribute to Ayckbourn that his plays could succeed not only at a popular level, but within a National repertoire. But it could be argued that there was no reason why the National should produce Ayckbourn's play, which was more or less guaranteed a London production in any case.

A more troubling case was the proposed production of William Douglas Home's *The Kingfisher*, which Home had written for Sir Ralph Richardson. Home's reputation among critics was less solidly based than Ayckbourn's, although his popularity with West End audiences was undeniable. Previously, Home's plays had been staged in the West End by various commercial impresarios, with Peter Saunders normally having the first refusal. It seemed highly unlikely that *The Kingfisher* would only receive comparatively few performances in repertoire at the National, whereas its commercial life in the West End might have been for a year's solid run—or more. Was the National therefore contemplating that situation envisaged in Blakemore's statement— whereby a play rehearsed on public money and receiving comparatively few performances at the National would transfer to the West End, with its director collecting something like 4 per cent of the box-office proceeds? It seemed, at one time, that this would be the case, and even perhaps that *The Kingfisher* would not open at the National at all, but in the West End, due, as Hall explained, to the 'building delays' on the South Bank. But the West End commercial managements reacted sharply. One producer said,

> If the National starts being an impresario, it could put every commercial management out of a job. It is wrong to use the taxpayers' money to produce a play commercially [Article by Craig Seton, *The Times*, January 26th, 1977. Copyright *The Times*, London].

The production had to be shelved. Indeed, Home himself withdrew his play from the National and from West End managements until, as he put it, 'somebody becomes more sensible and gives up this ridiculous war with the National'. He was, however, persuaded to change his mind by one commercial management, John Gale.

A further example, on a more lowly level, concerned the arrival of the Hull Truck (fringe) company for a week's run of their production, *Bridget's House*, during the National Theatre season at the Young Vic. Hull Truck regarded the Bush Theatre as their 'London home', having appeared there for short seasons during the two previous years. They were due to appear at the Bush in November 1976, in *Bridget's House*, a long-standing engagement. The National, however, decided that it should be seen under their auspices at the Young Vic, and therefore offered Hull Truck £600 for a July engagement. This effectively meant that the National was cutting across the Bush's interests, for critics were unlikely to want to see *Bridget's House* twice and the Young Vic appearance could have taken audiences away from the run at the Bush. As it happened, however, the Hull Truck season at the Bush was highly successful; although the Bush's management still felt that the National's action was wrong in principle.

What mattered, however, was not the ethics of the National's behaviour, but rather what role the National should eventually play in the theatre system. Clearly, it should be complementary to other theatre managements and not in rivalry with them, for in any straight competitive battle, the odds unfairly favoured the National. The size of their subsidies, the new theatre and the very name of the National raised the National Theatre company above—and away from—the normal battles of the market-place. The National was intended to be a privileged theatre; but circumstances seemed to have drawn the National away from undertaking the sort of work which its particular status had originally been intended to provide. In time, no doubt, the National would find its role, but in the summer and autumn of 1976, it still seemed far from such a discovery. It was not a 'library' theatre, as Granville Barker and Shaw had intended, containing classical and good modern works, for its repertoires ranged from plays which could be put on by almost any commercial company to those which might have been selected by almost any fringe group. The idea that the National's programmes should be selected within 'the wisdom and calmness of confluent opinion' (in Irving's phrase) had, in a sense, been jettisoned—perhaps because in the Britain of the 1970s it was so hard to decide what that confluent opinion was. Nor was it a sort of advanced drama school, bringing the young professionals into touch with the best traditions and the most experienced actor-teachers of their day. Nor indeed had Hall's rather different plans for the National taken root— for sheer poverty had prevented that constant flow of touring productions pouring out of the National Theatre and the building delays had prevented the development of the company, as he had hoped.

Hall's task, therefore, as he approached the Arts Council for another £1 million of public money, was not an easy one. There was tough talking ahead. In October, there was an interim agreement whereby the Arts Council agreed to raise the 1976–7 National Theatre grant to £2 million, while adding a further 'rolling guarantee' against loss of £250,000. This meant that there was an increase of £350,000 in the National Theatre's grant, which was taken from a sum of £500,000 given 'by way of special provision from the Government to meet the estimated requirements of the National Theatre'. The remaining £150,000 from that reserve fund was kept by the Council until the last quarter of the financial year; and not formally offered to the National Theatre.

This left the National Theatre with an anticipated deficit of £540,000, which they hoped to reduce by means of economies over the remaining four months of the financial year together with increases in seat prices on January 1st. The draft document prepared by the Arts Council and based on the findings of the Peat, Marwick, Mitchell & Company report had indicated areas where the National could make economies. In general, the Arts Council officers considered that there had been no conspicuous signs of extravagance at the National; but that the losses had been caused by the building delays, the standards of production required by Hall and the management, and by special conditions laid down governing National Theatre productions by local authorities and the unions. Nevertheless, the National Theatre and the Arts Council were agreed that there were signs of over-staffing and that additional economies would have to be made. For 1977–8, the National planned to reduce the number of productions at the Olivier Theatre from eight to five (plus one revival) and at the Lyttelton from six to four (plus one revival); and also to use the company more intensively than had been possible in 1976.

These discussions took place in November; and it was hoped that the deficit would be reduced by half before March 31st, 1977. It was an unsatisfactory compromise agreement, for it delayed the expansion of Hall's plans as he had intended them to develop, without imposing tougher restrictions on the National, as some members of the drama panel (and even on the Arts Council itself) would have liked. But it served its purpose of helping to cover the nagging deficit; and in time perhaps, when oil came gushing in from the North Sea, an expansion of the National's plans could once again be contemplated.

When all was said and done, however, the National Theatre was open—both auditoria—the culmination of 128 years of sporadic effort. 'Getting in', said Peter Hall in March 1976, 'is the only real achievement I'd lay claim to, just at present.' The business of settling down was still to come. On October 25th, the theatre received its royal launching.

It was raining miserably that night, thus giving the funfair erected on the patch of ground behind the National a singularly forlorn appearance. Nothing, however, could dampen Richardson's Rocket, an instant tradition invented by Sir Ralph, which consisted of letting off a firework on the roof to let London know that the curtain was going up on the National. The crowds waiting for the Queen, the Duke of Edinburgh and the royal party huddled under the lee of Lasdun's walkways and raised terraces; and there was a warm, slightly sodden feeling of muddling through amicably, to the strains of a military band outside.

The Queen arrived at 6.30, and was welcomed by the Mayor and Mayoress of Lambeth, before moving into the entrance foyer, where she was met by Lord Cottesloe, Lord and Lady Rayne, Lord Olivier and Peter Hall. The opening ceremony was very simple: a short speech from Lord Cottesloe as he welcomed the Queen and handed over the building on behalf of the South Bank Theatre Board to the National Theatre Board—another short speech from the Queen as she unveiled the memorial plaque—and a few words from Lord Rayne as he thanked the Queen and accepted the building. The royal party then divided, with the Queen and the Duke of Edinburgh visiting the Olivier Theatre, to watch *Il Campiello*, and Princess Margaret attending a performance of *Jumpers* at the Lyttelton.

Before the Queen arrived in the Olivier, the waiting audience noticed Sir Denys Lasdun slipping quietly into his seat at the side of the auditorium. He was recognized and cheered; but perhaps the most moving moment came, after the National Anthem had been played, and the audience had settled down to watch the production, when a familiar figure walked on to the stage with a certain graceful shyness: Olivier. He was given a standing ovation, and then he welcomed the Queen:

> It is an outsize pearl of understatement to say that I am happy to welcome you at this moment in this place. For this moment we must be grateful for the timing and durable cladding of Mr Peter Hall's foot, when he put it in the door. For this place, we must be grateful to many another party besides him.

He listed some of the names—the Lytteltons, Jennie Lee, Lord Goodman, Lord Cottesloe, Sir Carl Meyer and others—and concluded with a parting message to the company.

There is an unkind dictum which decrees that no true artist may expect satisfaction from his work. What shall I wish them then? Only perhaps a sense of the kind of dedication that was once inspired, some years ago, by Lilian Baylis—and others before her.

For a theatre conceived, as Hall once pointed out, at a time of comparative affluence and opening in a period of comparative poverty, such dedication was clearly going to be needed.

21

Postscript

CAREFUL readers may have noticed a trace of scepticism creeping into this narrative from time to time. Nicholas Tomalin must not be blamed for this, although his capacity for doubt was kept well-polished. The other author, John Elsom, accepts responsibility for this tone, which some who have worked hard to establish the National may find unfortunate, if not offensive. To those, he would like to offer a word of explanation:

When I started this book, I already possessed a certain image of what a national theatre could be like; and as events seemed to draw the National away from this vision, it was hard for me not to feel a sense of disappointment, even perhaps of feeling cheated.

I have been, and remain, a supporter of the National Theatre's cause, as I understand it to be. Not least among my reasons for being so is the belief that London needs a modern repertory theatre capable of housing a major company. The value of such a theatre is not that it would necessarily provide productions of unparalleled excellence: no theatre can ever guarantee to do that. Nor need it be a focal point for the entire theatre system, nor a place for experimentation, nor a South Bank catalyst. Its purpose is to provide a flowing repertoire of the world's best plays, in good productions, so that those living in Britain would have a better chance than before of forming their theatrical tastes by experiencing a wide range of what (for want of a better word) we might call masterpieces.

Sophisticated playgoers often do not realize how difficult it is, even today, for ordinary members of the public to see even the better-known plays of Molière, even in London; and one could select a list of some 300 to 400 plays which have formed an important part of Western literature, and which ought to be seen in Britain at fairly regular intervals. This repertoire may sound stuffy and somewhat unfashionable; but it cannot be provided on a commercial basis or in a theatre without large resources. For the National Theatre in any way to tackle this range, and indeed to use fully the theatre complex which the nation has provided, it needs to be able to offer an output of productions (excluding fringe events) of some thirty to forty plays a year, in the three auditoria.

This means that there has to be a large permanent company and at least five associate directors; for no director can be expected to tackle more than four or five main productions a year, and even that may be too many. The remaining productions could be tackled by guest directors. The National Theatre has been designed to contain three auditoria and stages of essentially different types; and it would be a mistake to regard the Cottesloe as just a studio for low-cost or experimental productions. In one formation, the Cottesloe provides an ideal Georgian theatre, in another theatre-in-the-round. And so for the first time in Britain, we have a single theatre complex capable of staging plays from very different genres and societies; and the stage equipment designed for it, particularly in the Olivier, combines a very high degree of flexibility with great sensitivity — although at the time of writing, it is still not completely installed. It would be a mistake to assume that each associate director would want to work in one theatre, rather than another, and should thus be assigned a theatre within the complex as part of his special responsibility. The advantage of having three theatres in one building is precisely that it allows actors and directors to swop around, testing their dramatic imaginations in different environments.

Because five associate directors would be occupying the same building, casting perhaps from the same group of actors and using the same essential facilities, conflicts of interest are bound to occur. If one of these directors is at the same time in charge of the whole operation, then his judgment will always be questioned, however magnanimous he may be, as being that of an interested party. It therefore seems better in principle to have an *Intendant* at the head of the organization, someone who is not personally involved in the business of directing plays, but whose role would primarily be that of assessing the needs of individual directors, allocating resources and acting as an impartial adviser.

Such a theatre and company would inevitably be expensive to run, requiring a total subsidy of probably between £3½ and £4 million. It is one of those cases, however, where more money might mean greater cost-effectiveness, in that for less than twice its current subsidy requirements, the National would be able to more than double its output of productions.

One factor which has dogged the National's history has been that, even when its basic cause was won, the general political will has never been so confidently present that the theatre could be built and endowed without further question and as it needed. This reflects both the penalties and advantages of living in what is still a pluralist society. Nothing has become the National so well as the cautious, sceptical and uncertain process by which it arrived at the South Bank. It reflects the checks and balances of power, the difficulties of being fair to everyone, the problems of being democratic and effective at the same time, and the determination not to be fooled by enthusiasts.

To get anything done under such conditions, however, and in particular to tackle a large and ambitious project like the National, which will win few votes at election time, it is usually necessary to out-manoeuvre your opponents—sometimes by bluff, sometimes by rhetoric and sometimes by a touch of blackmail. Once those habits have started, and in effect been accepted as part of the game, it is tempting for others to adopt the same tactics. Repeatedly, the cost of building the National was underestimated. Repeatedly, the burden of austerity fell on the shoulders of some of the contractors and sub-contractors, who, having scrambled for the jobs in the first place—for prestige reasons—then found that they had taken on more than they could handle within their contract tenders. This meant that some tried to take advantage of loopholes in their contracts, while others had to disperse their labour to take on other work—and the whole project became more and more delayed until, in desperation, opening dates had to be fixed in order to confront the contractors with the spectacle of public disaster, should they fail to deliver on time.

Thus, the climate of opinion surrounding the building of the National became soured; and traces of that souring can perhaps be seen in the building—in work inadequately finished, or perhaps not finished at all, because the money ran out. In the event, however, the nation is lucky to have acquired a theatre for about £16 million which, in almost any other European country, would have cost twice as much. And the contractors and designers, too, have gained experience and knowledge which should raise them to the ranks of the German civic theatre builders, capable of competing well in international markets. Once more we muddled through.

Somewhat similar controversies are almost bound to surround the annual subsidies given to the National. I have indicated that, in my opinion, the National is currently undersubsidized, though not for what we are now receiving in the way of productions. For the National to receive larger subsidies, however, it is necessary not only to find more money, new money, not taken from other subsidized theatres, but to change a certain public attitude towards the National. Within the theatrical profession, it must never be thought that the National trespasses upon the interests of other managements, fringe, commercial or subsidized. The National's budgets and financing, its salary scales for actors and directors alike, including that of the Director himself, must be openly known: and indeed publicized. There must be no concealed incomes from West End transfers or tours. The production budgets must be seen not to be excessive or extravagant. This is not mere catering to public inquisitiveness. It is almost a condition for the National's survival, for if it is thought that anybody in the company is using the National simply for his personal financial advantage, then further sums of public money will be increasingly hard to get approved.

This openness puts restrictions on everyone, from actors who may not wish their National Theatre incomes to be declared, to designers who might not want the public to know that their sets had to be scrapped, to the unions and their National Theatre members on or behind the stages. What sort of people would even want to work under such conditions? My belief is that eventually a kind of dignity should settle around that place, a pride in belonging to the National Theatre company, a sense of responsibility and a willingness to forgo other rewards in order to be known as a National Theatre member. Esteem, public and private, may seem again an old-fashioned idea; and it is something which, at best, can only come after a long tradition of artistic success which the National has not had time to acquire. Responsibility, however, is a state of mind which can sometimes be encouraged by allowing a nucleus of company members (equivalent perhaps to the *sociétaires* of the Comédie-Française, though without the inflexibilities of that system) to take part in major policy decisions—such as the appointment of associate directors and a right to veto a National Theatre Board selection of an *Intendant*.

For the time being, however, such a reorganization of the National will not take place; and it may be that those days are past, when such a repertory theatre, presenting a standard and perhaps over-conventional range of major plays, would be regarded as a national asset. Perhaps even the name, National Theatre, is anachronistic; for nationalism itself was born of nineteenth-century anti-royalism, and it no longer has the appeal of the days when the idea of a National Theatre was born.

Peter Hall's contract was renewed at the end of 1976, for another four years, until 1980; and his task will be to mould the National to the demands, as he sees them, of the age. The technology of the National will, during that time, come to his assistance—instead of holding him back; and the birth pangs of the National will be forgotten. But perhaps the British wariness, which so delayed the establishment of the National, could be an even more valuable quality now that it is here. It could prevent us from believing that state art is necessarily good art; and, by not suspending our disbelief too easily, we could encourage the National to earn our approval by the quality and range of its work, not by the mere fact of its existence.

Bibliography

ADDENBROOKE, D., *The Royal Shakespeare Company* (William Kimber, 1974)
ARCHER, W., *The Foundation of the National Theatre* (British Drama League, 1922)
ARCHER, W., and GRANVILLE BARKER, H., *A National Theatre: Scheme and Estimates* (Duckworth, 1907)
ARNOLD, M., 'The French Play in London', *The Nineteenth Century*, August 1879
BARKER, F., *The Oliviers* (Hamish Hamilton, 1953)
BRERETON, A., *The Life of Henry Irving* (Longmans, 1908)
BURTON, H. (ed.), *Great Acting* (B.B.C. Publications, 1967)
—— *Acting in the Sixties* (B.B.C. Publications, 1970)
LORD CHANDOS, *The Memoirs of Lord Chandos* (The Bodley Head, 1962)
COOK, J., *The National Theatre* (Harrap, 1976)
COTTRELL, J., *Laurence Olivier* (Weidenfeld and Nicolson, 1975)
EVERSHED-MARTIN, L., *The Impossible Theatre* (Phillimore, Chichester, Sussex, 1971)
FAIRWEATHER, V., *Cry God For Larry* (Calder and Boyars, 1969)
FINDLATER, R., *Lilian Baylis, The Lady of the Old Vic* (Allen Lane, 1975)
FORSYTH, J., *Tyrone Guthrie* (Hamish Hamilton, 1976)
GOURLAY, L. (ed.), *Olivier* (Weidenfeld and Nicolson, 1973)
GRANVILLE BARKER, H., *A National Theatre* (Sidgwick and Jackson, 1930)
GUTHRIE, T., *Theatre Prospect* (Wishart, 1932)
—— *A New Theatre* (McGraw Hill, New York, 1954)
HOLYOAKE, G., *Sixty Years of an Agitator's Life* (T. Fisher Unwin, 1892)
KOTT, J., *Shakespeare Our Contemporary* (University Paperbacks, Methuen, 1965)
LANDSTONE, C., *Off Stage* (Elek, 1953)
LYTTELTON, E., *Alfred Lyttelton* (Longmans, Green and Co., 1917)
LYTTON, V., *Life of Bulwer, First Lord Lytton* (Macmillan, 1913)
PILBROW, R., *Stage Lighting* (Studio Vista, 1970)
ROBERTS, P., *The Old Vic Story* (W. H. Allen, 1976)
TYNAN, K. (ed.), *The Recruiting Officer: The National Theatre Production* (Rupert Hart-Davis, 1965)
TYNAN, K., *A View of the English Stage* (Davis-Poynter, 1975)
—— *The Sound of Two Hands Clapping* (Jonathan Cape, 1975)
WHITE, E. W., *The Arts Council of Great Britain* (Davis-Poynter, 1975)
WHITWORTH, G., *The Making of a National Theatre* (Faber and Faber, 1951)
WILLIAMS, H., *Old Vic Saga* (Winchester Publications, Winchester, 1940)

Anon., *In Memory of Effingham Wilson* (published privately, Effingham Wilson, 1868)
'National Theatre', *The Architectural Review*, January 1977
Annual Reports: South Bank Theatre and Opera House Board (1962–1967); South Bank Theatre Board (1967/8–1975/6); National Theatre Board (1963–1976)
Hansard: April 23rd, 1913; March 23rd, 1948; November 18th, 1948; March 21st, 1968; November 7th, 1974

Acknowledgments

A LIST of those who have contributed valuable insights to this book would be long indeed; but I must record particularly my warm thanks to those who have spent considerable time talking to Nicholas Tomalin and me, who have written to us and have allowed extracts from correspondence and tapes to be included in this book — among them, Michael Blakemore, Richard Brett, Lord Cottesloe, Patrick Donnell, Frank Dunlop, Anthony Easterbrook, Richard Findlater, Lord Goodman, Sir Peter Hall, Sir Denys Lasdun, Sir Joseph Lockwood, Iain Mackintosh, Jonathan Miller, Victor Mishcon, Lord Olivier, Richard Pilbrow, Joan Plowright, Lord Rayne, Simon Relph, John Spurling, Peter Stevens, Kenneth Tynan and Richard York. The British Drama League have given access to the S.M.N.T. papers, and permission for an early design for a National Theatre to be published. The Society of Authors (as literary representatives of the estate of John Masefield), Heinemann and *The Times* have given permission for me to quote Masefield's short poem, written to mark the original laying of the National Theatre's foundation stone in 1951; the Society of Authors has also, on behalf of the Bernard Shaw estate, given permission to quote extracts from plays, speeches and letters by Shaw. I also thank Weidenfeld and Nicolson and Stein & Day for permission to quote from Logan Gourlay's *Olivier* and Faber and Faber for permission to quote from Geoffrey Whitworth's *The Making of a National Theatre*.

The illustrations are reproduced by permission of the following: Mander & Mitchenson Theatre Collection, Plates 5, 7, 12, 16–18; The Radio Times Hulton Picture Library, nos 2, 3, 6, 13–15; Shakespeare Memorial National Theatre Trust, nos 8–11; Denys Lasdun & Partners, nos 28–30; Keystone Press, nos 19, 27, 31; James Holmes, nos 32, 34, 41; Anthony Crickmay, nos 39, 40; Philip Sayer (George Harrap & Co.), nos 33, 36; the Press Association, nos 21, 26a; the Guildhall Library, City of London, no. 1; Bassano (Camera Press) no. 4; Brian O'Rorke, no. 20; *The Times*, no. 22; Chris Arthur, no. 23; British Home Entertainment, no. 24; Carl Samrock, no. 25; Jon Blau (Camera Press) no. 26b; Colin Davey (Camera Press) no. 26c; Steve Stephens, no. 35; London Weekend Television, no. 37; Sport & General, no. 38; Nobby Clark, no. 42; and Donald Cooper, no. 43; Figures nos 1 and 2 are from A. S. G. Butler, *The Architecture of Sir Edwin Lutyens*, vol. III (Country Life); and Figures 3–5 are by Denys Lasdun & Partners. The photography of Plates 1, 5, 8, 9 and 10 is by Stuart Windsor; and of Plate 11 and Figures 1 and 2 by John Freeman & Co.

John Goodwin, Bill Allen and the National Theatre's press department have been of continual help and assistance; while Anna Splawska has taken the full burden of acquiring and organizing the photographs. My special thanks to them.

Index

337

339